RELIGION AND PUBLIC DISCOURSE
IN AN AGE OF TRANSITION

Bahá'í Studies
SERIES

This series publishes monographs and other works of distinction in Bahá'í Studies, including the study of the Sacred Texts, theology, law, teachings, and principles of the Bahá'í Faith as well as the history of the Bahá'í religion (including its precursor movements, the Shaykhí school and the Bábí religion), its central figures, and the development of the Bahá'í community. Bahá'í Studies also encompasses the application of Bahá'í teachings and principles to the contemporary needs of humanity including (but not limited to) peace, human rights, ethics, governance, development, gender and family, the environment, the arts, race and ethnic relations, and Aboriginal peoples.

Books in the Bahá'í Studies series are published for the Association for Bahá'í Studies – North America by Wilfrid Laurier University Press.

For more information about the Bahá'í Studies series, please contact the series co-editors:

John S. Hatcher, PhD
Association for Bahá'í Studies
34 Copernicus Street
Ottawa, ON K1N 7K4 Canada
Phone: (613) 233-1903
Fax: (613) 233-3644
Email: series@bahai-studies.ca

RELIGION AND PUBLIC DISCOURSE IN AN AGE OF TRANSITION
REFLECTIONS ON BAHÁ'Í PRACTICE AND THOUGHT

GEOFFREY CAMERON & BENJAMIN SCHEWEL
EDITORS

WILFRID LAURIER
UNIVERSITY PRESS

Wilfrid Laurier University Press acknowledges the support of the Canada Council for the Arts for our publishing program. We acknowledge the financial support of the Government of Canada through the Canada Book Fund for our publishing activities. This work was supported by the Research Support Fund.

Library and Archives Canada Cataloguing in Publication

    Religion and public discourse in an age of transition : reflections on Bahá'í practice and thought / Geoffrey Cameron and Benjamin Schewel, editors.

(Bahá'í studies series)
Includes bibliographical references and index.
Issued in print and electronic formats.
ISBN 978-1-77112-330-3 (softcover).—ISBN 978-1-77112-331-0 (PDF).—
ISBN 978-1-77112-332-7 (EPUB)

    1. Bahai Faith. I. Cameron, Geoffrey, 1983–, editor II. Schewel, Benjamin, 1986–, editor III. Series: Bahá'í studies series

BP330.R45 2017   297.9'3   C2017-903165-1
                                                                                          C2017-903166-X

Front-cover image: *Canticle*, by Mark Tobey (Smithsonian American Art Museum, accession no. 1986.6.79). Gift of the Sara Roby Foundation. Reproduced with permission of Smithsonian American Art Museum. Book design by Daiva Villa, Chris Rowat Design.

© 2018 Association for Bahá'í Studies
© 2018 Wilfrid Laurier University Press
Waterloo, Ontario, Canada
www.wlupress.wlu.ca

Every reasonable effort has been made to acquire permission for copyright material used in this text, and to acknowledge all such indebtedness accurately. Any errors and omissions called to the publisher's attention will be corrected in future printings.

No part of this publication may be reproduced, stored in a retrieval system, or transmitted, in any form or by any means, without the prior written consent of the publisher or a licence from the Canadian Copyright Licensing Agency (Access Copyright). For an Access Copyright licence, visit http://www.accesscopyright.ca or call toll free to 1-800-893-5777.

CONTENTS

Preface
vii

Introduction
Geoffrey Cameron and Benjamin Schewel
1

ONE
Religion in an Age of Transition
Benjamin Schewel
13

TWO
Religion, Spiritual Principles, and Civil Society
David A. Palmer
37

THREE
Media and Public Discourse: Normative Foundations
Michael Karlberg
71

FOUR
Education and Moral Empowerment: Raising Capacity for Participation in Public Discourse
Sona Farid-Arbab
97

FIVE
An Inquiry into the Harmony of Science and Religion
Farzam Arbab
131

SIX
Bahá'í Participation in Public Discourse: Some Considerations Related to History, Concepts, and Approaches
Shahriar Razavi
163

SEVEN
Contributions to International Development Discourse: Exploring the Roles of Science and Religion
Matthew Weinberg
191

EIGHT
A New Politics of Engagement: The Bahá'í International Community, the United Nations, and Gender Equality
Julia Berger
221

NINE
The Bahá'í Community and Public Policy: The Bahá'í Refugee Resettlement Program (1981–1989)
Geoffrey Cameron
255

About the Authors
281

Index
283

PREFACE

This volume began as an idea discussed on a walk in suburban London, England. It evolved through countless exchanges over email and phone, and at workshops in Washington DC and West Palm Beach. In the course of this project, our families have each grown by one. So to Theodore and Elliott: we hope this modest endeavour contributes to the creation of a better world for you.

The preparation and editing of this volume has relied upon the advice and support of a number of close collaborators. We would like to thank Holly Hanson and Louis Venters, who contributed at its formative stages. Gerald Filson was a friendly critic throughout the process, reading everything and sending thoughts and revisions at all hours of the day and night. Ken Bowers followed each iteration of the chapters and contributed to deliberations over the volume's development with warm encouragement. We would also like to thank participants in several breakout sessions at Association for Bahá'í Studies annual conferences for their comments, questions and feedback on various chapters. Three anonymous reviewers and members of the ABS-WLUP Bahá'í Studies series editorial committee provided helpful remarks on the text, as did several staff at the Bahá'í World Centre. We have Jennifer Janechek to thank for her careful copyediting. As our editors with the Bahá'í Studies series, Pierre-Yves Mocquais helped to get the project off the ground, and John Hatcher skilfully stewarded the volume through its many twists and turns. Our gratitude also goes to each of the chapter authors, who helped to turn this collection into a more coherent whole. We would like to extend a special thanks to the National Spiritual Assembly of the Bahá'ís of Canada for its support throughout this project. Most of all, we wish to dedicate this book to the Universal House of Justice, whose love and guidance have enabled and illumined this path of inquiry.

Geoffrey Cameron, Hamilton, Canada
Benjamin Schewel, Amsterdam, Netherlands

INTRODUCTION

GEOFFREY CAMERON AND BENJAMIN SCHEWEL

Humanity is becoming increasingly connected in virtually every sphere of life, and the transition to a more integrated global society calls for new discourses about our collective future. It has become commonplace to say that humanity is undergoing a process of globalization; however, beneath this simple statement lies a more complex social reality. The rapid expansion of global economic ties, the accelerating movement of populations, and the growing density of communication links have generated unprecedented wealth and opportunity, but they have done so in a way that concentrates these benefits in the hands of certain people, classes, and nations. Globalization, as it has proceeded, is not simply a natural phenomenon that can be left to chart its own evolutionary course. Instead, public deliberation should inform political processes capable of harnessing these powerful forces to serve the interests of humanity. This calls for a robust, inclusive, and meaningful discourse on humanity's collective future.

There is, as yet, no "global public sphere" where citizens can deliberate on issues of worldwide concern and be heard by institutions that can translate public opinion into public policy. Of course, transnational discourses proceed in various settings throughout the world today. There is, for example, an ongoing conversation among academic, political, and business elites that informs the work of international institutions. Additionally, new technologies enable social movements to mobilize across borders, allow previously subordinated groups to organize themselves into influential "counter-publics," and diaspora communities to engage directly in the political affairs of their home countries.[1] What is sometimes referred to as a "global civil society," however, still largely reflects the interests and ideas of the wealthy and empowered social classes and tends to be dominated by the assumptions animating a liberal Western worldview. To make these observations is not to express pessimism about humanity's future but rather to underscore the point that the transition toward a more interdependent world calls for a truly globalized political existence.

This volume brings together contributions from authors who address various aspects of this challenge within the context of Bahá'í thought and practice, which are both oriented toward the goal of laying foundations for a new world civilization that harmonizes the spiritual and material aspects of human existence. In this regard, the Bahá'í teachings view religion as a source of enduring insight that can enable humanity to repair and transcend patterns of disunity, foster justice within the structures of society, and advance the cause of peace. Accordingly, a central concern of the chapters that follow is the role that religion can and ought to play in the broader project of creating a pattern of public discourse capable of supporting humanity's transition to the next stage in its collective development.

Throughout history, the peoples of the world have regularly turned to religion in order to to establish broader bases for collective life. In his acclaimed study of secularism, Charles Taylor mentions how the Buddha called upon His followers to abandon caste divisions and enter into a universal Sangha, Christians sought to realize a pattern of community life in which there was "neither Jew nor Greek, slave nor free, man nor woman," and Muslims worked to establish a global Ummah in which former tribal and national allegiances would play no part.[2] As systems of thought and practice with their own institutions and social disciplines, these religions helped generate conversations of sufficient complexity, coherence, and scope to sustain vast multilingual, multicultural, and multinational civilizations. However, notwithstanding these positive historical influences, we see many religious communities today reproducing the very patterns of conflict, exclusion, and domination that their founders originally sought to transcend. Should we therefore conclude that the ability of religion to help establish the foundations for more expansive patterns of collective life has been exhausted, or at least reached its limit, in the present age?

The influential theory of "secularization" proposes an affirmative answer to this question. Initially articulated by the founding figures of modern sociology, secularization theory involves three interrelated claims about the changing place of religion in the modern world.[3] First, there is the differentiation thesis, which contends that religion will no longer ground modern social reality but rather will operate as one functional sphere among others (e.g., politics, economics, ethics, and family life). Second, there is the privatization thesis, which holds that modern religion will gradually vacate public life and be relegated to the domain of private concern. And third, there is the decline of religion thesis, which claims that religion will gradually lose its ability to influence the thought and action of modern peoples. Classical secularization theorists derived these claims by analyzing modern Western Europe, yet they believed that all other cultures and peoples would eventually follow the same path as they continued to develop and advance.[4]

The spread of secularization theory played a significant role in encouraging the efforts of many intellectuals and political leaders to undermine the social influence of religion around the world. The result, as three political scientists explain, was that "like dying supernovae, every major religion on every continent seemed to be rapidly losing its influence on politics, economics, and culture."[5] They continue: "Apostles of nationalism, socialism, and modernization—such as Fidel Castro of Cuba, David Ben-Gurion of Israel, Gamal Abdel Nasser of Egypt, and the Shah of Iran—were 'men of the future.' Mullahs, monks, and priests, with their dogmas, rites, and hierarchies, were creatures of an increasingly irrelevant past."[6] It is not surprising, then, that during this period, for many social analysts, secularization theory went from being a "speculative academic theory" to an apparently "immanent global reality."[7]

During the last decades of the twentieth century, however, it became increasingly clear that a "straightforward narrative of progress from the religious to the secular" was flawed and problematic.[8] An important influence on this development was the recognition of the prominent role that religion continued to play in many instances of political conflict and revolution throughout the world, including the 1979 Iranian Revolution, the overthrow of communism in Eastern Europe and the "third wave" of democratization, Latin American revolutionary movements, the spread of conservatism in the United States, and the rapid ascent of extremist movements in the Middle East.[9] Growing awareness of the fact that secularization was not an inexorable historical force but rather a "political-economic project" that Western-educated elites who identified with Enlightenment values consciously pursued also played a significant role in undermining the authority of secularization theory.[10]

Nevertheless, there is, as yet, no consensus on how we should think about the potential of religion to contribute to an inclusive and meaningful pattern of worldwide public discourse after such challenges to secularization theory. Theorists debating these questions tend to cluster around one of three positions. The first position, which we describe as "rationalist," equates public discourse with the use of secularized reason and holds that religious believers can best contribute to the enhancement of public discourse by striving to present whatever ideas they have in wholly secular terms. Religious participants in public discourse are therefore assigned the task of adapting to the secular demands of deliberation by using non-religious terminology to describe their concepts and ideas. This requirement derives from the underlying belief that social unity and consensus can be achieved only by engaging in secular, rational-critical deliberation on the common good.

The second, "traditionalist," position starts from the same premise as the rationalist one—that the modern public sphere is largely a space of secular language and rationality—but claims that the absence of religion is precisely what has caused the deterioration of public discourse during the modern period. The only way to regenerate public discourse, then, is to revitalize engagement with a traditional pattern of religious practice and belief. For instance, Alasdair MacIntyre has argued that the erosion of modern public life is related to the abandonment of the classical tradition of "virtue ethics," which had been safeguarded by Catholic thought. During the Enlightenment, modern thinkers rejected the virtue tradition but sought to preserve some of its moral precepts within a secular, naturalistic worldview. Yet this Enlightenment project, he contends, failed to achieve its stated aims and left the modern public sphere in a state of moral relativism. MacIntyre thus argues that the only way to repair public discourse is to dedicate ourselves to reconstructing and repairing this lost tradition of moral and ethical thought.[11]

The third, "pluralist," position states that we can cultivate vibrant public discourses only by recognizing the incommensurable differences that characterize the constituent groups of modern society. The guiding idea here is that public discourse is strengthened by the sheer volume and authenticity of participation, as well as by the inclusion of groups with identities and views that are underrepresented in public life. The current challenge, therefore, is not to devise some way of achieving social unity through public consensus, whether secular or religious, but rather to develop appropriate means for validating different views and managing the conflicts that inevitably arise in maximally constructive ways. From this angle, religion becomes relevant to the public sphere not so much because of the particular insights it offers but rather because it is an important source of identity and meaning for many people throughout the world today.[12]

The rationalist, traditionalist, and pluralist approaches have each enriched recent discussions concerning the place of religion in the public sphere, but none has been sufficiently convincing on its own. Of course, most participants in this conversation, particularly the most sophisticated ones, cannot be easily reduced to one of these positions. However, they represent coherent positions that frame an ongoing conversation about the role of religion in our present age of transition toward a more globalized social existence.

Some prominent thinkers have begun considering new ways of approaching the debate within a growing literature on "post-secular" societies and discourse. The term "post-secular" refers to the apparent failure of secularization theory's prediction that the influence of religion in public life would steadily diminish. The enduring importance of religious belief, thought, and practice within historically "secularized" societies raises new questions about the ongoing role of religion in society. One of these questions is the following: If religious discourses are to be accepted alongside secular perspectives in public deliberation on the common good, how do we make sure that everyone understands one another and maintains an openness in their opinions? Therefore, as various scholars have noted, "post-secular" can also refer to the challenge of working out norms of public discourse that foster complementary learning processes between citizens employing religious and secular modes of discourse.[13] This task involves a search for an approach to politics that upholds certain norms that have historically been associated with secularism but allows religious perspectives to enter freely into public discourse.[14] Joseph Camilleri argues that such post-secular projects seek "to achieve a new reconciliation of unity and difference" by learning to accommodate "overlapping and competing religious and non-religious identities and allegiances" in the "vastly altered circumstances of the early twenty-first century."[15]

Without wanting to align this volume with either the concept of the post-secular or the thinkers associated with it, each of the chapters that follow can be seen as an attempt to offer new perspectives about the role of religion in the public sphere—a line of inquiry opened by post-secular literature.

We proceed in this direction by engaging with perspectives informed by the teachings of the Bahá'í Faith and the collective experiences of the worldwide Bahá'í community. Having emerged in nineteenth-century Persia and subsequently spread to nearly every country of the world, the Bahá'í Faith envisions religion as a progressive force that can and must play a central role in the construction of a just, peaceful, and unified world civilization that is characterized by material and spiritual prosperity. The goal of promoting an expansive and constructive worldwide discourse on the welfare of humankind is an explicit feature of the Bahá'í vision of how such a civilization can emerge. Many of the Bahá'í teachings therefore articulate principles, methods, and norms that should characterize the collective conversations of the human race, and the Bahá'í writings include ideas about the establishment of institutional structures that can promote and protect the integrity of these conversations. Additionally, during the past few decades, the Bahá'í community has developed an increasingly sophisticated understanding of how such principles, methods, norms, and institutional structures can be implemented in practice. For all these reasons, the teachings and experiences of the Bahá'í Faith should be seen as highly relevant to ongoing academic discussions of the role of religion in the public sphere in the context of humanity's transition to a more global society.

Alongside the aim of contributing to certain academic conversations, however, another goal of this volume is to make a modest contribution to the intellectual life of the Bahá'í community by correlating certain aspects of the Bahá'í teachings, as well as the rapidly accumulating experiences of the worldwide Bahá'í community, with contemporary research. All the chapter authors have been engaged in the efforts of the Bahá'í community to contribute to public discourse in a number of national and international settings. These experiences have shown us the need to engage at a deeper level with new currents of thought. Of course, the thoughts presented in this volume are only initial forays along paths of inquiry and learning that must be much more thoroughly pursued. However, each of the contributions that follow can help future researchers advance in their understanding of some of the relevant concepts, issues, and concerns.

Having clarified the broader contexts in which this volume seeks to intervene, we briefly summarize each of the chapters that follow. The first five chapters take up a number of important conceptual and theoretical issues within contemporary debates about the role of religion in public discourse. Chapter 6 marks an inflection point in the book, where Shahriar Razavi turns our attention to the features of Bahá'í history, belief, and thought that informs the Bahá'í community's participation in public discourse. It presents the context for the final three chapters, which analyze recent experiences of the Bahá'í community and its institutions as they have entered into public discourse at the national and international levels.

In chapter 1, Benjamin Schewel examines the various historical dilemmas that shape our ability to think about the place of religion in the current period of transition. Schewel begins by considering the Bahá'í concept of progressive revelation, which is organized around the idea that the periodic appearance of universal Educators or Manifestations of God is one of the prime drivers of civilizational advance. He proceeds to elaborate the major narratives of religious history that philosophers and social scientists are currently putting forth. His main purpose in discussing these narrative concepts is to illuminate the forces and ideas that shape many contemporary discussions of religion, as well as to show how many facets of these discussions align with the vision of religious history that is put forth by the writings of the Bahá'í Faith. Schewel additionally considers the influential concept of the "axial age" in order to help readers consider the broader academic viability of some of the insights contained in the concept of progressive revelation.

David A. Palmer continues in chapter 2 by focusing on the concept of civil society, which seeks to describe the set of intermediate social institutions that generate and organize public discourse. He notes that civil society is generally considered to be an unalloyed good for the public sphere because it reflects values of solidarity that are often lacking in political power struggles and market exchange. Within civil society, people contribute to countering oppressive social forces by developing voluntary relationships of cooperation and reciprocity, as well as norms and practices of deliberation on the common good. The position of religion in relation to civil society is ambiguous because, on the one hand, it is an important force for the promotion of civil society's transcendent values and communities of solidarity and, on the other hand, many forms of religious identification and practice violate those very values. Palmer proposes that a discourse on "spiritual principles" that relate to assumptions about human nature and visions of an ideal society can contribute to overcoming the discursive gap between visions and practices of solidarity in religion and in civil society and lead to a critical reflection on the means of building solidarity in both spheres. He subsequently argues that in order to expand the bases of human solidarity, we must gain a clearer understanding of the nature of these spiritual principles and the means by which they can be implemented in the field of social action, and he invites renewed consideration of the possible role that religion can play in stimulating these endeavours.

In chapter 3, Michael Karlberg focuses on questions concerning the media and the public sphere. He observes that contemporary media scholarship "is occurring within increasingly isolated coteries that lack common assumptions or even a common vocabulary." Nevertheless, normative assumptions are always present beneath the surface. Karlberg argues that the lack of attention to these normative assumptions has held back the advancement of knowledge in the field of media studies. Where they have received focused attention, they often reflect the perspective of Western liberal democratic theory, which emphasizes conflict and competition as the engine of public deliberation. Karlberg advances an alternative set of normative principles, oneness and justice, which are further articulated through practices of consultation. These principles, he suggests, are more adaptive for a global age of mutuality and interdependence, where a healthy public sphere demands a different kind of media than that which prevails today. A consultative framework can support public discourse in both its rational and affective dimensions, as well as transcend the liberal requirements for a strictly secular rationalism in public discourse. New questions and lines of inquiry about the possibilities for transformation in media systems and practices are raised through the application of this framework.

In chapter 4, Sona Farid-Arbab considers the basic elements of an educational framework that is capable of building capacity to participate in a global conversation on the advancement of material and spiritual civilization. Her deliberations are organized around a vision of "moral empowerment" in which educational processes seek to harmonize the urge to pursue one's own intellectual and moral development with the motivation to contribute to the advancement of society. To this end, Farid-Arbab argues that there are non-competitive dimensions to power—notably those expressing the nobility of the human spirit—that need to be recognized by such educational endeavours. She then proceeds to articulate notions of identity, capability, understanding, and fostering spiritual qualities that are commensurate with this view of education.

Farzam Arbab presents an inquiry into the harmony between science and religion in chapter 5. The facts and values upon which we construct our common life are intrinsically related to the knowledge generated by science and religion, yet faith and reason are frequently and falsely dichotomized. In response to this dilemma, Arbab seeks to redescribe science and religion as systems of knowledge and practice, which can be viewed as two ways of looking at reality. He situates his inquiry within the philosophy of science, particularly within discussions about the nature of science, the role of science in society, and the metaphysical foundations of scientific research. This inquiry leads to a discussion of Thomas Nagel's ideas about the existence of an "extended reality," which, Arbab suggests, enables us to "enter an arena where the dichotomy between faith and reason has lost its grip on our minds." Arbab proceeds to outline a number of avenues for future inquiry into the complementary relationship between science and religion, and he details the practical implications of this research for effective participation in discourses associated with the emergence of a world civilization.

In chapter 6, Shahriar Razavi examines more closely certain principles and norms that animate the Bahá'í community's evolving efforts to participate in public discourse. This chapter departs from many of the conceptual and theoretical issues informing the earlier chapters and presents a line of thought that is shaped by the author's experience working with senior Bahá'í institutions at the Bahá'í World Centre. Razavi begins this inquiry by considering the history of Bahá'í involvement in public discourse and then examines some of the key concepts and approaches that have informed these efforts. He considers to how the participation of the Bahá'í community in public discourse is shaped by a systematic and collaborative approach to generating knowledge as well as by the idea that humanity stands at the threshold of a profound collective transformation, as well as by a systematic and collaborative approach to generating knowledge. This chapter serves as essential background for the subsequent chapters, which narrate and analyze cases of Bahá'í participation in public discourse at the national and international levels.

Matthew Weinberg presents in chapter 7 a case study of how the Bahá'í community has consciously sought to reframe and broaden the current discourse on socio-economic development. In particular, Weinberg focuses on the Bahá'í community's efforts to nurture and create an international discourse on science, religion, and development when it found that one did not already exist. This decade-long, multi-country initiative was a modest attempt to raise questions about the salient assumptions of the development process and identify avenues of research and action in relation to these questions. The learning emanating from this experience, however, illustrates the deep relevance of religious practices and ideas to the exigencies of the contemporary world.

In chapter 8, Julia Berger examines the contributions of the Bahá'í International Community (BIC) to the United Nations discourse on gender equality. Berger emphasizes how the BIC's commitment to Bahá'í teachings concerning the oneness of humankind led it to consciously avoid the limitations of certain aspects of current UN discourse on gender equality, such as its oppositional climate, its tendency toward binary readings of reality, its distrust and resentment of religious actors and perspectives, as well as its enduringly patriarchal structures and processes. She also considers how concepts introduced by the BIC stimulated consideration of different facets of gender equality, such as its significance within the broader context of the oneness of humanity and the attainment of peace, the role of women and girls as protagonists of development, the dynamic coherence between the material and the spiritual, the lack of gender distinctions at the spiritual level, and the role of education in the advancement of women.

Finally, in chapter 9, Geoffrey Cameron examines aspects of the Bahá'í community's approach to public policy processes within the context of the development of an international refugee resettlement program in the 1980s. From 1981 to 1989, more than eight thousand stateless Bahá'ís were resettled in some two dozen countries. This program was the result of the participation of Bahá'í community representatives in policy processes that led to cooperative approaches to resettlement. Through a careful analysis of interactions between Bahá'í representatives, institutions, and public officials, Cameron shows how "Bahá'í beliefs and principles shaped the approach of Bahá'í institutions and actors to engaging with public policy processes." He emphasizes that this approach is marked by a commitment to a set of guiding principles rather than strategic choices about achieving policy influence. Some of the lessons gleaned through the experience of the Bahá'í community with this program may have wider application to the efforts of groups, whether religious or secular, that are trying to find new ways of engaging independently and constructively with public policy processes.

Notes

1. For a discussion of some of these post-Habermasian engagements with the idea of a public sphere, see Craig Calhoun, ed., *Habermas and the Public Sphere* (Cambridge: MIT Press, 1992); Kate Nash, ed., *Transnationalizing the Public Sphere* (Cambridge: Polity Press, 2014).
2. Charles Taylor, *A Secular Age* (Cambridge, MA: Harvard University Press, 2007), 576. See also Armando Salvatore, *The Public Sphere: Liberal Modernity, Catholicism, and Islam* (New York: Palgrave Macmillan, 2007) and Hannah Arendt, *The Human Condition* (Chicago: University of Chicago Press, 1958), 53. Taylor ultimately concludes that all the great religiously inspired "axial" traditions, which additionally include Confucianism, Daoism, Greek rationalism, Zoroastrianism, and Judaism, contributed in their own way to the emergence of expansive spaces of social solidarity and interaction. See Taylor, "What Was the Axial Revolution?" in *The Axial Age and Its Consequences*, ed. Robert Bellah and Hans Joas (Cambridge, MA: Belknap Press, 2012), 35.
3. We refer here to Auguste Comte, Karl Marx, Max Weber, and Émile Durkheim. See José Casanova, *Public Religions in the Modern World* (Chicago: University of Chicago Press, 1994).
4. Auguste Comte went so far as to claim that secularization was the basic law of human history upon which an exact social science could be built. For more on this, see Comte, *Auguste Comte and Positivism: The Essential Writings*, ed. Gertrud Lenzer (New York: Harper & Row, 1975).
5. Monica Duffy Toft, Daniel Philpott, and Timothy Samuel Shah, *God's Century: Resurgent Religion and Global Politics* (New York: Norton, 2011), 1.
6. Ibid.
7. Ibid., 78.
8. Talal Asad, *Formations of the Secular: Christianity, Islam, and Modernity* (Stanford, CA: Stanford University Press, 2003), 1.
9. Toft, Philpott, and Shah, *God's Century*, 82–120; Casanova, *Public Religions*, 1–19.
10. Asad, *Formations of the Secular*, 14. See also Peter Berger, "The Desecularization of the World: A Global Interview," in *The Desecularization of the World: Resurgent Religion and World Politics*, ed. Peter Berger (Washington, DC: William B. Eerdmans, 1999), 10–11; Elizabeth Shakman Hurd, *The*

Politics of Secularism in International Relations (Princeton, NJ: Princeton University Press, 2009).
11 Alasdair MacIntyre, *After Virtue: A Study in Moral Theory*, 3rd ed. (Notre Dame, IN: University of Notre Dame Press, 2007).
12 Implicit in this approach to religion and public discourse is the claim that rationalist visions of public discourse are elitist because they exclude the views of those who lack a sophisticated secular vocabulary in which to express themselves.
13 See Craig Calhoun, Eduardo Mendieta, and Jonathan VanAntwerpen, *Habermas and Religion* (Cambridge, UK: Polity, 2013), 8; Jürgen Habermas, *Between Naturalism and Religion* (New York: John Wiley & Sons, 2014), 348; Habermas, *Between Facts and Norms* (Cambridge, MA: MIT Press, 1996); and Rainer Forst, *The Right to Justification: Elements of a Constructivist Theory of Justice* (New York: Columbia University Press, 2007).
14 See Jürgen Habermas, ed., *An Awareness of What Is Missing: Faith and Reason in a Post-Secular Age* (Cambridge, UK: Polity, 2010).
15 Joseph Camilleri, "Postsecularist Discourse in an 'Age of Transition,'" *Review of International Studies* 38, no. 5 (2012): 1038.

Bibliography

Arendt, Hannah. *The Human Condition*. Chicago: University of Chicago Press, 1958.
Asad, Talal. *Formations of the Secular: Christianity, Islam, Modernity*. Stanford, CA: Stanford University Press, 2003.
Berger, Peter. "The Desecularization of the World: A Global Overview." In *The Desecularization of the World: Resurgent Religion and World Politics*, edited by Berger, 1–18. Washington, DC: William B. Eerdmans, 1999.
Calhoun, Craig, ed. *Habermas and the Public Sphere*. Cambridge, MA: MIT Press, 1992.
Calhoun, Craig, Eduardo Mendieta, and Jonathan VanAntwerpen, ed. *Habermas and Religion*. Cambridge, UK: Polity, 2013.
Camilleri, Joseph. "Postsecularist Discourse in an 'Age of Transition.'" *Review of International Studies* 38, no. 5 (2012): 1019–39.
Casanova, José. *Public Religions in the Modern World*. Chicago: University of Chicago Press, 1994.
Comte, Auguste. *Auguste Comte and Positivism: The Essential Writings*. Edited by Gertrud Lenzer. New York: Harper & Row, 1975.
Forst, Rainer. *The Right to Justification: Elements of a Constructivist Theory of Justice*. New York: Columbia University Press, 2007.
Habermas, Jürgen. *Between Facts and Norms*. Cambridge, MA: MIT Press, 1996.
———. *Between Naturalism and Religion*. New York: John Wiley & Sons, 2014.
Habermas, Jürgen, ed. *An Awareness of What Is Missing: Faith and Reason in a Post-Secular Age*. Cambridge, UK: Polity, 2010.

Hurd, Elizabeth Shakman. *The Politics of Secularism in International Relations.* Princeton, NJ: Princeton University Press, 2009.

MacIntyre, Alasdair. *After Virtue: A Study in Moral Theory,* 3rd ed. Notre Dame, IN: University of Notre Dame Press, 2007.

Nash, Kate, ed. *Transnationalizing the Public Sphere.* Cambridge, UK: Polity Press, 2014.

Salvatore, Armando. *The Public Sphere: Liberal Modernity, Catholicism, and Islam.* New York: Palgrave Macmillan, 2007.

Taylor, Charles. *A Secular Age.* Cambridge, MA: Harvard University Press, 2007.

———. "What Was the Axial Revolution?" In *The Axial Age and Its Consequences,* edited by Robert N. Bellah and Hans Joas, 30–46. Cambridge, MA: Belknap Press, 2012.

Toft, Monica Duffy, Daniel Philpott, and Timothy Samuel Shah. *God's Century: Resurgent Religion and Global Politics.* New York: Norton, 2011.

CHAPTER ONE

RELIGION IN AN AGE OF TRANSITION

BENJAMIN SCHEWEL

When considering how religion can contribute to the construction of a more ideal pattern of global public discourse, one key dilemma is historical in nature. Religion has clearly transformed during the preceding millennia and continues to do so today. Yet it is not clear what forces have driven this process forward. Has religion been locked into a process of gradual marginalization and decline? Or has it somehow developed and improved? Perhaps religion progressed up to a certain point and then fell into decline. Or maybe it has undergone a series of neutral transformations, neither better nor worse, only different, from age to age. Or again, it may be that the same religious dynamics simply reappear in each period of history. It should not be hard to see how each of these views, advanced by thoughtful and learned people today, alter our understanding of religion's role in the public life of our globalizing age.

The question is more straightforward when addressed within the context of the Bahá'í writings, which describe religious history as animated by the periodic appearance of Divine Messengers, such as Buddha, Jesus, Muhammad, and Bahá'u'lláh, Who manifest the attributes of God and reveal God's purpose and will to humanity. Although a distinct community of believers forms around each of these Figures and begins working to translate its Founder's teachings into a new social reality, the coming of each Divine Messenger or Manifestation exerts an influence on the entire human race. Within the Bahá'í schema, it reflects an "inadequate recognition of the unique station of Moses, Buddha, Zoroaster, Jesus, Muhammad—or of the succession of Avatars who inspired the Hindu scriptures—to depict their work as the founding of distinct religions."[1]

They should rather be understood as the "spiritual Educators of history" and the "animating forces in the rise of the civilization."[2]

Following this premise, the chaotic transformations that are sweeping the world today can be viewed as emanations of the transformative potential released by the coming of a new Manifestation of God, Bahá'u'lláh, during the middle of the nineteenth century. It is from this angle that the Universal House of Justice describes the present as a tumultuous "age of transition" in which humanity is being forced to abandon patterns of social organization that were suited to the needs of earlier epochs and to develop over time a new pattern of life that can lay the foundation for a peaceful and prosperous world civilization.[3] Thus, although crises and chaos currently abound, the Bahá'í writings suggest that future generations will look back on the current period as "the crowning stage in a millennia-long process which has brought [humanity] from its collective infancy to the threshold of maturity."[4] "Behind so much of the turbulence and commotion of contemporary life," then, Bahá'ís see "the fits and starts of a humanity struggling to come of age."[5]

As will be elaborated in subsequent chapters, this view of history, which is described in the Bahá'í writings as "progressive revelation," leads the Bahá'í community to orient its efforts in the realm of public discourse toward the goal of broadening the basis of society and fostering the gradual unification of the human race. "The supreme need of humanity," 'Abdu'l-Bahá explains, "is cooperation and reciprocity. The stronger the ties of fellowship and solidarity amongst men, the greater will be the power of constructiveness and accomplishment in all the planes of human activity."[6] Indeed, the Bahá'í writings go so far as to suggest that the very purpose of religion is to "unite all hearts and cause wars and dispute to vanish from the face of the earth."[7] Hence, "should religion become the cause of contention and enmity, its absence is preferable."[8]

This notion of religion as a unifying force is attractive for many today. Yet it can be difficult for some to accept the underlying concept of progressive revelation. For as briefly mentioned above, scholarship on religious history presents a wide variety of seemingly incompatible views. To what extent are these competing narratives of religious history compatible with the Bahá'í concept of progressive revelation? This chapter argues that each of the overarching narratives of religious history can be seen to cohere in certain ways with the vision of history provided by the Bahá'í writings. Additionally, there is at least one prominent theory of religious history that resonates with the central premise of the concept of progressive revelation, namely, that the periodic appearance of Divine Educators stimulates the advancement of human civilization.

Seven Narratives of Religion

Philosophers and social scientists working on the role of religion in society employ—either explicitly or implicitly—one of seven narratives of religious history, which I describe respectively as the (1) subtraction, (2) renewal, (3) transsecular, (4) postnaturalist, (5) construct, (6) perennial, and (7) developmental narratives.[9] Each of these narratives advances certain important yet limited insights about the broader course of religious history. I trace the influence of each of these narratives on the work of a number of prominent thinkers.

The Subtraction Narrative

Subtraction narratives claim that religion emerged as a means of coping with the conditions of ignorance and powerlessness that plagued early human existence. Hence, as people overcome these conditions, like they seem to be doing in today's world, they ought to become less religious. Or, put more simply, subtraction narratives claim that modernity and religion are inversely related: the more modern we are, the less religious we should be, and vice versa.

Auguste Comte presented one of the first subtraction narratives when he argued that humanity has gradually overcome its initial tendency to interpret everything as caused by human-like subjects. According to Comte, tribal societies believed that all natural objects possessed an individual mind, while archaic societies later claimed that the world was governed by a collection of semi-transcendent deities. "Higher religions," like Judaism and Christianity, subsequently rejected the idea of multiple divinities and embraced the concept of a single, transcendent God. Early modern peoples eventually lost faith in this God and posited instead deistic notions of a rationally creative force.[10] Finally, truly modern peoples began to see through supernaturalism outright and to embrace a positivist worldview that focuses entirely on the immanent features of the natural world.

Daniel Dennett has presented a revised version of this Comtean subtraction narrative. Dennett claims that religious ideas arise from the combination of the human tendency to see more agency in the world than actually exists and our desire to continue interacting with departed loved ones.[11] In order to counteract the inevitable falsification of religious ideas, early leaders worked to make their beliefs immune from empirical critique. This project of protective theology has since been the prime mover of religious history, as it has led people to develop increasingly abstract notions of divinity. This drive toward religious abstraction culminated during the Enlightenment when deist philosophers conceptualized God as little more than an abstract lawgiver. Deism then enabled a small group of thinkers to posit that "God" was a mere placeholder for the system of blind laws that actually governs nature. According to Dennett, this way of thinking inaugurated a period of unprecedented intellectual advancement by helping people abandon religion outright and embrace a naturalistic worldview. Admittedly, although growing numbers are accepting naturalism today, the overwhelming majority of the world's population remains, by any definition, highly religious. Yet for Dennett, this fact does not undermine naturalism. It rather demonstrates that the decline of religion is not a foregone conclusion but instead a difficult goal that must be energetically pursued.[12]

The Renewal Narrative

Renewal narratives accept the subtractivist claim that modernizing forces propel the decline and marginalization of religion. However, instead of characterizing this process as an integral feature of social progress, renewal narratives present it as a disaster that needs to be repaired. Most renewal narratives therefore argue that all the major problems of the modern world arose precisely because people abandoned the true religious path. Accordingly, the only way to solve our contemporary problems is to somehow renew our engagement with an older religious truth. Fundamentalists who idolize "some perfect embodiment of the true religion in the past" embrace a version of this renewal narrative.[13] Yet so too do numerous sophisticated thinkers who find fault with modern Western civilization and look favourably upon instances of our collective religious past.

Alasdair MacIntyre is one among this latter group.[14] MacIntyre argues that the "virtue tradition" of moral inquiry, which arose in ancient Greece and culminated in Thomistic Catholicism, generated what we now identify as the best features of modern Western morality. Yet modern Westerners rejected the foundational teachings of the virtue tradition during the Enlightenment and sought to rearticulate its moral insights within a secular, naturalistic worldview. As a result, modern Western civilization has fallen into a cycle of moral and intellectual decay. Indeed, MacIntyre concludes that the West's plight has become so severe that those who recognize the virtue tradition's truth should abandon modern societies and began working instead to construct new "local forms of community within which [the virtue tradition] can be sustained through the new dark ages which are already upon us."[15]

Martin Heidegger advances a less conventional, yet still influential, renewal narrative. His basic argument is that pre-Socratic Greek polytheism cultivated a benevolently pluralistic spiritual orientation by encouraging people to remain open to the many ways the gods could shape the world.[16] However, Plato transformed this orientation by binding the concept of God to the idea that the world displays a single, unchanging order.

The entirety of Western civilization originated in this Platonic conceptual shift.[17] Western societies have therefore long worked to find ways to uncover the world's order and then use this knowledge to reorganize nature and human life. Thus, during the medieval period, many Christians claimed that the world's order could be understood by correctly interpreting Holy Scripture. In the early modern period, this conviction evolved into the notion that humans participated directly in the divine life and could therefore discover truth by rigorously using their rational-cognitive faculties. Finally, during the later stages of modernity, the idea arose that "God" was a mere concept that people used to give order to their lives and the world.[18] Although many thinkers have worked to remedy the late modern collapse of belief, Heidegger suggests that the only way to do so is to go back beyond the Platonic beginnings of Western civilization and creatively revitalize the more pluralistic spiritual tradition of the pre-Socratic Greeks.[19]

The Transsecular Narrative
In contrast to both subtraction and renewal narratives, transsecular narratives claim that the forces of modernization do not cause religion's marginalization and decline but rather its transformation. Transsecular narratives accept the idea that modern phenomena like democracy, science and technology, and capitalism permanently disrupt pre-modern forms of religion. But they also preserve the renewalist claim that religion has a vital and enduring role to play in modern affairs. Many transsecular narratives advance their arguments by emphasizing how modern socio-political transformations create novel conditions of religious diversity. The core idea, then, is that the pluralization of modern religious life fundamentally undermines pre-modern religious structures without demolishing religion's ability to exert a significant influence on thought, action, and culture in the contemporary world.

Charles Taylor's recent work exemplifies elements of this transsecular narrative. He argues that the processes of modernization fundamentally altered the "conditions of belief" in Western culture.[20] Thus, whereas every aspect of medieval Western culture referenced God, modern Western culture has learned to approach reality in a way that is compatible with a wide variety of religious and non-religious perspectives. Admittedly, the rise of atheism played a central role in stimulating this development. Yet it is not "religion" as such that declined in the modern West, but rather only the kind of unproblematic and homogenous religious life that characterized the pre-modern world.[21] Modern peoples therefore must now choose from an ever-expanding variety of religious and non-religious perspectives.[22]

The Postnaturalist Narrative

Although the postnaturalist narrative could plausibly be placed within the trans-secular domain, it has gained such prominence in contemporary debates that it is worth considering on its own. Postnaturalist narratives argue that modern science disrupted theologically oriented views of nature, but science has since become falsely bound up with the ideology of naturalism. They therefore claim that modern ideas about the conflict between science and religion have less to do with science and religion as such than with the attempts of those who embrace a naturalistic worldview to claim modern science as their own. Some postnaturalist narratives go further still and contend that recent advancements in natural-scientific theory and the philosophy of science actually help us begin investigating non-material realities with more profundity and rigor than ever before.

Thomas Nagel's critical engagements with reductive naturalism employ this line of thought.[23] Nagel argues that "neo-Darwinian" naturalism hinders our ability to make sense of the scientifically known world by forcing us to discount any ideas that may seem to legitimize religious worldviews.[24] Nagel expresses particular concern about how neo-Darwinism prohibits people from seriously considering the quite obvious fact that the mind is an irreducibly subjective phenomenon.[25] The neo-Darwinians' reasoning on this front is clear: if we accept the irreducible subjectivity of mind, then we must also accept the idea that subjectivity somehow resides in the metaphysical structure of the world, and this claim seems to legitimize religious worldviews. Hence, they conclude, it cannot be true.[26] According to Nagel, however, it might just be that the kind of teleological ideas that many religious thinkers have used to make sense of the world can help us understand nature's apparent tendency to produce ever-greater states of complexity, spontaneity, and mental life. Himself an avowed atheist, Nagel decries the pervasive influence of reductive naturalism and encourages us to consider more openly the plausibility of teleological ideas.

The Construct Narrative

Construct narratives explore how the concept of "religion in general," which is to say the idea that religion is a general phenomenon that is variously instantiated throughout history and around the world, arose, or at least acquired a more determinate shape, during the modern period. These narratives debate whether or to what extent this new concept of religion was an illusion, a discovery, the mask of an expansionary political endeavour, or a mix of all three.

Brent Nongbri, for one, claims that the concept of religion was created during the post-Reformation fragmentation of European Christianity.

Following the so-called European Wars of Religion, he argues, the idea emerged that "different religions stand in tension" with one another and offer fundamentally "competing ways to salvation."[27] Early modern Europeans then applied this framework to the great cultural diversity they were encountering around the world during their early colonial endeavours. Nongbri thus presents the gradual development of the notion of "world religions" as, to quote Peter Harrison, a "projection of Christian disunity onto the world."[28] Nongbri accordingly recommends that we avoid using the term "religion" and simply recognize instead that rituals, beliefs about divinity, and other such phenomena are part and parcel of what it means to inhabit most non-Western and pre-modern societies.[29]

Proceeding somewhat differently, Jason Josephson explores how the Japanese constructed a general concept of religion during early modernity through their efforts to placate aggressive Western powers without opening their country to what they saw as the destructive influence of Christianity.[30] The idea of Shintoism, he shows, was invented during this period and differentiated from "religions" like Christianity and Buddhism in order to preserve a spiritualized Japanese vision of public life without violating the new Western-enforced dictates of religious freedom. This "Shinto secular," as Josephson calls it, helped the Japanese de-Christianize Western science and politics while presenting these phenomena as confirmations of their own ancient Shinto ways. Josephson thus uses the Japanese example to undermine the idea that all general concepts of religion have been created in and exported by the West.[31]

Articulating another angle still, Guy Stroumsa argues that "religion" was one of the most significant discoveries of the early modern period. He suggests that it was only after encountering previously unknown (e.g., Native American) and highly advanced (e.g., Chinese) civilizations, learning to read and historically locate a wider range of ancient texts through new philological methods, and questioning Christianity's superiority after many years of violent sectarian struggle that the idea of "religion" as a general category that is variously instantiated throughout history and around the world emerged.[32] This is not to say that early modern scholars conceptualized religion correctly; indeed, Stroumsa shows how many pursued their inquiries within a narrow biblical lens. Nevertheless, he explains that their underlying belief in the unity of humankind and their use of richly interdisciplinary and cross-cultural methods helped them steadily improve their conceptualization. Stroumsa even suggests that contemporary researchers would benefit by reincorporating elements of this approach into their understanding of religion today.[33]

The Perennial Narrative
Perennial narratives claim that all the world's religions display common core characteristics. For some readers, the word "perennial" immediately brings to mind the *philosophia perennis*, or perennial philosophy, which holds that all religions are partial manifestations of a higher mystical path. This perspective, which gained prominence through Jewish, Christian, and Islamic engagements with Neoplatonic thought during the ancient and medieval periods, was revitalized in modern West by figures like Aldous Huxley and H. P. Blavatsky.[34] The spread of perennial philosophical thought played a key role in stimulating the New Age movement and the idea of being "spiritual but not religious."[35] However, a much wider range of positions also falls within the perennial narrative's domain. Arnold Toynbee and Ibn Khaldûn, for example, highlight the perennial patterns that characterize the emergence and decline of religious civilizations, while Søren Kierkegaard and contemporary Buddhist thinkers emphasize the common existential structures that all religious systems display.[36] And still others claim that all the world's religious traditions interact with the same transcendent reality, albeit within different cultural and historical contexts.

John Hick's philosophy of religion exemplifies this latter variant of the perennial narrative. He claims that each of the world's major religions arose as some segment of humanity responded to an encounter with transcendence.[37] Because of the unique context of each group, their religious responses differed in significant ways. We therefore see important differences between the world's religions. Yet because they also all encountered the same transcendent reality, they came away with many of the same insights and ideas. Hence, the world's religions also display many important similarities. For these reasons, Hick concludes that we should abandon the idea that there is one true religion and see instead that all religions constitute legitimate and structurally similar responses to the same transcendent reality.[38]

The Developmental Narrative
Developmental narratives claim that religion has proceeded through several stages of historical development. These narratives were initially advanced in the West in order to show how all other religions were steps along a progressive ladder that culminated in European Christianity. G. W. F. Hegel provided what is still one the most extensive and sophisticated versions of this Euro- and Christo-centric developmental perspective.[39] Though one still encounters such developmental narratives today, most contemporary thinkers advance much more globally nuanced and open-ended conclusions.[40]

Robert Bellah's *Religion in Human Evolution* has made an influential contribution to this new line of developmental thought. His main argument is that religion has long played a central role in stimulating humanity's cognitive development. He demonstrates this by highlighting the isomorphism between the mimetic, mythic, and theoretic stages of human cognitive capacity and the tribal, archaic, and axial phases of religious history.[41] This isomorphism between cognitive capacity and religious form exists, he suggests, because religion tends to sacralize those aspects of culture that sustain the accumulation of knowledge and social complexity. Thus, during the tribal phase of history, religion helped launch the process of human learning and cultural evolution by establishing sacred rituals, as it was only through indefinitely preserved ritual that early humans could generate collective knowledge. During the archaic phase of religious history, religion facilitated the emergence of encompassing myths that enabled people to generate more intricate, universal, and historically extended kinds of knowledge. Hence, during the archaic period, we witness the appearance of more complex and powerful civilizations like the Aztec, Yoruba, Hawaiian, Egyptian, and Mesopotamian empires. Yet during the subsequent "axial" period, marginal prophets arose and criticized these mythological systems. Their teachings were then preserved in written texts and used to launch traditions of philosophical, scientific, and theological inquiry. It was therefore largely via the religious transformations of the axial age that humanity gained the ability to think in abstract conceptual terms.[42]

Progressive Revelation

Limitations of space prohibit me from examining the strengths and weaknesses of all seven narratives. However, it should not be hard to see that each one offers important insights that the others do not contain. It is therefore impossible to say that one and only one narrative framework is true. Rather, the challenge is to find a way to weave their respective insights together into a broader and more nuanced narrative whole.

I suggest that the Bahá'í concept of progressive revelation provides us with a fruitful perspective from which to pursue this task. Accordingly, I draw from Bahá'í sources to substantiate my application of this concept to the field of religious history. Progressive revelation posits that the advancement of human civilization is stimulated by the periodic appearance of Divine Messengers Who manifest the attributes of God, disclose His will and purpose to humankind, and release fresh measures of spiritual potency into the world. Thus, while each Messenger has a unique mission and appears in a distinctive cultural and historical context, all of Them—as well as the communities and traditions that arise in response to Their appearance—are expressions of a universal process of the advancement of human civilization. Although this vision of religious history may appear to resonate primarily with the developmental narrative lens, it also embraces many of the processes and dynamics emphasized by the other six narratives.

The perspective of progressive revelation leads one to reject the subtractivist claim that the forces of modernization fundamentally undermine religion. However, it also recognizes that many facets of previous religious epochs will be abandoned as human civilization continues to progress. "If long-cherished ideals and time-honoured institutions," Shoghi Effendi explains, "if certain social assumptions and religious formulae have ceased to promote the welfare of the generality of mankind, if they no longer minister to the needs of a continually evolving humanity, let them be swept away and relegated to the limbo of obsolescent and forgotten doctrines. Why should these, in a world subject to the immutable law of change and decay, be exempt from the deterioration that must needs overtake every human institution?"[43]

At the same time, the renewalist insight that the modern decline of religion has caused many of the most pressing crises in the world today finds support in Bahá'í texts. As the Universal House of Justice wrote in a public statement to the leaders of the world:

> However vital a force religion has been in the history of mankind, and however dramatic the current resurgence of militant religious fanaticism, religion and religious institutions have, for many decades, been viewed by increasing numbers of people as irrelevant to the major concerns of the modern world. In its place they have turned either to the hedonistic pursuit of material satisfactions or to the following of man-made ideologies designed to rescue society from the evident evils under which it groans.... How tragic is the record of the substitute faiths that the worldly-wise of our age have created. In the massive disillusionment of entire populations who have been taught to worship at their altars can be read history's irreversible verdict on their value. The fruits these doctrines have produced, after decades of an increasingly unrestrained exercise of power by those who owe their ascendancy in human affairs to them, are the social and economic ills that blight every region of our world in the closing years of the twentieth century.[44]

The perspective of progressive revelation also affirms aspects of the transsecular narrative by emphasizing that humanity is currently proceeding through an unprecedented period of transition that is characterized by processes of religious and political transformation:

The catastrophic fall of mighty monarchies and empires in the European continent, allusions to some of which may be found in the prophecies of Bahá'u'lláh; the decline that has set in, and is still continuing, in the fortunes of the Shí'ih hierarchy in His own native land; the fall of the Qájár dynasty, the traditional enemy of His Faith; the overthrow of the Sultanate and the Caliphate, the sustaining pillars of Sunní Islám, to which the destruction of Jerusalem in the latter part of the first century of the Christian era offers a striking parallel; the wave of secularization which is invading the Muḥammadan ecclesiastical institutions in Egypt and sapping the loyalty of its staunchest supporters; the humiliating blows that have afflicted some of the most powerful Churches of Christendom in Russia, in Western Europe and Central America; the dissemination of those subversive doctrines that are undermining the foundations and overthrowing the structure of seemingly impregnable strongholds in the political and social spheres of human activity; the signs of an impending catastrophe, strangely reminiscent of the Fall of the Roman Empire in the West, which threatens to engulf the whole structure of present-day civilization—all witness to the tumult which the birth of... the Religion of Bahá'u'lláh has cast into the world—a tumult which will grow in scope and in intensity as the implications of this constantly evolving Scheme are more fully understood and its ramifications more widely extended over the surface of the globe.[45]

There are many resonances between postnaturalist perspectives and Bahá'í teachings about the role of science and religion in the current age of transition. According to 'Abdu'l-Bahá, the insights and methods of modern science help us think in a more balanced and rigorous way about the spiritual features of reality. "Religious teaching which is at variance with science and reason," He explains, "is human invention and imagination unworthy of acceptance, for the antithesis and opposite of knowledge is superstition born of the ignorance of man. If we say religion is opposed to science, we lack knowledge of either true science or true religion, for both are founded upon the premises and conclusions of reason, and both must bear its test."[46] At the same time, Bahá'í sources decry the growing influence of voices of "dogmatic materialism" that claim "to be the voice of 'science'" and that systematically endeavour to "exclude from intellectual life all impulses arising from the spiritual level of human consciousness."[47]

The construct narrative contains a number of relevant insights. The Bahá'í International Community (BIC) has acknowledged the "confusion that surrounds virtually every aspect of the subject of religion" and has suggested that the situation is so dire that humanity must find ways to "recast the whole conception."[48] It goes on to challenge in particular the idea "that by 'religion' is intended the multitude of sects currently in existence."[49] That said, the Bahá'í writings avoid the overly constructivist conclusion that "religion" is merely the false creation of modern Western intellectuals by suggesting that a clear understanding of the "unity of religion" is an essential facet of any mature pattern of collective, global thought.[50]

Perennial narrative perspectives align quite directly with the historical perspective of progressive revelation. Thus, we find Bahá'u'lláh describing His own Message as but the most recent expression of "the changeless Faith of God, eternal in the past, eternal in the future," while 'Abdu'l-Bahá states that "the Prophets and Manifestations of God bring always the same teaching."[51] Bahá'u'lláh furthermore explains that "the difference between the ordinances under which [different cultures and religious traditions] abide should be attributed to the varying requirements and exigencies of the age in which they were revealed. All of them, except a few which are the outcome of human perversity, were ordained of God, and are a reflection of His Will and Purpose."[52]

Although the above reflections move swiftly through both the Bahá'í writings and contemporary scholarship, they illustrate several ways in which the concept of progressive revelation can be applied to reconcile various insights that are advanced within the literature on religious history. This is intended to be only the first step toward a long and broad path of inquiry that can elaborate elements of a Bahá'í perspective on history and correlate them with relevant lines of contemporary scholarship.

Of course, one element of this perspective is the idea that the advancement of civilization is propelled by the periodic appearance of Divine Messengers. Although on the surface this can appear to be a controversial claim to make within the field of religious history, there is a growing body of scholarship on the idea of the axial age that helps us to appreciate its plausibility.

The Idea of an Axial Age

German philosopher Karl Jaspers articulated the axial age thesis in 1949. Calling into question the widespread belief that Christianity was the axis or turning point of human history, he argued that the axis of human history can alternatively be found in the collection of religious-philosophical movements that appeared throughout the world during the first millennium BCE. He explains that "the most extraordinary events are concentrated in this period."[53]

Confucius and Lao-tse were living in China, all the schools of Chinese philosophy came into being.... India produced the Upanishads and Buddha and, like China, ran the whole gamut of philosophical possibilities down to scepticism, to materialism, sophism and nihilism; in Iran Zarathustra taught a challenging view of the world as a struggle between good and evil; in Palestine the prophets made their appearance, from Elijah, by way of Isaiah and Jeremiah to Deutero-Isaiah; Greece witnessed the appearance of Homer, of the philosophers—Parmenides, Heraclitus and Plato—of the tragedians, Thucydides and Archimedes. Everything implied by these names developed almost simultaneously in China, India, and the West, without any one of these regions knowing of the others.[54]

These movements, he continues, collectively established "the fundamental categories within which we still think today," as well as the philosophical and religious traditions "by which human beings still live."[55] In fact, he suggests that, despite the profundity and scope of later movements like Christianity, Islam, Mahayana Buddhism, neo-Confucianism, and Hellenism, even these remained within the parameters set by the classical axial breakthroughs.

Jaspers goes on to argue that the first fundamentally new thing to emerge after the classical axial period was modern science. Nevertheless, science can never provide us with a full-fledged worldview, as "the sum-total of the sciences does not give us reality in its entirety," but rather provides us with a "mobile," "manifold," and "forever incomplete" system of methods and concepts that help us more effectively navigate the world.[56] The most important result of modern science has therefore been the production of technologies that facilitate the material unification of the world. Although members of the different axial civilizations interacted with one another by, for example, engaging in long-range trade or by participating in intercivilizational military campaigns, the normal state of affairs was one of isolation. Yet since the advent of modern technologies like the steam engine and the telegraph, people have found their lives "filled with the daily news that comes... from all parts [of the world]."[57] Indeed, reflecting on the rapid advancement of globalizing technologies, Jaspers concludes that "today, for the first time, there is a real unity of mankind which consists in the fact that nothing essential can happen anywhere that does not concern all."[58] "The unity of the earth has arrived," he continues, as "all the crucial problems have become world problems, the situation a situation of mankind."[59]

The emergence of a global civilization has proven quite challenging, as neither the ideologies that animate the modern West nor the systems of practice and thought that arose during the axial age have been able to integrate the endeavours of the entire human race. Jaspers therefore concludes that humanity stands in need of a new socio-spiritual revolution, which can be likened in its effect to the net impact of all the axial breakthroughs.

He envisions two ways that such a second axial age could emerge. First, it might arise when one or several individuals successfully reorganize humanity's individual and collective affairs through the power of a "fresh revelation from God."[60] Jaspers considers this route unlikely. Alternatively, the second axial age could come about when humanity develops a new pattern of global public discourse that is capable of investigating the spiritual dimensions of reality and human life and of applying the insights gained thereby to the task of constructing a new world civilization. Although Jaspers considers this second route more plausible, he readily admits that the reality of the second axial age must remain "beyond our powers of imagination" until it has actually appeared.[61]

The resonances between Jaspers's axial age thesis and the Bahá'í concept of progressive revelation should not be hard to see: both reconceptualize the variety of religious traditions that exist around the world as expressions of a deeper and unified process of civilizational development, posit that many of the major moments of development have been stimulated by the appearance of spiritually illumined individuals, envision the profound spiritual transformation of our emerging global society, and claim that humanity must establish a new pattern of global discourse in which the knowledge systems of science and religion are both considered valid and important sources of insight.

Of course, there are also many significant differences between the two. Among the most obvious is the fact that Jaspers rejects the idea that humanity requires a new revelation to reach the next stage of collective evolution, whereas the Bahá'í writings see Bahá'u'lláh as the Divine Educator Who has come precisely to accomplish this task. Furthermore, while Jaspers's axial age thesis focuses on the Eurasian religious-philosophical movements that arose during the period of 800–200 BCE, the Bahá'í writings affirm a much broader and less stage-like view of religious history. In this regard, the Bahá'í writings focus less on the idea of distinct religious ages and more on the role that individual Manifestations of God play in the gradual advancement of civilization.

Concerning this latter point, it is interesting to note that scholars have subsequently developed Jaspers's theory in ways that align more with the concept of progressive revelation. Civilization was forever changed by ancient-mythological empires, the so-called axial renaissance movements, and the forces of modernization that have swept the world during the last several centuries. Why, then, one might ask, should we insist upon presenting the collection of religious-philosophical movements that arose during the period of 800–200 BCE as the axis of human history? Eric Voegelin describes the implications of this line of thought well:

> In order to elevate the period from 800 to 200 B.C., in which the parallel outbursts occur, to the rank of the great epoch in history, Jaspers had to deny to the earlier and later spiritual outbursts the epochal character which in their own consciousness they certainly had... [But if] spiritual outbursts were to be recognized as the constituents of meaning in history, the epiphanies of Moses and Christ, or of Mani and Mohammed, could hardly be excluded from the list; and if they were included, the axis time expanded into an open field of spiritual eruptions extending over millennia.[62]

Following this critique, John D. Boy and John Torpey have concluded that the only way to preserve the insights of the axial age thesis is to abandon the idea of a distinct axial age and focus instead on a broader concept of "axiality," which allows for the various moments of socio-spiritual breakthrough that have emerged throughout the ages.[63]

Suffice it to say, the purpose of this section has not been to claim that the Bahá'í concept of progressive revelation can somehow be equated with a more advanced version of the axial age thesis. To the contrary, my goal has simply been to help readers see how at least one plausible academic theory of religious history resonates with a core element of the Bahá'í view of history—that the periodic coming of Divine Messengers is a key driving force of human history. Indeed, in my estimation, the Bahá'í writings ought not to be engaged as the source of specific theories that can be either falsified or confirmed but rather as a reality of towering complexity and scope toward which finite minds can turn in order to derive insight and inspiration for the theories they must perpetually cast, refine, and recreate.

This chapter has initiated an inquiry into the "particular conception of history, its direction and course," that is presented in the Bahá'í writings and that informs the efforts of the Bahá'í community to contribute to public discourse.[64] It proceeded with this task by first elaborating seven narratives of religious of history that are used to make sense of the changing place of religion in the modern world and then showing how the Bahá'í teachings resonate with facets of each of these narratives. The chapter then considered how the increasingly prominent axial age thesis resonates with the core

Bahá'í idea that the periodic coming of Divine Messengers stimulates the advancement of civilization.

Numerous lines of inquiry emerge from the arguments presented above. However, two appear particularly significant. First, other researchers could consider more closely the insights and limitations of each of the seven narratives of religious history described above, as well as how they respectively illuminate the broader vision of history that is contained in the Bahá'í teachings. For instance, Dennett grounds his analysis of the subtractive dynamics of religious history in the idea that religious leaders have historically encouraged people to embrace increasingly abstract notions of divinity in order to protect the very idea of the divine from falsification.[65] The Bahá'í teachings obviously do not endorse Dennett's basic conclusions on this front. Nevertheless, Dennett's arguments do help us appreciate the Bahá'í claim that religious leaders often precipitate periods of religious decline by equating their own theological constructs with revealed divine truth. Although this is but one brief example, one can see how approaching the work of a growing number of thinkers who operate within the parameters of the subtraction narrative, as well as within the parameters of the other six narratives, could expand our understanding of the vision of religious history contained in the Bahá'í writings and increase the ability of the Bahá'í community to contribute to the broader academic and public discourses on religion.

A second line of inquiry could consider more closely the concept of the axial age, both as initially articulated by Jaspers and as subsequently developed by the likes of S. N. Eisenstadt, Marshall Hodgson, Robert Bellah, Charles Taylor, Lewis Mumford, and Eric Voeglin, among others. Future research could examine at greater length the nature and impact of the various moments of socio-spiritual "axiality" that have arisen throughout the longer arch of human history. When and where have such moments of axiality taken place? How are they correlated with the appearance of figures that the Bahá'í writings identify as Divine Messengers? How would we understand the historical influence of Islam in this light? How about the modern European breakthrough? And what arguments and historical trajectories might lead us to conclude that contemporary humanity will undergo another axial revolution? Such research can productively draw upon the expanding field of world history, in which figures such as William H. McNeill, Jürgen Osterhammel, C. A. Bayly, and John Darwin have advanced a wide variety of useful conceptual and empirical perspectives.

Notes

1. Bahá'í International Community, "One Common Faith" (Haifa, Israel: Bahá'í World Centre, 2005), 33–34.
2. Ibid., 34.
3. Universal House of Justice to the Conference of the Continental Board of Counsellors, December 28, 2010, http://www.bahai.org/library/authoritative-texts/the-universal-house-of-justice/messages/#d=20101228_001&f=f1-51.
4. Universal House of Justice to the Bahá'ís of Iran, March 2, 2013, http://www.bahai.org/library/authoritative-texts/the-universal-house-of-justice/messages/#d=20130302_001&f=f1.
5. Ibid.
6. 'Abdu'l-Bahá, *The Promulgation of Universal Peace*, ed. Howard MacNutt, 2nd ed. (Wilmette, IL: US Bahá'í Publishing Trust, 1982), 338.
7. 'Abdu'l-Bahá, *Paris Talks*, ed. Sara Louisa Blomfield (London: UK Bahá'í Publishing Trust, 1972), 131.
8. 'Abdu'l-Bahá, *Promulgation*, 298.
9. For a more expansive account of the framework of seven narratives, see Benjamin Schewel, *Seven Ways of Looking at Religion* (New Haven, CT: Yale University Press, 2017).
10. August Comte, *The Positive Philosophy of Auguste Comte*, ed. Harriet Martineau (Cambridge, UK: Cambridge University Press, 2009), 231.
11. Daniel C. Dennett, *Breaking the Spell: Religion as a Natural Phenomenon* (New York: Penguin, 2006), *passim*.
12. Ibid.
13. Steve Bruce, *Fundamentalism* (Malden, MA: Polity, 2000), 12–13.
14. See Alasdair MacIntyre, *After Virtue: A Study in Moral Theory*, 3rd ed. (Notre Dame, IN: University of Notre Dame Press, 2007). For other significant renewal narratives, many of which emphasize different religious traditions, see Muhammad Iqbal, *The Reconstruction of Religious Thought in Islam* (Stanford, CA: Stanford University Press, 2013); Mircea Eliade, *The Sacred and the Profane: The Nature of Religion* (San Diego, CA: Harcourt, 1987); Jens Zimmermann, *Humanism and Religion: A Call for the Renewal of Western Culture* (New York: Oxford University Press, 2012); and R. Ward Holder, *Crisis and Renewal: The Era of the Reformations* (Lousville, KY: Westminster John Knox, 2009).
15. MacIntyre, *After Virtue*, 263.
16. Mark Wrathall and Morganna Lambeth, "Heidegger's Last God," *Inquiry* 54, no. 2 (2011): 174.
17. Martin Heidegger, "Plato's Doctrine of Truth," in *Pathmarks*, ed. William McNeill (Cambridge, UK: Cambridge University Press, 1998), 164.
18. Mark Wrathall, *Heidegger and Unconcealment* (Cambridge, UK: Cambridge University Press, 2011), 218–21.

19 Heidegger, "Plato's Doctrine of Truth," 178–79.
20 Charles Taylor, *A Secular Age* (Cambridge, MA: Belknap Press, 2007), 3.
21 Other examples of transsecular narratives include Stephen Gaukroger, *The Emergence of a Scientific Culture: Science and the Shaping of Modernity 1210-1685* (New York: Oxford University Press, 2006); David Sorkin, *The Religious Enlightenment: Protestants, Jews, and Catholics from London to Vienna* (Princeton, NJ: Princeton University Press, 2008); Andrew Preston, *Sword of the Spirit, Shield of Faith: Religion in American War and Diplomacy* (New York: Random House, 2012).
22 Taylor, *A Secular Age*, 542.
23 For a summary of the controversy surrounding Nagel's work, see Andrew Ferguson, "The Heretic: Who Is Thomas Nagel and Why Are So Many of His Fellow Academics Condemning Him?" *Weekly Standard* (Washington, DC), March 2013, http://www.weeklystandard.com/articles/heretic_707692.html.
24 As he says, "The political urge to defend science education against the threats of religious orthodoxy, understandable though it is, has resulted in a counter orthodoxy, supported by bad arguments, and a tendency to overstate the legitimate scientific claims of evolutionary theory. Skeptics about the theory are seen as so dangerous, and so disreputably motivated, that they must be denied any shred of legitimate interest." See Thomas Nagel, *Secular Philosophy and the Religious Temperament: Essays 2002–2008* (Oxford, UK: Oxford University Press, 2009), 42.
25 See Nagel, *The View from Nowhere* (Oxford, UK: Oxford University Press, 1986).
26 Nagel, *Secular Philosophy*, 16–17. For other influential postnaturalist narratives, see David Bohm, *Wholeness and the Implicate Order* (New York: Routledge, 1980); Bernard d'Espagnat, *On Physics and Philosophy* (Princeton, NJ: Princeton University Press, 2006); John Polkinghorne, *Belief in God in an Age of Science* (New Haven, CT: Yale University Press, 2003); Henry P. Stapp, *Mind, Matter, and Quantum Mechanics*, 3rd ed. (New York: Springer, 2009); Pim van Lommel, *Consciousness beyond Life: The Science of the Near-Death Experience*, ed. Laura Vroomen (New York: HarperCollins, 2010); and Alfred North Whitehead, *Science and the Modern World* (New York: Free Press, 1997).
27 Brent Nongbri, *Before Religion: A History of a Modern Concept* (New Haven, CT: Yale University Press, 2012), 86.
28 Peter Harrison, *"Religion" and the Religions in the English Enlightenment* (Cambridge, UK: Cambridge University Press, 1990), 174.
29 Nongbri, *Before Religion*, 154–160.
30 Jason A. Josephson, *The Invention of Religion in Japan* (Chicago: University of Chicago Press, 2012).
31 Ibid., 1–22.

32 Guy G. Stroumsa, *A New Science: The Discovery of Religion in the Age of Reason* (Cambridge, MA: Harvard University Press, 2010).
33 Ibid., 1–14.
34 See Aldous Huxley, *The Perennial Philosophy: An Interpretation of the Great Mystics, East and West* (New York: Harper Perennial Modern Classics, 2009) and H. P. Blavatsky, *The Secret Doctrine*, ed. Boris de Zirkoff (Wheaton, IL: Theosophical Society in America, 1978).
35 Robert C. Fuller, *Spiritual, but Not Religious: Understanding Unchurched America* (New York: Oxford University Press, 2001).
36 See Ibn Khaldûn, *The Muqaddimah: An Introduction to History*, ed. N. J. Dawood and Franz Rosenthal (Princeton, NJ: Princeton University Press, 2004); Arnold Toynbee, *A Study of History*, vols. 1 and 2, ed. D. C. Somervell (Oxford, UK: Oxford University Press, 1987); Søren Kierkegaard, *The Concept of Anxiety: A Simple Psychologically Orienting Deliberation on the Dogmatic Issue of Hereditary Sin*, ed. Reidar Thomte and Albert B. Anderson (Princeton, NJ: Princeton University Press, 1980); and Steve Hagan, *Buddhism Plain and Simple* (Boston, MA: Broadway Books, 1997).
37 John Hick, *An Interpretation of Religion: Human Responses to the Transcendent*, 2nd ed. (New Haven, CT: Yale University Press).
38 Ibid., 1–20.
39 G. W. F. Hegel, *Lectures on the Philosophy of Religion, One-Volume Edition: The Lectures of 1827*, ed. and trans. Peter C. Hodgson (Oxford, UK: Oxford University Press, 2006).
40. See, for instance, Rodney Stark, *Discovering God: The Origins of the Great Religions and the Evolution of Belief* (New York: HarperCollins, 2007).
41 Robert N. Bellah, *Religion in Human Evolution: From the Paleolithic to the Axial Age* (Cambridge, MA: Belknap Press, 2011), *passim*.
42 Ibid.
43 Shoghi Effendi, *The World Order of Bahá'u'lláh* (Wilmette, IL: US Bahá'í Publishing Trust, 1991), 41.
44 Universal House of Justice, "The Promise of World Peace" (Haifa, Israel: Bahá'í World Centre, 1985), 5.
45 Shoghi Effendi, *World Order*, 155–56.
46 'Abdu'l-Bahá, *Promulgation*, 107.
47 Bahá'í International Community, *Century of Light* (Haifa, Israel: Bahá'í World Centre, 2001), 136, http://reference.bahai.org/en/t/bic/COL.
48 Bahá'í International Community, "One Common Faith," 11.
49 Ibid., 9.
50 Shoghi Effendi, *World Order*, 38–39.
51 Bahá'u'lláh, *The Kitáb-i-Aqdas*, ed. Shoghi Effendi and the Research Department of the Universal House of Justice (Haifa, Israel: Bahá'í World Centre, 1992), 85; 'Abdu'l-Bahá, *'Abdu'l-Bahá in London: Addresses and*

Notes of Conversations, ed. Eric Hammond (London: UK Bahá'í Publishing Trust, 1982), 57.
52 Bahá'u'lláh, *Proclamation of Bahá'u'lláh*, ed. Research Department of the Universal House of Justice (Wilmette, IL: US Bahá'í Publishing Trust, 1967), 114.
53 Karl Jaspers, *The Origin and Goal of History*, trans. Michael Bullock (New Haven, CT: Yale University Press, 1953), 2. It was first published in German in 1949.
54 Ibid.
55 Ibid.
56 Ibid., 84–86.
57 Ibid., 117.
58 Ibid., 139.
59 Ibid., 127.
60 Ibid., 227.
61 Ibid., 97.
62 Eric Voegelin, *Order and History*, vol. 4, ed. Michael Franz (Columbia, MO: University of Missouri Press, 2000), 49.
63 John D. Boy and John Torpey, "Inventing the Axial Age: The Origins and Uses of a Historical Concept," *Theory and Society* 42, no. 3 (March 24, 2013): 256.
64 Universal House of Justice to the Bahá'ís of Iran, March 2, 2013.
65 Dennett, *Breaking the Spell*, passim.

Bibliography

'Abdu'l-Bahá. *'Abdu'l-Bahá in London: Addresses and Notes of Conversation*. Edited by Eric Hammond. London: UK Bahá'í Publishing Trust, 1982.

———. *Paris Talks*. Edited by Sara Louisa Blomfield. London: UK Bahá'í Publishing Trust, 1972.

———. *The Promulgation of Universal Peace*. Edited by Howard MacNutt, 2nd ed. Wilmette, IL: US Bahá'í Publishing Trust, 1982.

Bahá'í International Community. *Century of Light*. Haifa, Israel: Bahá'í World Centre, 2001. http://reference.bahai.org/en/t/bic/COL/.

———. "One Common Faith." Haifa, Israel: Bahá'í World Centre, 2005.

Bahá'u'lláh. *The Kitáb-i-Aqdas*. Edited by Shoghi Effendi and the Research Department of the Universal House of Justice. Haifa, Israel: Bahá'í World Centre, 1992.

———. *Proclamation of Bahá'u'lláh*. Edited by the Research Department of the Universal House of Justice. Wilmette, IL: US Bahá'í Publishing Trust, 1967.

Bellah, Robert N. *Religion in Human Evolution: From the Paleolithic to the Axial Age*. Cambridge, MA: Bellknap Press, 2011.

Berger, Peter. "The Desecularization of the World: A Global Overview." In *The Desecularization of the World: Resurgent Religion and World Politics*, edited by Peter Berger, 1–18. Washington, DC: Wm. B. Eerdmans, 1999.

Blavatsky, H. P. *The Secret Doctrine*. Edited by Boris de Zirkoff. Wheaton, IL: Theosophical Society in America, 1978.

Bohm, David. *Wholeness and the Implicate Order*. New York: Routledge, 1980.

Boy, John D., and John Torpey. "Inventing the Axial Age: The Origins and Uses of a Historical Concept." *Theory and Society* 42, no. 3 (March 24, 2013): 241–59.

Bruce, Steve. *Fundamentalism*. Malden, MA: Polity, 2000.

Comte, Auguste. *The Positive Philosophy of Auguste Comte*. Edited by Harriet Martineau. Cambridge, UK: Cambridge University Press, 2009.

Dennett, Daniel C. *Breaking the Spell: Religion as a Natural Phenomenon*. New York: Penguin, 2006.

d'Espagnat, Bernard. *On Physics and Philosophy*. Princeton, NJ: Princeton University Press, 2006.

Eliade, Mircea. *The Sacred and the Profane: The Nature of Religion*. San Diego, CA: Harcourt, 1987.

Ferguson, Andrew. "The Heretic: Who Is Thomas Nagel and Why Are So Many of His Fellow Academics Condemning Him?" *Weekly Standard* (Washington, DC), March 2013. http://www.weeklystandard.com/heretic/article/707692.

Fuller, Robert C. *Spiritual, but Not Religious: Understanding Unchurched America*. New York: Oxford University Press, 2001.

Gaukroger, Stephen. *The Emergence of a Scientific Culture: Science and the Shaping of Modernity 1210–1685*. New York: Oxford University Press, 2006.

Hagan, Steve. *Buddhism Plain and Simple*. Boston, MA: Broadway Books, 1997.

Harrison, Peter. *"Religion" and the Religions in the English Enlightenment*. Cambridge, UK: Cambridge University Press, 1990.

Hegel, G. W. F. *Lectures on the Philosophy of Religion: One-Volume Edition: The Lectures of 1827*. Edited and translated by Peter C. Hodgson. Oxford, UK: Oxford University Press, 2006.

Heidegger, Martin. "Plato's Doctrine of Truth." *Pathmarks*, edited by William McNeill. Cambridge, UK: Cambridge University Press, 1998, pp. 155–82.

Hick, John. *An Interpretation of Religion: Human Responses to the Transcendent*, 2nd ed. New Haven, CT: Yale University Press, 2005.

Holder, R. Ward. *Crisis and Renewal: The Era of the Reformations*. Louisville, KY: Westminster John Knox, 2009.

Huxley, Aldous. *The Perennial Philosophy: An Interpretation of the Great Mystics, East and West*. New York: Harper Perennial Modern Classics, 2009.

Iqbal, Muhammad. *The Reconstruction of Religious Thought in Islam*. Stanford, CA: Stanford University Press, 2013.

Jaspers, Karl. *The Origin and Goal of History*. Translated by Michael Bullock. New Haven, CT: Yale University Press, 1953.

Josephson, Jason A. *The Invention of Religion in Japan*. Chicago: University of Chicago Press, 2012.

Khaldûn, Ibn. *The Muqaddimah: An Introduction to History*. Edited by N. J. Dawood and Franz Rosenthal. Princteon, NJ: Princeton University Press, 2004.

Kierkegaard, Søren. *The Concept of Anxiety: A Simple Psychologically Orienting Deliberation on the Dogmatic Issue of Hereditary Sin.* Edited by Reidar Thomte and Albert B. Anderson. Princeton, NJ: Princeton University Press, 1980.

MacIntyre, Alasdair. *After Virtue: A Study in Moral Theory.* 3rd ed. Notre Dame, IN: University of Notre Dame Press, 2007.

Nagel, Thomas. *Secular Philosophy and the Religious Temperament: Essays 2002–2008.* Oxford, UK: Oxford University Press, 2009.

———. *The View from Nowhere.* Oxford, UK: Oxford University Press, 1986.

Nongbri, Brent. *Before Religion: A History of a Modern Concept.* New Haven, CT: Yale University Press, 2012.

Polkinghorne, John. *Belief in God in an Age of Science.* New Haven, CT: Yale University Press, 2003.

Preston, Andrew. *Sword of the Spirit, Shield of Faith: Religion in American War and Diplomacy.* New York: Random House, 2012.

Schewel, Benjamin. *Seven Ways of Looking at Religion: The Major Narratives.* New Haven, CT: Yale University Press, 2017.

Shoghi Effendi. *The World Order of Bahá'u'lláh.* Wilmette, IL: US Bahá'í Publishing Trust, 1991.

Sorkin, David. *The Religious Enlightenment: Protestants, Jews, and Catholics from London to Vienna.* Princeton, NJ: Princeton University Press, 2008.

Stapp, Henry P. *Mind, Matter, and Quantum Mechanics.* 3rd ed. New York: Springer, 2009.

Stark, Rodney. *The Triumph of Christianity: How the Jesus Movement Became the World's Largest Religion.* New York: HarperCollins, 2011.

Stroumsa, Guy G. *A New Science: The Discovery of Religion in the Age of Reason.* Cambridge, MA: Harvard University Press, 2010.

Taylor, Charles. *A Secular Age.* Cambridge, MA: Harvard University Press, 2007.

Toynbee, Arnold. *A Study of History.* Vols. 1 and 2. Edited by D. C. Somervell. Oxford, UK: Oxford University Press, 1987.

Universal House of Justice. Letter to the Conference of the Continental Board of Counsellors, December 28, 2010, http://www.bahai.org/library/authoritative-texts/the-universal-house-of-justice/messages/#d=20101228_001&f=f1-51.

———. Letter to the Bahá'ís of Iran, March 2, 2013. http://www.bahai.org/library/authoritative-texts/the-universal-house-of-justice/messages/#d=20130302_001&f=f1.

———. "The Promise of World Peace." Haifa, Israel: Bahá'í World Centre, 1985.

Van Lommel, Pim. *Consciousness beyond Life: The Science of the Near-Death Experience.* Edited by Laura Vroomen. New York: HarperCollins, 2010.

Voegelin, Eric. *Order and History.* Vol. 4. Edited by Michael Franz. Columbia, MO: University of Missouri Press, 2000.

Whitehead, Alfred North. *Science and the Modern World*. New York: Free Press, 1997.
Wrathall, Mark. *Heidegger and Unconcealment*. Cambridge, UK: Cambridge University Press, 2011.
Wrathall, Mark, and Morganna Lambeth. "Heidegger's Last God." *Inquiry* 54, no. 2 (March 25, 2011): 160–82.
Zimmermann, Jens. *Humanism and Religion: A Call for the Renewal of Western Culture*. New York: Oxford University Press, 2012.

CHAPTER TWO

RELIGION, SPIRITUAL PRINCIPLES, AND CIVIL SOCIETY

DAVID A. PALMER

The public sphere of collective global discourse is emerging within social spaces that are often referred to as "civil society." This sphere usually is understood as one that is rooted in the people; that enjoys some degree of autonomy from direct state control, from market forces, and from particularistic interest groups; and that contains a great diversity of groups, associations, networks, and movements that self-organize, act to improve or transform social conditions, and participate in public discourses.

Civil society is generally considered to be a good thing. A vibrant civil society is seen to be a desirable goal; it is actively pursued and promoted by international foundations, government policies, development organizations, UN agencies, and academic institutions. "Global civil society" has become institutionalized in many international forums, UN conferences, and transnational alliances on specific issues. Why this nearly universal legitimation of civil society? Civil society seems to be conceptualized as the arena within which a host of positive values are spontaneously manifested in the popular realm. These values include solidarity, participation, volunteerism, altruism, generosity, and justice. Civil society thus becomes a realm of freedom, where people take voluntary initiatives, self-organize at the grassroots to address social issues, participate in public affairs, and sacrifice their narrow interests for the common good. It is considered to have the dynamism and flexibility to solve social problems without the cost and inefficient bureaucracy of the state, and it can draw on moral and cultural resources to counterbalance the harsh realities of the market in meeting social needs. Indeed, current discourses on civil society tend to stress its complementarity to the state and the market, compensating for the limitations of both: as an arena for the expression of popular voices and interests in the face of state authority; as an aggregate of flexible actors who, being close to the grassroots, are more capable of providing social services than inefficient bureaucracies; and as a space of altruism and philanthropy, making up for the cold rationality of market efficiency.[1]

The Bahá'í teachings and the community's pattern of social engagement generally predispose Bahá'ís to support and identify with those elements of civil society that promote the enhancement of human dignity and reinforce unity and solidarity within and among communities. Indeed, civil society organizations and movements have been at the forefront of advancing some of the social teachings that were promulgated by Bahá'u'lláh and 'Abdu'l-Bahá as part of the core principles and mission of the Bahá'í faith over a century ago—lessons on establishing peace, unity, and justice among the peoples of the world; overcoming racism and prejudice of all kinds; building equality between men and women; reducing economic inequality; promoting universal education; and establishing world citizenship. From the early twentieth century onward, Bahá'ís have been active in movements for women's rights and racial equality. Following the spread of the Bahá'í Faith to countries outside the Middle East and North Atlantic regions in the second half of the twentieth century, Bahá'í communities in regions such as South America and India began initiatives in literacy, health, agricultural technology, and grassroots education. The Universal House of Justice, in a message to the Bahá'ís of the world on October 20, 1983, stated that the growth and expansion of the Bahá'í community had reached the point where processes of social and economic development "must be incorporated into its regular pursuits"; shortly afterward, an Office of Social and Economic Development was established at the Bahá'í World Centre to promote these efforts and to collect, consolidate, and disseminate learning.[2] In the course of these endeavours, many Bahá'ís, typically in an individual capacity, worked for or established their own non-governmental organizations (NGOs), and some projects evolved into sustained Bahá'í-inspired development organizations that fostered long-term interactions and collaborations with other organizations and institutions of civil society. In its 1985 statement "The Promise of World Peace," the Universal House of Justice remarks that the rise of humanitarian organizations and "the spread of women's and youth movements calling for an end to war" and of "widening networks of ordinary people"—all of which may be seen as components of civil society—are a sign of the constructive processes that lay the foundations of the universal peace "for which from age to age the sacred scriptures of mankind have constantly held the promise."[3]

While the Bahá'í community is organized under the authority of a single institutional structure whose governing bodies are elected at the local, national, and international levels, its affairs are decentralized to the greatest extent possible. There is no clergy. Consultation on community affairs is a core aspect of religious practice. Individual initiative is encouraged, and universal participation in the expansion, consolidation, and administration of the community is a fundamental goal and principle. Over the past few decades, the Universal House of Justice, in a series of global plans, has encouraged Bahá'ís around the world to learn how to apply and develop these approaches through a focus on community building that extends to all members of a neighbourhood, village, or social space regardless of religious affiliation. As they gain experience in this process, Bahá'ís undertake social actions of increasing duration, scale, and complexity for the purpose of improving the spiritual, social, and material conditions of life, and they endeavour to contribute to the prevalent discourses of society. The Bahá'í International Community (BIC) was one of the first NGOs to be given consultative status at the United Nations in 1947; as discussed in Julia Berger's contribution to this volume, the BIC has become one of the most active participants in the UN's consultations with civil society organizations, and it was the BIC's representative to the UN who was elected to represent global civil society at the UN's Millennium Summit in 2000.

The Bahá'í Faith, from its core teachings to its organizational structure and from its historical experience to its contemporary modes of social engagement, clearly has deep affinities with civil society as a space for the expression of its values and teachings. It is strongly committed to fostering people's capacity to associate at the grassroots. Its purpose is to develop a new social order that will emancipate humans from all forms of oppression, and it hopes to bring its teachings and experience to bear on the deliberations of the public sphere. While the Bahá'í Faith defines itself as a religion based on divine revelation with its specific articles of faith, laws, and practices, it considers its social principles to be equally important to and inseparable from its teachings on individual spiritual life and ethics. Thus it does not recognize itself in the conventional framing of religion in modern secular societies as restricted to the private domain of individual subjectivity, whose social expression should be limited to congregational gatherings of people sharing the same faith. However, since the Bahá'í teachings forbid involvement in partisan politics and any attempt to seize the levers of political power, the social engagement of Bahá'ís does not take the form adopted by some modern religious movements that have challenged the privatization of religion by reasserting the role of religion in the political realm.[4] Instead, civil society is the preferred space within which

Bahá'ís tend to collectively engage with other social actors at the national and the global level. Given the great diversity of forms of organization, discourse, and action that can be found within civil society, the application of Bahá'í principles to social engagement has become an important area of inquiry among Bahá'í practitioners and institutions. Through reflection and consultations informed by both experience in the field and research on the relevant Bahá'í writings and teachings, an increasingly coherent body of knowledge has begun to emerge that not only helps guide Bahá'ís in their own involvement in civil society, but also can contribute to broader debates and discussions on the role of religion in civil society.

In this chapter, I hope to bring some insights from this body of knowledge into dialogue with the academic discourse on civil society, which is derived from several disciplinary and theoretical traditions, primarily in sociology, political science, and development studies. It is but a preliminary outline of a set of problems and lines of inquiry that have been the subject of discussions and consultations among Bahá'ís for many years but that may also be of interest to the broader community of researchers and practitioners who approach civil society from either secular or religious perspectives.

I begin by considering current normative conceptualizations and social configurations of civil society, discussing its associational, deliberative, symbolic, and emancipatory dimensions and the possibilities and limitations thereof. I define civil society as social spaces for the voluntary and expansive expression of values of human solidarity and explain why religion occupies an ambiguous position in relation to such spaces. Religion is a key source of values and commitment to human solidarity in individual and community life; at the same time, many forms of prevalent religious discourse and action ignore or even undermine the values of solidarity that underpin civil society. I propose that this dilemma can be overcome through the application of "spiritual principles"—principles of ethics and modes of action derived from certain ontological assumptions about the spiritual dimension of human nature and about the nature of an ideal society. While spiritual principles do not eliminate the distinction between religion and civil society, they provide a language and lines of inquiry that can be applied within both religious and secular spaces. I explore the implications for civil society actors of explicitly reflecting on the foundations of their action as based on spiritual principles such as the oneness of humanity, justice, and participation in the generation and application of knowledge, and of operationalizing these principles in all aspects of the deliberations and actions of civil society networks and organizations. But religion, as well, needs to question its role and build its capacity to become a social vehicle for nurturing, upholding, and applying spiritual principles. To the extent to which both religion and civil society are able to operate according to these principles, they will be able to expand the social space of voluntary and expansive solidarity.

Four Dimensions of Civil Society
Academic and public discourse on civil society is rich and complex, with many different understandings of what civil society is. Without providing a lengthy review of these debates, we can see that different authors have focused on four different dimensions, types, or functions of civil society, which can be described respectively as the "associational," the "deliberative," the "symbolic," and the "emancipatory."[5]

The Associational Dimension
The "associational" fabric of civil society, first described by Alexis de Tocqueville, is based on voluntary associations—flourishing, lively groups that are spontaneously organized among the people; this is the soil and the social space in which people learn to self-organize, to work together with civility, and to cooperate across different associations.[6] Associational activity is the very baseline of what civil society is—people interact and create clubs, organizations, churches, parent-teacher associations, sports clubs, history societies, environmental groups, support groups, and so on. As long as there is a diversity of lively non-governmental, voluntary associations, the thought goes, civil society flourishes and social capital can grow. And inversely, as lamented by Robert D. Putnam, if people do not participate in such associations, there will be a declining social capital and civil society.[7]

There seems to be an assumption that popular self-organization is always in the direction of social progress and solidarity. Although much contemporary discourse tends to idealize or even romanticize the popular or "democratic" nature of civil society associations and NGOs, the reality is that they are not accountable to anyone but themselves and their funders.[8] Many voluntary groups are violent, racist, extremist, or intolerant.[9] What if, in some societies, much of the associational self-organizing is in the service of xenophobia, fanaticism, violence, or the suppression of women or minority groups? Such "anti-civil" organizations have, in recent decades, increased their influence in places as varied as the United States, Western Europe, the Islamic world, and East Asia.[10] Clearly, the significance of civil society must reside in more than the empirical fact of people's capacity to form associations. What, then, are the values that these associations should embody?

The Deliberative Dimension

The "deliberative" concept of civil society, which can be linked to Jürgen Habermas's public sphere, focuses on the social spaces and discursive practices within which public discourse, common norms, values, and ideals are debated and elaborated.[11] Within certain social spaces, through their rational conversations on issues of mutual concern, people are drawn out of their private and particularistic interests, converse and engage with each other with civility, and accept people of different opinions and backgrounds into the conversation. They develop an inclusive language and norms of communication and debate on and elaborate common ideals and moral values based on the inherent dignity of each participant and the equal application of justice to all. The discourses emerging from this deliberative sphere influence other political, legal, and social institutions, which gradually embody and reinforce those values. Deliberative civil society operates at the level of discourse and of the rules of discourse, which is to say that it takes shape as a discourse on values, the practice of those values, and their institutional reinforcement.

The Symbolic Dimension

Michael Karlberg discusses the concept of the public sphere in chapter 3, so I will not further elaborate here on the deliberative dimension of civil society. I will instead turn to Jeffrey Alexander's proposal of the "civil sphere" as a more empirically grounded and realistic alternative to the abstract rationalism and universalism of Habermas's vision. Alexander's conceptualization focuses on the symbolic structures and dynamics of civil society. It points to the historical processes of cultural change by which, within a given society, the symbolic codes that define the boundaries of the sphere of social solidarity are contested and expanded, until, to varying degrees, civic values become normative for other spheres of society such as the family, the state, and the economy.

Alexander asserts that "societies are not governed by power alone and are not fuelled only by the pursuit of self-interest. Feelings for others matter, and they are structured by the boundaries of solidarity."[12] He defines civil society as this sphere of solidarity "in which a certain kind of universalizing community comes to be culturally defined and to some degree institutionally enforced."[13] Associations, the law, and the media give institutional structure to sustain and protect the civil sphere, which also depends on the practice of civility, criticism, and mutual respect. A central component of the dynamics of the civil sphere is the historically contingent expansion and contraction of the "boundaries of solidarity" through binary codes that define civic virtues and anti-civic vices and incorporate or stigmatize populations based on their purported capacity to express them. Thus, in the United States, the civil sphere was initially restricted to white, property-owning, Christian men who upheld values of universalistic solidarity but excluded much of the human race on the grounds that they lacked the civil qualities of rationality, autonomy, self-control, altruism, trustworthiness, and so on. Throughout the nineteenth and twentieth centuries, the boundaries of solidarity were expanded to include categories such as women, black people, and Jews, to the extent that there was a shift in the meanings and boundaries of the binary codes, and these populations were accepted within the civil sphere as being equally capable of embodying civic qualities. Essential to the success of these cultural transformations was that movements for the rights of these populations were able to translate their particular grievances into the language of universal civic values and thus to appeal to the broader society's feelings of solidarity. Thus, while exclusionary cultural binary codes create boundaries around the civil sphere, those boundaries are susceptible to be challenged and expanded by invoking the values of solidarity that underpin it.

Another key set of boundaries distinguishes the civil sphere from what Alexander calls the "noncivil" spheres of the state, the economy, religion, the family, and the local community. These spheres are "fundamental to the quality of life and to the vitality of a plural order, and their independence must be nurtured and protected," but they have their distinctive cultural codes and institutions and embody sectoral rather than societal interests, particularistic rather than universal values, and/or coercive hierarchies rather than voluntary, horizontal solidarity.[14] The civil sphere is thus a space that is independent of these other spheres but that is always in productive tension with them. Noncivil spheres can bring what Alexander calls "positive inputs," but also "negative intrusions," into the civil sphere. Thus, the market economy, for example, has undermined essentializing social hierarchies and divisions by seeing all humans as individuals equally capable of engaging in production, consumption, and exchange and by instilling habits of work, fairness, and autonomy that are conducive to civil relations. On the other hand, the market economy generates economic inequalities, class divisions, and an ideology of self-centred accumulation that are destructive to the civil sphere. It is precisely from the standpoint of the civil sphere and its values of solidarity that these phenomena are seen as problems and that a critical discourse emerges that calls on governments and corporations to restrict the unfettered intrusion of economic criteria into all domains of social life. The civil sphere also expands the reach of its values of solidarity into noncivil spheres, such as, for example, when civil associations, movements, and discourses devoted to women's liberation succeeded in institutionalizing norms of gender equality in the political and economic spheres and even, to varying degrees, in the spheres of the family and religion.[15]

Grounded in the often agonistic transformation of culture in the direction of a utopian solidarity, the civil sphere concept raises many questions. Since the civil sphere is based on culturally coded binary oppositions between populations identified as civil and anticivil, is it possible to have a civil sphere that does not define itself in opposition to some cultural other? And while the trajectory for Western societies has been, over the past few centuries, a bumpy and tortuous process of expanding the boundaries of the civil sphere to become more inclusive, is there not the possibility, increasingly evident today, of those boundaries shrinking back toward self-enclosed, antagonistic communities, each of which sees itself as more civil than the others? And even the expansion of the civil sphere, in Alexander's account, is a process of incorporating groups into a set of values and an understanding of solidarity that have very specific roots in Euro-American history and its institutions of liberal democracy. How feasible can this be in the emergence of a truly global civil sphere, which would necessitate the social instantiation, on a worldwide scale, of the values of solidarity that are needed to bind a progressively interconnected world? Is it necessary or even possible for the whole world to make a detour through Western liberalism in order to build a global sphere of solidarity?

The Emancipatory Dimension
The fourth, "emancipatory" dimension of civil society is highly relevant to these questions. The incorporation of groups into the civil sphere represents not only the expansion of the sphere of solidarity, but also liberation from political, social, and cultural oppression. The emancipatory vision of civil society is derived from several distinct intellectual traditions, which have different historical points of origin but share a focus on how civil society organizations can counter and even overturn structures of political hegemony and oppression. One strand, associated with the Marxist tradition and critical thinkers such as Antonio Gramsci, sees contemporary civil society as an adjunct to capitalism but also argues that it provides the soil out of which countervailing spaces can grow.[16] Another strand, exemplified by Adam Michnik, draws on the example of the collapse of communist totalitarianism in Eastern Europe in order to show how civil society activity can prepare people's consciousness and lay the foundations for the end of authoritarianism and the establishment of liberal democracy.[17]

Growing appreciation of the emancipatory function of civil society generates many of the expectations that people place on civil society; they hope that the advancement of civil society can help create different types of social spaces in which people can be freed from structures of oppression. This emancipatory vision of civil society is especially salient in social and political discourses outside of the North Atlantic countries and highlights the specific historical origin and spread of civil society as a conceptual and institutional construct. For in North America and Western Europe, civil society has emerged in parallel with modern social and political institutions, has long been part of the socio-political mainstream, and is now a fully institutionalized and legitimate component of the liberal-democratic order. From the West, models of civil society have spread to other regions, where they exist in tension with more traditional forms of associational life and public discourse and, often, with non-liberal political regimes. Since the 1990s, transnational flows have led to the emergence of a "global civil society" that is closely associated with the institutional infrastructures of international organizations such as the UN, as well as global meetings and forums, but that also remains largely Western centred. Funding tends to flow from the West outward, and the international NGOs that often act as intermediaries and brokers between global civil society, Western funders, and local groups and populations also tend to be Western based.

Thus, the emancipatory promise of civil society needs to be considered within the historical and geopolitical location of global and national civil societies. Indeed, although Western civil society organizations may promote counter-hegemonic discourses, advocate for the emancipation of specific populations, and engage in actions and social movements related to specific issues, they tend to take the Western liberal order for granted, are rather generally content (or resigned) to operate within its framework, and often consider their mission to be the defense or strengthening of that very order. However, in other countries, civil society may be highly contentious because its discourses may challenge the entire political order of a country. In these contexts, civil society organizations appear to provide the dynamic organizational infrastructure of transformative social movements.

Whether consciously or not, analyses of the emancipatory potential of civil society organizations still tend to present Western liberal democracies as the normative standard for emancipation. It is true that many civil society organizations, in the West and elsewhere, might strongly object to such a statement. Some simply work for human betterment, while others are highly critical of the Western social order. But the fact is that since the collapse of the socialist ideals that sustained many groups and movements until around the 1980s, the vast majority of civil society organizations and discourses have no vision of a progression beyond Western liberal democracy. Notwithstanding the cultural idealization of protest, subversion, and postcolonial critiques of the West in some quarters of civil society and intellectual discourse, the default position of civil society discourse is to erect the Western social, political, and economic system as the standard and ideal of emancipation toward which all societies should strive.[18]

The Western-centred emancipatory vision of civil society is problematic on two counts. First, it falsely assumes that Western liberal democracies represent the "end of history," the goal toward which all societies aspire. Second, it ignores that the freedom of Western liberal democracies is but a component of a global economic and geopolitical order, that it is structurally inseparable from the oppression of other regions, and that the West uses the economic, political, and cultural tools of soft power to sustain a global hegemony that is increasingly challenged by other powers.[19] Indeed, since the 1990s, Western governments and foundations have made use of civil society organizations as geopolitical tools, both in the provision of development aid and in the promotion of political reform.[20] Many groups that have benefited from such funding or participated in such projects are aware of the dangers of being instrumentalized; they have taken measures to protect their independence and are often highly critical of the governments that fund them. Nonetheless, it is important to recognize the role that partisan geopolitical and ideological forces play in shaping of civil society. The acknowledgment of these dynamics has led the legitimacy and the emancipatory potential of civil society to be questioned in many circles.[21]

We can better appreciate these complex facets of the contemporary discourse on civil society by understanding how this discourse arose in the 1980s and 90s, in the context of the decline of the traditional left-wing political project and of third world liberation movements, and the rise of global neoliberalism since the end of the Cold War. Under the "Washington consensus" of a strong neoliberal ideology and policies aiming to shrink the state and to expand the reach of the market, civil society came to be seen as an arena that could be opened up in parallel with the market, with charities and NGOs taking up functions of grassroots organization and social service provision that had previously been provided by the state, left-wing political parties, trade unions, and churches.[22] Some scholars have thus written about the role of NGOs and civil society as actors of "neoliberal governance."[23] With the breakdown of Marxist ideology, social organizations needed a new grounding. Revolution was no longer the order of the day; the path that was now open to them was to professionalize and to survive on grants from private foundations or international aid agencies. Both the left and the right converged in their support for civil society under the new consensus: because the state was seen as incapable of solving problems and, in many countries, was drastically pared down under structural adjustment programs imposed by the International Monetary Fund, society could be left to self-organize under the market and civil society.[24] At the same time, the associational fabric of civil society could generate social mobilization to keep governments in check or even topple authoritarian regimes. The growth of civil society was thus envisioned as an important condition for the establishment of liberal democracy.

The contemporary normative discourse of civil society is thus closely tied with the expansion of capitalism and Western-style democracy.[25] Civil society has been mythologized in counter-hegemonic discourses as stirring the seeds of anti-authoritarian movements and "colour revolutions" in Eastern Europe, Iran, Russia, the Middle East, Taiwan, Hong Kong, and elsewhere, with the promise of ushering in pro-Western democratic regimes or Western-style electoral systems.[26] For precisely this reason, civil society organizations have been fiercely fought by anti-Western forces that have become increasingly adept at deploying their own strategies of popular organization and mobilization against them; the end result, as seen in Russia, China, and the Arab world, has often been a renewed and more assertive authoritarianism, fractured societies, or total social disintegration.[27] Civil society in its current structural configuration is thus being instrumentalized in a set of broader ideological struggles and geopolitical conflicts that undermine its legitimacy and regenerative force.

Civil society organizations operating in non-Western settings thus find themselves in a difficult position. Groups that see themselves as critical or even opposed to Western powers and interests often have little choice but to receive much-needed support from foundations and governments that have no interest in transforming the Western socio-political order and may be actively committed to entrenching it.[28] As a result, regardless of how they use such resources, these groups often end up, whether directly or indirectly, consciously or not, being perceived as serving a Western geopolitical agenda. The emancipatory function of civil society is therefore undercut by its association with Western hegemony, which leads authoritarian regimes to strive to prevent the growth of an independent civil society, in the Western liberal understanding of the term.

In this section, I have reviewed four different conceptions of civil society that can be identified in the academic literature. This overview has undoubtedly oversimplified the great diversity of views on the roles, dimensions, and structures of civil society. For the present purposes, and drawing on insights from the conceptualizations I have discussed above, I will define civil society as referring to *social spaces for the voluntary and expansive expression of values of human solidarity*. Because it is made up of social spaces, civil society is structured by norms and institutions that define human interactions. The solidarity expressed in these spaces is voluntary—a manifestation of freely chosen bonds and aspirations—rather than imposed by tradition, regulation, or ideology. It is expansive, in the sense that while such spaces may be composed of very specific groups of people, the boundaries of such groups are not seen as essential but as temporary conditions in a collective aspiration for an ever-widening solidarity. The spaces of civil society are made up of people working together and enacting solidarity in and between groups and associations. In these spaces, participants learn to transcend particularistic interests in the course of mutual deliberations on the common good, and the values of solidarity are articulated, defended, and translated into societal, cultural, economic, and political realms. From this perspective, many of the shortcomings and limitations that have been pointed out in the discourse on civil society can be linked to a common problem, which is the tearing apart of the values of solidarity that underpin civil society, whether caused by associations whose values, ideals, or practices are damaging to an expansive solidarity; divisive forms of public discourse; exclusionary cultural codes; or co-optation by political forces or geopolitical interests.

The Role of Religion
What is the role of religion in civil society thus defined as spaces of solidarity? Its position is ambiguous and fraught with potential tensions. On the one hand, religion is a key source of the values associated with universal solidarity. It enjoins us to transcend our self-centred ego and to expand our sphere of concern to include all humans, all sentient beings, or even the entire cosmos. Religion does not content itself with ideas on universal love and compassion but attempts to express, embody, and disseminate these values through living communities. Creating expansive spaces of solidarity, one might argue, is of the very essence of religion. Religion is undoubtedly the origin of many of the core values of civil society.[29]

On the other hand, the transcendental source and authority at the root of the world religions, which generates intense bonds of solidarity expressed through a common faith, religious identity, ritual practices, and communal life, is also what separates religion from a complete identification with civil society. The solidarity of civil society is one of horizontal immanence, of free association among people and groups who may not share any common transcendental referent, while religious solidarity derives from a common connection and alignment to a transcendental divinity or spiritual reality. This faith automatically implies the possibility of its absence—of people who are, by definition, not bound by the same ties of solidarity. Civil society, on the other hand, calls on solidarity between religious and non-religious people, or between people of different religious communities.

Thus the problem: religion is an indispensable contributor of values and communities of solidarity, but it is also potentially one of the greatest obstacles to the nurturing of spaces of ever-expansive solidarity. Throughout history and around the world, religious communities have constituted the first and most widespread forms of self-governing groups that have been based on values of solidarity, which they have striven to embody in forms of collective life. And today, in many places, local religious communities such as congregations, parishes, temples, and mosques contribute in large measure to the associational and cultural dimensions of civil society by providing a strong fabric of grassroots community life.[30] They have also been the founders of the earliest charities, philanthropic organizations, and volunteer movements, as well as many movements for social and civil rights and some of the largest social service organizations and international NGOs.[31]

However, other aspects of religious culture can be obstacles to expanding spaces of solidarity. The traditional forms and habits of many religious groups are often based on patriarchal or authoritarian forms of leadership that are contrary to civic values, while the traditional scope of religious activity may divert people away from reaching out to broader spheres of solidarity around issues of common social concern. Religion too often remains associated with the oppression of women and the sanctification of ethnic, cultural, and national prejudice, all of which are severely damaging to civil society. Additionally, sectarianism and overemphasis on divisive religious identities often undermine the ability of many religious communities to build social solidarity, as does the tendency for many local religious organizations to be influenced by political forces and ideologies.[32]

In response to these limitations, some have sought to advance an individualistic spirituality that strongly rejects any hint of the divisive aspects of organized religion. But this new brand of spirituality has proven itself almost entirely unable to resist co-optation by the forces of the market and thus has given way to a "spiritual marketplace" of books, seminars, courses, and experiences that are consumed by people in pursuit of personal spiritual gratification and that cannot sustain community. While such a commodified, individualistic spirituality does tend to promote ideals of harmony, it is limited in its capacity to create meaningful and sustainable solidarity in social practice.

Another form of religious engagement with civil society is through faith-based charities, philanthropies, NGOs, and social service agencies. These efforts and contributions still form the bedrock of civil society in many places. Nevertheless, like many other civil society organizations, they often end up being co-opted by the state and transformed into purveyors of social services on its behalf. Worse, they may become unwitting palliatives that, by alleviating the worst forms of suffering, simply reinforce the oppressive structures of the dominant political and economic system.

Religiously inspired socio-political movements, which have arisen especially in many Christian, Muslim, and Hindu nations, can be seen as a final form of religious social engagement. These movements saw their origins in attempts to draw on religious teachings in order to challenge existing structures of social and political oppression and to propose utopian formulations of social solidarity. Yet as recent history shows, such movements are liable to end up becoming ensnared in political contests for power and thus made to be the servants of partisan and geopolitical dynamics that completely undermine any potential these movements may have initially possessed to reinforce social solidarity.

There is, to be sure, much to be learned from the various approaches to faith-based engagement mentioned above, ranging from individual spiritual growth to local community building, from agencies dedicated to serving the common good to movements aiming to generate a profound social transformation. But it is clear that even as there is a growing recognition of the potential role of religion in strengthening civil society, there is much to be questioned as well. Religion and civil society in the modern era are thus characterized by a dialectical tension and mutual intrusions. Religion contributes values, resources, and networks to civil society, but civil society pushes back against the influence of religiously sanctioned patriarchy, sectarianism, extremism, and prejudice—not only on the broader society, but even, with varying degrees of success, within religious communities themselves. For example, many churches have become tolerant of other religions, mindful of social justice and the rights of women, and find inspiration within scripture and theology for these moves toward a more all-encompassing solidarity. These changes and reforms have taken place at least partly in response to criticism and new norms of solidarity emanating from a secular civil sphere. As such, the dialectical relationship between religion and civil society has, to a great degree, been a productive one. But is it possible to move beyond these tensions and find a solid common ground and line of communication between religious and civil values of solidarity? In the next section, I argue that this common ground can be located by questioning prevalent assumptions about human nature; by exploring the spiritual dimension of human nature and its expression through solidarity-building values and initiatives in civil society; and by identifying and applying the spiritual principles that can guide public discourse and social action to build solidarity.

The Spiritual Foundations of Civil Society

From a Bahá'í perspective, any reflection on social action—e.g., its motivation, its methods, its purpose, and its effectiveness—must begin with an understanding of human nature. What is the ontological foundation of social action and its ideal of solidarity? What implicit assumptions do civil society actors make about human nature and aspirations? Such beliefs and ontological premises are rarely the subject of explicit discourse in civil society, but to avoid such a critical reflection may result in civil society actors being unconsciously governed by implicit assumptions or ideologies that are at odds with their own deepest aspirations for solidarity, or it may ultimately reinforce the very oppressive social structures that civil society organizations are trying to change or alleviate.

Questioning Prevailing Assumptions on Human Nature
Prevalent understandings of human nature fail to account for both the ultimate values of civil society and for the behavioural motivation of many civil society actors. Clearly, there is something that motivates people to commit their time and money to philanthropic aims, to volunteering, to mutual help, and to activism. The large and growing range and scale of civil society activity and organization and the persistence of civil society actors in the face of challenges, restrictions, and lack of resources are a testament to the power of the values of solidarity, participation, altruism, generosity, and justice—a power that the Universal House of Justice says is "not a finite entity that is to be 'seized' and 'jealously guarded'" but rather a "limitless capacity to transform" that can be "released," "encouraged," or "enabled" because it springs forth from the deepest roots of human nature.[33]

Many social theories and public policy frameworks employ a concept of human nature that assumes that human beings are self-interested and competitive and that all human behaviour can be explained in reference to an unquenchable thirst to satisfy material needs. Although such assumptions and theories can account for much human behaviour in the realms of politics and commerce, they fail to adequately account for the higher capacities, powers, and inclinations that are so conspicuously on display in the realm of civil society.

For example, the concept of *homo economicus* is based on a strong ontological claim about human nature—that the essence of human beings is to maximize self-interest. While this theory was developed to describe market behaviour, it has acquired an increasingly hegemonic and normative status in a growing number of disciplines and social domains.[34] A central assumption in economic theory has become an ideology that, through the institutions of education, politics, the economy, and the media, shapes people's subjective sense of self-identity as being driven by self-interest. But is it possible to build solidarity on the basis of this understanding of human nature? What is demonstrated by the record of the past several decades, during which the assumptions of *homo economicus* have increasingly been applied beyond the market to guide decisions, policies, and planning in government, civil society, and even sometimes religion? To what extent have civil society organizations, their funders, their members, and the policy-makers who regulate their activities, consciously or unwittingly structured civil society along the assumptions of *homo economicus*?

Similar questions arise in response to the equally widespread assumption that society is instituted entirely by competitive relations of power and that the only means of overcoming oppression is to engage in adversarial struggle.[35] Is it possible to build sustainable peace and solidarity, universal participation, and grassroots empowerment if all the actors of society are engaged in a perpetual struggle for domination? Embracing adversarial movements of protest and political struggle undermines civil society's emancipatory promise in what Michael Karlberg has called "the paradox of protest."[36] When civil society generates protest movements in the name of emancipation, these often trigger backlashes and counter-movements supporting powerful interests. The result is either a deepening of social divisions or a strengthened determination and capacity of vested interests to perpetuate their power. Or, if the social movement is successful, the "victors" occupying positions of power may end up either replicating the oppressive structures against which they had originally fought or creating new ones.[37]

The Spiritual Dimension of Human Nature
A sustainable and transformative solidarity must be grounded in an understanding of human nature that is at once critical, realistic, empowering, and ontologically consistent. From a Bahá'í perspective, although human nature cannot be boiled down to a simplistic formula, the range of potential human motivation and behaviour can be understood through a dual understanding of the self as including both a lower, more material and self-interested dimension and a higher spiritual dimension that is motivated by a sense of oneness with and love for all humanity, for all creation, and for the source of creation.[38] To put the point in other terms, as a product of biological evolution, the human body is driven by instincts to survival and self-preservation; when the powers of the mind are subordinated to these instincts, the self-centred and self-interested ego becomes the driving force of human motivation. Yet humans also have a spiritual essence that provides us with an innate desire and potential to strive for transcendence; to expand the sphere of concern beyond the self to the family, to the community, and

ultimately to all of humanity and even all beings; and to express spiritual capacities such as self-sacrifice, generosity, compassion, detachment, justice, the exercise of free will, and the earnest search for truth. When the powers of the human mind strive to express a higher spiritual potential, true transformation becomes a realistic possibility.

In Bahá'í discourse, the term "spiritual" is used to describe a reality that underlies and transcends the material world; reflects divine perfection; operates according to laws and principles that can, to a certain extent, be apprehended by human reason; and is the ultimate source and goal of human consciousness and aspiration. Attraction to and alignment with spiritual reality is manifested by humans in the form of virtuous qualities and ethical behaviours such as care and compassion for fellow beings, both human and non-human, and striving for unity and solidarity. Although great variations in intensity and expression appear throughout history and around the world, the attraction to spiritual reality and perfection is a universal quality of human nature.

According to this conception of human nature, which is, in various formulations, shared by all religious traditions and present in the deepest beliefs of most of humanity, a lower and a higher nature exist in all humans in latent form, and it is through the combined effects of social conditioning, education, and individual effort that they can be either strengthened or suppressed. Personal prayer and meditation is only one, albeit essential, aspect of spiritual growth and training. Spiritual development must also be pursued through the practice of social engagement. Indeed, the Bahá'í writings explicitly posit a twofold moral purpose for human life—a striving for both personal and collective transformation, each of which is a necessary condition for the other. Seen from this perspective, the social space of civil society acquires deep significance. For engagement in civil society provides an ideal space in which human beings can express their essential spiritual nature and develop its infinite latent potentials.

To be sure, human motivations are complex, and the self-centred ego raises its head in all endeavours. Civil society actors are often, to lesser or greater extents, motivated by personal ambitions or the desire for worldly gain. They often also operate according to principles of competitive power struggle. Real-world civil society organizations, movements, and discourses usually combine spiritual and material (including economic and political) values and mix self-interested and altruistic motivations. But, undoubtedly, much of the power driving civil society's yearning for solidarity reflects the spiritual desires to transcend the ego, to seek a higher purpose and meaning, and to follow the inner urges to do something for the good of humanity and to build a better society. From this perspective, the stirrings of solidarity, compassion, and desire for justice that are at the origin of the founding of many civil society groups and movements are expressions of the spiritual promptings of the soul. Most of the time, however, these spiritual motivations remain implicit or inchoate. Accordingly, lacking consciousness and coherence, such motivations can easily fall prey to the self-centred promptings of the ego or to the many powerful ideologies and social forces that aggressively promote our lower nature.

Although most civil society actors do not explicitly define their values and principles as "spiritual," it is important to acquire a conscious awareness of the spiritual foundations of solidarity. For if the discourse and practice of social solidarity lack a coherent foundation, they may become vulnerable to the intrusion of other hegemonic discourses that are based on contradictory and spiritually impoverishing assumptions. Such hegemonic discourses shape self-understanding, actions, structures, and policies in much of contemporary civil society. These include discourses and practices of entrepreneurship, professionalism, management, enterprise, and client relations that are derived from the world of business. Perhaps more controversially, from a Bahá'í perspective, they also include the discourses and tactics of adversarial struggle—advocacy, protest, occupation, and political campaigning. As I argued above, social action inspired by and striving for solidarity, participation, and emancipation cannot be premised on assumptions of self-interested humans craving unlimited accumulation of wealth and participating in contests of power.

Spiritual Principles

The concept of "spiritual principles" provides us with a useful lens through which to think about the contexts in which the spiritual yearning for solidarity can be properly developed and expressed. Bahá'í discourse often discusses the oneness of humankind, justice, the equality of men and women, and environmental stewardship, among others, as "spiritual principles."[39] What makes these widely accepted principles specifically *spiritual*? The term "spiritual principles" refers in this discourse to a certain set of normative concepts that are expressions of a deeper spiritual reality; as such, they link ontological foundations and practical action. The concept of spiritual principles ties motivation, goals, and action to an ontological foundation that is understood as spiritual. First, it describes an aspect of spiritual reality. Second, it refers to the consciousness of this reality within us, which causes a deep yearning of our soul. Third, it describes an outer social state in which this inner consciousness finds its expression; it thus refers to the motivation and imperative to translate consciousness into social reality. Fourth, it guides our action in the realization of the inner yearning toward its outer expression.

For example, the oneness of humankind, taken as a spiritual principle, describes the idea that it is (1) a reflection of divine reality; (2) an inner spiritual consciousness of and yearning for oneness and unity among all people; (3) a social ideal that manifests our inner aspiration for oneness; and (4) a guiding principle, according to which any effort to build more peace and oneness must itself follow the requirements and realities of the principle of oneness—the ends do not justify the means. The principle of the oneness of humankind thus sets a standard that both protects the spiritual integrity of actors who seek to be guided by its light while also providing a clear and useful orientation for various forms of social action.

Spiritual principles shape our consciousness, our inner motivations, our social goals, and our efforts to pursue actions that help us express our motivations and realize our goals. Furthermore, they are mutually reinforcing and inseparable from each other, as, for example, the equality of men and women is inseparable from the broader principles of justice and the oneness of humankind.

Applying Spiritual Principles

According to the Bahá'í writings, contemporary religion should strive to contribute to the emergence of a socially and politically integrated global civilization by systematically infusing spiritual values and principles into all dimensions of social life. Civil society can be seen as a space in which humans' individual and collective capacity to channel the powers of their spiritual nature toward the realization of the social ideals of justice, solidarity, and oneness can be developed and explored in relation to various populations, issues, and discourses. And then as this capacity develops and grows, it can be used to guide deepening engagement in other spheres, such as the realms of economy and governance.

This is not to say that spiritual values and principles cannot simultaneously and immediately be infused into these other spheres. Indeed, although I have emphasized the spiritual foundations of civil society in the above discussion, it is important to mention that the Bahá'í writings equally insist on the need to establish spiritual foundations for the economy and governance, which is to say for the production and distribution of material resources and for the administration of order and justice in society. Many individuals and organizations working in the fields of business and public administration, including Bahá'ís and others, strive to apply spiritual principles in their respective realms. However, in the current configuration of the world, norms and ideologies of material acquisition and power struggle have established a powerful hegemony over the practices of economics and government. Yet in the sphere of civil society, insofar as it is based on values of solidarity that can resist such hegemony, there is more space for experimentation with and learning about establishing social relations based on spiritual principles.

Taking this perspective, let us now reconsider the operation of civil society in its associational, deliberative, cultural, and emancipatory functions. At the associational level, we can see how face-to-face social interaction in the context of working together for the common purpose of bettering the community can provide a training ground for the development of spiritual qualities and the building of solidarity at a local level, outside the matrix of the family. Of particular importance here are informal groups that are rarely considered in much of the contemporary discourse on civil society. Indeed, it is often in the absence of formal organization and procedures and in response to specific problems or needs that most initiatives of solidarity and cooperation arise, and it is in such informal, local spaces that interpersonal trust and resilience in the face of obstacles, among other spiritual qualities, are exercised and trained. Although such initiatives are rarely noticed and are always very small in scale, their importance cannot be overemphasized.

It is therefore important to think at greater length about how these small-scale associational dynamics can be fostered and enabled to mature. How, we might ask, can such spaces become venues for learning and empowerment? How can the kinds of small acts of service that address concrete needs be understood in a broader vision of building solidarity through individual and social transformation? How can institutions and communities provide nurturing spaces and support for these kinds of local initiatives without imposing ready-made packages from above? How can these initiatives and acts of service contribute to the strengthening of our higher nature? How can capacities such as self-sacrifice, detachment, consultation, and mutual accompaniment be nurtured? How can learning processes characterized by consultation, action, and reflection be integrated into such small-scale grassroots initiatives?

Moving to the formal organizations of civil society, the main issue is the extent to which they provide a structure for the systematic nurturing and application of spiritual qualities. Numerous challenges exist in this regard. In their eagerness to do more or to become bigger, civil society organizations are inevitably tempted to act according to forms of instrumental rationality that treat human beings—whether the populations being served, the members of the organization, or its staff and volunteers—as mere instruments to attain institutional outcomes. Furthermore, funding agencies, governments, and regulatory bodies, as well as the general sociopolitical environment, often pressure civil society organizations to adopt structures, procedures, and objectives that may not align with a spiritual understanding of human nature and purpose. Finally, while civil society organizations are usually established to address a specific social need or problem, the spiritual principle of the oneness of humanity places the resolution of specific problems in the context of the general progress of humanity. Actions taken to address a particular problem or to aid a specific population are entry points for service to humanity as a whole. Civil society organizations, however, face the challenges of retaining this broader perspective and of avoiding the tendencies to become, at best, entrenched special interest organizations committed to a single issue or community and, at worse, groups concerned primarily with their own self-perpetuation.

In order to address such issues, we must consider questions concerning how civil society organizations can evolve from small-scale groups and initiatives into formal organizations while retaining their role as spaces for the development of spiritual qualities and capacities in situations of increasing organizational complexity. How can civil society groups remain true to spiritual principles while engaging constructively with government agencies, funding bodies and foundations, and other civil society organizations? How can the expansion of the scope and complexity of their activities be tied to a growing capacity to connect specific issues or populations to broader processes of constructive social transformation, thus aiming for the betterment of humanity taken as a whole? And how can civil society organizations become vehicles and repositories of collective learning in which all of their action is undertaken with a posture of learning, seeking to involve all participants in the process of knowledge generation through consultation, action, and reflection?

Such types of questions form the basis of a research program that should not be limited to professional researchers, but rather should be driven by civil society practitioners as they reflect on their own experiential learning. This brings us to the second, deliberative dimension of civil society. Developing spiritual virtues and qualities can contribute to enhancing the deliberative capacity of groups and populations, and learning to deliberate for the common good is an important arena for training spiritual qualities. Here I will limit myself to mentioning the importance of nurturing this capacity at the grassroots level. Public discourse should not be seen as restricted to the public spaces for elites at the international, national, or regional levels, but rather as a process that also involves general humanity, as friends, family, neighbours, and community members engage in meaningful conversations about issues of common concern and about the material, social, intellectual, and spiritual progress of their communities.

In this context, it is important to consider how civil society groups can strengthen the quality and frequency of deliberation within both their organizations and the broader community. How can such deliberative processes be conducted in a mode of learning and sincere consultation, rather than as the representation and defense of competing interests? How can they contribute to the generation and application of knowledge regarding material, social, and spiritual reality at the grassroots level? And how can this process connect with public discourse at wider levels and even on a global scale?

Nurturing the spiritual qualities that strengthen people's capacity to build solidarity through associative and deliberative activity as outlined above implies a process of cultural transformation—which brings me to the third, symbolic dimension of civil society. A civil sphere based on spiritual principles would be one that does not define itself in opposition to "uncivil" outside groups. Spiritual principles, as defined in this essay, help to identify what types of motivations and actions are appropriate to building solidarity and which ones are not. In that sense, spiritual principles help draw limits that define what fits into the sphere of solidarity and what does not. But such principles and limits are not identities that can be ascribed to specific individuals and groups; they are guidelines for reflection and action. They replace binary cultural codes. Being rooted in transcendence, they are the property of no single person or group; in fact, they have never been realized fully anywhere. They belong to no culture or nation; they can only guide and inspire; their latent and partial expression can be found in any culture. In this context, we would need to consider how to nurture the capacity, within individuals and groups, to define and strengthen solidarity on the basis of spiritual principles. How can people learn to identify, appreciate, and release their spiritual consciousness, and the deep roots of solidarity that are present in their culture, without developing a parochial sense that their group has a higher level of civility or spirituality than others?

The emancipatory dimension of civil society—the search for justice motivated by solidarity with the weak and the oppressed—then, can find expression through the release of the powers of the human spirit, rather than through power struggles. The Bahá'í writings present justice as, among other things, a capacity and expression of the human soul. In this context, justice, as a spiritual principle, leads the heart to feel pain and anger at the sight of the unjust suffering of our fellow human beings, motivates us to act to overcome injustice, provides us with a moral compass that helps us exercise independent and critical judgment about social conditions, and gives us a standard to guide our efforts to build just social relations.[40]

Undoubtedly, many of the actions, initiatives, organizations, and movements of civil society are motivated by such promptings of justice. But after they have become large and highly institutionalized and have grown too close to positions of worldly power, even organizations and movements that actively strive to realize social justice can end up reproducing the very structures of domination that they had originally set out to transform. Indeed, one might even say that the more successful a civil society organization is, the more temptations it faces to betray its founding ideals.[41]

From a spiritual perspective, the root of such conflicts can be found in the attempt of many organizations to pursue the promptings of the soul to seek justice within a framework that explicitly denies the spiritual dimension of human life. Thus, it is important to ask how civil society can become a space within which people's spiritual yearning for justice can be strengthened and trained.

A first step in this direction would be to deepen our understanding of the spiritual and material dimensions of both justice and injustice. Otherwise, the initial stirrings of the soul may be easily manipulated by propaganda, vested interests, or popular fads and ultimately lead to disillusionment, cynicism, and apathy.

There are many forms of oppression in the world—the oppression of women by men, of the poor by the rich, and of one race, nation, ethnic group, or religion by another, to name but a few. All these forms of oppression have a common foundation in the habit of dividing humanity into opposing groups in order to justify the elevation of one group over another. At its core, then, injustice involves the violation of human unity and solidarity. By extension, true justice and emancipation entail the realization in thought, action, and social structure of the oneness of humanity. Some common expressions of oneness are the equality of men and women, the reduction of economic disparities, and the harmony between racial, ethnic, and religious communities.

Many attempts to overcome injustice fall short of this realization by framing their efforts as struggles against specific populations, groups, organizations, or institutions that are identified as being the causes of oppression. As a result, they end up reproducing the structural root of injustice, which is the tearing apart of the oneness of humanity. To be sure, material conditions of inequality that generate and reinforce divisions need to be changed. But we cannot effectively promote oneness in material conditions by using ideologies and methods that are predicated on division and struggle between groups. Reproducing the same structural divisions by inverting them, or by generating new divisions, thus fails to contribute to the important goal of establishing lasting justice.

Another key dimension of injustice is ignorance. When people are unaware of the social forces that shape their reality, they are deprived of the capacity to reflect effectively and to transform and improve it. The concentration of knowledge and the means for its generation and application in the hands of a small class of specialists in wealthy nations is therefore one of the most fundamental and pervasive forms of oppression in the world. For universal participation in the creation and use of knowledge is an essential condition for the emancipation of humanity. And such knowledge cannot be only material, as nothing is a greater form of oppression than keeping people ignorant of their spiritual nature. Ideologies that aggressively teach children and adults that they are little more than animals, pleasure-seeking hedonists, or selfish players in a ruthless contest of power and influence therefore deprive humans of the capacity to think and act in any meaningful way, to know themselves, and to improve the human condition. An essential component of social justice is thus to create the conditions for universal participation in the generation and application of material and spiritual knowledge at the grassroots level.

Reconceptualizing Religion

If we are to conceive of civil society as an expression of the spiritual nature of humanity and envision it as a space to channel the powers of spiritual reality into social solidarity, then civil society organizations and actors might wish to better understand spiritual reality and to learn how to operate according to its principles. This would seem to suggest the need to turn to the wisdom and knowledge provided by religion. But if religion is seen by its own adherents and by society at large as consisting primarily of subjective belief, forms of personal and collective worship, and rules of personal behaviour, then it becomes difficult to contribute meaningfully to a broader discourse on spiritual principles and their potential application outside of closed religious communities.

In order to overcome this discursive chasm, a new understanding of religion will be required. Over the past decades, within their communities and in their interactions with civil society actors, Bahá'ís have been working to develop such a new vision of religion, which could provide appropriate and effective knowledge, concepts, and experience for the benefit of the broader society. Although Bahá'ís would not claim to be able to provide simple solutions to the issues presented above, they have gradually developed a principled conceptual framework that guides their endeavours.

In this context, religion can be considered as an evolving system of discourse, knowledge, and practice that is concerned with understanding spiritual reality, applying its principles, and releasing its powers for the dual purpose of individual and collective transformation. This vision of religion is admittedly partial, and it does not deny the central role of faith, worship, laws, and community. But it helps us appreciate the continuity through history of humanity's many efforts to understand spiritual reality and to apply these insights to human life and society. It also enables us to see how religion must be dynamic and embrace change in its ongoing effort to understand the spiritual dimension of reality and to communicate effectively and apply its insights and ideas in the constantly changing domains of social reality.

Still, many questions must be asked about how religion, so conceived, can be protected from the many intrusive dynamics that have been considered and explored above. What attitudes, understandings, and capacities can individuals acquire from their personal relationship with their Creator that help them become better servants of humanity? What forms of religious life and institutional organization are most conducive to nurturing the qualities of unity, justice, and solidarity that religion seeks to bring to the world? What types of social service and action are most conducive to the welfare and solidarity of humankind? How can profound processes of structural transformation be set in motion and sustained? How can religious communities see themselves as catalysts and vehicles for such processes?

An inquiry into the social expression of our spiritual nature, as well as into the identification and application of spiritual principles, is just as important in the exploration of these questions pertaining to religion as it is to the challenges facing civil society. Such a discourse is one that can be applied equally within the spheres of religion and civil society. In either sphere, it prompts a critical reflexivity on widely held assumptions and practices and leads to a rethinking of the nature and purposes of both religion and civil society. As a common language, it can facilitate communication and mutual learning, and it makes possible a conceptual and practical coherence for actors who operate simultaneously in both spheres.

There is, of course, a certain tension between this discourse on spiritual principles and prevalent modes of thought in both the religious and the secular domains. In the secular sphere of civil society, it may appear to be a religious intervention to the extent that it assumes the existence of a transcendent spiritual reality and the spirituality of human nature. But the ideals of solidarity, justice, and peace, here considered to be expressions of a spiritual reality, are widely shared in the secular realm. It is thus possible for religious and non-religious actors to consult together on the means of achieving these ideals, and to search for principles to motivate and guide action. In the religious domain, a discourse on spiritual principles may appear as a secular intervention to the extent that it focuses on a rational exploration of social structures and realities that are often seen, even by religious people, as marginal or irrelevant to spiritual life and salvation. But both traditional religious discourses and those on spiritual principles derive from the search for knowledge of the divine reality and the means to align our lives to it. It is thus possible to engage in productive dialogues on how the accumulated religious wisdom of humanity can be understood, re-examined, and extended into new domains of social life. Ultimately, from a Bahá'í perspective, all these tensions are caused by false dichotomies that are produced by the limitations of our languages and modes of thinking. It is thus important, if a discourse on spiritual principles is to be productive and inclusive of people of different backgrounds, to allow for a certain degree of ambiguity—avoiding, for instance, hair-splitting metaphysical discussions of spiritual reality on the one hand, and excessively precise programs of social reform on the other. This is not to deny the academic value of such elaborations in other contexts. But the purpose of a discourse on spiritual principles is to guide consultation, analysis, and planning in the context of action and reflection on action, providing direction and flexibility in a complex and rapidly changing social reality.

The approach I have outlined is, to be sure, not one that will appeal to everyone. For some religious groups, the only form of solidarity that matters is the one that derives from their own religious identity and community. For some civil society actors, struggle is the only realistic path to a future solidarity. And for others, the only legitimate form of public discourse is one that excludes any reference to spiritual ideals. All these perspectives need to be respected within the big tent of civil society, and their constructive contributions need to be honoured. At the same time, the experience of the Bahá'í community, in its own work and in its collaborations with actors from other religious traditions and from civil society, demonstrates that another path is possible.

The aim of this chapter has been to argue that the values of solidarity that define civil society are ultimately expressions of our spiritual nature—the part of us that yearns for oneness with all beings, that cannot bear to see others suffering pain or injustice, and that is willing to give generously, to reach out, and to work hand in hand with others. It prompts us to join with others to build the better community or the better world of which all people dream—a vision that leads us to act for the transformation of society and for the emancipation of its peoples, and that motivates us to engage in public discourses in order to deliberate on the content of our collective dreams and the means of achieving them.

But if these spiritual foundations are not adequately channelled and nurtured, both civil society and religion become vulnerable to forces that are destructive to the core values of solidarity. Indeed, the empirical reality of civil society is far from a pure expression of such noble sentiments and ideals. But it is these ideals of solidarity, emanating from the soul, that are the ultimate source of the power that makes civil society distinct from other spheres such as the market and partisan politics, with their logics of material accumulation and domination. The question for both religion and civil society, then, is how those spiritual values and capacities can be better understood, how their dynamics can be apprehended, how they can be nurtured in individuals, how they can be applied in the field of social action, and how they can be systematically and sustainably fostered through appropriate educational and institutional arrangements. Guided by spiritual principles, religion and civil society can work hand in hand to expand and consolidate the domain of human solidarity.

Notes

This chapter draws on research funded by the Hong Kong Research Grants Council (Project: "Volunteering in Contemporary China: Moral Discourse and Social Spaces") and the Hong Kong Jockey Club/University of Hong Kong Initiative on Excellence and Capacity Building for Entrepreneurship and Leadership in the Third Sector (Project: "Spiritual Values in the Third Sector"), whose support is gratefully acknowledged.

1. See for example, D. C. Korten, *Getting to the 21st Century: Voluntary Action and the Global Agenda* (West Hartford, CT: Kumarian Press, 1990). See also Neera Chandhoke, "The Limits of Global Civil Society," in *Global Civil Society 2002*, ed. Marlies Glasius, Mary Kaldor, and Helmut Anheier (Oxford, UK: Oxford University Press, 2002); Manuel Castells, "The New Public Sphere: Global Civil Society, Communication Networks, and Global Governance," *Annals of the American Academy of Political and Social Science* 616, no. 1 (March 2008); Marlies Glasius, "Dissecting Global Civil Society: Values, Actors, Organizational Forms," last modified November 2, 2010, http://www.opendemocracy.net/5050/marlies-glasius/dissecting-global-civil-society-values-actors-organisational-forms; and Rebecca Todd Peters, *In Search of the Good Life: The Ethics of Globalization* (New York: Continuum, 2004), 156.
2. Universal House of Justice to the Bahá'ís of the World, October 20, 1983, http://www.bahai.org/library/authoritative-texts/the-universal-house-of-justice/messages/#d=19831020_001&f=f1.

3 Universal House of Justice, "The Promise of World Peace" (Haifa, Israel: Bahá'í World Centre, 1985).
4 On religious re-engagment in political life, see José Casanova, *Public Religions in the Modern World* (Chicago: University of Chicago Press, 1994).
5 This categorization is loosely inspired by Jeffrey Alexander's review of theories of civil society in *The Civil Sphere* (New York: Oxford University Press, 2006).
6 Alexis de Tocqueville, *Democracy in America* (Chicago: University of Chicago Press, 2000).
7 Robert D. Putnam, *Bowling Alone: The Collapse and Revival of American Community* (New York: Simon & Schuster, 2000).
8 See, for example, Chandhoke, "The Limits of Global Civil Society"; Jens Steffek and Kristina Hahn, "Transnational NGOs and Legitimacy, Accountability, Representation," in *Evaluating Transnational NGOs: Legitimacy, Accountability, Representation*, ed. Jens Steffek and Kristina Hahn (Basingstoke, UK: Palgrave Macmillan, 2010), 1–25.
9 See J. H. Mittelman and R. Johnston, "The Globalization of Organized Crime, the Courtesan State, and the Corruption of Civil Society," *Global Governance* 5 (1999): 103–26; and Mary Kaldor and Diego Muro, "Religious and Nationalist Militant Groups," in *Global Civil Society 2003*, ed. Marlies Glasius, Mary Kaldor, and Helmut Anheier (Oxford, UK: Oxford University Press, 2003), 151–84.
10 Jan Aart Scholte, "Global Civil Society: Changing the World?" (May 1999), http://www.sites.google.com/a/usnayar.com/www2/GlobalCivilSociety-ChangingtheWorldJ.pdf.
11 Jürgen Habermas, *The Structural Transformation of the Public Sphere: An Inquiry into a Category of Bourgeois Society*, trans. Thomas Burger (Cambridge, MA: MIT Press, 1989).
12 Alexander, *The Civil Sphere*, 3.
13 Ibid., 31.
14 Ibid., 7.
15 Ibid., 205–09.
16 See Antonio Gramsci, *Selections from the Prison Notebooks of Antonio Gramsci* (New York: International Publishers, 1971); Alexander, *The Civil Sphere*; and Joseph A. Buttigieg, "Gramsci on Civil Society," *Boundary 2* 22, no. 3 (1995): 1–32.
17 Adam Michnik, "Towards a Civil Society: Hopes for Polish Democracy: Interview with Erica Blair (John Keane)," in *Letters from Freedom: Post-War Realities and Perspectives* (Berkeley, CA: University of California Press, 1998), 96–113.
18 See Alexander, *The Civil Sphere* and Chandhoke, "The Limits of Global Society," 52.
19 See Joseph S. Nye, "Soft Power," *Foreign Policy* 80 (1990): 153–71; Nye, "What China and Russia Don't Get about Soft Power," *ForeignPolicy.com*, last modified April 29, 2013, http://foreignpolicy.com/2013/04/29/what

-china-and-russia-dont-get-about-soft-power/?wp_login_redirect=0; and Jie Chen, *Transnational Civil Society in China: Intrusion and Impact* (Cheltenham, UK: Edward Elgar Publishing, 2012).

20 Pawel Stefan Zaleski, "Global Non-governmental Administrative System: Geosociology of the Third Sector," in *Civil Society in the Making*, ed. Dariusz Gawin and Piotr Glinski (Warsaw, Poland: IFiS Publishers, 2006).

21 See, for example, Jai Sen, "Interrogating the Civil. Engaging Critically with the Reality and Concept of Civil Society," in *Worlds of Movement, Worlds in Movement*, ed. Jai Sen and Peter Waterman (New Delhi: OpenWord, 2010).

22 Chandhoke, "The Limits of Global Civil Society," 43.

23 See Mitchell Dean, *Governing Societies* (New York: McGraw Hill Open University Press, 2007) and Lidia Lo Sciavo, "Governance, Civil Society, Governmentality. The 'Foucauldian Moment' in the Globalization Debate: Theoretical Perspectives," *International Journal of Humanities and Social Science* 4, no. 13 (November 2014): 181–97.

24 See Michael Edwards and David Hulme, eds., *Too Close for Comfort? Donors, NGOs and States* (London: Palgrave Macmillan, 1996); Alison Van Rooy, ed., *Civil Society and the Aid Industry* (London: Earthscan, 1998); and Ian Smillie and Henny Helmich, eds., *Stakeholders: Government–NGO Partnerships for International Development* (London: Earthscan, 1999).

25 Stephen Hopgood, "Reading the Small Print in Global Civil Society: The Inexorable Hegemony of the Liberal Self," *Millennium: Journal of International Studies* 29, no. 1 (2000): 1–25.

26 See Armine Ishkanian, "Democracy Promotion and Civil Society," in *Global Civil Society 2007–08*, ed. Marlies Glasius, Mary Kaldor, and Helmut Anheier (Oxford, UK: Oxford University Press, 2008), 58–85.

27 See Gzegorz Ekiert, Elizabeth Perry and Yan Xiaojun, eds., *Ruling by Other Means: State-Mobilized Social Movements* (Cambridge: Cambridge University Press, forthcoming).

28 See David Chandler, "Building Global Civil Society 'From Below?'" *Millennium: Journal of International Studies* 33, no. 2 (2004): 313–39; Chandhoke, "The Limits of Global Civil Society," 45; Frances Pinter, "Funding Global Civil Society Organizations," in *Global Civil Society 2001*, ed. Helmut Anheier, Marlies Glasius, and Mary Kaldor (Oxford, UK: Oxford University Press, 2001), 195–217.

29 See Robert Wuthnow, "Can Religion Revitalize Civil Society? An Institutional Perspective," in *Religion as Social Capital: Producing the Common Good*, ed. Corwin E. Smidt (Waco, TX: Baylor University Press, 2003), 191–210.

30 Corwin E. Smidt, ed., *Religion as Social Capital: Producing the Common Good* (Waco, TX: Baylor University Press, 2003).

31 See World Economic Forum, "The Future Role of Civil Society," *World Scenario Series* (2013): 13–14, available online at http://www3.weforum.org/docs/WEF_FutureRoleCivilSociety_Report_2013.pdf.

32 See Abdullahi An-Na'im, "Religion and Global Civil Society: Inherent Incompatibility or Synergy and Interdependence?" in *Global Civil Society 2002*, ed. Marlies Glasius, Mary Kaldor, and Helmut Anheier (Oxford, UK: Oxford University Press, 2002), 55–73.
33 Universal House of Justice to the Bahá'ís of Iran, March 2, 2013, http://www.bahai.org/library/authoritative-texts/the-universal-house-of-justice/messages/#d=20130302_001&f=f1.
34 Daniel Cohen, *Homo Economicus: The (Lost) Prophet of Modern Times* (London: Polity Press, 2014).
35 On the sociological theory of Pierre Bourdieu, see, for example, Roger Friedland, "The Endless Fields of Pierre Bourdieu," *Organization* 16, no. 6 (2009): 1–31.
36 Michael Robert Karlberg, *Beyond the Culture of Contest: From Adversarialism to Mutualism in an Age of Interdependence* (Oxford, UK: George Ronald, 2004).
37 Ibid.
38 'Abdu'l-Bahá, "The Two Natures in Man," in *Paris Talks* (London: UK Bahá'í Publishing Trust, 1972), 60.
39 See, for example, Farzam Arbab, "Promoting a Discourse on Science, Religion and Development," in *The Lab, the Temple, and the Market: Reflections at the Intersection of Science, Religion and Development*, ed. Sharon Harper (Ottawa, ON: Kumarian Press, 2000), 177–205.
40 Arbab, "Promoting a Discourse on Science, Religion and Development," 200–01; William S. Hatcher, *Love, Power, and Justice* (Wilmette, IL: Bahá'í Publishing Trust, 2002).
41 Michael Hardt and Antonio Negri, *Empire* (Cambridge, MA: Harvard University Press, 2001), 133.

Bibliography

Alexander, Jeffrey. *The Civil Sphere*. New York: Oxford University Press, 2006.
'Abdu'l-Bahá. "The Two Natures in Man." In *Paris Talks*, 60–62. London: UK Bahá'í Publishing Trust, 1972.
An-Na'im, Abdullahi. "Religion and Global Civil Society: Inherent Incompatibility or Synergy and Interdependence?" In *Global Civil Society 2002*, edited by Marlies Glasius, Mary Kaldor, and Helmut Anheier, 55–73. Oxford, UK: Oxford University Press, 2002.
Arbab, Farzam. "Promoting a Discourse on Science, Religion and Development." In *The Lab, the Temple, and the Market: Reflections at the Intersection of Science, Religion and Development*, edited by Sharon Harper, 177–205. Ottawa, ON: Kumarian Press, 2000.
Buttigieg, Joseph A. "Gramsci on Civil Society." *Boundary 2* 22, no. 3 (1995): 1–32.
Casanova, José. *Public Religions in the Modern World*. Chicago: University of Chicago Press, 1994.

Castells, Manuel. "The New Public Sphere: Global Civil Society, Communication Networks, and Global Governance." *Annals of the American Academy of Political and Social Science* 616, no. 1 (March 2008): 78–93.

Chandhoke, Neera. "The Limits of Global Civil Society." In *Global Civil Society 2002*, edited by Marlies Glasius, Mary Kaldor, and Helmut Anheier, 35–53. Oxford, UK: Oxford University Press, 2002.

Chandler, David. "Building Global Civil Society 'From Below?'" *Millennium: Journal of International Studies* 33, no. 2 (2004): 331–39.

Chen, Jie. *Transnational Civil Society in China: Intrusion and Impact*. Cheltenham, UK: Edward Elgar Publishing, 2012.

Cohen, Daniel. *Homo Economicus: The (Lost) Prophet of Modern Times*. London: Polity Press, 2014.

Dean, Mitchell. *Governing Societies*. New York: McGraw-Hill Open University Press, 2007.

Edwards, Michael, and David Hulme, eds. *NGOs, States and Donors: Too Close for Comfort?* London: Palgrave Macmillan, 1996.

Friedland, Roger. "The Endless Fields of Pierre Bourdieu." *Organization* 16, no. 6 (2009): 1–31.

Glasius, Marlies. "Dissecting Global Civil Society: Values, Actors, Organizational Forms." Last modified November 2, 2010. http://www.opendemocracy.net/5050/marlies-glasius/dissecting-global-civil-society-values-actors-organisational-forms.

Gramsci, Antonio. *Selections from the Prison Notebooks of Antonio Gramsci*. New York: International Publishers, 1971.

Habermas, Jürgen. *The Structural Transformation of the Public Sphere: An Inquiry into a Category of Bourgeois Society*. Translated by Thomas Burger. Cambridge, MA: MIT Press, 1989.

Hardt, Michael, and Antonio Negri. *Empire*. Cambridge, MA: Harvard University Press, 2001.

Hatcher, William S. *Love, Power, and Justice*. Wilmette, IL: Bahá'í Publishing Trust, 2002.

Hopgood, Stephen. "Reading the Small Print in Global Civil Society: The Inexorable Hegemony of the Liberal Self." *Millennium: Journal of International Studies* 29, no. 1 (2000): 1–25.

Ishkanian, Armine. "Democracy Promotion and Civil Society." In *Global Civil Society 2007–08*, edited by Marlies Glasius, Mary Kaldor, and Helmut Anheier, 58–85. Oxford, UK: Oxford University Press, 2008.

Kaldor, Mary, and Diego Muro. "Religious and Nationalist Militant Groups." In *Global Civil Society 2003*, edited by Marlies Glasius, Kaldor, and Helmut Anheier, 151–84. Oxford, UK: Oxford University Press, 2003.

Karlberg, Michael Robert. *Beyond the Culture of Contest*. Oxford, UK: George Ronald, 2004.

Korten, David C. *Getting to the 21st Century: Voluntary Action and Global Agenda*. West Hartford, CT: Kumarian Press, 1990.

Michnik, Adam. "Towards a Civil Society: Hopes for Polish Democracy: Interview with Erica Blair (John Keane)." In *Letters from Freedom: Post–Cold War Realities and Perspectives*, edited by Irena Grudzinska Gross, 95–113. Berkeley, CA: University of California Press, 1998.

Mittelman, J. H. and R. Johnston. "The Globalization of Organized Crime, the Courtesan State, and the Corruption of Civil Society." *Global Governance* 5 (1999): 103–26.

Nye, Joseph S. "Soft Power." *Foreign Policy* 80 (1990): 153–71.

———. "What China and Russia Don't Get about Soft Power." Last modified April 29, 2013. http://foreignpolicy.com/2013/04/29/what-china-and-russia-dont-get-about-soft-power/?wp_login_redirect=0.

Peters, Rebecca Todd. *In Search of the Good Life: The Ethics of Globalization*. New York: Continuum, 2004.

Pinter, Frances. "Funding Global Civil Society Organizations." In *Global Civil Society 2001*, edited by Helmut Anheier, Marlies Glasius, and Mary Kaldor, 195–217. Oxford, UK: Oxford University Press, 2001.

Putnam, Robert D. *Bowling Alone: The Collapse and Revival of American Community*. New York: Simon & Schuster, 2000.

Sciavo, Lidia Lo. "Governance, Civil Society, Governmentality. The 'Foucauldian Moment' in the Globalization Debate: Theoretical Perspectives." *International Journal of Humanities and Social Science* 4, no. 13 (November 2014): 181–97.

Scholte, Jan Aart. "Global Civil Society: Changing the World?" (May 1999). http://www.sites.google.com/a/usnayar.com/www2/GlobalCivilSociety-ChangingtheWorldJ.pdf.

Sen, Jai. "Interrogating the Civil. Engaging Critically with the Reality and Concept of Civil Society." In *Worlds of Movement, Worlds in Movement*, edited by Sen and Peter Waterman. New Delhi: OpenWord, 2010.

Smidt, Corwin E., ed. *Religion as Social Capital: Producing the Common Good*. Waco, TX: Baylor University Press, 2003.

Smillie, Ian, and Henny Helmich, eds. *Stakeholders: Government–NGO Partnerships for International Development*. London: Earthscan, 1999.

Steffek, Jens, and Kristina Hahn. "Transnational NGOs and Legitimacy, Accountability, Representation." In *Evaluating Transnational NGOs: Legitimacy, Accountability, Representation*, edited by Steffek and Hahn, 1–25. Basingstoke, UK: Palgrave Macmillan, 2010.

Tocqueville, Alexis de. *Democracy in America*. Chicago: University of Chicago Press, 2000. First published 1835 by Saunders and Otley.

Universal House of Justice. Universal House of Justice to the Bahá'ís of Iran, March 2, 2013. http://www.bahai.org/library/authoritative-texts/the-universal-house-of-justice/messages/#d=20130302_001&f=f1.

———. Universal House of Justice to the Bahá'ís of the World, October 20, 1983. http://www.bahai.org/library/authoritative-texts/the-universal-house-of-justice/messages/#d=19831020_001&f=f1.

———. "The Promise of World Peace." Haifa, Israel: Bahá'í World Centre, 1985.
Van Rooy, Alison, ed. *Civil Society and the Aid Industry*. London: Earthscan, 1998.
World Economic Forum. "The Future Role of Society." *World Scenario Series* (2013): 13–14. http://www3.weforum.org/docs/WEF_FutureRoleCivilSociety_Report_2013.pdf.
Wuthnow, Robert. "Can Religion Revitalize Civil Society? An Institutional Perspective." In *Religion as Social Capital: Producing the Common Good*, edited by Corwin E. Smidt, 191–210. Waco, TX: Baylor University Press, 2003.
Zaleski, Pawel Stefan. "Global Non-governmental Administrative System: Geosociology of the Third Sector." In *Civil Society in the Making*, edited by Dariusz Gawin and Piotr Glinski, 113–43. Warsaw, Poland: IFiS Publishers, 2006.

CHAPTER THREE

MEDIA AND PUBLIC DISCOURSE: NORMATIVE FOUNDATIONS

MICHAEL KARLBERG

We live in an age of existential insecurity. The threats of climate change, weapons of mass destruction, economic collapse, political instability, forced migration of populations, global health pandemics, and other crises indicate the need for fundamental transformations in the way we live together on an increasingly interdependent planet. Among other things, we need to develop more thoughtful and mature modes of public discourse so that we can deliberate collectively on the exigencies of the age and the means for addressing them. To do this, one of the factors we need to consider is the role of the media in shaping public discourse.

As we consider this, we would do well to remind ourselves that all media systems and practices are socially constructed. They are brought into existence through collective human agency, and they can be reformed through such agency. Moreover, all processes of social construction rest on implicit or explicit normative assumptions because human agency is intrinsically value-laden. This chapter argues that contemporary media need to be constructed on more coherent normative foundations that correspond to the exigencies of the age in which we live. Articulating foundational principles is, however, only half of our challenge. We also need to learn how to apply such principles consciously and purposefully to the construction of media systems and practices. This entails the development of a process for the systematic generation and application of knowledge about media systems.

Such a process will undoubtedly need to include policy-makers who shape media systems, media organizations that operate within such systems, professionals who work within media organizations, as well as those who generate and consume media content. But those who formally study media systems and practices have a central role to play in this regard. With this point in mind, this chapter focuses primarily on the domain of media studies. But it invites a much wider conversation regarding the normative foundations of media and the generation of knowledge based on those foundations.

The chapter begins by elaborating the need for coherence in media studies and by examining the inherently value-laden nature of media systems and practices. Then it invites the reader to consider a set of foundational normative principles that can bring coherence to the study and social construction of media systems and practices. In turn, the chapter discusses how these principles can resolve several long-standing tensions in the field. It concludes by outlining some broad lines of inquiry that derive from these normative principles along with some of the challenges that will arise in this context.

Before proceeding, a note is in order regarding how the concept of *social construction* is used in this chapter. This concept is widely invoked today in the humanities and social sciences. It suggests that human knowledge, as well as the social phenomena associated with any given body of knowledge, are constructed by groups of people within systems of shared meaning. But this broad concept can be understood in different ways depending on the underlying ontological assumptions at play. If one assumes there are no normative truths underlying and informing social reality, then the concept of social construction leads to an extreme relativism in which there is no way to assess or compare the merits of different social constructs. There are thus no foundational truths to which one can appeal in struggles to overcome oppressive social norms, and there is no ontological basis for the idea of social progress. On the other hand, if one assumes there are normative truths underlying and informing social reality—no matter how dimly we understand them at present—this creates the potential for constructing social realities that embody normative truths to lesser or greater degrees. This logic opens the possibility—indeed, the imperative—of struggling for real social progress.

This chapter employs the latter conception of social construction. The reasons for this are threefold. First, the extreme relativism associated with the first version is logically self-contradictory. It asserts that one can make no universal truth claims about the normative dimensions of social reality, yet this assertion constitutes a universal truth claim about the normative dimensions of social reality. Second, it is irrational to deny the possibility of social progress because this denial promotes a self-fulfilling prophecy that renders the alternative—the possibility of social progress—untestable. It is more rational to operate from the premise that social progress is possible because this is the only way this notion can be tested empirically over time. Third, although we do not understand the essential nature of normative truths, we can infer their existence by observing their effects. By analogy, physicists do not understand the essential nature of gravity or electromagnetism, yet they assume these forces exist because they can observe their effects. If one ignores the laws of gravity or electromagnetism while constructing an airplane, the result are calamitous. Likewise, if one ignores foundational normative truths in the construction of social systems, the results are disastrous—as we can see in the existential crises currently facing humanity.

The Need for Coherence in the Social Construction of Media

As alluded to above, media systems are among the many social systems that need to be constructed on coherent normative foundations. Media studies has a role to play in articulating these foundations and developing methodologies for the generation of knowledge that embody these foundational commitments. But the field of media studies has much work to do in this regard.

The field of media studies traces back roughly a century. In that time, it has embraced countless lines of inquiry grounded in diverse disciplinary and theoretical matrices resting on a range of implicit or explicit normative commitments. The field is thus characterized by a wide array of rich yet fragmented insights that prevent it from advancing in a systematic manner. As Shearon Lowery and Melvin DeFleur explain:

> Research on mass communication has been particularly unsystematic. It has never been a precisely defined field, and those who have studied the media in the past have come from several different disciplines. One consequence is that researchers have seldom developed their research efforts in a "programmatic" manner.... Such research seldom leads to theoretically significant results.[1]

Against this backdrop, the most comprehensive effort to formulate a coherent framework for media studies was undertaken by James Potter in his 2009 book, *Arguing for a General Framework for Mass Media Scholarship*. Following an ambitious meta-review of the media studies literature, Potter argues that the field is deeply fragmented because it is characterized by widespread definitional variations; by little translation between, or synthesis among, diverse approaches; by inadequate levels of theory-driven and programmatic research; and by categorical thinking that leads to polarized and unproductive debates. He concludes that media studies scholars have, so far, tended to operate in exploratory, inductive, and generative modes that have yielded diverse insights and findings but little coherence. He thus asserts that a more theory-driven and deductive mode is now needed, and he proposes his *lineation general framework* for this.[2] Within this framework, Potter prescribes four broad but interconnected domains of inquiry that should be explored in a mutually informing manner: the study of media organizations, media audiences, media messages, and media effects. In relation to each of these, he sketches out specific lines of inquiry that can contribute to the systematic advancement of a more unified body of knowledge.

Potter's framework contains much to be admired. However, at the core of it is a subtle normative contradiction that arises from his definition of mass media as "technological channels of distributing messages by organizations with the purpose of creating and maintaining audiences."[3] Potter implies that this definition is value neutral. "When our scholarly purpose is to understand how the media operate," he writes, "normative models fall out of bounds.... It would seem far better to accept the nature of the mass media as they exist and judge their performance on their fundamental nature."[4] "In short," he concludes, "let's treat the media for what they are—economic entities."[5] These definitional assertions obscure the fact that the commercialization of media organizations, along with the commodification of media content and media audiences, are all, in themselves, normative social constructs with a distinct political history. These constructs were consolidated in the United States by the mid-twentieth century through a series of heavily lobbied media policy decisions that have since been exported around the world in concert with efforts to defund public service media.[6]

Potter's framework is thus premised on a culturally normalized conception of media coupled with a naïve empiricism that obscures the inherently normative nature of media studies, including his own framework. In the contemporary social sciences and humanities, this kind of empiricism, and the broader tradition of positivism associated with it, has been widely criticized for its construction of a false dichotomy between facts and values and a subsequent tendency to reproduce uncritically inherited and oppressive social formations.[7] Indeed, this is one of the central concerns of critical media studies, which Potter dismisses when he rejects normative commitments as a basis for the field.

The Inherently Value-Laden Nature of the Field

The most prominent normative conceptions of media derive from public sphere theory. In its broadest sense, *the public sphere* tends to be understood as a discursive space in which citizens explore issues of common concern in the process of public opinion formation, foster the emergence of collective will, and inform the legitimate exercise of institutional authority.[8] In any large population of people, the mass media are among the most important discursive spaces for this purpose—at least potentially. Critical media studies demonstrate that this potential is rarely realized in the modern world. On the contrary, dominant forms of media, which are increasingly commercial and frequently financed by advertising, often undermine or distort the deliberative function of the public sphere and tend to serve instead as instruments of commercial or political hegemony.[9] This is an inherent normative bias of the commercial model on which Potter premises his framework.

The structural causes of this distortion of public deliberation have been examined extensively by scholars who study the political economy of media. This body of scholarship analyzes how political and economic forces shape media organizations and content in ways that align with the interests of powerful social classes.[10] This occurs most fundamentally, but not exclusively, at the level of media policies and the political processes that determine them. These processes are largely invisible to the average citizen in countries dominated by commercial media because commercial media rarely report on media policy processes—as it would require them to expose their own extensive lobbying machinery and motives.[11]

In democratic countries, media policies determine, among other things, the extent to which media organizations are structured as public service organizations or for-profit organizations, the degree to which for-profit media organizations have public interest obligations, the extent to which commercial media ownership is concentrated or diversified, whether commercial media organizations can be co-owned by other industries with material interests that conflict with media obligations to serve the public interest, the relative freedoms or constraints placed on advertisers, tax incentives or disincentives for advertising, the presence or absence of public funding for non-commercial media, and the relative freedoms or constraints placed on partisan political propaganda. Increasingly, media policies also determine the extent to which the Internet functions as a public utility or a commercial venture, how access-neutral it remains, the relative freedoms or constraints placed on privacy violations and personal data collection, and other emerging issues.[12] At the moment, as a result of powerful corporate lobbying efforts, media policy trends in many countries are moving toward the neoliberal model of deregulation and hyper-commercialization that dominates the US media landscape.

Political economy scholars have also critiqued the exploitation of audiences within advertising-financed media systems. In such systems, the audience becomes a commodity that is manufactured and sold to advertisers through formulas designed to maximize industry profits rather than public goods.[13] This is accomplished in part through the lure of cheap spectacle—entertaining forms of conflict, violence, and sexual titillation that can be produced at minimal expense to attract maximal audiences. In this context, the customer of the media industry becomes the advertiser, not the public, and it is primarily the advertiser whose interests are being catered to. In the process, advertising-financed media tend to promote and naturalize deeply materialistic worldviews. This is another normative bias of such media.

The political economy of advertising-financed media has also given rise to practices that undermine and distort meaningful public deliberation—especially in televised public affairs programming.[14] This is a function of profitable programming formulas characterized by partisan disputation, dramatic social confrontations, episodic violence, tragedy, and disaster. In this context, the ideal of "objectivity" is frequently reduced to constructing stories as binary oppositions that give equal voice to two dramatically conflicting positions.[15] This often includes balancing one set of partisan political claims against another. It can also entail balancing the consensus of entire scientific fields against the propaganda of self-interested industries that seek to cast doubt on public-interest science.[16] Thus we can see another normative bias of advertising-financed media.

Critical studies have also exposed the problematic relationship between representation and identity in commercial media, which further distorts the public sphere. In general, research has found that the frequency with which different social groups are represented and the positive or negative nature of those representations correlate with a group's position in the social hierarchy.[17] The most powerful and privileged segments of society tend to be represented more frequently and more favorably than those with less power and privilege. The voices, values, interests, and perspectives of the most powerful segments of society thus tend to dominate public discourse. When less powerful voices are heard, they often are trivialized or marginalized. This is another normative bias of advertising-financed media and some other commercial models.

Yet another area of concern in critical media studies pertains to new and emerging media—from the Internet to social media to mobile devices. Foremost among these are concerns regarding privacy violations, surveillance, and the manipulative use of big data by governments and industries.[18] An inseparable concern is the increasing colonization of new media by advertising and the way this further undermines substantive public deliberation while reinforcing the ideology of consumer capitalism.[19]

Foundational Normative Principles
The issues discussed above illustrate the inherently value-laden nature of media systems and practices and, in turn, of media studies. What is needed, therefore, are coherent normative principles that can inform the inseparable processes of knowledge generation and social construction in these domains. To date, most efforts to articulate explicit normative foundations of media have focused on journalism and the press. Such efforts trace back to Enlightenment philosophers such as John Milton and John Stuart Mill who established freedom of the press as a normative principle in liberal democracies.[20] Subsequent normative theories of the press began to be elaborated in the 1940s and 1950s, in the aftermath of European fascism and against the backdrop of an emerging Cold War.[21] This work focused on the relationship between press freedom and social responsibility within the context of Western liberal democracies, and its normative emphasis was on the flow of trustworthy information and the circulation of diverse opinions as requisites of democracy.

Media policy debates in the 1970s and 1980s reflected an increasingly complex array of normative issues. In his book *Media Performance*, Denis McQuail synthesizes the concerns, principles, and values most commonly invoked in these policy discourses.[22] He identifies three basic normative principles: *freedom, justice/equality*, and *order/cohesion*. He then correlates these broad principles with a set of subordinate principles: *independence, access, diversity, objectivity, solidarity, social control*, and *symbolic culture*.

The authors of *Normative Theories of the Media* distill normative media theory so that it accounts for four basic roles of the press in democratic societies.[23] The first is a *monitorial role*, which entails seeking, collecting, and publishing a wide range of information that serves the public interest. The second is a *facilitative role*, which involves supporting the deliberate processes of civil society. The third is a *radical role*, which that entails challenging authority and voicing support for progressive reform. The fourth is a *collaborative role*, which involves forming partnerships between journalists, the state, and other centres of power to advance mutual interests.

Each of the preceding theories offers valuable insights regarding the normative functions of the press. However, they all reflect the biases of Western liberal democratic theory. In contrast, Achal Mehra and the contributors to *Press Systems in ASEAN States* explore the normative implications of Asian cultural values for the press, leading to a decidedly non-Western emphasis on *duty, consensus,* and *social harmony*.[24] Still, most normative media theory has developed within the context of Western liberal democracy.

Although prevailing systems of liberal democracy represent valuable historical accomplishments, the Bahá'í teachings suggest that they represent a transitory stage in an ongoing process of social evolution.[25] And Bahá'ís are not alone in recognizing the limitations of liberal democracy. Similar views can be seen in the growing alienation of diverse people in the West and around the world, especially young people and marginalized populations, who recognize that liberal democracies are proving incapable of ensuring equal opportunities and shared prosperity, of addressing legacies of racism, sexism, xenophobia, and other forms of oppression or social exclusion, and of combating the existential threat of climate change and other pressing environmental concerns.

Explicating the underlying causes of these problems is beyond the scope of this chapter. Suffice it to say that when governance is organized as a contest for power and authority within and between nation states, interest group competition and the corrupting expressions of power it invites impede our advancement toward a more peaceful, just, and sustainable social order.[26] Thus the premises of liberal democracy do not provide an adequate basis for a normative theory of the media in an age of global interdependence. Neither, however, do the traditional Asian values identified by Mehra and colleagues. History has amply demonstrated that these latter values, by themselves, are easily invoked to stifle legitimate struggles for social justice.

Oneness and Justice
This chapter argues that the most fruitful basis for the study and construction of media systems and practices is the principle of the oneness of humanity and its reciprocal principle of justice. Bahá'ís understand these principles not as relativistic values or beliefs, but as ontological truths that underlie and inform social reality—every bit as real as the laws of gravity or electromagnetism in the domain of physical reality—as alluded to at the outset of this chapter. These normative truths about social reality cannot be ignored without consequence. Therefore, they must become embodied, to ever-increasing degrees, in every social system and practice within an emerging global civilization. In this sense, oneness and justice are latent truths that become manifest in social realities through processes of social construction that are informed by the conscious application of these principles.

If one accepts these rational premises, it becomes imperative to ask how media systems and practices can embody these principles to a much greater degree than they currently do in order to minimize the prolongation of conflict and suffering in the world and contribute to the goals of peace, justice, and shared prosperity. In this respect, the Bahá'í community can be understood as a vast social laboratory that is systematically testing the validity of these premises. One can also see tentative evidence in support of these premises across the entire range of human experience in the myriad consequences that accrue from the acceptance or rejection of the principles of oneness and justice.

Other chapters in this volume elaborate these principles in some depth, so it is not necessary to do so here.[27] In brief, the principle of the oneness of humanity enables us to recognize our organic unity and interdependence on a global scale. It helps us see that the well-being and development of every individual and group is inextricably linked to the well-being and development of the entire body of humanity. However, the principle of oneness becomes legitimate only when it is informed by the principle of justice. Otherwise, appeals to unity can be invoked to stifle diversity, critical thought, and transformative agency in the name of a specious and oppressive social harmony that serves the narrow interests of privileged elites.[28]

In this context, justice can be understood in part as a latent faculty of human consciousness that, when developed, enables people to recognize that the interests of the individual and those of society are inseparably linked. Commitments to justice prompt individuals and groups to exercise judgment in fair-minded and unprejudiced ways. The principle of justice is thus an indispensable guide for fair and equitable decision-making at individual and collective levels. The cause of justice is advanced when every individual and group is given the fullest opportunity to develop their latent capacities to contribute to the well-being of the entire social body. Hence justice must become the central organizing principle of a unified and mutually prosperous society.

Bahá'ís believe these truths about social reality are gradually permeating human consciousness across the planet. In this regard, Bahá'ís share a teleological understanding of history. Humanity has been advancing through a collective process of social evolution leading toward the emergence of a global civilization that embodies the principles of oneness and justice to a historically unprecedented degree. Currently, it is passing through a critical transitional period, much like the turbulent period of adolescence, leading toward our collective maturity. This transitional period is characterized by the accelerating disintegration of anachronistic social structures and behavioural norms. At the same time, the emergence and integration of more mature structures and norms can be discerned. But these integrative processes are not automatic. They advance only through human agency. The more prolonged this period of transition is, the more suffering humanity will experience on its path toward maturity.

Consultation
The twin principles of oneness and justice have profound implications for the study and construction of media systems and practices. The discussion that follows will focus primarily on the deliberative functions of media as a forum for public discourse. However, it is important to note that the functions of media cannot be reduced to public deliberation. For instance, art is an important function of media, and the principles of oneness and justice have profound implications for the media arts. Moreover, the arts contribute to deliberative public discourse in significant ways so one cannot easily disentangle the arts from deliberative discourse. Nonetheless, a substantive exploration of the media arts is beyond the scope of this chapter.

As for the deliberative functions of the media, the implications of oneness and justice are brought into focus by examining the Bahá'í practice of *consultation*. Consultation is an approach to collective inquiry and deliberation that seeks to be unifying rather than divisive. Participants are encouraged to exercise freedom of expression and engage in informed, probing, critical analysis. At the same time, they are called to express themselves with care and moderation while remaining detached from preconceived opinions and positions. In the process, they strive to apply spiritual principles—such as the principles of oneness and justice—to the analysis of shared concerns. Diversity is regarded as an asset in this process. Diverse perspectives, insights, and interpretations are therefore solicited to make the process as informed as possible. However, once ideas are expressed, they are no longer identified with the individuals who express them; in this way, ideas become collective resources that can be adopted, refined, or discarded freely according to the emergent wisdom of the group, without the entangling complications of ego or self-interested ambition.

Bahá'ís have demonstrated the efficacy of this deliberative model in tens of thousands of communities across the planet—on local, national, and international scales, and in formal and informal settings. Yet Bahá'ís view consultation not merely as an internal community practice. They see it as a mode of collective inquiry and deliberation that must increasingly characterize a maturing humanity. As Bahá'u'lláh writes, "For everything there is and will continue to be a station of perfection and maturity. The maturity of the gift of understanding is made manifest through consultation."[29]

Consultation can be understood as a model for communication across the public sphere, including the mass media. The Universal House of Justice expresses this clearly in its statement that "the code of conduct of the press must embrace the principles and objectives of consultation . . . to make its full contribution to the preservation of the rights of the people and become a powerful instrument in the consultative processes of society, and hence for the unity of the human race."[30]

The implications of this statement extend beyond the printed word to public discourse more broadly. This theme was explored in a previous article correlating the Bahá'í teachings on the press with those on consultation.[31] Although the full details of that analysis and the primary sources supporting it will not be reproduced here, key insights from it are revisited in the discussion that follows.

In brief, the broadest objectives of consultation can be understood as the collective investigation of reality, or the collective pursuit of truth, in a manner that promotes unity and justice. Within these broad objectives, consultation serves distinct functions in different contexts. In some contexts, it is *exploratory* in nature, with the purpose of generating collective awareness, insight, and understanding regarding an issue of common interest or concern. In other contexts, it is *advisory* in nature, with the purpose of providing advice, feedback, suggestions, or constructive criticism to those who will be making decisions. And in other contexts, it is *decisional* in nature, with the purpose of making a decision, rendering a judgment, or determining a course of action. All these functions can be expressed in formal and informal ways, through communicative processes playing out in an ongoing manner at all levels of community life.

The first two of these functions—*exploratory* and *advisory* consultation—are directly relevant to media and public discourse. Modern societies require ongoing public spaces in which questions and issues of common concern can be raised; data, evidence, and context can be offered and examined; and diverse perspectives, interpretations, and suggestions can be shared. In some cases, the purpose will be to generate collective awareness, insight, and understanding. In others, the purpose will be to inform the subsequent decision-making processes of individuals or institutions. Each of these processes are essential to the progress of all communities, from the local to the global. Media of mass communication are a primary means of extending these consultative processes across space and time.

Resolving Long-Standing Tensions in Public Sphere Theories

This model of consultative public discourse shares some elements in common with liberal democratic models of the public sphere, such as the value placed on the circulation of diverse perspectives. However, liberal democratic theories rest on the premise that competition is the best way to promote social well-being, so diverse perspectives are often understood in a competitive manner. The result tends to be divisive, exclusive, and dysfunctional modes of public discourse—as is evident today throughout the public sphere. Consultative norms of discourse, structured on the premises of oneness and justice, offer a more unifying, inclusive, and functional alternative. Consultative norms also resolve several long-standing tensions inherent in liberal democratic theories of the public sphere. Should the public sphere be characterized by the dynamics of mutualism and cooperation or agonism and contestation? Should public discourse be characterized by a strictly analytical rationality or other modes of expression? And what role, if any, should religion play in the public sphere? Each of these questions is addressed below.

The Relational Dynamics of Public Discourse

The most prominent exponent of public sphere theory is Jürgen Habermas. Habermas's initial conception of the public sphere was largely epistemic. He viewed it as a deliberative space characterized by the advancement of reasoned arguments and counterarguments, supported by logic and evidence, leading to the formation of public opinion and collective will.[32] In this regard, Habermas conceptualized discourse within the public sphere as a relatively cooperative endeavour between equals seeking to arrive at a shared understanding regarding issues of common concern.

This conception has been criticized by scholars who point out that Habermas's bourgeois conception of the public sphere excluded many marginalized or oppressed social groups such as women, racial minorities, and the poor.[33] Such groups have historically been unable to participate in the public sphere as equals, if at all. Their views and interests are also frequently in conflict with the hegemonic assumptions and conceptions governing societies. Some theorists thus have reconceptualized the public sphere as an essentially conflictual or agonistic space (or spaces) characterized by publics and counter-publics or hegemonic and subaltern voices.[34] Scholars continue to debate the question of whether the public sphere should be characterized by mutualistic or agonistic dynamics.

Although these debates continue, agonistic dynamics tend to characterize the contemporary public sphere because they reflect the competitive premises that underlie liberal democracy. Moreover, the wider culture of contest that has arisen from these premises tends to perpetuate the oppression of marginalized social groups.[35] The reason for this is not difficult to understand. When social practices, relationships, and institutions are structured as contests for power, this typically serves the narrow self-interests of powerful social groups because such contests inherently privilege those with the most power. To promote justice, what is needed is to move beyond the culture of contest, recognize the inherent unity and interdependence of the entire social body, and develop more mutualistic relationships, practices, and institutions that reflect our organic oneness. To this end, conceptions of identity will need to expand to include the entire social body, conceptions of power will need to broaden to allow for mutual empowerment, and the dynamics of public discourse will need to mature in a corresponding manner—along mutualistic lines informed by the principle of consultation.[36]

Reason, Emotion, and Inclusivity in Public Discourse
Habermas originally conceptualized the public sphere as a largely epistemic space characterized by the advancement of reasoned arguments and counterarguments supported by logic and evidence. This notion has been criticized for its excessive rationalism; its failure to allow for emotional, narrative, and other forms of expression; and its consequent exclusion of individuals or groups without the inclination or training to communicate in appropriately "rational" ways.[37] Public sphere theorists continue to grapple with the issue of rationalism in public discourse; with the role emotion, narrative, and other modes of expression should play; and with the question of whether participation in the public sphere should be contingent on specific communication competencies.

Like Habermas's conception, the consultative model outlined earlier in this chapter is a model of rational deliberation. But within this model, rational deliberation need not preclude emotion. Emotion is fundamental to human experience and perception, and efforts to foster mutual understanding cannot ignore it. Emotions can uplift, inspire, and motivate. Even painful emotions convey dimensions of human experience—such as the experience of oppression—that must be acknowledged if mutual understanding, empathy, and justice are to prevail. However, within the consultative model, participants strive to convey the emotional dimension of their experience in a constructive manner, without the offensive and defensive posturing that has become so characteristic of media discourse today.

It is also rational to ensure that, in the consideration of complex issues, all relevant individuals and groups can give voice to their diverse perspectives and experiences—even if they do not conform to narrowly construed notions of "rational" speech. In this context, freedom of expression is a bedrock principle of consultation, regardless of cultural background, educational attainment, or communicative competency. At the same time, participants are encouraged, to the best of their ability, to express their views with courtesy, dignity, care, and moderation; to consider the timeliness and impact of their contributions; and to adopt an "etiquette of expression worthy of the approaching maturity of the human race."[38]

Prescriptions for a mature etiquette of expression therefore do not serve as a licence to dismiss or exclude any person or group as coarse, uneducated, or irrational. Etiquette of expression is not a prerequisite for participating in consultation. Rather, the capacity to participate is understood in a developmental manner, and consultation is seen as an inclusive process through which people collectively learn and refine constructive modes of expression. Moreover, in large consultative groups that require facilitation, there is much that a skilful facilitator can do to set a positive tone, foster an inclusive atmosphere, draw out diverse views, and reframe sensitive issues in constructive ways—without silencing any voices. Likewise, there is much the media can do, along the same lines, as facilitators of public discourse across entire populations.

The developmental perspective alluded to above, in which participants learn through experience, also helps us recognize the need for educational processes outside the media that support these aims by helping prepare citizens to participate in public discourse. One of their aims must be to foster modes of expression that allow diverse perceptions and concerns to be examined critically in ways that render difficult problems as soluble challenges. This is not the same as learning to gloss over conflicts by remaining silent or speaking with artificial civility in the name of a superficial harmony.

Finally, it is important to acknowledge that formal deliberation is not in itself the only means by which informed public opinion and collective will can form. Inspirational appeals, aspirational statements, affective expressions, and other modes by which the human spirit communicates and perceives also play an essential role. It is partly for this reason that the media arts are such powerful forces in processes of awareness raising, opinion formation, and mobilization. It is also for this reason that symbolic forms of public action can play a catalyzing role at critical historical moments. Today, the arts and symbolic forms of public action are in many cases the only means by which marginalized people can exercise their voices within a public sphere that tends to exclude or misrepresent them. For all these reasons, the significance of the media cannot be reduced to its epistemic role as a forum for rational discourse, narrowly conceived. The consultative model accommodates an understanding that the public sphere is a forum of rich and multi-layered exchange, with both rational and affective dimensions, through which systems of shared knowledge and meaning evolve.

The Role of Religion in Public Discourse

Habermas's initial conception of the public sphere was also characterized by a purely secular rationality. This understanding was subsequently criticized for excluding large segments of society and reflecting a narrow conception of modernity.[39] Habermas has since begun to explore how religion can play a constructive role within the public sphere, and a growing number of post-secular theorists are grappling with the same question.[40]

The normative principles outlined in this chapter suggest that religion can make significant contributions to the advancement of knowledge about the construction of social realities—if religious voices meet certain conditions. To understand this potential, it is important to return to the issue of relativism. Within consultation, diverse perspectives are viewed as a means of arriving at a more comprehensive understanding of multi-faceted realities in the pursuit of unity and justice. In the absence of these foundational normative commitments, diversity results in extreme relativism. And extreme relativism leads to a normative impasse that makes social progress impossible, as mentioned at the outset of this chapter. This impasse cannot be avoided unless one assumes the existence of foundational normative truths, or what Bahá'ís refer to as spiritual principles, which underlie and inform the construction of social realities.

Based on these premises, it is possible to conceive of the relative embodiment of foundational normative truths in diverse social constructs and of efforts to increase this relative embodiment. Consider, for instance, the way spiritual principles such as oneness and justice can be embodied in socially constructed systems of rights. Slavery fails to manifest these principles in any meaningful way. The caste system and feudal systems embody these principles in ways that are only marginally better. The bills of rights adopted by various democratic states today, or the Universal Declaration of Human Rights, manifest these principles to a much higher degree. And it should be possible to construct future systems of rights that embody these underlying normative truths to even higher degrees.

The same can be said for all socially constructed systems. And in relation to all processes of social construction, the public sphere serves an essential epistemic function. It is a sphere in which diverse voices must be able to contribute their perspectives and participate in the generation of knowledge regarding efforts to increase the embodiment of normative truths in social realities. But this cannot be understood merely at the level of individual voices speaking in idiosyncratic ways. It also needs to be understood at the level of epistemic frameworks. The generation and application of knowledge, whether scientific or religious, advances systematically only within evolving conceptual frameworks that provide a coherent means for the collective investigation of reality. Hence public discourse must be characterized by conditions in which diverse frameworks can be articulated and explored, in which they can be tested against reality, and in which their relative fruitfulness can, over time, be assessed.

These insights point to a constructive role for religion in the public sphere. Religion can, at its best, be understood as a system for generating knowledge about the application of spiritual principles—or normative truths—to the advancement of civilization. Understood in this manner, religious voices and interpretative frameworks should be welcome in the public sphere to the extent that they are seeking to apply spiritual principles thoughtfully to the betterment of society. Like all contributions, they should be held to basic standards of civility (i.e., they should not promote violence or sectarian animosities) as well as basic standards of rationality (i.e., they should be consistent with reason and scientific knowledge). When they meet these conditions, religious contributions should be welcome in a consultative public sphere and should be assessed according to their fruitfulness.

A skeptic might argue that these conditions are unrealistic because they are so frequently violated. Yet religious systems of thought and practice have always had an evolutionary character in relation to the underlying truths on which they are founded. This is a function of the hermeneutic, or interpretive, nature of religious systems in relation to such truths. At this critical juncture in history, when the entire human population is becoming increasingly interdependent and the exigencies of the age require us to address unprecedented global challenges, religious systems of thought and practice must continue to evolve.

What is called for in this regard is a sustained, probing, normative public discourse on religion itself. What are the standards by which religious thought and practice will be held to account in the public sphere? What systems of meaning even warrant the appellation "religion" in an age of global interdependence? Why should we continue to associate any irrational, fanatical, or violent truth claims with this term? After all, when mid-twentieth-century fascists asserted equally irrational, fanatical, and violent truth claims in the name of "science," they ultimately were denied this validating appellation within the scientific community and throughout the global public sphere.

We would therefore do well to recall that the advancement of science has been driven by a parallel normative discourse that has been playing out for several centuries now. It is only through the insights and commitments generated through the normative discourse on science that we increasingly distinguish pseudoscience, junk science, and the perversion or abuse of science from valid scientific thought and practice. Why should religion not be driven to advance in a parallel manner? This will be possible, however, only if thoughtful and reflective religious voices are welcomed as full participants in a consultative public sphere—as was the case with the normative discourse on science. Only in this way can valid religious contributions to social progress be distinguished from the dogmatic beliefs, divisive postures, anti-scientific assertions, and triumphalist rhetoric that often masquerade in the name of religion.

As primary gatekeepers and facilitators of the public sphere, the media have a crucial responsibility in this regard. But this responsibility becomes fully apparent only when media systems and practices are conceptualized in a consultative manner that embodies the principles of oneness and justice.

Learning Our Way Forward

This chapter has argued that media systems and practices, along with the field of media studies that participates in their construction, need more coherent normative foundations. To this end, it invites the reader to consider the reciprocal principles of oneness and justice, and the practice of consultation that derives from them, as coherent foundations.

To build upon these foundations, it will help to consider briefly some specific lines of inquiry that will need to be pursued. One important question is how to enact and refine policies that support the construction of more consultative media systems and practices. Another is how to raise the internal capacity of media organizations to better facilitate consultative modes of public discourse. Yet another is how to raise the capacity of individuals, of non-media institutions, and of communities to engage public discourse in more consultative modes. It also will be important to determine how to advance processes of technological innovation and adoption in conscious ways that support consultative modes of public discourse. Ultimately, all these lines of inquiry are intimately connected, but each points to distinct long-term processes that will need to be systematically pursued if media systems and practices are to realize their full potential to contribute to the establishment of a more peaceful, just, and prosperous social order.

These considerations raise important methodological questions that also need to be explored. In the social sciences, the legacy of positivism continues to exert a powerful influence on methodology. By asserting a strict dichotomy between the domain of facts and values, positivism has led to the dominance of allegedly value-neutral methodologies. Although critiques of positivism are increasingly common and the myth of value-neutral methodologies in the social sciences has been widely challenged, the absence of shared normative foundations has led to the problem of value relativism among those who reject positivism—including within the field of media studies. For media studies—and all social sciences—to advance more systematically, post-positivist methodologies will need to be developed on shared, coherent, and normative foundations.

Finally, when considering the possibility of normative, epistemological, and methodological progress in the social construction of media systems and practices, we cannot be naïve. Powerful vested interests will feel threatened by these processes and will seek to undermine them. Indeed, they already do, even though these processes are in such nascent stages. If we accept the principles of oneness and justice as foundational truths, the challenge will be to employ unifying and constructive approaches to social change in the pursuit of social justice.[41] Only in this way will the means of social change become congruous with the ends. The question of how to actualize this methodology will need to be pursued consciously and systematically in response to the exigencies of the age.

Notes

1 Shearon A. Lowery and Melvin L. DeFleur, *Milestones in Mass Communication Research: Media Effects*, 3rd ed. (White Plains, NY: Longman, 1995), 5. Refer also to a discussion of this theme in James Potter, *Arguing for a General Framework for Mass Media Scholarship* (Los Angeles, CA: SAGE, 2009).
2 Potter, *Arguing*, passim.
3 Ibid., 32.
4 Ibid., 54.
5 Ibid., 55.
6 For overviews of this history and discussions of the social consequences of these policy decisions refer to Paul Starr, *The Creation of the Media: Political Origins of Modern Communications* (New York: Basic Books, 2004); Daniel Rossides, *Communication, Media, and American Society* (New York: Rowman & Littlefield, 2003); Robert McChesney, *The Problem of the Media: U.S. Communication Politics in the 21st Century* (New York: Monthly Review Press, 2004); Mark Lloyd, *Prologue to a Farce: Communication and Democracy in America* (Chicago: University of Illinois Press, 2006); and Sasha Costanza-Chock, "The Globalization of Media Policy," in *The Future of Media*, ed. Robert McChesney, Russell Newman, and Ben Scott (New York: Seven Stories Press, 2005), 259–74.

7 See Evelyn Fox Keller and Helen Longino, *Feminism and Science* (Oxford, UK: Oxford University Press, 1996); Hilary Putnam, *The Collapse of the Fact/Value Dichotomy and Other Essays* (Cambridge, MA: Harvard University Press, 2002); and Janet Kourany, *Philosophy of Science after Feminism* (Oxford, UK: Oxford University Press, 2010).

8 Jostein Gripsrud and Martin Eide, *The Idea of the Public Sphere: A Reader* (Lanham, MD: Lexington Books, 2010), xiii–xiv, 114–15.

9 See Robert McChesney, *Rich Media, Poor Democracy* (New York: New Press, 2015); Douglas Kellner, "Habermas, the Public Sphere, and Democracy," in *Re-Imagining the Public Sphere: The Frankfurt School in the 21st Century*, ed. Diana Boros and James Glass (New York: Palgrave Macmillan, 2014); Richard Butsch, ed., *Media and Public Spheres* (New York: Palgrave Macmillan, 2007); and Benjamin Page, *Who Deliberates? Mass Media in Modern Democracy* (Chicago: University of Chicago Press, 1996).

10 See, for example, Janet Wasko, Graham Murdock, and Helena Sousa, eds., *The Handbook of Political Economy of Communications* (Oxford, UK: Wiley Blackwell, 2014); Vincent Mosco, *The Political Economy of Communication*, 2nd ed. (London: SAGE, 2009); Robert McChesney, *The Political Economy of Media: Enduring Issues, Emerging Dilemmas* (New York: Monthly Review Press, 2008); and Edward Herman and Noam Chomsky, *Manufacturing Consent: The Political Economy of the Mass Media* (New York: Pantheon Books, 1998).

11 For an analysis of how extensive the media lobby is in the US, along with the unreported influence it exerts on media policies, refer to John Dunbar, "Who Is Watching the Watchdog?" in *The Future of Media*, ed. Robert McChesney, Russell Newman, and Ben Scott (New York: Seven Stories Press, 2005), 127–40.

12 See Robert McChesney, *Digital Disconnect: How Capitalism Is Turning the Internet Against Democracy* (New York: New Press, 2013) and Susan Crawford, *Captive Audience: The Telecom Industry and Monopoly Power in the New Gilded Age* (New Haven, CT: Yale University Press, 2013).

13 See Dallas Smythe, *Dependency Road: Communications, Capitalism, Consciousness, and Canada* (Norwood, NJ: Ablex, 1981); Sut Jhally, *The Codes of Advertising: Fetishism and the Political Economy of Meaning in the Consumer Society* (New York: St. Martin's Press, 1987); and William Leiss et al., *Social Communication in Advertising: Consumption in the Mediated Marketplace*, 3rd ed. (New York: Routledge, 2005).

14 See Peter Dahlgren and Colin Sparks, *Communication and Citizenship: Journalism and the Public Sphere in the New Media Age* (New York: Routledge, 1991) and McChesney, *Rich Media, Poor Democracy*.

15 Robert Hackett and Yuezhi Zhao, *Sustaining Democracy?: Journalism and the Politics of Objectivity* (Toronto: Garamond Press, 1998), 45.

16 Naomi Oreskes and Erik Conway, *Merchants of Doubt: How a Handful of Scientists Obscured the Truth on Issues from Tobacco Smoke to Global Warming* (New York: Bloomsbury Press, 2011), *passim.*
17 See Pamela Shoemaker and Stephen Reese, *Mediating the Message in the 21st Century* (New York: Routledge, 2014); Susan Ross and Paul Lester, *Images That Injure: Pictorial Stereotypes in the Media*, 3rd ed. (Oxford, UK: Praeger, 2011); and Gail Dines and Jean M. Humez, *Gender, Race, and Class in Media: A Critical Reader* (Thousand Oaks, CA: SAGE, 2003).
18 See Mark Andrejevic, "Surveillance in the Digital Enclosure," *Communication Review* 10, no. 4 (2007): 295–317; Marc Rotenberg, Jeramie Scott, and Julia Horwitz, *Privacy in the Modern Age* (New York: New Press, 2015); Neil Richards, *Intellectual Privacy: Rethinking Civil Liberties in the Digital Age* (Oxford, UK: Oxford University Press, 2015); and Tim Dwyer, *Convergent Media and Privacy* (New York: Palgrave Macmillan, 2016).
19 McChesney, *Digital Disconnect* 146-158.
20 See John Milton, *Areopagitica: A Speech of Mr. John Milton for the Liberty of Unlicenc'd Printing to the Parliament of England* (London, 1644) and John Stuart Mill, *On Liberty* (London: John W. Parker & Son, 1859).
21 See, for example, Robert Hutchins, *A Free and Responsible Press: Report of the Commission on Freedom of the Press* (Chicago: University of Chicago Press, 1947); Royal Commission on the Press, *Report, Command 7700* (London: His Majesty's Stationary Office, 1949); and Fred Siebert, Theodore Peterson, and Wilbur Schramm, *Four Theories of the Press: The Authoritarian, Libertarian, Social Responsibility and Soviet Communist Concepts of What the Press Should Be and Do* (Urbana, IL: University of Illinois Press, 1956).
22 Denis McQuail, *Media Performance: Mass Communication and the Public Interest* (London: SAGE, 1992), 67.
23 Clifford Christians et al., *Normative Theories of the Media: Journalism in Democratic Societies* (Urbana, IL: University of Illinois Press, 2009).
24 Achal Mehra, ed., *Press Systems in ASEAN States* (Singapore: AMIC, 1989).
25 Universal House of Justice to the Followers of Bahá'u'lláh in the United States of America, December 29, 1988, http://www.bahai.org/library/authoritative-texts/the-universal-house-of-justice/messages/#d=19881229_001&f=f1.
26 For a discussion of these themes by this author refer to *Beyond the Culture of Contest* (Oxford, UK: George Ronald, 2004) and "Western Liberal Democracy as New World Order?" in *The Bahá'í World: 2005–2006*, ed. Robert Weinberg (Haifa, Israel: World Centre Publications, 2007), 133–56.
27 Refer especially to the chapter by Shahriar Razavi in this volume.
28 Refer to discussions of this theme in Bertrand de Jouvenel, *On Power: The Natural History of Its Growth* (Indianapolis, IN: Liberty Fund, 1993); Laura Nader, "Harmony Models and the Construction of Law," in *Conflict Resolution: Cross-Cultural Perspectives*, ed. K. Avruch et al. (New York: Greenwood

Press, 1991), 41–60; and Laurel Rose, *The Politics of Harmony* (Cambridge, UK: Cambridge University Press, 1992).

29 Bahá'u'lláh, *Compilation of Compilations*, vol. 1 (Mona Vale, Australia: Bahá'í Publications Australia, 2000), 93.

30 Universal House of Justice to the Followers of Bahá'u'lláh in the United States of America, December 29, 1988. Beyond this statement on the code of conduct of the press, the issue of responsible media practice was emphasized from the inception of the Bahá'í Faith in the writings of Bahá'u'lláh. For a fuller discussion of this theme see Michael Karlberg, "The Press as a Consultative Forum: A Contribution to Normative Press Theory," *Bahá'í Studies Review* 16 (2010): 29–42.

31 Karlberg, "The Press as a Consultative Forum: A Contribution to Normative Press Theory."

32 Jürgen Habermas, *The Structural Transformation of the Public Sphere: An Inquiry into a Category of Bourgeois Society*, trans. Thomas Burger (Cambridge, MA: MIT Press, 1989) xi–xii, 25–31.

33 See Craig Calhoun, *Habermas and the Public Sphere* (Cambridge, MA: MIT Press) and Bruce Robbins, *The Phantom Public Sphere* (Minneapolis, MN: University of Minnesota Press, 1993).

34 See Nancy Fraser, "Rethinking the Public Sphere"; Chantal Mouffe, "Deliberative Democracy or Agonistic Pluralism?" *Social Research: An International Quarterly* 66, no. 3 (1999): 745–58.

35 Karlberg, *Beyond the Culture of Contest*, see discussion in chapter 3.

36 Ibid., see discussion in chapter 5.

37 See Nancy Fraser, "Rethinking the Public Sphere: A Contribution to the Critique of Actually Existing Democracy," in *The Phantom Public Sphere*, ed. Bruce Robbins (Minneapolis, MN: University of Minnesota Press, 1993), 1–32; Mary P. Ryan, "Gender and Public Access: Women's Politics in Nineteenth-Century America," in *Habermas and the Public Sphere*, ed. Craig Calhoun (Cambridge, MA: MIT Press, 1994), 259–88; Jane Mansbridge, "Feminism and Democracy," *American Prospect* 1 (Spring 1990): 126–39; Lynn Sanders, "Against Deliberation," *Political Theory* 25, no. 3 (1997): 347–75; and Johanna Meehan, ed., *Feminists Read Habermas: Gendering the Subject of Discourse* (New York: Routledge, 1995).

38 Universal House of Justice to the Followers of Bahá'u'lláh in the United States of America, December 29, 1988.

39 See, for example, David Zaret, "Religion, Science, and Printing in the Public Spheres in Seventeenth-Century England," in *Habermas and the Public Sphere*, ed. Craig Calhoun (Cambridge, MA: MIT Press, 1994), 212–35; José Casanova, *Public Religions in the Modern World* (Chicago: University of Chicago Press, 1994); and Armando Salvatore, *The Public Sphere: Liberal Modernity, Catholicism, Islam* (New York: Palgrave Macmillan, 2007).

40 See Habermas, "Notes on Post-Secular Society," *New Perspectives Quarterly* 25, no. 4 (2008): 17–29; Judith Butler et al., *The Power of Religion in*

the Public Sphere (New York: Columbia University Press, 2011); and Craig Calhoun, Eduardo Mendieta, and Jonathan VanAntwerpen, eds., *Habermas and Religion* (Cambridge, UK: Polity, 2013).

41 For discussions of this theme, refer to Karlberg, "The Paradox of Protest in a Culture of Contest," *Peace & Change* 28, no. 3 (2003): 319–47 and "Constructive Resilience: The Bahá'í Response to Oppression," *Peace & Change* 35, no. 2 (2010): 222–57.

Bibliography

Andrejevic, Mark. "Surveillance in the Digital Enclosure." *Communication Review* 10, no. 4 (2007): 295–317.

Bahá'u'lláh. *Compilation of Compilations*. Vol. 1. Mona Vale, Australia: Bahá'í Publications, 2000.

Boros, Diana, and James M. Glass, eds. *Re-imagining Public Space: The Frankfurt School in the 21st Century*. New York: Palgrave Macmillan, 2014.

Butler, Judith, et al. *The Power of Religion in the Public Sphere*. New York: Columbia University Press, 2011.

Butsch, Richard, ed. *Media and Public Spheres*. New York: Palgrave Macmillan, 2007.

Calhoun, Craig. *Habermas and the Public Sphere*. Cambridge, MA: MIT Press, 1992.

Calhoun, Craig, Eduardo Mendieta, and Jonathan VanAntwerpen, eds. *Habermas and Religion*. Cambridge, UK: Polity, 2013.

Casanova, José. *Public Religions in the Modern World*. Chicago: University of Chicago Press, 1994.

Christians, Clifford, et al. *Normative Theories of the Media: Journalism in Democratic Societies*. Urbana, IL: University of Illinois Press, 2009.

Costanza-Chock, Sasha. "The Globalization of Media Policy." In *The Future of Media*, edited by Robert McChesney, Russell Newman, and Ben Scott, 259–74. New York: Seven Stories Press, 2005.

Crawford, Susan. *Captive Audience: The Telecom Industry and Monopoly Power in the New Gilded Age*. New Haven, CT: Yale University Press, 2013.

Dahlgren, Peter, and Colin Sparks. *Communication and Citizenship: Journalism and the Public Sphere in the New Media Age*. New York: Routledge, 1991.

Dines, Gail, and Jean M. Humez. *Gender, Race, and Class in Media: A Critical Reader*. Thousand Oaks, CA: SAGE, 2003.

Dunbar, John. "Who Is Watching the Watchdog?" In *The Future of Media*, edited by Robert McChesney, Russell Newman, and Ben Scott, 127–40. New York: Seven Stories Press, 2005.

Dwyer, Tim. *Convergent Media and Privacy*. New York: Palgrave Macmillan, 2016.

Fraser, Nancy. "Rethinking the Public Sphere: A Contribution to the Critique of Actually Existing Democracy." *The Phantom Public Sphere*, edited by

Bruce Robbins, 1–32. Minneapolis, MN: University of Minnesota Press, 1993.

Gripsrud, Jostein, and Martin Eide. *The Idea of the Public Sphere: A Reader.* Lanham, MD: Lexington Books, 2010.

Habermas, Jürgen. "Notes on Post-Secular Society." *New Perspectives Quarterly* 25, no. 4 (2008), pp. 17–29.

———. *The Structural Transformation of the Public Sphere: An Inquiry into a Category of Bourgeois Society.* Translated by Thomas Burger. Cambridge, MA: MIT Press, 1989.

Hackett, Robert, and Yuezhi Zhao. *Sustaining Democracy?: Journalism and the Politics of Objectivity.* Toronto: Garamond Press, 1998.

Herman, Edward, and Noam Chomsky. *Manufacturing Consent: The Political Economy of the Mass Media.* New York: Pantheon, 1998.

Hutchins, Robert. *A Free and Responsible Press: Report of the Commission on Freedom of the Press.* Chicago: University of Chicago Press, 1947.

Jhally, Sut. *The Codes of Advertising: Fetishism and the Political Economy of Meaning in the Consumer Society.* New York: St. Martin's Press, 1987.

Jouvenel, Bertrand de. *On Power: The Natural History of Its Growth.* Indianapolis, IN: Liberty Fund, 1993.

Karlberg, Michael. *Beyond the Culture of Contest: From Adversarialism to Mutualism in an Age of Interdependence.* Oxford, UK: George Ronald, 2004.

———. "Constructive Resilience: The Bahá'í Response to Oppression." *Peace & Change* 35, no. 2 (2010): 222–57.

———. "The Paradox of Protest in a Culture of Contest." *Peace & Change* 28, no. 3 (2003): 319–47.

———. "The Press as a Consultative Forum: A Contribution to Normative Press Theory." *Bahá'í Studies Review* 16 (2010): 29–42.

———. "Western Liberal Democracy as New World Order?" In *The Bahá'í World: 2005–2006,* edited by Robert Weinberg, 133–56. Haifa, Israel: World Centre Publications, 2007.

Keller, Evelyn Fox, and Helen Longino, *Feminism and Science.* Oxford, UK: Oxford University Press, 1996.

Kellner, Douglas. "Habermas, the Public Sphere, and Democracy." In *Re-imagining the Public Sphere: The Frankfurt School in the 21st Century,* edited by Diana Boros and James M. Glass, 19–43. New York: Palgrave Macmillan, 2014.

Kourany, Janet. *Philosophy of Science after Feminism.* Oxford, UK: Oxford University Press, 2010.

Leiss, William, et al. *Social Communication in Advertising: Consumption in the Mediated Marketplace.* 3rd ed. New York: Routledge, 2005.

Lloyd, Mark. *Prologue to a Farce: Communication and Democracy in America.* Chicago: University of Illinois Press, 2006.

Lowery, Shearon A., and Melvin L. DeFleur. *Milestones in Mass Communication Research: Media Effects.* 3rd ed. White Plains, NY: Longman, 1995.

Mansbridge, Jane. "Feminism and Democracy." *American Prospect* 1 (1990): 126–39.

McChesney, Robert. *Digital Disconnect: How Capitalism Is Turning the Internet Against Democracy*. New York: New Press, 2013.

———. *The Problem of the Media: U.S. Communication Politics in the 21st Century*. New York: Monthly Review Press, 2004.

———. *Rich Media, Poor Democracy*. New York: New Press, 1999.

McQuail, Denis. *Media Performance: Mass Communication and the Public Interest*. London: SAGE, 1992.

Meehan, Johanna, ed. *Feminists Read Habermas: Gendering the Subject of Discourse*. New York: Routledge, 1995.

Mehra, Achal, ed. *Press Systems in ASEAN States*. Singapore: AMIC, 1989.

Mill, John Stuart. *On Liberty*. London: John W. Parker & Son, 1859.

Milton, John. *Areopagitica: A Speech of Mr. John Milton for the Liberty of Unlicenc'd Printing to the Parliament of England*. London, 1644.

Mosco, Vincent. *The Political Economy of Communication*. 2nd ed. London: SAGE, 2009.

Mouffe, Chantal. "Deliberative Democracy or Agonistic Pluralism?" *Social Research: An International Quarterly* 66, no. 3 (1999): 745–58.

Nader, Laura. "Harmony Models and the Construction of Law." *Conflict Resolution: Cross-Cultural Perspectives*, edited by K. Avruch et al., 41–60. New York: Greenwood Press, 1991.

Oreskes, Naomi, and Erik Conway. *Merchants of Doubt: How a Handful of Scientists Obscured the Truth on Issues from Tobacco Smoke to Global Warming*. New York: Bloomsbury, 2011.

Page, Benjamin. *Who Deliberates?: Mass Media in Modern Democracy*. Chicago: University of Chicago Press, 1996.

Potter, James. *Arguing for a General Framework for Mass Media Scholarship*. Los Angeles, CA: SAGE, 2009.

Putnam, Hilary. *The Collapse of the Fact/Value Dichotomy and Other Essays*. Cambridge, MA: Harvard University Press, 2002.

Richards, Neil. *Intellectual Privacy: Rethinking Civil Liberties in the Digital Age*. Oxford, UK: Oxford University Press, 2015.

Robbins, Bruce. *The Phantom Public Sphere*. Minneapolis, MN: University of Minnesota Press, 1993.

Rose, Laurel. *The Politics of Harmony*. Cambridge, UK: Cambridge University Press, 1992.

Ross, Susan, and Paul Lester. *Images That Injure: Pictorial Stereotypes in the Media*. 3rd ed. Oxford, UK: Praeger, 2011.

Rossides, Daniel. *Communication, Media, and American Society*. New York: Rowman & Littlefield, 2003.

Rotenberg, Marc, Jeramie Scott, and Julia Horwitz. *Privacy in the Modern Age*. New York: New Press, 2015.

Royal Commission on the Press. *Report, Command 7700*. His Majesty's Stationary Office, 1949.

Ryan, Mary P. "Gender and Public Access: Women's Politics in Nineteenth-Century America." In *Habermas and the Public Sphere*, edited by Craig Calhoun, 259–88. Cambridge, MA: MIT Press, 1994.

Salvatore, Armando. *The Public Sphere: Liberal Modernity, Catholicism, Islam*. New York: Palgrave Macmillan, 2007.

Sanders, Lynn. "Against Deliberation." *Political Theory* 25, no. 3 (1997): 347–75.

Shoemaker, Pamela, and Stephen Reese. *Mediating the Message in the 21st Century*. New York: Routledge, 2014.

Siebert, Fred, Theodore Peterson, and Wilbur Schramm. *Four Theories of the Press: The Authoritarian, Libertarian, Social Responsibility and Soviet Communist Concepts of What the Press Should Be and Do*. Chicago: University of Illinois Press, 1956.

Starr, Paul. *The Creation of the Media: Political Origins of Modern Communications*. New York: Basic Books, 2004.

Smythe, Dallas. *Dependency Road: Communications, Capitalism, Consciousness, and Canada*. Norwood, NJ: Ablex, 1981.

Universal House of Justice. Universal House of Justice to the Followers of Bahá'u'lláh in the United States of America, December 29, 1988. http://www.bahai.org/library/authoritative-texts/the-universal-house-of-justice/messages/#d=19881229_001&f=f1.

Wasko, Janet, Graham Murdock, and Helena Sousa, eds. *The Handbook of Political Economy of Communications*. Oxford, UK: Wiley Blackwell, 2014.

Zaret, David. "Religion, Science, and Printing in the Public Spheres in Seventeenth-Century England." *Habermas and the Public Sphere*, edited by Craig Calhoun, 212–35. Cambridge, MA: MIT Press, 1994.

CHAPTER FOUR

EDUCATION AND MORAL EMPOWERMENT: RAISING CAPACITY FOR PARTICIPATION IN PUBLIC DISCOURSE

SONA FARID-ARBAB

Widespread participation in a global conversation on the advancement of material and spiritual civilization requires capacity building among diverse populations. In this chapter, we propose an inquiry into the nature of a conceptual framework for educational processes that can contribute to such a capacity. Many elements of this framework were initially introduced into the Bahá'í community's discourse on education through the experience of Fundación para la Aplicación y Enseñanza de las Ciencias (FUNDAEC)—in English, the Foundation for the Application and Teaching of the Sciences—a Bahá'í-inspired organization in Colombia engaged in learning about education for development.[1]

To call an educational endeavour "Bahá'í-inspired" assumes a particular relationship between the Bahá'í Faith and education. The influence of religion on education often is perceived either in terms of the inculcation of beliefs among groups of adherents or the incorporation of ethical teachings drawn from religion in programs of secular moral training. There is, however, another way in which religion can exert influence on the field of education. When viewed as a system of knowledge and practice that develops in harmony with science, religion can provide a source of inspiration for a conceptual framework within which educators can act and reflect. This is the relationship between the framework being discussed here and the Bahá'í teachings. Such a framework has been evolving through a dynamic process of action and reflection on action that benefits from insights gleaned from the critical analysis of various theories and practices in the field of education; its elements continue to be elaborated in an ongoing conversation among participants in a growing network of Bahá'í-inspired educational endeavours.

The concept that integrates the various elements of the above framework into a consistent whole is that of "moral empowerment." The present chapter begins with a preliminary discussion of this concept and suggests that educational processes concerned with moral empowerment should seek to harmonize the urge to pursue one's own intellectual and moral development with the motivation to contribute to the advancement of society. Every effort toward the empowerment of a group of people has to deal rigorously with the question of power. A conception of power proper to education as moral empowerment is thus the first element of the framework discussed here. A brief examination of the concept of political power, focused on how it shapes approaches to citizenship education and cultivation of critical consciousness, leads to the conclusion that there are other dimensions to power—notably those expressing the nobility of the human spirit—that need to be recognized. To draw upon these sources of power, education must pursue vigorously the aim of nurturing "understanding" not only as an achievement, but also as a process in which one advances and as a faculty of the human soul with endless potentialities. Furthermore, to nurture understanding adequately, one must deal in an integrated manner with the "subject of understanding", the "object of understanding", and the "process of understanding" and avoid the common error of emphasizing one at the expense of the others. In the search for the desired characteristics of the subject of understanding—the protagonist of moral empowerment—this chapter takes a cursory look at a few major theories in education and ethics. What we find is that each offers a partial and, at times, less than suitable picture of the subject of understanding. Our protagonist is not the emotivist self or the radical constructivist of extreme subjectivism, nor the programmed computer-like entity of the cognitive movement. He or she cannot be characterized merely by a set of virtues, competencies, or skills and needs to be viewed in terms of states of *being, knowing,* and *doing* that are the manifestations of the qualities and powers inherent in the human spirit. The notion of capability as developed by FUNDAEC proves central to a way of thinking that enables us to describe the progress of the subject of understanding on the path of moral empowerment, where individual growth and contribution to social transformation are inseparably linked. Emphasis on *being, knowing,* and *doing* demands that attention be given to attributes of the subject of understanding beyond those addressed in the usual deliberations on virtues. Thus, the concept of spiritual qualities as defining attributes of the human soul comes into play. What is proposed here is that nurturing understanding, so crucial in the process of moral empowerment, is inseparable from fostering spiritual qualities. The conception of the reciprocal relationship between the two is yet another element of the framework explored in this chapter. Only those elements of the framework that are particularly relevant to the overall theme of this publication are being examined here, namely, an expanded notion of power, the nature of understanding, the identity of the protagonist of moral empowerment, and a conception of capability and the relationship between nurturing understanding and fostering spiritual qualities.[2] This chapter concludes with some thoughts on the characteristics of an appropriate language that can be used by the protagonist of moral empowerment to participate fruitfully in public discourse.

A Twofold Moral Purpose

The term "moral empowerment" as employed in this chapter applies to both the process and the goal of educational endeavours that seek to endow individuals with a twofold moral purpose: to pursue their own intellectual and spiritual growth and to contribute to the transformation of society. It is a premise of this chapter that the adoption of such a twofold purpose by an increasing number of people is necessary if a dynamic global conversation on the advancement of civilization is to penetrate the grassroots of society.

The notion of moral empowerment advanced here receives inspiration from two interrelated sets of Bahá'í convictions. The first pertains to the principle of the oneness of humankind and the second to the evolution of human society. The oneness of humankind is the pivotal principle around which all the teachings of the Bahá'í Faith revolve. However, oneness should not be misinterpreted to mean uniformity, and "the consciousness of the oneness of humankind" should not be construed as "a mere outburst of ignorant emotionalism" or "an expression of vague and pious hope."[3] The principle implies "an organic change in the structure of present-day society, a change such as the world has not yet experienced."[4]

As to the evolution of society, the teachings of the Bahá'í Faith suggest that humanity's collective life can be seen in terms of stages analogous to infancy, childhood, adolescence, and maturity in the life of a human being. Accordingly, the agitations of today's society are understood as the necessary manifestations of an age of transition from childhood to maturity. The forces operating in the world, both destructive and constructive, are associated with parallel processes of disintegration and integration of a society in rapid transformation; they compel humanity to abandon the habits of childhood and to embrace ways commensurate with its approaching maturity.

The interplay of these two sets of convictions—having to do with the oneness of humankind and the evolution of society—gives shape to a twofold moral purpose, requiring the individual to pursue the development of the virtues and powers that should characterize a member of the human race entering its age of maturity and, at the same time, to contribute to organic change in the structure of society.

The idea of a twofold purpose implies that there is no tension between the pursuit of one's own development and one's contribution to the transformation of society; these are two interwoven aspects of one necessary movement. Advancing in both requires a change in the essential relationships that define societal existence—among individuals and groups and between the individual, community, and institutions of society. Underlying these relationships are humanity's ties to nature and, even more fundamentally, the bonds that connect the human being with God. As the transition to maturity advances, humanity must move away from the vision of society as an arena of negotiation and competition among people defending personal or group interests. The condition in which the State, as the embodiment of collective will, would crush individuality to defend what is considered to be a higher purpose is also incompatible with the principle of the oneness of humankind. The advancement of the human race need not occur at the expense of human individuality. "As social organization becomes more complex, the scope for the expression of the capacities latent in each human being should correspondingly expand. Because the relationship between the individual and society is a reciprocal one, the transformation now required must occur simultaneously within human consciousness and the structure of social institutions."[5] The following words express this point succinctly:

> We cannot segregate the human heart from the environment outside us and say that once one of these is reformed everything will be improved. Man is organic with the world. His inner life moulds the environment and is itself deeply affected by it. The one acts upon the other and every abiding change in the life of man is the result of these mutual reactions.[6]

Examining the Concept of Power

The framework governing educational endeavours that aim to raise capacity to pursue a twofold purpose must make explicit the conception of power that informs the process of moral empowerment. Given the centrality of power to the way relationships among individuals, groups, and the institutions of society take shape, and taking into consideration the long-established association of the very notion of power with domination, competition, and conflict, it seems reasonable to suggest that the anticipated transformation in these relationships demands a fundamental revision of the way in which power itself is understood. Prevalent views of political power clearly do not exhaust the meaning of power in all the relationships into which a human being enters. There are other manifestations of power—notably those expressing the nobility of the human spirit—that a process of moral empowerment would have to recognize and bring into play. But appealing to these expressions alone does not prove to be sufficient. The conception of political power itself needs to undergo transformation if relationships among the participants in the envisioned global conversation are to be free from incessant conflict and manipulation.

Steven Lukes's treatment of power in its "three dimensions" is a helpful source of insight into the nature of political power.[7] In explaining the one-dimensional view of power, Lukes cites Robert Dahl's "intuitive idea of power" according to which "A has power over B to the extent that he can get B to do something that B would not otherwise do."[8] When introducing the two-dimensional view, Lukes draws on the analysis made by Bachrach and Baratz that power has a second face; it also is present when persons or groups limit the scope of the issues to be considered, allowing room for only those matters that are not detrimental to their set of preferences.[9] The one- and two-dimensional views both place undue emphasis on "observable" conflict, be it overt or covert, and both are fundamentally individualistic.

To overcome the shortcomings of these two views, Lukes argues that the hidden face of power in its three-dimensional representation should be exposed.[10] Although latent, power in its third dimension operates by securing willing compliance. Certain Marxist thinkers seek to provide an explanation of this phenomenon through the idea of "false consciousness." Antonio Gramsci's elaboration of the concept underscores the consciousness developed by the subordinated social groups who borrow their conception of the world from the ideology of dominant groups and internalize it. Their internalization is evident either in the form of belief in the ideology in question or in the inability to conceive of alternatives to it.[11]

This brief overview of Lukes's analysis helps us identify views of power implicit in educational approaches concerned with political empowerment. Citizenship education in liberal democracies provides a good example. It emphasizes that in order to resolve conflict and achieve some degree of consensus in a pluralistic society, "appreciation of the paramount importance of democratic decision-making" has to be cultivated.[12] Citizens should be politically empowered to participate in the processes of decision-making, to identify those policies and practices that are biased toward certain groups and to bring them to the attention of the public. The parameters of this type of empowerment, one can argue, are defined largely by the value placed on free and fair competition. The kind of power with which the citizen is to be invested belongs to the one- and two-dimensional views of power.

Paulo Freire has proposed what is perhaps the best-known educational approach in which one can recognize Lukes's three-dimensional representation of power. Given that in this representation, both observable and unobservable conflicts are to be considered, any attempt at empowerment would necessarily involve the cultivation of critical consciousness. Freire examines how the oppressed can defeat the false consciousness they have adopted. According to him, human beings begin in a state of "semi-intransitive" consciousness, solely concerned with "survival" on a biological level, lacking "a sense of life on a more historical plane."[13] They enter a "transitive" state as they "amplify their power to perceive and respond to suggestions and questions arising in their context" and as they "increase their capacity to enter into dialogue not only with other men but with their world."[14] However, this is only a "naïve transitive" state in which "developing capacity for dialogue is still fragile and capable of distortion."[15] Consciousness must therefore progress from a naïve to a "critical transitive" state, characterized, among other things, by depth in the interpretation of problems, the substitutions of causal principles for magical explanations, the testing of one's "findings," and openness to revision.[16] For Freire, only when the oppressed have reached a state of critical transitive consciousness will they have the power to change society. Elsewhere he criticizes the type of education he calls "banking education" as one in which the act of teaching and the relationship between the teacher and the students perpetuate an intransitive or naïve transitive state of consciousness, and he recommends a "problem-posing" pedagogy instead.[17]

With the above two examples in mind, we may now examine the extent to which the kind of capacity-building process being proposed here would need to include dimensions of power not addressed in approaches bent on political empowerment—dimensions that could in turn modify the operation of power in all three dimensions described by Lukes. The idea has often been expressed that, as Lukes puts it, "revisionary persuasive redefinitions" of power end up "concealing from view the (central) aspects of power which they define out of existence."[18] But what, we may ask, are these central aspects of power? Are they to be sought, as Hobbes suggested, through "riches joined with liberality," "friends," "success," "noble rank," "eloquence," "good looks," and "what quality soever maketh a man beloved or feared of many, or the reputation of such quality"?[19] Hobbes's characterization could be rejected as extreme. Yet the same pattern of thinking emerges in analyses that view human relations in purely materialistic terms. For even Foucault's brilliant attempt to "eschew the model of the Leviathan" does not ultimately diverge from Hobbes's vision of power and its omnipresence; it only shifts attention to the points at which power should be studied—not in its "central location," but at "its extremities, in its ultimate destinations," points "where it becomes capillary."[20]

The claim being made here is that assigning conflict and domination a central role in the discourse on power limits philosophical explorations of the theme to perspectives that belong to the stage of humanity's childhood. There are numerous rich metaphors in the Bahá'í writings that provide valuable insights into a conception of power that is congruent with the coming of age of the human race: a pure, kindly, and radiant heart is likened to a sovereignty ancient, imperishable, and everlasting; humility is said to exalt the human being to the heaven of glory and power; a thought of peace is regarded as more powerful than a thought of war; and idle disputation to advance oneself over one's brother is seen as unworthy of a human being.

Apart from the wisdom enshrined in such religious teachings, insights can be gained from the philosophical literature in which the subject of power is studied in new ways. When viewed as a substance that one or more people can possess, power appears to be a measurable and circumscribed quantity to be distributed. In other words, if A gets filled with so much power, then B must be emptied of a corresponding amount of it. Even in Lukes's three-dimensional conception, political emancipation is meant to take power away from the "oppressors" and redistribute it among the "oppressed." There are, however, dimensions of power that are tied to limitless resources. Drawing on such resources enhances reciprocity and interconnectedness—conditions that are necessary if public discourse is not to become trapped in irresolvable debate. Hannah Arendt reminds us that power is always a "potential and not an unchangeable, measurable, and reliable entity like force and strength."[21] It is actualized when people are together "in the manner of speech and action" and when, in their association, they have reached a state in which "word and deed have not parted company,... words are not empty and deeds not brutal,... words are not used to veil intentions but to disclose realities, and deeds are not used to violate and destroy but to establish relations and create new realities."[22] Power in the sense that Arendt describes is inexhaustible and inextricably bound up with action. It is the condition of unity that ties power to action: "power corresponds to the human ability not just to act but to act in concert. Power is never the property of an individual; it belongs to a group and remains in existence only so long as the group keeps together."[23] It is this power that is the antithesis of violence. She further suggests that "the will to power, as the modern age from Hobbes to Nietzsche understood it in glorification or denunciation, far from being a characteristic of the strong, is, like envy and greed, among the vices of the weak."[24]

Understanding

A premise of the argument presented in this chapter is that moral empowerment needs to occur in the context of participation in the generation, application, and diffusion of knowledge—a process driven by the twofold purpose of pursuing personal growth and contributing to the transformation of society—and not in the struggle for power per se. For such participation to lead to moral empowerment, the intellectual excellence associated with the acquisition of knowledge should be freed from the chains of self-centredness. Knowledge has to be acquired in light of a profound understanding of social reality by one intimately involved in its ongoing transformation. A proper conception of understanding and how it is to be nurtured, then, is another element of the framework considered here.

That the field of education suffers from alarming superficiality is a widely lamented fact. The blurring of the distinction between understanding of concepts and assimilation of information is partly responsible for this lack of depth. But when concepts do become the focus of attention, profound ones and trivial ones end up receiving equal treatment. The problem is further exacerbated when understanding is confused with the mastery of learning techniques—techniques often taught with the help of trivial examples, assuming that their application is the key to the understanding of complex concepts as well.[25] And even deeper problems appear when understanding itself is reduced to mere achievement and its boundlessness as a process in which one continuously advances is ignored. These interrelated challenges can be met only if issues related to the powers of the human spirit and the interconnection between nurturing understanding and the development of these powers are adequately addressed.

Understanding seems to be a notion that defies definition. It is not synonymous with how the human mind sorts out and processes information. It is not merely a culminating point at which one arrives once certain facts are assimilated. It is not simply the conclusion reached after following one procedure or another, nor is it reducible to sound judgments based on the beliefs one holds. Understanding differs from physical action—say, planting a tree—and mental occupation—say, thinking about what to do. It is also distinct from mental activity related to gathering and sorting information. All these contribute to understanding, especially when carried out purposefully, but they do not make up the process in its entirety.

An exploration of understanding can start with the innocent statement that "the verb *to understand* assumes a subject and an object."[26] The verb also implies a process through which one advances, at least in relation to substantive concepts, as well as significant moments of insight and the grasp of specific facts and meanings. The process can be likened to moving forward along a path that, although marked by certain milestones, does not have a predetermined end. What is required to advance is not independent of the object of understanding. Attempts to reduce the process of understanding of every object to the application of a single approach—cognitive, cultural, empirical, constructivist, and so on—is the cause of great difficulty in educational theory and resultant pedagogies. Conceptualizing the process of understanding without any reference to the qualities of the subject of the verb "to understand" creates its own problems. And it is counterproductive to sharply separate the subject from the object of understanding.

Despite the positive response that many would likely give to the above suggestions, the field of education continues to follow theoretical constructs that place one element of the complex process of understanding in opposition to another. The long-standing tension between two major positions—one predominantly concerned with knowledge and information and another primarily focused on the individual learner—is a case in point. In *Ethics and Education*, Richard S. Peters sheds light on what led to the sharp division between the learner and the content of education. The so-called "child-centred" movement emerged as a reaction to traditional teaching approaches that strive to fill up the brain with items, using coercive techniques if necessary. Alternative models offered by proponents of progressive trends have focussed on the *manner* rather than the *matter* of education. Peters argues that although, on moral grounds, students should be accorded respect and their liberty preserved, the manner in which these principles are upheld cannot serve as a substitute for content.[27] In other words, there is no foundation holding up the assumption that an emphasis on worthwhile content must be accompanied by a "rigid" and "unreflective" method of education. On the contrary, Peters claims that all "the talk about growth, self-realization, and the development of the individual potentiality" has glossed over what is worthwhile for the child to learn.[28]

The unending debate about the merits of child-centred versus subject-centred approaches to teaching, as well as a number of other similar debates, seem unresolvable unless we learn to pay appropriate attention to the subject, the object, and the process of understanding in an integrated way. This proves extremely difficult in an environment that constantly creates tension between these elements. One challenge is to ensure that understanding itself is not equated with mastering some cognitive skills or achieving some predetermined narrow objectives. Any perspective on learning represents only a glimpse into the astonishing and often unpredictable power of understanding. But when a model is built merely on small fragments and supported by elaborate explanations of how such parts capture the whole, reality is sliced to fit the model. The subject, the object, and the process of understanding may all be included but shorn of their depth of meaning. The "behavioural objectives model," which continues to appear in different guises as education goes from one fad to another, is an instructive example in this respect.[29]

The Subject of Understanding

The way the process of understanding and its objects are analyzed in any educational approach invariably projects a vision of the subject of understanding. A search for the desired attributes of the protagonist of moral empowerment, then, would have to take into account the characteristics of the individual implied by major theories in education as well as those traits promoted by the prevalent culture. We will illustrate some of these characteristics by exploring the work of several authors.

Computationalism and Culturalism
Jerome Bruner describes two fundamental views that have altered "conceptions about the nature of the human mind in the decades since the cognitive revolution"—namely, the hypothesis that "mind could be conceived as a computational device" and the proposal that "mind is both constituted by and realized in the use of human culture."[30] The computational view is concerned with information processing, that is, "how finite, coded, unambiguous information about the world is inscribed, sorted, stored, collated, retrieved, and generally managed by a computational device."[31] It "takes information as its given, as something already settled in relation to some pre-existing, rule-bound code that maps onto states of the world."[32]

A computational approach to education, according to Bruner, does at least three things: it restates classical theories of teaching or learning in a computable form, it articulates a protocol of what transpires in the process of problem solving or mastering a particular body of knowledge, and it takes students through a process of re-description of the output of a prior operation—to "turn around" on the results of a procedure that has worked locally and to re-describe it in more general, simplified terms. However, bound as it is by "the constraints of computability" common to all information systems, the computational approach is unable to explain the "messy, ambiguous, and context-sensitive process of meaning making."[33] Bruner seeks to overcome this limitation by embracing culturalism, although he asks that the disagreements between the two not be exaggerated.

Culturalism proposes that in initiating the young into a culture, education must "partake of the spirit of a forum, of negotiation, and of the recreating of meaning."[34] For "although meanings are 'in the mind,' they have their origins and their significance in the culture in which they are created."[35] Culturalism adds new dimensions to computationalism, according to which the candidate for the subject of understanding could not be more than a highly complex computer. It recognizes the significance of context in the process of understanding and acknowledges the collective dimension of understanding. It thus moves away from an exclusive focus on the workings of the brain and envisions education as contributing to the creation and re-creation of culture. The learner, or subject of understanding, becomes a participant in forum-like processes of meaning-making in a constantly changing environment.

There are, however, limitations to this conception of the subject of understanding. One particular difficulty arises from Bruner's "constructivism tenet." Culturalism, according to him, should be counted among the "sciences of the subjective."[36] It concentrates on how individuals "construct realities and meanings."[37] The social dimension of the mind must, of course, be acknowledged. Yet the constructivist thread running through Bruner's account commits him to models of learning that tend to forsake "a sensible realism in which minded beings inhabit a world which is, to a large extent, not of their making."[38] Although constructivism can be dressed up in appealing forms, its illusions can best be identified in its radical version. Ernst von Glasersfeld, for instance, has argued that we should reject "the naïve commonsense perspective" that the elements constituting the complex environment in which knowledge is created "belong to a *real* world of unquestionable objects, as real as the student."[39] The results of "our cognitive efforts," he insists, "have the purpose of helping us cope in the world of experience, rather than the traditional goal of furnishing an objective representation of a world as it might 'exist' apart from us and our experience."[40] However, as D. C. Phillips has rightly pointed out, this view overlooks the fact that "teachers and parents and siblings and so forth—no less than the atoms and molecules and forces of the external physical universe—are part of the realm external to the knower that von Glasersfeld is so skeptical about."[41] Further, Phillips has argued that we should be cautious about the tendency to "treat[] the justification of our knowledge as being entirely a matter of sociopolitical processes or consensus."[42] It is necessary to recognize that "nature exerts considerable constraint over our knowledge-constructing activities, and allows us to detect (and eject) our errors about it. This still leaves plenty of room for us to improve the nature and operation of our knowledge-constructing communities, to make them more inclusionary and to empower long-silenced voices."[43] Such criticisms of radical constructivism are suggestive of the care one would have to exercise were one to incorporate certain characteristics of constructivism in the vision of the protagonist of moral empowerment.

Excessive Subjectivism
Radical constructivism clearly places undue emphasis on the subjective dimensions of understanding. Excessive subjectivism has been keenly criticized by Alasdair MacIntyre, among others. MacIntyre's account of its modern manifestation in the "emotivist" self is particularly revealing. He charts the rise of emotivism—the doctrine that all evaluative judgments are nothing but the expressions of attitude or feeling—from the late seventeenth century to the present. He attributes the interminable character of disagreements in the moral sphere to "conceptual incommensurability" pertaining to underlying premises, disagreements that are irresolvable by appeals to a rational set of arguments.[44] This interminability of public argument goes hand in hand with the appearance of a disquieting arbitrariness in the private domain. A "paradoxical air" surrounds the contemporary moral debate in the public sphere, which, despite the subjective nature of so many of its statements—assertions of personal feelings and preferences—aspires to express itself in a language that invokes some independent and impersonal standard of objectivity.[45] That "we simultaneously and inconsistently treat moral argument as an exercise of our rational powers and as mere expressive assertion" is symptomatic of "moral disorder."[46]

MacIntyre views Søren Kierkegaard's *Either/Or* as one of the intellectual sources that contributed to the emergence of the emotivist self. Kierkegaard's book vividly describes the characteristics of two individuals—one embodying the "aesthetic" and another the "ethical." While it may appear that his descriptions make clear which of the two modes of life should ultimately be considered superior, according to MacIntyre, this is not what *Either/Or* is about; rather, it advocates for the primacy of the subjective choice. For the emotivist self, then, it is not the choice between good and bad that is significant but the act of choosing itself.[47]

Independent of our opinion on the accuracy of his historical analysis, we can find in MacIntyre's description of the emotivist self numerous insights into the ascendant culture of our time. We see that the social world is all too often viewed as "the meeting place for the individual wills, each with its own set of attitudes and preferences," while so many "understand that world solely as an arena for the achievement of their own satisfaction" and "interpret reality as a series of opportunities for their enjoyment and for whom the last enemy is boredom."[48] Indeed, in the present culture, the sense of what constitutes candid and non-manipulative social relations is often lost because personal preferences and impersonal evaluation are collapsed together. Sentences are used in arguments to persuade others of the superiority of one's own preferences. The individual does not perceive the discrepancy between the meaning of a sentence and how it is used. In such an environment, meaning is no longer the property of concepts but a mere shadow that allows the agent to use words and sentences to achieve his goals. He can then claim that he is appealing to independent criteria even though all he is doing is expressing his feelings in a manipulative way.

Clearly, the emotivist self is a poor choice for the subject of understanding. On the one hand, lacking the ability to distinguish between statements expressing personal preference and those containing propositional knowledge, the emotivist self cannot properly connect to an object of understanding. On the other hand, its mode of understanding cannot be trusted, as it is prone to be manipulated and to perpetuate manipulation in social relations. The failure of the once prevalent "values clarification" approach to achieving moral clarity among students is but an indication of the havoc created in the field of education when it is invaded by the culture of emotivism.[49]

The Communitarian Self

Having rejected the emotivist self as a candidate for the subject of understanding, we might explore the extent to which the characteristics of the "self" promoted by communitarian worldviews that emphasize rootedness in social soil may enter into our vision of the protagonist of moral empowerment. The communitarian view of the self is often presented in contrast to the "liberal self." From a liberal perspective, individuals are not defined by their membership in social institutions and social practices; they can at any time stand out and question their loyalty to and participation in them and, if necessary, relinquish them. In this view, the self exists prior to its social roles and relationships. Communitarians, in contrast, present the self as embedded or situated in existing social practices and social roles. Our self-perception, they argue, stems from such societal dynamics. For them, even notions such as freedom and self-determination are empty when considered outside the context of community.

It is important to note that the contrast between the communitarian and the liberal views of the self is not as sharp as it initially seems. According to Will Kymlicka, the distinction made between the "unencumbered" liberal self, which is prior to any end, project, or social commitment, and the "embedded-self" of the communitarian, "constituted by its ends," represents a false dichotomy.[50] As a communitarian, Michael Sandel, for example, admits that the boundaries imposed by ends that constitute the self are flexible; they can be redrawn, incorporating new ends and excluding others. He states that "a certain faculty of reflection" and "a certain capacity for self-knowledge" are necessary if the subject is to be "empowered to participate in the constitution of its identity." It is therefore necessary to regard "the bounds of the self as open" and "the identity of the subject as the product rather than the premise of its agency."[51] The adherent to the liberal view, too, can accept that what is essential is not that we perceive in abstract "a self prior to its ends" but that "we understand ourselves to be prior to our ends in the sense that no end or goal is exempt from possible re-examination."[52] Thus, as Kymlicka puts it, the differences between the two positions "hide a more fundamental identity; both accept that the person is prior to her ends. They disagree over where, within the person, to draw the boundaries of the self."[53]

There is a more profound dichotomy underlying the false division between the individual and the collective, which has to do with how the subject of understanding is envisioned to relate to the world. As mentioned before, the field of education has long struggled to overcome the tension between approaches that emphasize educational content and those that focus on the individual learner. The corresponding debate is fed by the assumption that there is a fundamental gap between the subjective self and an objective world. This sharp separation does not allow for the type of relationship that must flourish between the two if education is to engender understanding. The subject of understanding must engage in a great deal of introspection and reflection in order to understand. But much of what should be understood is found in fields and disciplines of human knowledge with varying degrees of claim to objectivity.

The candidates we have examined thus far do not by themselves measure up to our expectations of a protagonist of moral empowerment. The intellectual powers needed to think deeply about the problems facing humanity are not cultivated in education focused on algorithms and technique. The relativism that many constructivist approaches inculcate in students can at best take them to a fragile state in which they tolerate differences, but it cannot help them move beyond tolerance to comprehend the implications of the oneness of humankind. And surely, the ability to investigate reality together with others and trace paths of progress cannot be developed in an emotivist environment characterized by myriad forms of manipulation.

However, our discussion of various perspectives has given us insights into the kind of characteristics that should or should not enter our conception of the subject of understanding in educational processes that seek moral empowerment—one aim of which would be to create capacity among the diverse peoples of the world to engage in public discourse on the advancement of civilization in a growing number of spaces, from the grassroots of society to global consultative forums.

Capability

Educational processes seeking moral empowerment have the challenge of addressing *being*, *knowing*, and *doing* in a coherent way. The strategy suggested by FUNDAEC for making appropriate pedagogical choices in this respect involves the notion of capability, defined here as the "developed capacity to think and act in a particular sphere of activity and according to an explicit purpose."[54] Capabilities in this sense refer to "complex spheres of thought and action."[55] A capability is not something a student either has or does not have. It develops progressively as one masters a set of interrelated skills and abilities, assimilates the necessary information, advances in the understanding of relevant concepts, and acquires certain attitudes, habits, and spiritual qualities. To be useful in making pedagogical choices, a given capability does not need to have a definable or measurable existence as might a skill, an attitude, or the knowledge of something. The attributes that contribute to it should not be considered its components; a capability is not reducible to a list of such attributes.

The word *capability* can, of course, be used in many ways. One could be considered capable of identifying types of nutrients in foods being bought in the market or could be deemed capable of critical thinking. To be useful in formulating objectives corresponding to a given educational aim, only capabilities in a certain range of "sizes" and levels of specificity would be admissible. For example, "typing" is too small in size and would be relegated to the realm of skills; "critical thinking" is too broad, and the capabilities that assist in its gradual realization would each be formulated in relation to more specific objectives.

The universe of concepts, information, skills, habits, attitudes, and spiritual qualities is not being divided here into subsets, each corresponding to a capability. The term *capability* is used heuristically to allow for a way of thinking about the attributes of the subject of understanding as one tries to formulate objectives and elaborate a curriculum for an educational program of specified aims. There is no call for a taxonomy of desired attributes. A given attribute clearly contributes to more than one capability; thus, there is overlap among capabilities. Relationships, however, are not simple. The treatment of an attribute—say, understanding a certain concept or possessing a certain spiritual quality—varies as one focuses on different capabilities in the same curriculum. For example, the quality of honesty has to be addressed in the context of the capability of managing personal and community affairs with rectitude of conduct, together with related concepts, skills, and attitudes, as well as the knowledge of issues involved in specific instances when the capability is to be exercised. Fostering the same quality needs to be treated together with another set of attributes in the context of unity building, and yet another in relation to engagement in scientific inquiry. In the totality of these contexts, honesty as a spiritual quality is endowed with far more meaning than when it is addressed in the context of a single capability. In an appropriate pedagogy, then, the conception of capability serves to integrate theoretical and practical knowledge, simultaneously addressing *knowing*, *being*, and *doing* in the context of a dual process of individual and societal transformation.

There is much more to say about the notion of capability that is outside the scope of this chapter. The term has been employed extensively by others, notably Amartya Sen and Martha Nussbaum.[56] However, it is important to mention that there are fundamental differences between the way they use the concept and FUNDAEC's elaboration of it.[57] FUNDAEC has applied its conception of capability to organize curricula for various programs concerned with community building and social and economic development. One such program for the training of "Promoters of Community Well-Being" has met with great success and is being widely implemented in a number of countries in Latin America, Africa, and Asia. A careful examination of the program shows that the curriculum addresses three broad categories of capabilities: those related to the moral dimension of service to the community, those that have a direct bearing on the specific acts of service that give practical expression to the aims of the program, and those associated with the intellectual heritage of humankind.[58]

An area of service to the community for which the promoter takes responsibility involves raising consciousness about environmental issues and promoting the kind of learning within the population that leads to effective action. Since the environment is one of the themes of global conversation, a brief mention of the capabilities that the program helps develop in this area can serve to illustrate the relevance of the concept of capability to the empowerment of a group of people to participate in public discourse.

To help build unity of thought and to accompany others in their efforts without imposing one's own will on them are examples of capabilities related to the moral dimension of service in general, and students advance in them as they study, act, and reflect on their actions. Examples of capabilities in the second category are those that enable the promoter to engage in conversations that make explicit the knowledge and experience of the local inhabitants and to participate in collective action to improve processes of community life. Every sphere of activity requires yet another type of capabilities that have to do with the accumulated knowledge of humanity in one or more of its forms. In the case of the environment, the promoters need to develop capabilities that belong to the realm of scientific inquiry, particularly ecology and other environmental sciences, enabling them to accomplish tasks like making a diagnosis of the state of an ecosystem and searching for possible solutions to its problems.

All the above capabilities are of a "size" that allows for the formulation of objectives of curriculum units that impart sufficient knowledge of the environment, nurture a deep enough understanding of the relevant scientific and moral concepts, and cultivate desirable skills, habits, attitudes, and spiritual qualities. The objective of such units would not be the definitive acquisition of these capabilities; all that a student does is advance in them, and the units contribute to such progress. The capabilities need not be confined to the sphere of action at the level of the local community. The knowledge, skills, attitudes, habits, and spiritual qualities required of the promoter capable of raising the community's consciousness of environmental issues represent the beginnings of those attributes that would be needed if he or she were to become the executive of a sophisticated agency concerned with environmental policy at the national level.

A satisfactory treatment of the pedagogical approach based on capabilities requires an examination of theoretical positions on habit formation; skill acquisition; information processing; cognitive, affective, and moral development; among others. To illustrate the kind of exploration being proposed, the reciprocal relationship between nurturing understanding and fostering spiritual qualities in a process of moral empowerment is addressed briefly in the next section.

Nurturing Understanding and Fostering Spiritual Qualities
There is an infinite dimension to understanding. The notion of infinity here does not deny the limitations of human understanding; it simply suggests that understanding cannot be circumscribed in all instances—for example, in the ways computationalism and culturalism often imply. The boundlessness to be taken into account relates both to concept acquisition and to understanding as an attribute of the human soul with endless potentialities. To explore this vastness, an educational process inspired by religious conviction must look deep into its foundations where its conception of the human being takes shape. There, the physical universe is believed

to be embedded in a much larger reality to which all religious traditions have referred as spiritual. This larger reality has its own existence and is not merely an emergent set of physical qualities.

The corresponding conception of a human being does not necessarily endorse the Cartesian duality of body and mind, which has already been discredited. However, the worldviews that seek to offer alternatives to this mistaken notion are not persuasive either.[59] Bahá'í scriptures do not support the Cartesian duality: "The mind comprehendeth the abstract by the aid of the concrete.... It is by the aid of such senses as those of sight, hearing, taste, smell and touch that the mind comprehendeth."[60] But the exercise of the powers of the mind is not limited by the physical senses: "The other mode of the spirit's influence and action is without these bodily instruments and organs. For example, in the state of sleep, it sees without eyes, it hears without ears, it speaks without a tongue, it runs without feet.... For the spirit has two modes of travel: without means, or spiritual travel, and with means, or material travel—as birds that fly, or as being carried in a vehicle."[61] The mind, moreover, is regarded as "the power of the human spirit" and as "the perfection of the spirit and a necessary attribute thereof, even as the rays of the sun are an essential requirement of the sun itself."[62] The rational soul or the human spirit "encompasses all things and as far as human capacity permits, discovers their realities and becomes aware of the properties and effects, the characteristics and conditions of earthly things."[63] The human soul "did not descend into the body" because descent and entrance are characteristic of physical bodies.[64] There is a subtle relationship: "The connection of the spirit with the body is even as the connection of this lamp with a mirror. If the mirror is polished and perfected, the light of the lamp appears therein."[65]

The materialistic interpretation of reality, whether couched in the language of neuroscience or of evolutionary biology, is rich enough to allow for an extensive study of the brain and its functioning as well as an examination of the higher-order entity called culture. But underlying every explanation is the presupposition that the phenomenon being studied—physical, mental, social, moral, and even what a materialist might call spiritual—is ultimately the manifestation of interactions among atoms and molecules over time.

The assumption that spiritual reality has as much of an existence as material reality may not add anything to the operation of the natural sciences. But what if taking it into account does affect the pedagogical choices we should make to develop moral susceptibilities and powers? What if the nurturing of understanding in the context of pursuing one's own growth and contributing to the transformation of society—a society that, after all, slides deeper into a state of moral confusion every day—does depend on our assumptions about the existence of the human soul? Are we not justified, then, in at least exploring the idea of spiritual reality per se, taking every caution of course to avoid the close-mindedness and the obscurantism that has historically hampered religion's ability to deal with the ways of science? In such an exploration, we have to consider the truth that the mind comprehends many an abstract concept with the help of the concrete observed through the physical senses. The computational functions of the brain, as identical as they may be to those of a computer, do not cause us any difficulty. The pervasiveness of a constantly evolving culture need not be denied either. What does occur is that the language being used becomes broader, opening space for certain powers to be acknowledged and cultivated. Intelligence ceases to be defined merely as a capacity of the brain and comes to be understood as the combined capacity of a number of interacting faculties of the human soul. Objectives of curricula are formulated so as to include the sharpening of these faculties, allowing the powers of the spirit to flow and bring harmony and prosperity to the life of the individual and humanity. On a practical level, the introduction of such an assumption points to a promising terrain in the search for solutions to the ever-present challenge of motivation in education. When everything is reduced, explicitly or implicitly, to interactions between material entities, one can seek sources of motivation only externally, in social and economic achievements, or internally, in ill-defined notions such as self-esteem and self-satisfaction. But necessary as these may be in specific situations, motivation to learn is best sought in the realm of spirit, as an illumination that excites one or more of the faculties of the human soul.

Reflections such as these expand the concept of understanding. In addition to being viewed as a process and occasionally as an achievement, understanding is also considered an attribute of the human soul. There will continue to be facets of understanding tied to the world of the contingent, like processing information and negotiating meaning in a cultural context. Yet understanding as a whole will acquire permanence, not in the sense of storing and retaining knowledge in memory but through its connection with the human soul; it is the kind of permanence that the concept of soul brings to the contemplation of human existence. Permanence does not mean a static state; understanding will be an attribute endowed with its own dynamics of growth fed by the comprehension of concepts and assimilation of facts facilitated by the functioning of the brain.

When understanding is viewed in a broad sense as suggested above, it becomes necessary to explore its relationship with other attributes of the human soul, which, in addition to finite manifestations in action have an independent existence in the realm of being. Chief among these are attributes we call "spiritual qualities." Our assumption is that among all the virtues a human being can possess, those belonging to this category can be considered constituents of our being, and their development is of particular significance to moral empowerment. Whereas in popular discourse, an assortment of characteristics such as punctuality, amiability, alertness—and some modern creations like assertiveness—are discussed as virtues, spiritual qualities are distinct attributes fundamental to our identity as human beings. In fact, by them, a wide range of virtues gain significance. The sharing of one's resources with others in specific circumstances, for example, takes on new meaning when it is intimately connected to generosity as a divine perfection that one is to increasingly acquire. A kindly tongue as a manifestation of a kind heart has far greater value than the mere habit developed in conformity with the rules of etiquette. Tactfulness, to take another example, seems superficial when compared to qualities such as wisdom and humility. It is important, then, to explore the nature of this special category of human qualities and establish a reciprocal relationship between their development and the nurturing of understanding.

The exploration being proposed must necessarily begin with the analysis of the concept of virtue in its most general sense. MacIntyre's well-known account of virtues and practice is helpful in this respect—not as a theoretical framework but, like the works of other authors examined in this chapter, as a source of insight. Two concepts are crucial to his account: "practice" and "goods." The word *practice* refers to "any coherent and complex form of socially established cooperative human activity."[66] Tic-tac-toe and throwing a ball around are not considered practices; games such as chess and football are. Each practice holds within it a set of internal goods realized through the achievement of standards of excellence appropriate to that practice. Personal attitudes and preferences need to submit themselves to the authority of the best standards and rules of practice, even though "the standards are not themselves immune from criticism."[67]

Internal and external goods are distinct. If motivated by an external good such as candy, a child playing chess, for example, would have every reason to cheat in order to win. However, he would find a whole new set of reasons for playing if he came to recognize goods that are internal to the game: "a certain highly particular kind of analytical skill," "strategic imagination" and "competitive intensity."[68] External goods such as prestige and money are "contingently" attached to practices; one could always obtain them through alternative means. Internal goods, on the other hand, can be achieved only by engaging in a particular practice and are "identified and recognised by the experience of participating in the practice in question."[69]

Through discussion of internal goods and standards of excellence, MacIntyre presents a notion of virtues that embeds them in practices: "*A virtue is an acquired human quality the possession and exercise of which tends to enable us to achieve those goods which are internal to practices and the lack of which effectively prevents us from achieving any such goods.*"[70]

Although practices are vital to the development of virtues, MacIntyre emphasizes that they are not the only context within which virtues develop; there is also "the narrative order of a single human life" and "moral tradition."[71] Take the example of patience as a virtue. Its exercise would allow the practitioner to draw out the goods internal to a practice and preserve its integrity. But the meaning of patience is amplified in the context of a single human life. A parent, a potter, and a politician would each have to discover what role patience plays in life outside their respective practices and synthesize different understandings of this virtue.[72] As to the third context, virtues acquire specific significance and are graded differently across various moral traditions and within a particular age or cultural ethos. The virtue of patience viewed in this broadest context would mean something quite different in a modern industrial culture, where it can easily be regarded as an obstacle to progress, than in many ancient cultures, where it was among the most venerated qualities.

MacIntyre's account of virtue and practice provides a valuable set of concepts. Yet although attaching the development of many virtues—assorted abilities, attitudes, habits, moral dispositions, and mental as well as physical skills—to specific practices may be highly useful for some educational programs, are there not categories of virtues, one must ask, for which the relationship with practices is not so central a feature, but of secondary importance?

MacIntyre himself appears to be cognizant of this issue when he incorporates into his account the two other contexts within which the concept of virtues becomes intelligible. Beyond this, he feels obliged to identify virtues of justice, courage, and honesty "as necessary components of any practice with internal goods and standards of excellence," without which they will be only instruments for achieving external goods.[73] But even when the various dimensions of his narrative are taken into account, something more fundamental seems to be missing—namely, the possibility that certain virtues, apart from being instrumental in achieving internal goods in one or more practices, may be essential components of being human.[74]

Another difficulty that arises from the tendency to overemphasize the role of practices in developing virtues relates to motivation. Achieving internal goods can be a source of motivation for participants in a practice. But what is it in a child that recognizes the value of such internal goods, as opposed to the candy he may receive if he performs well? From the point of view of an educator, being motivated by internal goods is highly desirable. Yet no matter how much consideration is given to goods internal to a practice, the conditions internal to the learner that give rise to motivation cannot be sidestepped. In the case of the child learning to play chess, competitive intensity is one of the internal goods mentioned by MacIntyre. But what correspondence is there, one may ask, between competitive intensity in playing chess and competitiveness as an inner quality? Should competitiveness be nurtured within the child irrespective of how it could undermine certain other highly valued qualities—say, generosity and selfless love—only because it is considered an indispensable good to a given practice?

There are other problems with assigning a central role to the notion of practice in the exploration of virtues, but we need not address them here. Our intention is not to argue that educational processes concerned with moral empowerment should ignore the importance of practices to the development of human qualities. Rather, what is necessary is to be aware of the pitfall of falling prey to relativism. Acknowledging the great value of MacIntyre's account while allowing for other explanations that treat certain virtues like justice and honesty at a much more fundamental level increases our ability to resist moral relativism.[75]

We seem to be justified, then, in searching for an account of at least a subset of all virtues that would overcome some of the difficulties associated with the narrative of virtues wrapped up in practices. Once again we may look to FUNDAEC, which seems to have taken a few initial steps in this direction. As a first step, it tries to identify some of the forces that motivate a person to pursue a twofold moral purpose. Two forces stand out as of paramount importance. The first is "attraction to beauty," manifesting itself in myriad ways: in love for the majesty and diversity of nature; in the impulse to express beauty through the visual arts, music, and crafts; in the pleasure of beholding the fruits of these creative endeavours; in the stirrings within the human heart of noble emotions in response to the beauty of an idea, the elegance of a scientific theory, and the perfection of character in one's fellow human beings; and in longing for order and meaning in the universe and in social relations.[76]

Many scholars have elaborated different aspects of the notion of beauty. Iris Murdoch, for example, associates it with occasions in our surrounding for "unselfing". Beauty is something that nature and good art share; it gives a "fairly clear sense to the idea of quality of experience and change of consciousness."[77] There is a difference between forced, self-directed enjoyment of nature and a "self-forgetful pleasure in the sheer alien pointless independent existence of animals, birds, stones, and trees. 'Not how the world is, but that it is, is the mystical.'"[78] Good art, not self-consoling fantasy art, "both in its genesis and its enjoyment," is opposed to "selfish obsession."[79] "It invigorates our best faculties and...inspires love in the highest part of the soul."[80]

The world's great religious traditions see the vital force of attraction to beauty as ultimately directed toward the beauty of the Creator. By acknowledging it, their scriptures awaken and sustain the qualities that are inherent in the human soul. This they accomplish "not only by the standard of behaviour they uphold, the vision of human perfection they disclose, and the laws they promulgate, but also through the beauty of the language in which they express profound truths."[81]

The second force that, together with attraction to beauty, impels moral purpose is "thirst for knowledge." This force motivates "every human being to gain an understanding of the mysteries of the universe and its infinitely diverse phenomena, both on the visible and on the invisible planes. It also directs the mind to seek a fuller understanding of the mysteries within one's own self. Oriented by a vision of beauty and perfection, an individual who is motivated by a thirst for knowledge approaches life as an investigator of reality and a seeker after truth."[82]

Can an examination of the two forces given such prominence in FUNDAEC's thinking shed some light on the nature of spiritual qualities as a category of attributes that education would need to address? The task is not to define spiritual qualities but rather to point to some of the characteristics that would make it possible to distinguish them with sufficient clarity from other categories of virtues. One statement suggests itself: spiritual qualities are those attributes of the learner that are intimately involved in the operation of the two motivating forces, and without them the forces could be misdirected.

The Bahá'í writings consider qualities such as justice, love, generosity, and truthfulness to be reflections of divine attributes in the mirror of the human heart. They teach that the fundamental purpose of earthly existence is the acquisition of these qualities, which, as do physical organs developed in the womb of the mother for one's life after birth, define the capacity of the human soul in its infinite journey toward the source of all beauty and knowledge. Understanding, too, is a crucial determining factor of this capacity in the soul's eternal evolution. It is in this relationship with the divine that the profound connection between understanding and spiritual qualities should be sought. Understanding, in its infinite dimension and as a faculty of the human soul, is like the water that satisfies one's thirst for knowledge and the light that guides one's attraction to beauty.

Nurturing understanding and fostering spiritual qualities, therefore, need to be considered inseparable goals of education as moral empowerment.

Seeking an Appropriate Language

Clearly, reflection on the nature of each spiritual quality brings to mind a number of concepts, the understanding of which is integral to the acquisition of that quality. Nurturing such understanding requires an appropriate language that embraces an expanded rationality addressing both the material and the spiritual dimensions of human existence. This language should enable the student to explore moral issues while staying away from the relativism of approaches such as values clarification. It has to set a direction—a higher and a lower one—but avoid moralizing.

In this context, Charles Taylor's account of languages of qualitative contrast offers valuable insight. Although marginalized by utilitarianism and formalism, such languages acknowledge the "qualitative distinctions we make between different actions, or feelings, or modes of life, as being in some way morally higher or lower, noble or base, admirable or contemptible."[83] Sensitivity to these qualitative contrasts—which, borrowing from Bahá'í terminology, arises from "spiritual susceptibility"—motivates us to aspire to higher goals, to be less concerned with inferior ones, and to stay completely away from others. For example, according to Taylor, those who hold integrity, liberation, and charity as particularly worthy of pursuit often are ready to sacrifice for their sake the lesser goods of wealth, position, and comfort. Qualitative contrast can be expressed in a number of ways: through admiration for that which is higher and contempt for that which is lower, through a sensibility to the higher good that commands our awe and respect, and through an instrumental obligation to ordinary goals and a profound commitment to higher ones. Ordinary goals such as wealth or comfort require one to do a number of "instrumental" things, but they are dispensable in the sense that no one should be condemned for not having them, whereas higher goals such as integrity are indispensable—"those who lack them are not just free of some additional instrumental obligations which weigh with the rest of us; they are open to censure."[84] As Taylor points out, "it may well be that much of human behaviour will be understandable and explicable only in a language which characterises motivation in a fashion which marks qualitative contrasts and which is therefore not morally neutral."[85]

Another feature of the language that is to serve as a vehicle for understanding spiritual qualities, related to the one discussed above, is that it should convey a vision of human existence that extends beyond the requirements of day-to-day life. The understanding achieved should enable the student to distinguish between superficial and lasting results of one's words and actions, directing moral purpose toward that which has permanence. Pursuing the "lasting" has too often led to contempt for the world. The understanding of spiritual qualities as vital elements of human existence, it is assumed, can be nurtured in such a way that it leads not to asceticism, but to a coherent approach to one's own spiritual growth and contribution to the processes that transform society.

Furthermore, the language in question should address simultaneously the permanent existence of spiritual qualities and the evolutionary changes in their meanings over time. This would be congruent with the Bahá'í belief that religious truth is relative and revealed progressively. The human heart, for example, is prone to love. In the language used by FUNDAEC, "to love" is one of the "properties" of the human being.[86] On what we focus our love varies from occasion to occasion, and how we go about choosing one or another focus is determined by numerous social and cultural factors. Love, for example, can be expressed in increasingly larger contexts—within a friendship, family, clan, tribe, and nation. At a given historical moment, love for one's country may be the largest of these contexts and patriotism the highest expression of love, even demanding the sacrifice of some of its other manifestations. But if the hallmark of the age of maturity of the human race is the realization of the oneness of humankind, the potential for a much wider expression of love—a kind of universal love—must be emerging, and the fostering of this spiritual quality has to be a concern of education. Other loyalties are not to be forgotten, but they must take new meaning in the context of this larger loyalty. Yet all such expressions of love, even for the entire human race, are limited. In a certain sense, they are finite manifestations of infinite divine love. Creating consciousness of this infinite love is therefore essential to the fostering of love as it expresses itself in changing finite contexts.[87]

We should also remember that spiritual qualities are not independent of each other. Indeed, we could argue that the full exercise of one requires the presence of others. In our search for a more complete description of spiritual qualities, therefore, we have to explore the dynamic interaction among them, say, how love must interact with a host of other spiritual qualities such as purity, detachment, wisdom, and generosity if it is to manifest its endless potentiality, and how its expression is sullied when it becomes mingled with passion, jealousy, and possessiveness.

Although spiritual qualities ought to express themselves in action, the language in which they are described cannot merely focus on observable behaviour. Yet we do need at least a qualitative measure of how to advance in the acquisition of spiritual qualities. In pursuing a twofold moral purpose, the participants need to assess their own development through socially meaningful activity. Here is where the concept of service takes centre stage. As argued above, the development of capabilities that enable the individual to carry out progressively more complex acts of service in the community is indispensable to moral empowerment.

This brief and incomplete reference to the question of language points to a central feature of educational processes concerned with building capacity, particularly at the grassroots of society, for participation in public discourse. The issues humanity faces today arise from a complex reality, the material, social, and spiritual dimensions of which are intimately connected. The framework introduced here considers science and religion as complementary systems of knowledge and practice, a perspective also discussed in the next chapter. It calls on education to draw on both science and religion as sources of knowledge to develop the needed capacity to address the formidable challenges humanity is encountering. The complementarity between the languages of the two systems is essential to this proposal. Neither of the languages can be excluded from public discourse; space has to be opened for the operation of a wider rationality. The language of religion will not be taken seriously, however, as long as the mistaken notion of a duality between faith and reason persists. By the same token, the majority of humanity will not be able to contribute meaningfully to a conversation about the future of a global society without a developed capacity to use the language of science. The cultivation of a broader rationality helps counteract the emotivism with which much public discourse is infused. The two languages together have the potential to transform global conversation. The mere expression of personal and group positions and preferences in an arena where only power as "power to dominate" operates gives way to a consultative process in which profound insights into the human condition and the root of social ills are sought. Intellect is in need of spiritual qualities if it is to investigate reality; self-referential emotions have to yield to self-transcending sentiments such as compassion, respect, the sense of justice, and the concern for truth.[88] The protagonist of moral empowerment as a participant in public discourse is to employ a language that is endowed with the rigor of science and has moral clarity, a fruit of spiritual perception.

Notes

1 FUNDAEC was founded in 1974 by a group of scientists and professionals trying to understand the role of science, technology, and education in the social and economic development of a micro-region in Colombia. It

expressed its primary aim as the creation of a social space in which specific populations could actively engage in learning about their own path of development. In pursuance of this aim, FUNDAEC dedicated the first decade of its existence to action and research, helping various groups in the region to participate in the generation, application, and diffusion of knowledge about the different processes of community life and how to improve them. A set of some eighty textbooks based on this experience was prepared, constituting the core of a secondary education curriculum that, in the ensuing two decades, reached tens of thousands of students in several Latin American countries. The secondary school program became known as Sistema de Aprendizaje Tutorial (SAT); to make its implementation possible on a large scale, two other programs were also developed, one for the training of secondary school teachers and the other for raising human resources with competence at the master's level. In recent years, FUNDAEC has focused on a revised portion of the SAT curriculum to create a program for the training of "promoters of community well-being," a program that is now being adopted by a growing number of organizations in Africa, Asia, and the Pacific.

2 A more detailed treatment of the framework can be found in Sona Farid-Arbab, *Moral Empowerment: In Quest of a Pedagogy* (Wilmette, IL: US Bahá'í Publishing Trust, 2016).

3 Shoghi Effendi, "Summary Statement—The World Religion," 1947, http://www.bahai-library.net/english/index.php?option=com_content&view=article&id=71:summary-statement-the-world-religion&catid=3:shoghi-effendi&Itemid=4.

4 Ibid.

5 Bahá'í International Community, "The Prosperity of Humankind" (Haifa, Israel: Bahá'í International Community Office of Public Information, 1995), http://www.bahai.org/r/181834053.

6 Shoghi Effendi, *Compilation of Compilations Prepared by the Universal House of Justice, 1963–1990* (Maryborough, Victoria: Bahá'í Publications Australia, 1990), 84.

7 See Steven Lukes, *Power: A Radical View*, 2nd ed. (London: Palgrave Macmillan, 2005).

8 Robert Dahl, "The Concept of Power," *Behavioral Science* 2 (1957): 202–03, cited in Steven Lukes, *Power*, 16–17.

9 Bacharch and M.S. Baratz, *Power and Poverty: Theory and Practice* (Oxford University Press, 1970), 7–8, cited in Steven Lukes, *Power*, 20–21.

10 See Steven Lukes, *Power*, 108–52.

11 See Joseph V. Femia, *Gramsci's Political Thought: Hegemony, Consciousness and the Revolutionary Process* (Clarendon Press, 1981), 39–40.

12 J. Buckley and J. Erricker, "Citizenship Education in the Postmodern Moment," in *Spirituality and Ethics in Education*, ed. H. Alexander (Brighton-Portland, UK: Sussex Academic Press, 2004), 174.

13 Paulo Freire, *Education for Critical Consciousness*, trans. M. B. Ramos (New York: Continuum, 2000), 17.
14 Ibid.
15 Ibid., 18.
16 Ibid.
17 Freire, *Pedagogy of the Oppressed*, trans. M. B. Ramos (New York: Continuum, 1998), 56–66.
18 Lukes, *Power*, 34.
19 Thomas Hobbes, *Leviathan* (Toronto: Broadview, 2011), 94.
20 Michel Foucault, *Power/Knowledge: Selected Interviews and Other Writings* (New York: Pantheon, 1980), 96.
21 Hannah Arendt, *The Human Condition*, 2nd ed. (Chicago: University of Chicago Press, 1958), 200.
22 Ibid.
23 Arendt, *On Violence* (New York: Harcourt Brace, 1970), 44.
24 Arendt, *The Human Condition*, 203.
25 See, for instance, Anita Woolfolk, *Educational Psychology* (Upper Saddle River, NJ: Prentice Hall, 2010) for information about how instructors are advised to teach students concepts in general through an approach called "concept attainment" using the idea of fruit.
26 FUNDAEC, *Curriculum Development* (Cali, Columbia: Fundacion para la Aplicacion y Ensenanza de las Ciencias, 2005), 11.
27 Richard S. Peters, *Ethics and Education* (London: George Allen, 1966), 35–36.
28 Ibid., 35–36.
29 See an insightful analysis of the behavioural objectives model in Joseph Dunne, "Teaching and the Limits of Technique: An Analysis of the Behavioural-Objectives Model," *Irish Journal of Education* 22, no. 2 (1988): 66–90.
30 Jerome Bruner, *The Culture of Education*, 5th ed. (Cambridge, MA: Harvard University Press, 1999), 1.
31 Ibid.
32 Ibid.
33 Ibid., 8–11.
34 Ibid., 82.
35 Ibid., 3.
36 Ibid., 12.
37 Ibid., 11.
38 David Bakhurst, "Memory, Identity and the Future of Cultural Psychology," in *Jerome Bruner: Language, Culture, Self*, ed. Bakhurst and S. G. Shanker (Thousand Oaks, CA: SAGE, 2001), 195.
39 Quoted in D. C. Phillips, "The Good, the Bad, and the Ugly: The Many Faces of Constructivism," *Educational Researcher* 24, no. 7 (October 1995): 6.
40 Ibid., 8.
41 Ibid., 9.

42 Ibid., 11.
43 Ibid., 12.
44 Alasdair MacIntyre, *After Virtue* (Notre Dame, IN: University of Notre Dame Press, 1981), 8–10.
45 Ibid., 11.
46 MacIntyre further attributes the rise of the emotivist self to the failure of the Enlightenment project and the attempts of philosophers, particularly Immanuel Kant and David Hume, to find rational justification for morality outside a teleological framework.
47 MacIntyre, *After Virtue*, 24.
48 Ibid., 25.
49 For criticism of values clarification see, for example, John L. Elias, *Moral Education: Secular and Religious* (Malabar, FL: Krieger Publishing, 1989) and William Kilpatrick, *Why Johnny Can't Tell Right from Wrong: And What We Can Do about It* (New York: Simon & Schuster, 1993).
50 William Kymlicka, *Contemporary Political Philosophy: An Introduction*, 2nd ed. (Oxford, UK: Oxford University Press, 2002), 225–27.
51 Michael J. Sandel, *Liberalism and the Limits of Justice* (Cambridge, UK: Cambridge University Press, 1998), 152.
52 Kymlicka, *Contemporary Political Philosophy*, 225.
53 Ibid., 227.
54 FUNDAEC, *A Discourse on Social Action, Unit 2: Education* (Cali, Columbia: Fundacion para la Aplicacion y Ensenanza de las Ciencias, 2008), 47.
55 Ibid.
56 See, for example, Amartya Sen, "Capability and Well-Being," in *The Quality of Life: A Study Prepared for Development Economics Research (WIDER) of the United Nations University*, ed. Martha Nussbaum and Amartya Sen (Oxford, UK: Oxford University Press, 1993), 30–66; Sen, *Development as Freedom* (New York: Anchor Books, 1999); and Martha Nussbaum, *Women and Human Development: The Capabilities Approach* (Cambridge, UK: Cambridge University Press, 2000).
57 See Farid-Arbab, *Moral Empowerment*, 258–64.
58 See Farid-Arbab, *Moral Empowerment*, 264–74.
59 See David Bakhurst's criticism of two principal styles of anti-Cartesianism in Bakhurst, "Meaning, Normativity and the Life of Mind," *Language and Communication*, 17, no. 1 (1997): 38.
60 'Abdu'l-Bahá, "Tablet to Dr. Auguste Forel," 1921, http://www.bahai.org/r/638170569.
61 'Abdu'l-Bahá, *Some Answered Questions* (Haifa, Israel: Bahá'í World Centre, 1908), http://www.bahai.org/r/009799446.
62 Ibid.
63 Ibid.
64 Ibid.
65 Ibid.

66 MacIntyre, *After Virtue*, 175.
67 Ibid., 177.
68 Ibid., 175.
69 Ibid., 175–76.
70 Ibid., 178.
71 Ibid., 175.
72 Christopher Higgins, "MacIntyre's Moral Theory and the Possibility of an Aretaic Ethics of Teaching," *Journal of Philosophy of Education* 37, no. 2 (2003): 281.
73 MacIntyre, *After Virtue*, 178.
74 See, for example, G. E. M. Anscombe, "Modern Moral Philosophy," in *Ethics, Religion and Politics: Collected Philosophical Papers*, edited by G. E. M. Anscombe, vol. 3 (Minneapolis, MN: University of Minnesota Press, 1981), 38.
75 For arguments against attaching virtues to rival moral traditions see David Carr, "Character and Moral Choice in the Cultivation of Virtue," *Philosophy* 78 (2003): 231 and Nussbaum, "Non-Relative Virtues: An Aristotelian Approach," in *The Quality of Life*, ed. Martha Nussbaum and Amartya Sen (Oxford, UK: Oxford University Press, 1993), 250.
76 FUNDAEC, *A Discourse on Social Action, Unit 1: Basic Concepts* (Cali, Columbia: Fundacion para la Aplicacion y Ensenanza de las Ciencias, 2006), 23.
77 Iris Murdoch, "The Sovereignty of Good over Other Concepts," in *Virtue Ethics*, ed. Roger Crisp and Michael Slote (Oxford, UK: Oxford University Press, 1997): 104–05.
78 Ibid.
79 Ibid.
80 Ibid.
81 FUNDAEC, *A Discourse on Social Action, Unit 1: Basic Concepts*, 23.
82 Ibid., 31.
83 Charles Taylor, "The Diversity of Goods," in *Utilitarianism and Beyond*, ed. Amartya Sen and Bernard Williams (Cambridge, UK: Cambridge University Press, 1982), 132.
84 Ibid., 136.
85 Ibid.
86 FUNDAEC, *Primary Elements of Description*, Unit 1: Properties (Cali, Columbia: Fundacion para la Aplicacion y Ensenanza de las Ciencias, 2005), 51.
87 For a lengthier account of justice as a spiritual quality, see Farid-Arbab, *Moral Empowerment*, 101–17.
88 See Peters's descriptions of these two types of emotion in "The Education of Emotions," in *Education and Reason*, ed. R. F. Dearden, P. H. Hirst, and R. S. Peters (London: Routledge, 1972), 466–83.

Bibliography

'Abdu'l-Bahá. "Tablet to Dr. Auguste Forel." 1921. http://www.bahai.org/r/638170569.

———. *Some Answered Questions*. Haifa, Israel: Bahá'í World Centre, 1908. http://www.bahai.org/r/009799446.

Anscombe, G. E. M. "Modern Moral Philosophy." In *Ethics, Religion and Politics: Collected Philosophical Papers*, edited by G. E. M. Anscombe. Vol. 3, 26–42. Minneapolis, MN: University of Minnesota Press, 1981.

Arendt, Hannah. *The Human Condition*. 2nd ed. Chicago: University of Chicago Press, 1958.

———. *On Violence*. New York: Harcourt Brace, 1970.

Bahá'í International Community. "The Prosperity of Humankind." Haifa, Israel: Bahá'í International Community Office of Public Information, 1995. http://www.bahai.org/r/181834053.

Bacharch and M.S. Baratz, *Power and Poverty: Theory and Practice*. Oxford University Press, 1970.

Bakhurst, David. "Meaning, Normativity and the Life of Mind." *Language and Communication* 17, no. 1 (1997): 33–51.

———. "Memory, Identity and the Future of Cultural Psychology." In *Jerome Bruner: Language, Culture, Self*, edited by David Bakhurst and S. G. Shanker, 184–98. Thousand Oaks, CA: SAGE, 2001.

Bruner, Jerome. *The Culture of Education*. 5th ed. Cambridge, MA: Harvard University Press, 1999.

Buckley, J., and J. Erricker. "Citizenship Education in the Postmodern Moment." In *Spirituality and Ethics in Education: Philosophical, Theological, and Radical Perspectives*, edited by H. Alexander, 172–87. Brighton-Portland, UK: Sussex Academic Press, 2004.

Carr, David. "Character and Moral Choice in the Cultivation of Virtue." *Philosophy* 78 (2003): 219–32.

Dunne, Joseph. "Teaching and the Limits of Technique: An Analysis of the Behavioural-Objectives Model." *Irish Journal of Education* 22, no. 2 (1988): 66–90.

Dahl, Robert A. "The Concept of Power." *Behavioral Science* 2 (1957): 201–15.

Elias, John L. *Moral Education: Secular and Religious*. Malabar, FL: Krieger Publishing, 1989.

Farid-Arbab, Sona. *Moral Empowerment: In Quest of a Pedagogy*. Wilmette, IL: Bahá'í Publishing, 2016.

Femia, Joseph. *Gramsci's Political Thought: Hegemony, Consciousness and the Revolutionary Process*. Clarendon Press, 1981.

Foucault, Michel. *Power/Knowledge: Selected Interviews and Other Writings, 1972–1977*. New York: Pantheon, 1980.

Freire, Paulo. *Education for Critical Consciousness*. Translated by M. B. Ramos. New York: Continuum, 2000.

———. *Pedagogy of the Oppressed*. Translated by M. B. Ramos. New York: Continuum, 1998.

FUNDAEC. *Curriculum Development*. Cali, Columbia: Fundacion para la Aplicacion y Ensenanza de las Ciencias, 2005.

———. *A Discourse on Social Action, Unit 1: Basic Concepts*. Cali, Columbia: Fundacion para la Aplicacion y Ensenanza de las Ciencias, 2006.

———. *A Discourse on Social Action, Unit 2: Education*. Cali, Columbia: Fundacion para la Aplicacion y Ensenanza de las Ciencias, 2008.

———. *Primary Elements of Description*, Unit 1: Properties. Cali, Columbia: Fundacion para la Aplicacion y Ensenanza de las Ciencias, 2005.

Higgins, Christopher. "MacIntyre's Moral Theory and the Possibility of an Aretaic Ethics of Teaching." *Journal of Philosophy of Education* 37, no. 2 (2003): 279–92.

Hobbes, Thomas. *Leviathan*. Toronto Broadview, 2011. First published in 1651.

Kilpatrick, William. *Why Johnny Can't Tell Right from Wrong: And What We Can Do about It*. New York: Simon & Schuster, 1993.

Kymlicka, William. *Contemporary Political Philosophy: An Introduction*. 2nd ed. Oxford, UK: Oxford University Press, 2002.

Lukes, Steven. *Power: A Radical View*. 2nd ed. New York: Palgrave Macmillan, 2005.

MacIntyre, Alasdair. *After Virtue*. Notre Dame, IN: University of Notre Dame Press, 1981.

Murdoch, Iris. "The Sovereignty of Good over Other Concepts," in *Virtue Ethics*, edited by Roger Crisp and Michael Slote, 99–117. Oxford, UK: Oxford University Press, 1997.

Nussbaum, Martha. "Non-Relative Virtues: An Aristotelian Approach." In *The Quality of Life*, edited by Martha Nussbaum and Amartya Sen, 242–69. Oxford, UK: Oxford University Press, 1993.

———. *Women and Human Development: The Capabilities Approach*. Cambridge, UK: Cambridge University Press, 2000.

Peters, Richard S. "The Education of Emotions." In *Education and the Development of Reason*, edited by R. F. Dearden, P. H. Hirst, and R. S. Peters, 466–83. London: Routledge, 1972.

———. *Ethics and Education*. London: George Allen, 1966.

Phillips, D. C. "The Good, the Bad, and the Ugly: The Many Faces of Constructivism." *Educational Researcher* 24, no. 7 (October 1995): 5–12.

Sandel, Michael J. *Liberalism and the Limits of Justice*. Cambridge, UK: Cambridge University Press, 1998.

Sen, Amartya. "Capability and Well-Being." In *The Quality of Life: A Study Prepared for Development Economics Research (WIDER) of the United Nations University*, edited by Martha Nussbaum and Amartya Sen, 30–66. Oxford, UK: Oxford University Press, 1993.

———. *Development as Freedom*. New York: Anchor Books, 1999.

Shoghi Effendi. *Compilation of Compilations Prepared by the Universal House of Justice, 1963–1990.* Maryborough, Victoria: Bahá'í Publications Australia, 1990.

———. "Summary Statement—The World Religion." 1947. http://www.bahai-library.net/english/index.php?option=com_content&view=article&id=71:summary-statement-the-world-religion&catid=3:shoghi-effendi&Itemid=4.

Taylor, Charles. "The Diversity of Goods." In *Utilitarianism and Beyond*, edited by Amartya Sen and Bernard Williams, 129–44. Cambridge, UK: Cambridge University Press, 1982.

Woolfolk, Anita E. *Educational Psychology.* Upper Saddle Hill, NJ: Prentice Hall, 2010.

CHAPTER FIVE

AN INQUIRY INTO THE HARMONY OF SCIENCE AND RELIGION

FARZAM ARBAB

In exploring religion's contributions to a discourse on the advancement of civilization, we must necessarily examine its relationship with science. In the West, ideals of public discourse have been influenced by a conception of rationality that assumes a dichotomy between faith and reason. If this conception continues to be promoted globally, as has been done so persistently over the decades, the voice of religion will be finally heard only at the margins of relevance. What is needed is a suitably sophisticated picture of faith and reason that does not compel us to place science and religion in opposition.

This chapter is written as an invitation to potential participants in a program of inquiry into the nature of the harmony between science and religion that would draw inspiration from the writings of the Bahá'í Faith. Its arguments and conclusions, however, may also be of interest to a wider audience. Its goals are modest. It is no more than an outline, a brief discussion of a few features of the inquiry being suggested, the purpose of which is to explore the various ways in which science and religion can complement each other in contributing to the advancement of civilization. In this endeavour, care is exercised to avoid the kind of treatment of science that diminishes its legitimacy or casts doubt on the efficacy of its methods in order to open space for religion. Much of the discussion in this chapter, in fact, deals primarily with the characteristics of scientific knowledge, for complementarity is meaningful only between science in all its power and religion freed from superstition.

The chapter begins with the suggestion that science and religion can be considered systems of knowledge and practice that propel human progress, and it discusses several ways in which the relationship between the two can be conceptualized. It then briefly examines certain elements of post-positivist conceptions of science, focusing on the relationship between facts, observation, and scientific knowledge. Rigorous reflection on the nature of science is a well-established intellectual endeavour; an ongoing discourse addresses myriad issues related to such themes as demarcation criteria separating science from pseudo-science, the role of science in society, and the metaphysical foundations of science. It is a premise of this chapter that the inquiry being proposed must be fully informed of the wealth of ideas advanced in the discourse on science. Thus, several pages are dedicated to an overview of some of the breakthroughs in the philosophy of science achieved in the middle of twentieth century—this to underscore the imperative of moving away from simplistic conceptions of science. An examination of Thomas Nagel's arguments regarding objectivity and "expanded reality" follows, laying the ground for the investigation of complementarity between science and religion. The chapter closes by identifying three categories of questions that the proposed inquiry would need to address.

Two Systems of Knowledge and Practice

Issues related to science, religion, and their interactions may be approached from various directions. Bahá'ís see their participation in the discourses of society in the context of their contributions to the advancement of material and spiritual civilization, an intention that lends itself to a view of science and religion as complementary systems of knowledge and practice. The statement that science is, among other things, a system of knowledge is self-evident. That religion can be viewed as a system of knowledge is not as easily accepted; proposing it can create uneasiness in some religious, as well as strictly materialistic, circles. Among the religious, the proposal may arouse suspicion that it is circumscribing the power of religion, and in materialism, there is little room for the claim that religious beliefs can represent genuine knowledge. Both sets of objections, however, arise from a misunderstanding of the nature of the proposal. That religion may be examined in certain contexts as a system of knowledge and practice does not deprive the believer from holding it dear as something that transcends limited definitions. And the view that religion is being raised to an undeserved station often springs from a stubborn insistence that religion means fanaticism and superstition.

To regard science and religion as systems of knowledge and practice allows for a position of minimum theoretical commitment. Participants in the inquiry being proposed here will, of course, come with their own conceptions of science. They will know, for example, of grand theories such as relativity and evolution, and will see connections between the scientific and technological advances of our times. There will also be some awareness of the ongoing discourse on science that sheds light on the nature of scientific knowledge. One of the goals of our intended inquiry will be to deepen our understanding of this discourse while avoiding commitment to fixed theoretical positions—to be "Popperian" or "Kuhnian," for instance. Such a commitment is not necessary for the purposes of this inquiry; insights gained from various theoretical perspectives prove sufficient.

As to religion, commitment to certain views of its nature need to be made explicit, for there are so many apparent differences among the religions of the world that it is difficult to talk about religion in the same manner that one speaks of science. This difficulty can be overcome by stepping outside religion and examining it as a social phenomenon, an approach that is clearly fruitful and leads to valuable insights into the workings of religion. Religious communities are comprised of human beings; what they do with their Faiths and how they handle the influence of social, economic, and political forces on them can be studied with tools developed by scientific disciplines. But in our proposed inquiry, we need to look at religion—and, of course, at science—from the inside, to the extent possible. The central belief of at least each of the major world religions is that it originates in Divine Revelation, and that its connection with the Divine never ceases. Any attempt to ignore such a conviction or to explain it away will make our treatment of religion somewhat foreign to the perspective and experience of those who practise it.

Because our proposed inquiry is to be inspired by the Bahá'í teachings, we can choose another option and try to overcome the ambiguities of the term "religion" by committing ourselves to the idea of progressive revelation, as explained elsewhere in this book. This involves adopting the view that whatever the nature of Revelation, religious truth brought forth by the Founders of religions speaks to the needs of the time and is expressed according to the capacity of the people destined to receive it. To adopt this position, the believer has to take the crucial step of accepting religious truth as relative. This is not to deny the existence of the absolute but to recognize that a relativity in time is built into religion. Once this step is taken, it becomes possible to see at least the major religions of the world—say, Hinduism, Judaism, Zoroastrianism, Buddhism, Christianity, Islam and the Bahá'í Faith—as chapters of a single book to which, from time to time, new chapters are added. Focus now shifts from disagreements to the consideration of common themes running through the various chapters—themes expressed in diverse ways, each offering myriad meanings. It is also possible to see, if one is willing to do so, an overall evolution of ideas in historic time commensurate with the social evolution of humanity and the advancement of civilization.

The Relationship between Science and Religion

With the cautious attitude toward commitment to specific theories and with the adoption of certain basic elements of the doctrine of progressive revelation described above, we can move on to address two fundamental questions: What is the nature of the system of knowledge called science? And what is the nature of religion as a system of knowledge that is in harmony with science? Neither of these two questions admits easy and precise answers. What is possible is to agree on a vocabulary through which we can express the relationship between the two systems. In so doing, we are able to move away from naïve conceptions of science and set aside the myth of its inherent conflict with religion. Yet lack of conflict does not mean harmony; our inquiry has to go further and help us reach a deeper understanding of the relationship between science and religion. A few possibilities immediately suggest themselves.

In some schools of thought—secular, but willing to give room to the notion of spirituality—religion is considered a necessary aspect of human existence and a product of psychological and sociological forces. It is accepted that at any given time, religion can offer partial answers to mysteries that will be understood later as science advances. If one is willing to abandon religious convictions already disproved by successful scientific theories, one can hold on to the remaining ones and, in a vague sense, harmonize them with the scientific knowledge of the day. This is a version of harmony that minimizes the role of God and Revelation in religion.

It can also be argued that because religion is the outcome of God's Revelation, and because God is all-knowing, religion already contains every scientific truth, albeit in ways that are difficult to discover. This view seems to confuse God's knowledge with the understanding gained by a religious community of the knowledge expressed in a specific Revelation. That scientific progress receives its share of the impulse given to civilization by Revelation as it illumines humanity's spiritual and intellectual environment is supported by historical evidence, but to claim that science is a subsystem of religion, in the sense that human beings can discover the workings of the physical universe by reading religious scriptures, is to deny the indispensability of the methods of science.

Yet another possibility is that truths enshrined in science and religion cover two separate and mutually exclusive areas of experience. Science studies the material universe, including certain phenomena associated with human communities, institutions, and interactions. The knowledge it generates becomes the basis for technological progress, and technology is employed either for the good of humanity or to its detriment. No matter how far the social sciences advance, science itself has limited ability to determine the use to which its products should be put. Religion, on the other hand, is concerned with the spiritual dimension of human existence. Its purpose is to throw light on the inner life of the individual, to touch the roots of human motivation, and to engender a moral code to guide human behaviour. The civilizing process is dependent on both systems of knowledge; so long as each remains within the sphere of its own genius, there is no reason for them to come into conflict.

This last approach to attaining harmony between science and religion is valid, but mostly at the level of application, for ultimately science and religion are allowed to pursue their own ways separately. What assumes importance is the interaction between technology and morality. In this view, the metaphysical component of the paradigms within which scientific activity takes place and the vast number of questions of physical, social, and psychological existence that religion tries to address both receive fragmented attention. Yet it can hardly be denied that there is an overlap in the range of phenomena science and religion explore; after all, a sharp division between matter and spirit is impossible. Although it is often necessary and legitimate to consider the two systems separately, attempts to deny their interconnectedness, both in the mind of the human being and in society, rob them of the extraordinary powers they both possess.

If the aims of the inquiry being proposed here are valid, a reasonable choice before us is to consider science and religion as distinct systems of knowledge and practice with an overlap in the questions they address and the methods they employ. The claim being made in this chapter is that extensive examination of the elements of these two overlapping systems suggests a kind of complementarity between them, reminiscent of the notion as employed in quantum mechanics.[1] In physics, according to certain interpretations, the manifestations of the wave-particle duality, say, of the electron, are inherent to the process of scientific observation and measurement. It is not that the electron is sometimes a wave and sometimes a particle, nor that it is both or neither. One must go beyond the question of "either/or" and deal directly with the fact that under certain experimental setups, the electron will always behave as a particle, and under others it will always act as a wave. These two setups exhaust all possibilities of measurement. That is, it is not possible to establish an experiment that could answer the question "Is the electron really a wave or a particle?"

What we suggest here is not a direct application of the physical principle of complementarity to the relationship between religion and science, for attempts to transfer theoretical structures originating in physics to the realm of complex human and social phenomena should be regarded with suspicion. Yet whatever the interpretation of the wave-particle duality may be, it is true that at certain levels, nature lends itself to complementary descriptions. Given the intricacies of the process of measurement, the claim covers more than the objects being measured. Theoretical models elaborated by the human mind underlie the arrangement of instruments in the experimental setup. Therefore, complementarity seems to be saying something about two coexisting realities—human consciousness and physical reality—and their interactions. At some level, the human mind has to face aspects of the physical universe too complex to admit a single description. If this is the case, then it is not unreasonable to assume that when the object of exploration is the sum of both spiritual and physical reality—an object far more complex than the material universe—a single description would also prove inadequate. Is it not possible that to understand and explain this larger reality, humanity needs at least two ways of looking at things—the way of science and the way of religion? A positive answer to this question is as close as we need to get to the concept of complementarity in quantum mechanics without imagining a precise correspondence between wave-particle duality and the harmony between science and religion.

Facts, Observations, and Scientific Knowledge

One of the goals of our intended inquiry is to move away from simplistic conceptions of science and recognize the complexities being addressed in the prevailing discourse on scientific activity and knowledge. We can use as a starting point the common narrative that prior to the seventeenth century, science in the West was largely based on the authority of religious doctrine and the claims of certain illumined minds, such as Aristotle, and that a scientific revolution shifted the basis of science to facts originating in observation. There is truth to this statement, but unfortunately it has become a slogan in superficial treatments of science. The connection between facts and observation, in this narrative, is that the former are derived from the latter. In everyday conversation this notion remains vague, but behind it are elaborate attempts by empiricists and positivists to establish a firm ground on which knowledge could be constructed, with certain brands of empiricism giving the impression that the world simply implants facts in our minds through the senses.[2] The positivist position, with its arguments against "metaphysical nonsense," leaves no room for religion as a system of knowledge, for when all is said and done, scientific knowledge built from sensory perception through sound reasoning ends up being the only reliable knowledge. As humanity becomes imbued with this knowledge, so the argument continues, it will gradually free itself from the chains of ignorance, particularly the "ignorance of religious faith."

Historically, this naïve picture of scientific knowledge has played a significant role in legitimizing anti-religious sentiments, and although it has been discredited, it is surprising how it continues to prompt belligerence against religion today. Admittedly, sophisticated pictures of science do not automatically support the cause of religion. However, they do leave considerable room for it as long as we succeed in separating religion from superstition and blind imitation. A first step toward developing a realistic picture of science is the clarification of the nature of scientific facts at two levels: (1) at the level of the human mind and (2) at the level of belief systems that define ideologies, cultures, and civilizations.

(1) A great deal has been written about scientific facts that needs to be examined in our proposed inquiry. We may begin with the simple insight that some thinking always precedes observation. That we can see certain things in pictures only when we look for them, that most of us cannot see what a "trained eye" sees in an X-ray even before any interpretation is called for, that recognizing the information transmitted to the brain about specific combinations of shapes and colours representing common objects is not automatic and requires learning beginning in infancy—these are among the examples often cited. Attention is also drawn to the entire framework of language used to create observation statements that communicate personal experience among subjects. Some thinking, and therefore some theory, always precedes observation, and this simple truth alone destroys the infallibility attributed to scientific facts; an observation can be wrong when the thinking behind it is defective. It has been pointed out, for example, that an Aristotelian would make the observation statement "the fire rose" after watching flames in the air as a confirmation of his theoretical conception of fire as a substance.

The kind of argument summarized above is by no means revolutionary. Even Auguste Comte stated that "if it is true that every theory must be based on observed facts, it is equally true that facts cannot be observed without the guidance of some theory."[3] It is simply that acquiring a deeper understanding of what constitutes an "observation statement" is a first, necessary step toward a more realistic understanding of the nature of scientific inquiry. In its popularized form, the resulting account is enticing. Through the mental process of induction, the scientist moves from the repeated observations of an occurrence to "universal observation statements," the building blocks of scientific knowledge. Once such generalizations are made, hypotheses and ultimately theories can be constructed and tested. This involves the prediction of novel facts—employing the well-understood process of deduction—that are then confirmed by carefully designed experiments.

The various versions of a verificationist account of science are, of course, far more complex and more respectable than this simple statement implies.[4] They emerge from the work of brilliant minds that examine, sometimes in painful detail, such concepts as induction, deduction, prediction, hypothesis, experiment, explanation, and verification, and analyze how these enter into the process of scientific inquiry. At some point the concept of probability is introduced and attempts are made to show how the rules of the "scientific method" lead to choices that, although not absolutely certain, are highly probable. In our proposed inquiry, we would have to give attention to many arguments of this kind without the urge to prove them wrong. The mental and physical processes underscored by empiricist accounts in general are indeed among the elements of the system of knowledge and practice we call science. But by no means do they describe scientific activity in its entirety. Narratives that represent significant advances in the philosophy of science since the middle of the twentieth century are far more elaborate. Even without such sophistication, however, the picture of scientific knowledge based on verification is so full of uncertainties that one is forced to abandon the image of a scientific fact as a firmly established and secure basis for knowledge.

(2) The nature of scientific facts cannot be studied merely in terms of what happens in the mind of the observer. There is an enormous body of literature, including feminist critical examinations of science, that offers glimpses of how belief systems of a community of scientists—indeed, of an entire society—influence the formulation of scientific facts.[5] Some of the issues involved are discussed briefly in the following section on science and pseudo-science. But much more has to be said and examined in our inquiry about the "contextual" dimension of scientific knowledge.[6] Contextual factors affect "virtuous science" and not just "bad science" in a fundamental way, this in spite of heroic efforts to diminish their importance and save experience and logic as unassailable foundations of scientific knowledge. One such effort, known as the Hempel/Nagel tradition, introduces a distinction between a context of discovery and a context of justification. The first refers to that phase of activity that leads to the formulation of hypotheses. And why, it is asked, should one be concerned with the influence of individual and collective beliefs on this aspect of scientific inquiry? Let a hypothesis be discovered in a dream, for that matter. What really counts is the process through which it is confirmed in the context of justification. There, hypotheses are tested as they confront observation statements—results of carefully designed and

executed experiments—and there they are confirmed or rejected. But when everything is said and done, attempts to depict scientific knowledge as the fruit of experience and logic alone do not lead to convincing results, and there is no way to deny the influence of contextual factors on science.

The dependence of scientific knowledge on contexts larger than the operation of science per se undermines the credibility of positivist accounts, which, after all, are themselves sets of theoretical statements about science. As such, they were formulated, and presumably tested, in specific social and intellectual environments. It seems prudent, then, to inquire into the nature of some of the beliefs, in the context of which these theories were constructed. One context is clearly relevant to the way religion is perceived—the ongoing effort to secularize life in the West, a centuries-long project that involves more than the desire to make of science a producer of infallible knowledge. To free humanity from the yoke of religion has been a motivation explicit in various departments of Western life: politics, literature and the arts, and social organization in general. What were the criteria, we may ask, employed by those thinking and writing in this environment that helped them confirm their theories of science? How thorough were they in their exploration of what scientists actually do? How selective were they in their choices of evidence? What evidence is there for the claim that materialism is the only rational system of thought?

These questions are not rhetorical. The claim that science is proving religion wrong is alive today. New atheism is but one expression of it. Yet science does not prove the non-existence of God. The corroborating arguments are presented in the context of an account of science that allows scientific facts to be interpreted as evidence against religion. But the intention to do away with religion is one of the contextual factors that exert influence on the development of such an account of science in the first place. Thus, there is a degree of circularity in arguments that use the ascendance of science to talk humanity into abandoning God and religion.

Science and Pseudo-science

Any effort to gain a realistic understanding of science must necessarily take into account the rapid succession of ideas that entered the discourse on the nature of science in the middle of the twentieth century. A cursory look at the contributions of four outstanding philosophers—Karl Popper, Willard Van Orman Quine, Thomas Kuhn, and Imre Lakatos—illustrates what our intended inquiry has to achieve in this respect.

Popper's work is of singular importance to the evolution of thought on the nature of science, this despite the fact that he did not succeed in his effort to identify clear-cut demarcation criteria separating science from pseudo-science. Some of his arguments aim to refute views that equate the "logic of scientific discovery" with "inductive logic." His reasoning in this direction is instructive and sheds light on many of the problems of verificationism. Equally interesting is the way he brings to light certain positivist passions, for example, the intention to "prove that metaphysics by its very nature is nothing but nonsensical twaddle—'sophistry and illusion,' as Hume says, which we should 'commit to the flames'":

> If by the words "nonsensical" or "meaningless" we wish to express no more, by definition, than "not belonging to empirical science," then the characterization of metaphysics as meaningless nonsense would be trivial; for metaphysics is usually defined as non-empirical. But of course, the positivists believe they can say much more about metaphysics than that some of its statements are non-empirical. The words "meaningless" or "nonsensical" convey, and are meant to convey, a derogatory evaluation; and there is no doubt that what the positivists really want to achieve is not so much a successful demarcation as the final overthrow and the annihilation of metaphysics.[7]

Popper declares in no uncertain terms that his own intention is not to overthrow metaphysics. What he finds necessary is to define the concepts "empirical science" and "metaphysics" so that the two can be distinguished. It is well known that the criterion of demarcation he proposes is "falsifiability." His proposal takes into account the asymmetry between falsifiability and verifiability, "an asymmetry which results from the logical form of universal statements."[8] Singular statements of the form "a white swan was seen," no matter how numerous, do not prove the universal statement "all swans are white." But one singular statement, "a black swan was seen," does prove it wrong. Popper demands that for a theory to be scientific, there should exist a logically possible observation statement inconsistent with it so that, if the truth of such a statement is established, the theory is proven wrong. For many scientific statements, of course, falsification may never occur; all that is being asked is the logical possibility. "So long as a theory withstands detailed and severe tests and is not superseded by another theory in the course of scientific progress, it has 'proved its mettle'; it is 'corroborated.'"[9]

Falsifiability is an attribute of a system of statements, an attribute that Popper takes as the real criterion for the empirical character of those statements. But his arguments go further by claiming that falsification is the hallmark of scientific method, that which ensures the empirical nature of scientific activity. A problem with his position is that the generation of falsifiable statements is too weak a demarcation criterion. There are many examples of such statements in pseudo-science. Astrology, to take an obvious example, makes plenty of predictions that are not only falsifiable, but repeatedly falsified. Its practitioners refuse to abandon theories just because some of their predictions turn out to be wrong. And to require them to do so in order to win the distinction of being scientific proves to be too stringent a condition. History is replete with evidence indicating that scientists, too, are quite disinclined to abandon their theories once some of their statements have been falsified. There are many ways to save a theory when one of its predictions does not agree with an empirical fact. The construction of scientific knowledge cannot depend excessively on a process of falsification. Science cannot be reduced to an elaborate system of trial and error, the proposal of "bold hypotheses" ensued by a stream of efforts to disprove them.

The kind of inquiry proposed here requires a reasonable degree of familiarity with arguments for and against falsificationism. Criticisms of Popper are both logical and historical. On the logical side, a most notable and influential body of thought was presented by W. V. Quine. In his attempt to build a version of empiricism free of two false dogmas—one, the "belief in some fundamental cleavage between truths which are *analytic*, or grounded in meanings independently of matters of fact, and truths which are *synthetic*, or grounded in fact"; and two, "*reductionism*: the belief that each meaningful statement is equivalent to some logical construct upon terms which refer to immediate experience"—Quine offers breathtaking glimpses into the reality of science:

> The totality of our so-called knowledge or beliefs, from the most casual matters of geography and history to the profoundest laws of atomic physics or even of pure mathematics and logic, is a man-made fabric which impinges on experience only along the edges. Or, to change the figure, total science is like a field of force whose boundary conditions are experience. A conflict with experience at the periphery occasions readjustments in the interior of the field. Truth values have to be redistributed over some of our statements. Reevaluation of some statements entails reevaluation of others, because of their logical interconnections—the logical laws being in turn simply certain further statements of the system, certain further elements of the field. Having reevaluated one statement we must reevaluate some others, which may be statements logically connected with the first or may be the statements of logical connections themselves. But the whole field is so underdetermined by its boundary conditions, experience, that there is much latitude of choice as to what statements to reevaluate

in light of any single contrary experience. No particular experiences are linked with any particular statements in the interior of the field, except indirectly through considerations of equilibrium affecting the field as a whole. If this view is right, it is misleading to speak of the empirical content of an individual statement—especially if it is a statement at all remote from the experiential periphery of the field. Furthermore, it becomes folly to seek a boundary between synthetic statements, which hold contingently on experience, and analytic statements, which hold come what may. Any statement can be held true, come what may, if we make drastic enough adjustments elsewhere in the system. Even a statement very close to the periphery can be held true in the face of recalcitrant experience by pleading hallucination or by amending certain statements of the kind called logical laws. Conversely, by the same token, no statement is immune to revision.[10]

This particular statement of Quine's has received its share of philosophical scrutiny. It has been quoted and misquoted, used as a clarion call for relativism, and, as such, amply criticized. It has generated absurd as well as fruitful ideas. It has been combined with a weaker statement made by Pierre Duhem that does not involve the totality of science in empirical tests of hypotheses to constitute what is known as the "Duhem-Quine thesis."[11] Focusing on physics, Duhem pointed out half a century before Quine that "the physicist can never subject an isolated hypothesis to experimental test, but only a whole group of hypotheses; when the experiment is in disagreement with his predictions, what he learns is that at least one of the hypotheses constituting this group is unacceptable and ought to be modified; but the experiment does not designate which one should be changed."[12] "Underdetermination," the doctrine that empirical evidence by itself does not enable us to determine which theory among alternatives we should accept or reject, has been expressed in many ways, some rather weak and others excessively strong. The strong expressions point to directions we may not wish to follow in our inquiry, for we have no intention to argue for the harmony between religious knowledge and a scientific knowledge that has lost its close connection to the results of observation and experiment. It is true that we are trying to move away from accounts of science that present it as the provider of infallible truth, but we are equally wary of accounts that make of it a mere sociological phenomenon, its stability and growth over the centuries attributable to the collective decisions of its creators and users.

A weak sort of underdetermination, the statement that disagreement with experimental data does not necessarily lead to the refutation of a hypothesis and that, often, one or another auxiliary assumption can be, and is, changed to save a theory from falsification, is sufficient for our purposes. The conflict between science and religion is at times illustrated by the conflict between some statement of a religion—say, the story of Adam and Eve as related in the Bible and the Qur'án—and the findings of evolutionary biology. But all one has to do to remove this particular conflict is to change the auxiliary assumption that the story is to be taken literally to the assumption that it is an allegorical expression of spiritual truth. This can be done convincingly in many instances.

Thomas Kuhn added a historical dimension to the logical objections to Popper's defense of falsifiability as a demarcation criterion. It is widely known that Kuhn's account of science caused an upheaval in the philosophy of science. His work is of such significance that one can talk about the discourse on science before and after the appearance of *The Structure of Scientific Revolutions*. Although the totality of his argument—his brand of holism—does not stand the tests of history or logic, some of the concepts he introduced are here to stay in rational discourse on the nature of scientific knowledge. "Normal science" and "paradigm" are two such concepts.

Looking into history, Kuhn identified certain achievements that particular scientific communities have acknowledged as "supplying the foundation" for their further practice. He pointed to two essential characteristics of these achievements. They were "sufficiently unprecedented to attract an enduring group of adherents away from competing modes of scientific activity" and "sufficiently open-ended to leave all sorts of problems for the redefined group of practitioners to resolve."[13] Such achievements he called "paradigms," suggesting that "some accepted examples of actual scientific practice—examples which include law, theory, application, and instrumentation together—provide models from which spring particular coherent traditions of scientific research."[14] Ptolemaic or Copernican astronomy, Aristotelian or Newtonian dynamics, and corpuscular or wave optics are examples of such paradigms.[15]

Kuhn's definition of a paradigm is closely related to his conception of a "scientific community." According to him, the members of such communities "have undergone similar educations and professional initiations" and "have absorbed the same technical literature and drawn many of the same lessons from it."[16] They feel "uniquely responsible for the pursuit of a set of shared goals, including the training of their successors."[17] Among them, "communication is relatively full and professional judgment relatively unanimous."[18] Such communities exist at various levels: the community of natural scientists; the community of physicists, chemists, or biologists; and even smaller ones, say, the community of scientists focusing on organic chemistry, or solid state physics, and so on.[19]

Kuhn uses the term "normal science" to refer to the day-to-day activities of a scientific community working within a definite paradigm. The success of a paradigm, according to him, "is at the start largely a promise of success discoverable in selected and still incomplete examples. Normal science consists in the actualization of that promise."[20] Normal science is akin to "puzzle solving," but not all puzzles are addressed by a scientific community:

> one of the things a scientific community acquires with a paradigm is a criterion for choosing problems that, while the paradigm is taken for granted, can be assumed to have solutions. To a great extent these are the only problems that the community will admit as scientific or encourage its members to undertake. Other problems, including many that had previously been standard, are rejected as metaphysical, as the concern of another discipline, or sometimes as just too problematic to be worth the time.... One of the reasons why normal science seems to progress so rapidly is that its practitioners concentrate on problems that only their own lack of ingenuity should keep them from solving.[21]

Kuhn's contribution to the discourse on science would not have aroused as much interest had he confined himself to the description of normal science. What captured everyone's attention was his explanation of scientific advancement at times of paradigm change, a process that he claimed had characteristics of political revolutions and religious conversion. Kuhn's account of such revolutions is well known. In the course of normal science, difficulties arise as the community fails to solve certain problems. This in itself is not a source of concern, for the difficulty can be attributed to many factors and ultimately tolerated. There are always anomalies that create difficulty for a paradigm, but when one or more seem to question some of its fundamental tenets, and after repeated failures to remove them, the community enters a state of crisis. A new paradigm can then emerge and replace the old one.

That profound changes of paradigm occur in science is an undeniable fact supported by historical evidence. What is in question is the rationality of the process. The logical positivists had tried their best to explain the choice between rival theories within the confines of rationality as they defined it. Kuhn's initial statements, evoking such images as political revolution and religious conversion, on the other hand, seemed to indicate a disturbing lack of rationality. In the years that followed, a number of influential thinkers took the argument to the extremes of relativism, obliterating, in the end, the distinction between science and pseudo-science. But untenable extremes aside, what remained was a fruitful debate on the nature and degree of rationality in the choice between rival theories. Kuhn's own contribution to this debate has been subject to varied interpretations. He examines certain characteristics of a good scientific theory—mainly accuracy, consistency, scope, simplicity, and fruitfulness—as "standard criteria for evaluating the adequacy of a theory."[22] "Together with others of much the same sort," he states, "they provide *the* shared basis for theory choice."[23] But he does not consider the application of these criteria a straightforward matter. Citing historical examples, he argues that "every individual choice between competing theories depends on a mixture of objective and subjective factors, or of shared and individual criteria."[24] The question Kuhn asks his critics is one that cannot be ignored: How could philosophers of science "for so long have neglected the subjective elements which, they freely grant, enter regularly into the actual theory choices made by individual scientists? Why have these elements seemed to them an index only of human weakness, not at all of the nature of scientific knowledge?"[25]

The intricacies of a search for possible answers to this last question are matters to be explored in the inquiry being proposed here. Yet even at this early stage, and without altering our position of minimum commitment to theory, we may admit that we share Kuhn's pessimism toward any project that tries to "construct algorithms for theory choice."[26] The existence of criteria for such a difficult task cannot be denied. But we can easily agree with Kuhn that scientists choose these criteria as values that shape scientific practice and not as rules. In doing so, however, we should avoid the traps of narrow rationality. Values do not have to belong to some irrational mental activity; they do lend themselves to scrutiny by reason. Whatever the dynamics of choice at the time of Copernican Revolution, it, and not Ptolemy's views, triumphed, paving the way for the extraordinary advances made by Newtonian physics. Can anyone imagine a comparable way forward if their values had inclined our forefathers to insist on adherence to Ptolemy's astronomical theory?

Imre Lakatos, a critic of both Kuhnian revolution and Popperian falsification as the propellers of scientific progress, is the fourth philosopher whose work has particular relevance to this quick review of certain elements of what we may loosely call post-positivist conceptions of science. In a paper he presented first as a radio lecture in 1973, he states:

> In the last few years I have been advocating a methodology of scientific research programmes, which solves some of the problems which both Popper and Kuhn failed to solve.

> First, I claim that the typical descriptive unit of great scientific achievements is not an isolated hypothesis but rather a research programme. Science is not simply trial and error, a series of conjectures and refutations. "All swans are white" may be falsified by the discovery of one black swan. But such trivial trial and error does not rank as science. Newtonian science, for instance, is not simply a set of four conjectures—the three laws of mechanics and law of gravitation. These four laws constitute only the "hard core" of the Newtonian program. But this hard core is tenaciously protected from refutation by a vast "protective belt" of auxiliary hypotheses. And, even more importantly, the research programme also has a "heuristic," that is, a powerful problem-solving machinery, which, with the help of sophisticated mathematical techniques, digests anomalies and even turns them into positive evidence. For instance, if a planet does not move exactly as it should, the Newtonian scientist checks his conjectures concerning atmospheric refraction, concerning propagation of light in magnetic storms, and hundreds of other conjectures which are all part of the programme. He may even invent a hitherto unknown planet and calculate its position, mass and velocity in order to explain the anomaly.[27]

By introducing the concept of the research program, Lakatos made possible a most fruitful way of thinking about science. In doing so, he tried to carefully avoid the traps of relativism. All research programs are by no means equally valuable, and one can sort them out according to rational criteria that reveal whether they are progressive or degenerating:

> how can one distinguish a scientific or progressive programme from a pseudoscientific or degenerating one?
> Contrary to Popper, the difference cannot be that some are still unrefuted, while others are already refuted. When Newton published his *Principia*, it was common knowledge that it could not properly explain even the motion of the moon; in fact, lunar motion refuted Newton. Kaufmann, a distinguished physicist, refuted Einstein's relativity theory in the very year it was published. But all the research programmes I admire have one characteristic in common. They all predict novel facts, facts which had been either undreamt of, or have indeed been contradicted by previous or rival programmes. In 1686, when Newton published his theory of gravitation, there were, for instance, two current theories concerning comets. The more popular one regarded comets as a signal from an angry God warning that He

will strike and bring disaster. A little known theory of Kepler's held that comets were celestial bodies moving along straight lines. Now according to Newtonian theory, some of them moved in hyperbolas or parabolas never to return; others moved in ordinary ellipses. Halley, working in Newton's programme, calculated on the basis of observing a brief stretch of a comet's path that it would return in seventy-two years' time; he calculated to the minute when it would be seen again at a well-defined point in the sky. This was incredible. But seventy-two years later, when both Newton and Halley were long dead, Halley's comet returned exactly as Halley predicted. Similarly, Newtonian scientists predicted the existence and exact motion of small planets which had never been observed before.[28]

Lakatos agrees with Popper that "the hallmark of empirical progress is not trivial verifications."[29] He further states: "It is no success for Newtonian theory that stones, when dropped, fall towards the earth, no matter how often this is repeated."[30] But for him, "so-called 'refutations' are not the hallmark of empirical failure" either, "since all programmes grow in a permanent ocean of anomalies."[31] "What really count are dramatic, unexpected, stunning predictions: a few of them are enough to tilt the balance; where theory lags behind the facts, we are dealing with miserable degenerating research programmes."[32]

With regard to Kuhn's scientific revolutions, Lakatos claims that "if we have two rival research programmes, and one is progressing while the other is degenerating, scientists tend to join the progressive programme."[33] This, for Lakatos, "is the rationale of scientific revolutions."[34] Yet we should not forget, he reminds us, that "it is not dishonest to stick to a degenerating program and try to turn it into a progressive one."[35] As he suggests:

> the methodology of scientific research programmes does not offer instant rationality. One must treat budding programmes leniently: programmes may take decades before they get off the ground and become empirically progressive. Criticism is not a Popperian quick kill, by refutation. Important criticism is always constructive: there is no refutation without a better theory. Kuhn is wrong in thinking that scientific revolutions are sudden, irrational changes in vision. The history of science refutes both Popper and Kuhn: on close inspection both Popperian crucial experiments and Kuhnian revolutions turn out to be myths: what normally happens is that progressive research programmes replace degenerating ones.[36]

This brief account of the views of four prominent philosophers of science on the nature of scientific knowledge and the way it advances should give us a glimpse of the insights we can gain through our intended inquiry if we pay close attention to ongoing discourse about the nature of scientific knowledge. It is already possible to see that the question "What is science?" does not admit definitive answers. During the decades that separate us from the first publication of *The Structure of Scientific Revolutions*, the discourse on science has advanced on many fronts, and although a number of attempts have been made to address the question of demarcation between science and pseudo-science, the conclusion reached by most is that the search for absolute criteria needs to be abandoned. Yet it would be a mistake to assume that such a conclusion diminishes the significance or the worth of scientific knowledge. It took a long time for science to separate itself from religion and philosophy, and a crucial step was taken in sixteenth-century Europe when science began to take on the attributes that enables it today to endow humanity with a rich and powerful system of knowledge and practice. That these attributes defy reduction indicates strength and not weakness.

Objectivity and Expanded Reality
No matter how certain the methods characterizing a knowledge system may be, they will not prove adequate for the examination of all its elements. There will necessarily be underlying conceptions that cannot be explained fully by the very system that has been built upon them. These vital premises must lend themselves to the scrutiny of reason, but in the final analysis, they owe their credibility to the accomplishments of the system in its entirety. Inherent to the concept of knowledge is the existence of that which is to be known, and therefore the most basic premises of science and religion are those concerned with the nature of the reality they strive to comprehend.

A fundamental premise upon which the structure of science is built is the existence of an order that is upheld through the operation of specific laws of nature. And this order in the universe, it is believed, can and does reveal itself to the human mind. Science is precisely the faculty that makes it possible to discover the laws governing the physical world and at least some aspects of the human psyche and social existence. Yet there is no way to prove logically or show irrefutably through observation and experimentation the truth of such a premise. In fact, there have always been schools of philosophical thought that have questioned the very existence of an "external reality"; one can even go as far as solipsism and state that the entire world is nothing but the creation of one's own mind. Philosophy, of course, may wish to ask every imaginable question and explore every possible answer; science, on the other hand, tends to set aside what it considers fruitless speculation. As far as science is concerned, the physical universe exists; the nature of the mind and its connection to the material world are open questions.

The existence of order in the universe is only the first half of the premise under consideration. It is also assumed that the underlying order allows itself to be understood. The existence of an intelligible order is by no means obvious; nature shows such complexity, reveals such variability, and seems to behave so chaotically that immutable laws governing even some of its regular manifestations do not readily suggest themselves. What else but indomitable faith in such an order could have fuelled a process that culminated in the succession of statements elaborated by Johannes Kepler, Galileo Galilei, and Sir Isaac Newton—statements that would so elegantly explain the messy observed trajectories of heavenly bodies as well as innumerable instances of motion on earth? And without such a faith, how would Albert Einstein have been motivated to ask the kind of questions that led him to an account of space and time so far removed from ordinary human experience?

Belief in an order intelligible to the human mind requires that we go beyond the world of appearances—the initial impressions we receive about the universe from our senses—and investigate what we often call "objective reality," which exists independently of these impressions. It can hardly be denied that taking such a step involves faith. Yet it would be a mistake to equate the concept of faith here with blind acceptance. A definition given by 'Abdu'l-Bahá proves to be far more appropriate. According to Him, faith is, first, conscious knowledge and, second, practice of good deeds.[37] Far from being blind, faith in the existence of order in the universe, the laws of which are accessible to the human mind, is conscious knowledge ever present in the practice of science. This is not a faith that results from fuzzy thinking or from deep-rooted psychological needs. It is confirmed by the extraordinary success achieved by the system of knowledge and practice we call science. Here is an element of the system, essential for its functioning, receiving its legitimacy from the achievements of the the system itself. If it were not for science, belief in the existence of this specific type of order would not be defendable.

Religion shares this article of faith with science. The universe is real and exists within a prescribed order. Yet the perception of order and its expression varies from religion to religion. The way miracles are understood illustrates the point. At least in popular belief, the followers of most religions consider miracles to be acts of God, Who demonstrates His power by breaking the laws of nature. Such a belief would, as far as one can see, put religion in conflict with science. But the problem admits reasonable solutions. One can put aside numerous accounts of miracles as superstition, examine some as metaphors conveying profound meaning, and view others as extraordinary phenomena that only appear to break a poorly understood law of nature. And in the final analysis, religion can abandon its emphasis on miracles and focus on its transformative power, which is its real miracle.

At least in relation to knowledge that can be tested against rigorous observation—this with all the complexity we have described in previous sections—religion must be willing to measure the validity of its explanations in the balance of those of science. Thus, in relation to the material world and its manifestations, religion must depend on science to resist the human tendency toward superstition. This is not to say that scientific theories do not change. One could argue that the Christian belief in an earth-centred universe was in harmony with Ptolemy's science of the day. But once the Copernican Revolution occurred, Christianity had no choice but to change its view; that it did so gradually and blemished itself on the way does not diminish the significance of religion's ability to change certain interpretations of its scriptures when confronted with scientific evidence.

Religion, of course, is not primarily concerned with the workings of the physical universe. To the premise of an ordered and intelligible physical universe, monotheistic religions add faith in the existence of a purposeful Author and of a spiritual reality to which the human soul belongs. Clearly, these assumptions cannot be empirically proven. It can be argued, in fact, that "God exists" and "There is no God" are both statements of faith. But such arguments cannot be made haphazardly. While reductionist approaches that try to explain everything in terms of the laws governing the physical world as discovered, say, by physics or evolutionary biology can be readily set aside, our inquiry will have to be well informed of the claims of what we may call "sophisticated secularism." A brief discussion of a few ideas presented by Thomas Nagel, beginning with his treatment of objectivity, is helpful in this regard.

According to Nagel, objectivity is above all a method of understanding: "It is beliefs and attitudes that are objective in the primary sense. Only derivatively do we call objective the truths that can be arrived at in this way."[38] Thus when we use the word to refer to a certain kind of knowledge or to reality, we must remember that by objective knowledge or truth we mean that which has resulted from the application of a specific method of understanding, and by objective reality we mean reality that can be investigated through the application of that method. The broader our conception of objectivity, then, the larger the reality we are able to fathom. The starting point is what Nagel calls the physical conception of objectivity, "developed as part of our method of arriving at a truer understanding of the physical world, a world that is presented to us initially but somewhat inaccurately through sensory perception."[39] He writes:

> The development goes in stages, each of which gives a more objective picture than the one before. The first step is to see that our perceptions are caused by the action of things on us, through their effects on our bodies, which are themselves parts of the physical world. The next step is to realize that since the same physical properties that cause perceptions in us through our bodies also produce different effects on other physical things and can exist without causing any perceptions at all, their true nature must be detachable from their perceptual appearance and need not resemble it. The third step is to try to form a conception of that true nature independent of its appearance either to us or to other types of perceivers. This means not only not thinking of the physical world from our own point of view, but not thinking of it from a more general human perceptual point of view either: not thinking of how it looks, feels, smells, tastes, or sounds. These secondary qualities then drop out of our picture of the external world, and the underlying primary qualities such as shape, size, weight, and motion are thought of structurally.[40]

The approach described in this paragraph, when applied imaginatively, as it has been in physics, generates an enormous body of knowledge about the universe. But, at least as expressed in the summary above, it cannot result in a complete understanding of reality. For one thing, it leaves behind "perceptions and specific viewpoints" and has no account of the "mental activity of forming an objective conception of the physical world"; these, of course, exist and are part of reality.[41] Nagel aptly notes:

> Faced with these facts one might think that the only conceivable conclusion would be that there is more to reality than what can be accommodated by the physical conception of objectivity. But remarkably enough this has not been obvious to everyone. The physical has been so irresistibly attractive, and has so dominated ideas of what there is, that attempts have been made to beat everything into its shape and deny the reality of anything that cannot be so reduced.[42]

Throughout his work, Nagel presents argument after argument against forms of reductionism built on the assumption that "a particular conception of objective reality is exhaustive of what there is."[43] But his project is not to do away with the concept of objective reality. He seeks to broaden the notion of objectivity in a way that such phenomena as consciousness, reason, and even values can be understood as parts of reality as it is.

Nagel's systematic pursuit of an objectivity broader than the kind employed in the physical sciences is well known, particularly through two of his works, *The View from Nowhere* and *Mind and Cosmos*. In these books, he analyzes the possible features of the desired objectivity and the extended reality to which it points without ever claiming that he can make explicit the corresponding objective methods themselves; this task, he often intimates, will be made possible only in a distant and more advanced future. "Too much time is wasted," he observes, "because of the assumption that methods already in existence will solve problems for which they were not designed: too many hypotheses and systems of thought in philosophy and elsewhere are based on the bizarre view that we, at this point of history, are in possession of the basic forms of understanding needed to comprehend absolutely anything."[44]

Despite this absence of the necessary methods, Nagel manages to achieve a great deal in his search. Below are but three of his accomplishments:

1. His challenge to physicalism casts serious doubt on the validity of psychophysical explanations of the mind. He graciously concedes that physicalism has behind it an impulse, not unlike what motivates him, to "find a way of thinking about the world as it is, so that everything in it, not just atoms and planets, can be regarded as real in the same way: not just an aspect of the world as it appears to us, but something that is really there."[45] He argues convincingly, however, that it gives "distorted and ultimately self-defeating expression" to that impulse.[46]

   Nagel admits that "he may be thought unduly pessimistic about the capacity of physics to provide a complete understanding of reality."[47] But he finds no reason to accept the inductive argument that today's biochemical explanations of such phenomena as heredity, growth, metabolism, and muscle movement should convince us of the ultimate success of physics to explain the mind. The development of physics itself requires us to doubt such an argument. In the case of James Clerk Maxwell's theory of electromagnetism, for example, the concepts and instruments of Newtonian mechanics had proven inadequate and "new types of concepts" had to be elaborated for a new theory to emerge.[48] This, and the subsequent developments that explained phenomena at a deeper level of unity, would have been unthinkable "if everyone had insisted that it must be possible to account for any physical phenomenon by using the concepts that are adequate to explain the behaviour of planets, billiard balls, gases, and liquids."[49] Nagel reminds his reader that "the difference between mental and physical is far greater than the difference between electrical and mechanical," and he argues that "[o]nly if the uniqueness of the mental is recognized will concepts and theories be devised especially for the purpose of understanding it."[50]

2. Nagel goes far in convincing his reader of the existence of a centreless extended reality in which "the mental" exists as, say, space, time, matter, and energy exist in the physical universe. This is a rejection of psychophysical reductionism, rejection requiring a way of explaining the remarkable fact that an "arrangement of basic physical material" can have a range of mental capacities, "none of which can be accommodated by the physical conception of objective reality."[51] Nagel expresses clearly his unwillingness to consider the existence of a soul as the "bearer of mental properties, the subject of mental states, processes, and events."[52] His main objection to what he believes to be necessarily a kind of dualism is that "it postulates an additional, non-physical substance without explaining how it can support subjective mental states whereas the brain can't."[53] The falsity of physicalism, for him, does not require such a substance.

3. Nagel takes a significant step to argue that even his extended reality does not have to exhaust reality—that much of reality is beyond the scope of human understanding or even beyond entirely subjective imagination. He introduces a skepticism, not just in relation to knowledge, "not about what we know but about how far our thoughts can reach."[54] As he writes: "I shall defend a form of realism according to which our grasp on the world is limited not only in respect of what we can know but also in respect of 'what we can conceive. In a very strong sense, the world extends beyond the reach of our minds.'"[55] He further explains: "I want to resist the natural tendency to identify the idea of the world as it really is with the idea of what can be revealed, at the limit, by an indefinite increase in objectivity of standpoint."[56]

There is no need at this point to go through Nagel's analysis of the merits and difficulties of the alternatives he identifies and describes as he tries to place mental entities in the extended reality, the existence of which he has convincingly argued for. That must be left to other moments and phases in the process of our inquiry. Yet the mention of one feature of his thinking in this regard seems necessary. Nagel points out that any explanation of consciousness, cognition, or value as "components of reality not describable by the physical sciences" will have two elements: "an ahistorical constitutive account of how certain complex physical systems are also mental, and a historical account of how such systems arose in the universe from its beginnings."[57] The constitutive account will be either reductive or emergent, and the historical account causal, teleological, or intentional.

As to the constitutive, Nagel presents a compelling analysis of emergence that goes beyond the simplistic statement that "each mental event or state supervenes on the complex physical state of the organism in which it occurs."[58] "That," he points out, "would be the kind of brute fact that does not constitute an explanation but rather calls for explanation."[59] This aspect of his analysis, too, would have to be examined at some other time in our inquiry; it is his choice of the teleological as the historical account that is more relevant to our present exploration. Nagel accepts that teleological explanations have "serious problems" but considers them "no more serious than those of the alternatives."[60] And after looking at certain alternatives, he admits that he is drawn to what he calls "natural teleology":

> I am drawn to a fourth alternative, natural teleology, or teleological bias, as an account of the existence of the biological possibilities on which natural selection can operate. I believe that teleology is a naturalistic alternative that is distinct from all three of the other candidate explanations: chance, creationism, and directionless physical law.... Teleology means that in addition to physical law of the familiar kind, there are other laws of nature that are "biased toward the marvelous."[61]

Natural teleology, according to Nagel, would require two things: first, "that the non-teleological and timeless laws of physics—those governing the ultimate elements of the physical universe, whatever they are—are not fully deterministic"; and second, that "among those possible futures there will be some that are more eligible than others as possible steps on the way to the formation of more complex systems, and ultimately of the kinds of replicating systems characteristic of life."[62] To understand his position, we must distinguish his natural teleology from the intentional alternative that appeals to divine intervention:

> for theists there is the intentional alternative: divine intervention to create life out of the basic material of the world, and perhaps also to guide the process of evolution by natural selection, through the intentional production and preservation of some of the mutations on which natural selection operates along the way. This could be

combined with either a reductive or an emergent answer to the constitutive question. A creationist explanation of the existence of life is the biological analogue of dualism in the philosophy of mind. It pushes teleology outside of the natural order, into the intentions of the creator—working with completely directionless materials whose properties nevertheless underlie both the mental and the physical.[63]

It is important to note, however, that Nagel admits, as he should, that creationism is not the only alternative open to a believer in God:

My preference for an immanent, natural explanation is congruent with my atheism. But even a theist who believes God is ultimately responsible for the appearance of conscious life could maintain that this happens as part of a natural order that is created by God, but that it does not require further divine intervention. A theist not committed to dualism in the philosophy of mind could suppose that the natural possibility of conscious organisms resides already in the character of the elements out of which those organisms are composed, perhaps supplemented by laws of psychophysical emergence.[64]

Nagel is not the only philosopher who tries to account for the existence of consciousness, reason, and value outside the limits of psychophysical reductionism. There are other expressions of philosophical thought that discredit the fundamental assumptions of crude materialism that would also contribute significantly to the inquiry proposed here. But even this brief examination of Nagel's ideas allows us to express some of the fundamental premises upon which our conception of the harmony between science and religion can be built.

Let us begin, then, by accepting the validity of Nagel's last statement. It is possible for a believer in God to find some kind of natural teleology more credible than creationism. That would imply the operation of laws that make the appearance of the mind a likely outcome of physical evolution without any need for God to intervene in every step of the process. But an inquiry such as ours, inspired by the Bahá'í teachings, is not limited to the choice between a God who created the universe and then left it to its own and a God—an infinite version of the human being—who intervenes in every step of the evolution of life on earth. Contemplating the handiwork of an "Unknowable Essence" has its own dynamics. It allows for immutable laws of nature, including teleological ones, to be manifestations of the Will of God. But it also enables us to express the most intimate longings of the heart in a language that calls upon God as an ever-present and loving sustainer, One Who satisfies all things above all things. And as far as the laws of nature are concerned, there is no reason to doubt that as we discover the methods associated with an objectivity broader than the present "physical objectivity," we will be able to understand more and more of these laws and describe the mental at least as we do space and time. But why should we not want to achieve more?

Standing firm in his secular position, Nagel explicitly makes a choice to stay away from belief in a soul and the continuation of individual consciousness after death. But the choice made by a religious person is a different one. If what is at stake is the mere introduction of the concept of a soul as an "additional, non-physical substance without explaining how it can support subjective mental states," then his objection is well taken.[65] But there is much more to the existence of a spiritual world in which the material world is embedded as conceived by sophisticated religious thought free of the feared mind–body duality. There are a number of questions we can legitimately ask: Would we not advance substantially in our understanding of reality if we were to seek insights into the nature of an extended reality in the teachings of the Founders of world religions, this without denying the possibility of methods that would lead to some kind of objective knowledge of entities such as consciousness, reason, and value? Why should the only doors to understanding be opened through human reasoning? Why can there not be another phenomenon more complex than any one of us can imagine—namely Revelation, which opens other doors in ways that individual and collective reasoning alone are unable to do?

There is no justification for the assumption that the glimpses of spiritual reality offered by the revealed word would contradict reason. On the contrary, they allow reason to manifest its potentialities to a fuller degree. But from a religious point of view, such glimpses are available only to those who are disposed toward receiving them. Rationality defined in a narrow sense does not find enough "evidence" to "prove" the validity of spiritual perception. But the problem here is with the definition of rationality and not with spiritual reality. Reason, in a broader view, needs to be illumined by the spirit of faith, which, in turn, is illumined by the Holy Spirit emanating from an Unknowable Essence, God, through Revelation. Philosophers like Nagel go beyond the reductionist rationality of physicalism. The religious person can seek an even broader rationality, one that accommodates articles of faith receiving their legitimacy from an entire system of knowledge possessing impressive explanatory power—religion freed from superstition.

The powers of the human soul need to be focused not merely on the world of matter or, by extension, on the operation of the mind. Religious text asks the human mind to look beyond that which it learns from the senses and a limited use of reason and understand reality in light of that which the soul receives through the eyes of the spirit. Thus, Bahá'u'lláh speaks of attaining the "shores of true understanding":

> The essence of these words is this: they that tread the path of faith, they that thirst for the wine of certitude, must cleanse themselves of all that is earthly—their ears from idle talk, their minds from vain imaginings, their hearts from worldly affections, their eyes from that which perisheth. They should put their trust in God, and, holding fast unto Him, follow in His way. Then will they be made worthy of the effulgent glories of the sun of divine knowledge and understanding, and become the recipients of a grace that is infinite and unseen, inasmuch as man can never hope to attain unto the knowledge of the All-Glorious, can never quaff from the stream of divine knowledge and wisdom, can never enter the abode of immortality, nor partake of the cup of divine nearness and favor, unless and until he ceases to regard the words and deeds of mortal men as a standard for the true understanding and recognition of God and His prophets.[66]

Once we find plausible the existence of an extended reality that the human mind can penetrate, as appropriate methods corresponding to a broad conception of objectivity are gradually discovered, we enter an arena where the dichotomy between faith and reason has lost its grip on our minds. There, both science and religion can explore this extended reality, the existence of which they have accepted on faith, without contradicting each other. But religion would extend this element of faith further than science, convinced that the phenomenon of Revelation opens doors through which humanity can also receive glimpses of what it would consider spiritual reality. To dismiss this reality as "supernatural," and to assume believing in it involves a sharp separation between the physical and the mental, is to ignore the evolution of religious thought in the course of humanity's journey from childhood to maturity. The inquiry we are proposing here, then, has to face the formidable challenge of describing in some detail the conception of the spiritual—the way, for example, the brief discussion of spiritual qualities in the previous chapter seems to illustrate—in the kind of discourse on religion that can match the existing discourse on science.

Toward Complementarity

As mentioned above, our proposed inquiry has at least two important tasks to accomplish. In this chapter, we have mostly tried to clarify the nature of the first task, that of deepening our understanding of the prevalent discourse on science. Although there is much more to be done in this respect, our preliminary analysis already removes some of the obstacles that keep us from seeing harmony between science and religion. The brief discussion of a specific view of "sophisticated secularism" in the previous section has taken us a step further, opening the way for us to argue for the existence of spiritual reality and, therefore, some kind of complementarity between science and religion because of the nature of that which is to be known. Much of our work, however, has to be concerned with the second task before us, that of examining certain features of religion—divested from superstition and the creations of human fancy—as a system of knowledge and practice that is in a meaningful way complementary to science. This requires advancing on at least three parallel tracks, keeping in mind our purpose, which is to explore the part that religion in general—and the Bahá'í Faith in particular—must play in advancing civilization.

On one track, we need to examine scientific and religious knowledge. Myriads of questions present themselves. The vocabulary developed in the discourse on science should help us ask and explore the relevant questions. What role do facts play in religion as a system of knowledge and practice, and what is their nature? What is a religious explanation of a phenomenon and in what sense does it complement a scientific explanation? Which are the demarcation criteria that separate religion from superstition? What is the relation between philosophical reasoning and spiritual insight? These are but a few of the kinds of questions that would have to be addressed as we advance in this line of inquiry.

On a second track, we would have to examine issues related to the methods used in religion to generate knowledge. In what ways are such concepts as induction, deduction, prediction, justification, and verification/falsification to be applied in religion as a system of knowledge and practice? What is the role of experience, and how does reason enter into the construction of religious knowledge? How is the relationship between subjective and objective truth to be dealt with in religion? And, given the centrality of Revelation to religion, there is no doubt that two sets of issues, one related to language and the other to hermeneutics, will have to be among those to be given a great deal of attention.

On yet another track, we must strive to understand the civilization-building capacity of religion. What are the sources of transformational powers of religion, and how do these powers operate when religion acts as a force propelling civilization? What is the relationship with the science of the day in such instances? Can the notion of "progressive and degenerative research programs" be borrowed from the philosophy of science to explore the nature of the civilization-building projects of religious communities? What attributes of a religious community enhance its capacity to contribute to the advancement of civilization, and which retard it? Shoghi Effendi has stated that the Bahá'í Faith is scientific in its method.⁶⁷ Subsequently, the Universal House of Justice has asked its worldwide community to function in a learning mode.⁶⁸ How would the methods of science operate in a religious community, and what does it mean for such a community to approach its civilization-building projects in a posture of learning? These are, again, but a few of the relevant questions to be asked in this context.

What is being suggested in this chapter is that as we explore the above three categories of questions, a picture of the complementarity between science and religion, rich in insight, will emerge. The value of such a picture will not be only theoretical. The Bahá'í community needs to understand the nature of this complementarity and its practical implications in order to participate effectively in discourses associated with the emergence of a global civilization. And to the extent that other religious communities may find some of our arguments in accord with their beliefs, they, too, may wish to participate in the kind of inquiry being proposed here.

Notes
1 *Essays 1958–1962 on Atomic Physics and Human Knowledge* (New York: Interscience Publishers, 1963) gathers together a number of talks given by Niels Bohr on the development of quantum mechanics. Although all the talks contain highly technical passages, a consistent expression of complementarity repeats itself throughout, revealing how Bohr himself was thinking about the subject in the context of human knowledge.
2 Publications on positivist thought abound. A most widely read account, now for more than a century and a half, is John Stuart Mill, *Auguste Comte and Positivism* (London: N. Trübner, 1866). A critical view of positivism as applied to a range of disciplines, including the theory of law and literary history, is provided by Leszek Kolakowski in *The Alienation of Reason: A History of Positivist Thought*, trans. Norbert Guterman (New York: Doubleday, 1968).
3 Auguste Comte, *The Positive Philosophy of Auguste Comte*, trans. Harriet Martineau (Kitchener, ON: Batoche Books, 2000), 29.
4 A thorough examination of verificationism can be found in C. J. Misak, *Verificationism: Its History and Prospects* (London: Routledge, 1995).
5 For one such examination, see Lynn Hankinson Nelson, "On What We Say There Is and Why It Matters: A Feminist Perspective on Metaphysics and Science," in *New Metaphysical Foundations of Modern Science*, ed. Willis Harman and Jane Clark (Sausalito, CA: Institute of Noetic Sciences, 1994).
6 See, for example, Ludwik Fleck, *Genesis and Development of a Scientific Fact*, trans. Fred Bradley and Thaddeus J. Trenn (Chicago: University of Chicago Press, 1981).

7   Karl Popper, *The Logic of Scientific Discovery* (London: Routledge, 2002), 12.
8   Ibid., 10.
9   Ibid.
10 Willard Van Orman Quine, *From a Logical Point of View* (New York: Harper & Row, 1961), 20, 42–43.
11 See, for example, Sandra G. Harding, *Can Theories Be Refuted?: Essays on the Duhem-Quine Thesis* (Dordrecht, Netherlands: D. Reidel, 1976).
12 Pierre Duhem, *The Aim and Structure of Physical Theory*, trans. Philip P. Wiener (Princeton, NJ: Princeton University Press, 1991), 187.
13 Thomas S. Kuhn, *The Structure of Scientific Revolutions* (Chicago: University of Chicago Press, 1996), 10.
14 Ibid.
15 Ibid.
16 Ibid., 177.
17 Ibid.
18 Ibid.
19 Ibid.
20 Ibid., 24–25.
21 Ibid., 37.
22 Kuhn, *The Essential Tension: Selected Studies in Scientific Tradition and Change* (Chicago: University of Chicago Press, 1977), 322.
23 Ibid., 325.
24 Ibid.
25 Ibid., 325–26.
26 Ibid., 328.
27 Imre Lakatos, *The Methodology of Scientific Research Programmes* (Cambridge, UK: Cambridge University Press, 1980), 4.
28 Ibid., 5.
29 Ibid., 6.
30 Ibid.
31 Ibid.
32 Ibid.
33 Ibid.
34 Ibid.
35 Ibid.
36 Ibid.
37 Quoted in *Bahá'í World Faith—Selected Writings of Bahá'u'lláh and 'Abdu'l-Bahá* (Wilmette, IL: Bahá'í Publishing Trust, 1976), 449.
38 Thomas Nagel, *The View from Nowhere* (Oxford, UK: Oxford University Press, 1986), 4.
39 Ibid., 14.
40 Ibid.
41 Ibid., 16.
42 Ibid., 15.

43 Ibid., 16.
44 Ibid., 10.
45 Ibid., 16.
46 Ibid.
47 Ibid., 51.
48 Ibid., 52.
49 Ibid.
50 Ibid., 52, 53.
51 Ibid., 29.
52 Ibid.
53 Ibid.
54 Ibid., 90.
55 Ibid.
56 Ibid., 91.
57 Nagel, *Mind and Cosmos: Why the Materialist Neo-Darwinian Conception of Nature Is Almost Certainly False* (Oxford, UK: Oxford University Press, 2012), 54.
58 Ibid., 55.
59 Ibid.
60 Ibid., 88.
61 Ibid., 91.
62 Ibid., 92–93.
63 Ibid., 94.
64 Ibid., 95.
65 Nagel, *The View from Nowhere*, 29.
66 Bahá'u'lláh, *The Kitáb-i-Íqán*, trans. Shoghi Effendi (1931). http://www.bahai.org/r/966025582.
67 Shoghi Effendi, from a letter written by Shoghi Effendi to the High Commissioner of Palestine (June 1933).
68 See for example the Ridvan 2010 message of the Universal House of Justice to the Bahá'ís of the Word (2010).

Bibliography

Bahá'u'lláh. *The Kitáb-i-Íqán*. Translated by Shoghi Effendi. 1931. http://www.bahai.org/r/966025582.

Bahá'í World Faith—Selected Writings of Bahá'u'lláh and 'Abdu'l-Bahá. Wilmette, IL: Bahá'í Publishing Trust, 1976.

Bohr, Neils. *Essays 1958–1962 on Atomic Physics and Human Knowledge*. New York: Interscience Publishers, 1963.

Comte, Auguste. *The Positive Philosophy of Auguste Comte*. Translated by Harriet Martineau. Kitchener, ON: Batoche Books, 2000.

Duhem, Pierre. *The Aim and Structure of Physical Theory*. Translated by Philip P. Wiener. Princeton, NJ: Princeton University Press, 1991.

Fleck, Ludwik. *Genesis and Development of a Scientific Fact.* Translated by Fred Bradley and Thaddeus J. Trenn. Chicago: University of Chicago Press, 1981.

Harding, Sandra G. *Can Theories Be Refuted?: Essays on the Duhem-Quine Thesis.* Dordrecht, Netherlands: D. Reidel, 1976.

Kolakowski, Leszek. *The Alienation of Reason: A History of Positivist Thought.* Translated by Norbert Guterman. New York: Doubleday, 1968.

Lakatos, Imre. *The Methodology of Scientific Research Programmes.* Cambridge, UK: Cambridge University Press, 1980.

Kuhn, Thomas S. *The Essential Tension: Selected Studies in Scientific Tradition and Change.* Chicago: University of Chicago Press, 1977.

———. *The Structure of Scientific Revolutions.* Chicago: University of Chicago Press, 1996.

Mill, John Stuart. *Auguste Comte and Positivism.* London: N. Trübner, 1866.

Misak, C. J. *Verificationism: Its History and Prospects.* London: Routledge, 1995.

Nagel, Thomas. *Mind and Cosmos: Why the Materialist Neo-Darwinian Conception of Nature Is Almost Certainly False.* Oxford, UK: Oxford University Press, 2012.

———. *The View from Nowhere.* Oxford, UK: Oxford University Press, 1986.

Nelson, Lynn Hankinson. "On What We Say There Is and Why It Matters: A Feminist Perspective on Metaphysics and Science." In *New Metaphysical Foundations of Modern Science*, edited by Willis Harman and Jane Clark. Sausalito, CA: Institute of Noetic Sciences, 1994.

Popper, Karl. *The Logic of Scientific Discovery.* London: Routledge, 2002.

Quine, Willard Van Orman. *From a Logical Point of View.* New York: Harper & Row, 1961.

CHAPTER SIX

BAHÁ'Í PARTICIPATION IN PUBLIC DISCOURSE: SOME CONSIDERATIONS RELATED TO HISTORY, CONCEPTS, AND APPROACHES

SHAHRIAR RAZAVI

According to the Bahá'í teachings, the process by which the human race has developed over the centuries is best understood as the outcome of its response to the impulse imparted to the world by successive Divine Messengers. Known to the world as the founders of the recognized religious traditions, these defining historical figures are considered by Bahá'ís to manifest perfectly the attributes of God in the plane of material existence and to be appointed by Him as educators of humankind. The appearance of such a figure, in a particular place and at a particular point in history, is associated with the release of powerful moral and spiritual forces in society, which, in time, result in the emergence of a new civilization. Their influence stimulates the expansion of consciousness and the increase of human capacity; history itself is the record of the ebb and flow of those civilizations that blossom, flourish, and eventually age and decay as they lose the spiritual potency that characterized their origins. Thus, the advent of each successive manifestation of God signals the coming of a new era and makes possible the next stage of humanity's social evolution.

Viewed from this perspective, religion is not regarded as simply the set of beliefs, rituals, and forms of worship that characterize a particular people. It is conceived, rather, as the vehicle for spiritual forces that are capable of bringing about the transformation of the individual—at the level of heart and mind—and of society, where new patterns of interaction and order emerge. It can be considered the ultimate source of those moral imperatives of the age that eventually become norms of conduct and are codified in laws upheld by those institutions of society which are established for that end.

This conception of religion is fundamental to an understanding of why Bahá'ís place so significant an emphasis on their participation, as a community, in public discourse. Clearly, a different conception of religion—for instance, one where its interests are considered to rest wholly in the private life of the individual and personal salvation—would not provide grounds for the wholehearted involvement of a religious community in matters of public discourse. Such involvement cannot merely be an expression of civic duty; it goes to the very heart of what it means to practise one's faith. Indeed, in one of the most celebrated works of Bahá'u'lláh, the prophet-founder of the Bahá'í Faith, He exhorts His followers to occupy themselves with the pressing issues facing society: "Be anxiously concerned with the needs of the age ye live in, and centre your deliberations on its exigencies and requirements."[1]

Engagement with the problems of society complements activity directed toward the growth and development of the Bahá'í community, activity that aims to develop a pattern of community life and extend it to others, thereby increasing its resources and capacity for all the endeavours to be undertaken. In other words, there is no dichotomy between activities that contribute to the spread of the Faith and activities that engage with the issues facing society at large. Both contribute to the transformation of the individual and of society—that is, the inner life and external conditions of humankind—which, as stated above, is understood to be the essential reason that divine revelation occurs. Bahá'ís can be entirely at ease with conviction in the fundamental importance for humanity of the spiritual principles that lie at the heart of their faith while simultaneously recognizing that a society founded on those principles will not emerge exclusively through their own efforts. Ultimately, every nation and group must, to one extent or another, have the opportunity to make a contribution.

Bahá'í Participation in Public Discourse: A Historical Perspective
The origins of formal Bahá'í participation in public discourse can be traced back to the earliest days of the Faith. For instance, in an epistle addressed to Queen Victoria in the 1860s, Bahá'u'lláh touched on numerous themes that would have resonated strongly with society's preoccupations of that time, such as systems of governance, the benefits of international peace, the burden of taxation, and how corruption can frustrate efforts to bring about reform.[2] One of the most striking early examples of a contribution to public discourse, and one that continues to inform Bahá'í activity today, is the treatise entitled *The Secret of Divine Civilization*, which was written in 1875 by 'Abdu'l-Bahá—Bahá'u'lláh's son and appointed successor after His

passing—and addressed to the rulers and people of Persia. In this highly significant work, published anonymously at the time, 'Abdu'l-Bahá describes how Persia had declined relative to other nations of the world as a result of poor education, bad governance, ignorance of scientific advances, rejection of innovation, and the atrophy of the life of the mind. He encouraged the people of Persia to learn from other countries and to be open-minded to new ideas, while stressing that spiritual qualities provide the surest foundation for social progress. Further instances of contributing to the intellectual and moral life of society can be found in the public talks that 'Abdu'l-Bahá delivered to audiences in Europe and the United States, in which he frequently addressed topics central to contemporary thought, such as race relations, the equality of the sexes, religious prejudice, industrial strife, poverty, and excessive wealth. Examples are also to be found in his numerous encounters with leaders of thought—theological, political, scientific thought—with whom he engaged in sometimes extensive discussions related to current trends and developments in their respective fields.

Beyond these well-known examples of participation in public discourse by the central figures of Bahá'í history, the Faith's followers have always been urged to associate with like-minded groups and individuals. In his history of the first Bahá'í century, the Guardian of the Faith, Shoghi Effendi, examined how communities in various countries had gradually increased their size and the scope of their activities, drawing attention to "the participation, whether official or non-official, of representatives of these newly founded national Bahá'í communities in the activities and proceedings of a great variety of congresses, associations, conventions and conferences, held in various countries of Europe, Asia and America for the promotion of religious unity, peace, education, international cooperation, inter-racial amity and other humanitarian purposes."[3] He himself had given attention from the earliest stage of his leadership of the community to build institutional capacity for the community's engagement with society at both the international and national levels. As early as 1925, he encouraged the emergence of the International Bahá'í Bureau in Geneva, then the seat of the League of Nations. In 1947, soon after the creation of the United Nations Organization, the eight existing National Spiritual Assemblies—elected councils that administer the affairs of national Bahá'í communities—were able to constitute the Bahá'í International Community (BIC) and won accreditation for it as an international non-governmental organization, giving birth to an effective instrument for the community's participation in discourses on the international stage.

Capacity for this participation was enhanced further by a certain category of Shoghi Effendi's writings that, although addressed to the community itself and not directly to the public, constitutes a model for both a reading of contemporary society and an analysis of the operation of social forces in light of the Bahá'í teachings and of the Faith's conception of the development of history. It is in the light of that body of his exegesis and the worldview it presents that efforts of the Bahá'í community to apprehend more profoundly its principles and correlate them to the contemporary issues of the day take shape.

Following the establishment in 1963 of the Universal House of Justice, the elected body which governs the affairs of the Bahá'í world, the community's capacity to participate in public discourse at the international level continued to increase, and the scope of its activities widened as well. One indication of this occurred in 1970 when the BIC was given consultative status with the United Nations Economic and Social Council. Meanwhile, the Bahá'í community at large was being encouraged by the House of Justice to strengthen its ability to reach out to the society around it. Individuals, active in a variety of fields and disciplines, also were inspired to find ways of putting a Bahá'í perspective on an issue of particular moment before the public, without necessarily needing to focus on the source of their inspiration in all cases.

The community's capacity for engaging with topics of importance to society, then, has been built gradually over time, and its ability to articulate the role of religion in the world has developed in tandem. Whereas this capacity initially was most visible at the international level, in the 1980s it became a more recognizable feature of activity at every level. This coincided with a period when, following the appearance in October 1983 of a significant letter of the House of Justice, Bahá'ís began to increase their involvement in social and economic development, which would inevitably lead to their becoming more directly concerned with the serious questions and challenges confronting the society around them.[4] Another significant moment came in 1985 with the publication of a message of the Universal House of Justice addressed to the peoples of the world entitled "The Promise of World Peace." The statement set out a far-reaching analysis of the condition of the world and in particular of the shortcomings of the prevailing international order and the barriers to peace. It pointed to a paralysis of will brought on by the inescapable contradiction between the commonly accepted assumptions about human nature on one hand, and the expressions of hope and urgent effort in the search for peace and for solutions to ameliorate dangerous and deep-seated social maladies on the other. It aimed to raise the discourse on peace—at that time most often cast in the narrow terms of nuclear disarmament—to the level of spiritual principle. And to guard against the possible hasty rejection of its appeal to "spiritual" principle, the statement was careful to explain that by "human spirit" what was being evoked were those "endowments which distinguish the human race from all other forms of life," with the mind as its "essential quality."[5] The message presents certain foundational tenets of peace and prerequisites for its emergence based on insights derived from the teachings of the Baháʼí Faith and the experience of its adherents throughout the world. The indispensable role of religion as a vital social force is discussed, as are a number of interrelated concepts such as the equality of women and men, economic justice, and universal education. Ultimately, however, its call was for the recognition of the oneness of humankind and the acceptance of the profound implications that such a principle holds for the reorganization of the collective life of humanity and organic structural change. And as a practical means of assistance for the exploration of the subject, it offered the experience of the Baháʼí community itself, representing a microcosm of the human family, in its endeavours to apply the central idea of the oneness of humankind to its own collective life.

Quite apart from its influence on those to whom it was presented, the impact of this message on Baháʼís around the world was considerable. Baháʼí communities everywhere were galvanized into a kind of action that, until then, had been chiefly confined to the national and international arenas—not simply sharing the teachings of the Faith, but initiating conversations about the application of those teachings to the condition of the world. Appearing on the eve of the United Nations' International Year of Peace and at a time when the mindset of the Cold War and the imminent threats it aroused still dominated international affairs, "The Promise of World Peace" offered Baháʼís a powerful example of being "anxiously concerned with the needs of the age ye live in."[6] The perspicuity with which it diagnosed the root causes of society's ills, combined with the clear, dignified, but uncompromising language it used to communicate its message—drawing heavily on the archetypes of ʻAbduʼl-Baháʼs presentations on peace over seventy years earlier—meant that the statement offered the Baháʼí community an invaluable contemporary model of how to contribute to the discourses of society. It is a model that continues to inspire thought and action in today's world.

In the three decades since the publication of "The Promise of World Peace," there have been numerous instances of Baháʼís participating in international forums focused on particular topics, sometimes making a contribution at the level of thought and at other times contributing by way of helping to initiate consultation and bring about consensus. Not only at gatherings of religious representatives—such as the Parliaments of the World's Religions or, most notably, the Millennium World Peace Summit of Religious and Spiritual Leaders—but also at major conferences of the United Nations on themes such as women, development, and the environment, the BIC has been an active participant on the global stage. The number of documents available in the BIC's online library of statements, most of which were issued after 1985, now exceeds 250, and the diversity of topics they cover demonstrates the multitude of issues of significance to human welfare that Bahá'ís are learning to address.

Since 1996, the Bahá'í world has been guided by the Universal House of Justice to approach its various areas of endeavour in an increasingly systematic way, consciously seeking to learn from its experiences and, over time, develop its capacity for taking particular kinds of action. In the messages of the House of Justice, a connection has been made between systematic action and the demands of a world experiencing social and moral decline. In one such message, it explained that, for the Bahá'í community, systematization is "a necessary mode of functioning animated by the urgency to act."[7] Initially, the Bahá'í community focused its attention on the development of human resources for facilitating its own growth. As a result of these efforts, it learned much about how to sustain a long-term process. In 2008, the House of Justice encouraged the Bahá'í world "to extend the process of systematic learning... to encompass a growing range of human endeavours."[8] Especially as Bahá'í communities in certain parts of the world grew larger and stronger, it became evident that there were a number of dimensions to the Faith's interaction with society. These have been broadly defined by the House of Justice as encompassing three major spheres of action: the outreach through which the Bahá'í community actually grows and develops, involvement in social action, and "participation in the prevalent discourses of society."[9] The last of these is of particular interest to our present discussion.

Drawing on Elements of a Common Conceptual Framework
As discussed earlier, being involved in public discourse is not a peripheral activity. It should be closely associated with what it means to practise the Bahá'í Faith, which is understood to imply being active in the world, not removed from it—demonstrating one's faith primarily through good actions and not simply by professing one's adherence to particular doctrines. As such, Bahá'ís have to ensure that the methods and attitudes they adopt when contributing to formal conversations that occur in society are consistent with those that characterize their other major areas of endeavour. Thus, to describe a Bahá'í approach to participation in public discourse is to identify, from within the overarching conceptual framework that governs

the Bahá'í approach to every significant field of action, those elements that are most relevant to activity in this field.

The usefulness of adhering to a common conceptual framework has become increasingly apparent to the Bahá'í community in recent years. Indeed, a certain unity of thought and effectiveness of action that has become more visible during this time can be largely attributed to an increasing reliance on such a framework. It has encouraged the community to ensure that its various arenas of activity are coherent with one another and are each internally coherent. That is to say, Bahá'ís are striving to adopt a mode of thinking whereby the actions in a variety of domains remain consistent with the essential principles they profess. Naturally, the elements of the framework that are most relevant to each area of endeavour vary, as does the manner in which each element is expressed, and this needs to be learned over time. Understanding in terms of how best to apply the conceptual framework to the community's participation in public discourse is developing gradually, but although much remains to be learned and although efforts in this regard are still in their early stages, it can already be observed that some of the framework's elements have special resonance and that there is a dynamic interplay between them when undertaking action in this area.

The role of the Office of Public Discourse (OPD) at the Bahá'í World Centre deserves special mention here. The House of Justice announced the OPD's establishment in a 2013 message, stating that it had been created to assist National Spiritual Assemblies by "gradually promoting and coordinating activities and systematizing experience."[10] Since then it has established strong collaborative relationships with the external affairs agencies of a number of National Assemblies. These offices have increasingly come to conceptualize their work in terms of participation in the discourses of their society on the national stage and are being encouraged to work in a learning mode and to document their experiences. By drawing on, comparing, and evaluating what is being learned in different settings, the OPD is well positioned to be able to articulate insights of universal value for those who seek to participate in discourses more effectively and contribute to the emergence of a body of knowledge in this field of action. Although, as this article will explore later, Bahá'í participation in the discourses of society also occurs at the local and individual levels and has recognizable characteristics wherever it takes place, the process of learning has proved demonstrably fruitful in the national and international arenas, and the application of the conceptual framework to this field of endeavour has particular relevance for the actions taken in those domains.

The Oneness of Humanity

Among the elements of the conceptual framework that have proven to be fundamental to the Bahá'í approach to participation in public discourse are tenets so central to the Faith that it is difficult to imagine any significant field of Bahá'í activity not being directly influenced by them—for instance, the Bahá'í teachings about the true nature of the human being, the existence of God, His purpose for humanity, and the progressive nature of history. The oneness of humanity, the cornerstone of all the teachings of Bahá'u'lláh, is another such principle. Given its far-reaching implications for a profound change in social structures and all aspects of societal existence, which Bahá'ís believe the next stage of humanity's collective evolution requires, involvement in public discourse clearly cannot ignore it. The paramount value and importance of universal participation in the advancement of society is but one of its implications. For a conception of humanity that transcends divisions of nationality, ethnicity, creed, and class is not compatible with an approach to world affairs that excludes segments of the human race from any significant involvement. Nor can such involvement be reduced to tokenism or participation in a sterile listening exercise. Indeed, the greater the relevance of the discourse in question for the entire body of humanity, the more important it is that the opportunity to contribute to it is extended to as many people as possible, and the richer will that discourse be as a result.

Stated in these terms, such an approach would probably be seen by most people as unobjectionable. But when effected in practice, it quickly encounters obstacles. Human beings associate most readily with those who already share similar views and hold the same things dear. This trait of human nature is becoming even more pronounced in the modern age, given how easy it is for people to use the Internet to coalesce with individuals whose outlook on life matches their own. Being prepared to credit those with whose perspectives one differs deeply as being worth listening to can be a challenge in some quarters. Reaching out to them for meaningful dialogue can require considerable courage. But being willing to acknowledge some dimension of truth in their worldview, even if it finds expression through distorted means, and being open to develop one's own thinking as a result—this, in practice, and all too often, is a significant barrier to inclusive discourse and the cause of many an impasse in human affairs.

The efforts Bahá'ís make to overcome this challenge and transcend such differences in the search for consensus are founded on the principles essential to their worldview. To begin with, the fundamental unity of the world's religious traditions is an article of their faith, meaning that they are predisposed to see the points of agreement between their own views and those held by the follower of another religion. But the Faith's emphasis on the essential oneness of the human race itself broadens this inclusive attitude far beyond the confines of religious thought. Addressing Dr. Auguste-Henri Forel, a prominent European scientist and thinker, 'Abdu'l-Bahá explains:

> Every community in the world findeth in these Divine Teachings the realization of its highest aspirations. These teachings are even as the tree that beareth the best fruits of all trees. Philosophers, for instance, find in these heavenly teachings the most perfect solution of their social problems, and similarly a true and noble exposition of matters that pertain to philosophical questions. In like manner men of faith behold the reality of religion manifestly revealed in these heavenly teachings, and clearly and conclusively prove them to be the real and true remedy for the ills and infirmities of all mankind.[11]

If the members of every community are able to find in the teachings of Bahá'u'lláh the realization of their highest aspirations, it necessarily follows that the followers of Bahá'u'lláh should be able to identify in some way with the highest ideals and precepts cherished by each of the world's peoples. This extends to cases where those ideals and aspirations might not be readily apparent within a particular ideology or practice—sometimes, they might be almost totally obscured. In the context of participation in the discourses of society, such a perspective implies, among other things, that when involved in discussions between groups holding differing worldviews that risk spiralling downward into irreconcilable antipathy, it is necessary to maintain the conviction that by elevating a discourse to the level of principle and high ideals, it becomes possible to achieve unity and consensus. For this reason, a Bahá'í contribution to a prevalent discourse will often seek to reconceptualize the way in which it is being framed and will explore underlying assumptions that represent conceptual obstacles. An effort to reframe the discussion in this way is typically founded on the idea that unity is the critical prerequisite for fundamental progress and that acceptance of the principle of oneness can release moral capacities and induce a positive dynamic in a discourse and a will to find consensus.

Attaining Higher Levels of Unity
Closely associated with the concept of the oneness of humanity, then, is the principle that unity is a prerequisite for any undertaking dedicated to progress. 'Abdu'l-Bahá asserts that "[n]othing can be effected in the world, not even conceivably, without unity and agreement."[12] Such a conviction does not imply sympathy toward a relativistic worldview, where one is willing to

accept that everyone's perspective contains truth because one is prepared to deny the existence of any absolute truth. "As reality is one," 'Abdu'l-Bahá explains, "and cannot admit of multiplicity, therefore different opinions must ultimately become fused into one."¹³ At the opposite extreme, unity cannot be achieved through the suppression of contrary views. As will be discussed later, higher and higher levels of unity are attained if all opinions are given thoughtful consideration in a spirit of consultation.

As might be imagined, reaching this level of consensus is a considerable challenge with respect to any of the serious issues confronting society. The approach that is common to much of the public domain—whether in the context of international summits, parliamentary debates, academic conferences, panel discussions in the media, or other settings—is a confrontational one, and consensus is not necessarily the expected outcome. There is much in the Bahá'í teachings that urges a very different approach. Bahá'ís are exhorted not to quarrel with anyone, indeed, to "shun every form of dispute."¹⁴ Considered dispassionately, it can be seen that such an attitude flows logically from the premise that one engages in public discourse for the sake of promoting that which is conducive to the well-being of society. Whatever the merits of one's line of reasoning, common experience suggests—and wisdom confirms—that contentiousness will yield nothing. Without a shared desire to achieve consensus, unity will remain elusive; it cannot be imposed from without. In this respect, as in so many others, method and message are interwoven and inseparable. Unity is "the alpha and omega of all Bahá'í objectives."¹⁵ Accordingly, Bahá'ís hold that it is inconceivable for consensus and understanding, much less the betterment of society, to emerge from an atmosphere characterized by disunity. Bahá'u'lláh's emphasis in the following well-known statement is particularly relevant to this line of reasoning: "The well-being of mankind, its peace and security, are unattainable unless and until its unity is firmly established."¹⁶

Non-involvement in Partisan Politics
The importance attached to unity leads directly to the principle of non-involvement in politics, for it naturally follows that Bahá'ís cannot choose as a strategy methods and approaches that are appropriate for a system in which factions must compete for power and partisan interests each seek to increase their own influence relative to others'. Even when the motives that inspire the protagonists of various political systems are entirely benign, the system through which they seek to fulfil their aims necessarily involves a contest for power and ideological conflict, conditions that self-evidently can never bring about unity in a diverse population, even if they succeed in uniting a smaller group of people who hold a shared worldview. For anyone

whose ultimate objective is unity, then, involvement in partisan politics, even for sincere reasons, would entail resorting to means that would contradict the ends sought.

Nevertheless, it remains true that politics, in its broad expression rather than its more narrow partisan form, is generally the instrument by which decisions about social order are reached and attendant issues that confront society are debated. Any effort to contribute to the betterment of society thus sooner or later encounters the question of politics and needs to navigate it. In this regard, it is necessary to draw a clear distinction between, on the one hand, partisan political activity and, on the other, action and discourse aimed at bringing about constructive social change. The latter, though it might also be described as relating to the domain of "politics," is, as has already been explained, closely aligned with what it means to practise the Bahá'í Faith. The challenge for Bahá'ís, then, is to determine how they can actively contribute in spaces where meaningful subjects are deliberated without becoming associated with either the promotion of or the opposition to one partisan interest. In every situation, it is imperative to strive to be an unbiased and open-minded participant in a discourse.

The approach being put forward here implies openness to a broad range of views, and, at the same time, the rejection of adversarial or confrontational methods of reconciling contrary positions. How, then, can unity be realized when real differences exist?

Consultation
One of the means advocated by the Bahá'í teachings to reach unity of thought is consultation. This principle needs to be recognized as another element of the conceptual framework that is especially pertinent to participation in public discourse. It would not be possible to explore this theme fully without excessively lengthening this paper; the Bahá'í writings are replete with exhortations to resolve difficulties of all kinds through consultation and passages describing the conditions that are necessary for consultation to succeed. When Bahá'ís consider the concept of consultation, they most often do so in the context of deliberations that take place in various kinds of gatherings that form part of Bahá'í community life. However, there is growing awareness of the need to learn to employ the skills and sensibilities they develop in those settings when taking part in consultation *outside* the community. For participation in discourse calls for contributions not only at the level of content and ideas, but also at the level of process.

As indicated above, Bahá'ís are naturally predisposed to find points of agreement between conflicting views. A consultative approach does not involve adversarial debate, resulting in the triumph of whomever can advocate his or her view most forcefully; it directs energies away from contention and towards consensus. It would be a mistake to characterize this as a tendency to find compromise. Rather, a recognizable feature of the approach is a desire to identify principles on which agreement can be secured. Indeed, finding points of common agreement can serve as a means of building unity and elevating a given discourse to a level at which it "harmonizes with that which is immanent in human nature" and hence universal in human experience.[17] Fostering consensus around realities that have a universal application is a way of reaching increasingly higher levels of unity. Thus, a very useful contribution one can make to a consultative process is to encourage participants to remain focused on the highest purpose of the discourse, which is to aspire toward the best possible future for humanity. This tends to lead away from particularism and toward a recognition that all welfare is rooted in collective well-being, which, from a Bahá'í perspective, religion exists to safeguard. The strength afforded by unity will sooner or later prove hollow and lacking in vitality if it is brought about by uniting one group against the best interests of another.

Another dimension of the consultative spirit is that one is likely to be influenced by an argument that runs counter to one's own thinking only if one is persuaded that the proponent of the argument is an unbiased and sincere contributor to the discourse. As Bahá'u'lláh asserts in the Tablet of Wisdom, the power of human utterance to influence "is conditional upon refinement which in turn is dependent upon hearts which are detached and pure."[18] As such, value should be placed on discovering the truth, not on the assertion of a view, on proving its correctness, or on success in persuading people to accept it. Of course, the other extreme—where a person's contributions are presented without conviction—would also be self-defeating, for one's line of reasoning is unlikely to be taken seriously if one is not prepared to express some confidence in its value. But the desired approach nevertheless implies having humility and a sincere appreciation of the contribution each person can make on the basis of his or her own experience. Without such an attitude, efforts to advance a particular argument are unlikely to be fruitful, but when consultation proceeds in a spirit of sincere investigation without attachment to preconceived opinions, then the insights that arise are likely to be of mutual benefit to all the participants. 'Abdu'l-Bahá's explanation, offered in one of the talks he gave in America, is as follows:

> He who expresses an opinion should not voice it as correct and right but set it forth as a contribution to the consensus of opinion, for the light of reality becomes apparent when two opinions coin-

cide. A spark is produced when flint and steel come together. Man should weigh his opinions with the utmost serenity, calmness and composure. Before expressing his own views he should carefully consider the views already advanced by others. If he finds that a previously expressed opinion is more true and worthy, he should accept it immediately and not wilfully hold to an opinion of his own. By this excellent method he endeavours to arrive at unity and truth.... Therefore, true consultation is spiritual conference in the attitude and atmosphere of love.[19]

Essential to an understanding of consultation is to recognize that it is not an end in itself. It is, rather, a means for achieving consensus, heightening collective consciousness, and fostering unified action supported by the participants. It provides for the unfoldment of an iterative process through which contributions to a discourse are offered, discussed, considered in the light of scientific knowledge and other perspectives, refined, and presented, until they have been thoroughly examined and are ready to be offered more formally.

Commitment to an Unbiased Investigation of Reality
The foregoing exploration of the approach to consultation points in the direction of another element of the conceptual framework that has particular relevance for participation in public discourse, namely, the duty of each person to investigate reality.

God has given man the eye of investigation by which he may see and recognize truth. He has endowed man with ears that he may hear the message of reality and conferred upon him the gift of reason by which he may discover things for himself. This is his endowment and equipment for the investigation of reality. Man is not intended to see through the eyes of another, hear through another's ears nor comprehend with another's brain.[20]

These words, taken from a talk given by 'Abdu'l-Bahá, describe the attitude to which Bahá'ís aspire in their involvement in public discourse. Consciousness of the imperative that one must investigate reality with an unbiased mind helps maintain an inclusive, open-minded approach. But again, this does not provide grounds for a relativist worldview, nor does it imply that a Bahá'í lacks any confidence that the teachings of Bahá'u'lláh offer remedies for the ills of society. On the contrary, it is confidence in the universality of the Bahá'í teachings that encourages Bahá'ís to participate in societal discourse with humility, willing to acknowledge that their own understanding of those teachings is limited. Faith in the teachings of Bahá'u'lláh, then, does not suggest that a Bahá'í would insist on the correctness of his or her personal understanding of those teachings. Rather, Bahá'ís find that the experience of others can enrich their understanding and be vital to illuminating the inadequacies of their own reasoning. This is an outlook that can protect Bahá'ís from adopting an attitude of superiority or intellectual complacency. Similarly, they readily acknowledge that those who have no affiliation with the Faith may be motivated by intentions easily as pure as any in their own hearts. Indeed, in a certain sense, it is to enhance and give effect to the good intentions and goodwill of others that contributions to a discourse are offered by a Bahá'í.

The Sources of Knowledge
Any review of those elements of the conceptual framework which have special relevance to Bahá'í participation in public discourse cannot overlook the role of knowledge and its sources. Knowledge is central to the advancement of civilization, which Bahá'ís believe to be the purpose of religion. And it is the responsibility of every human being to participate in the generation, application, and diffusion of knowledge. This responsibility cannot be properly exercised without access to knowledge and the means to learn. If it is accepted that education is a fundamental right of every person, then it also follows that every people should have the opportunity to make a contribution to shared understanding.

With regard to the sources of knowledge, the Bahá'í teachings uphold the concept of harmony between science and religion. 'Abdu'l-Bahá's public statements on this subject were emphatic: "If we say religion is opposed to science, we lack knowledge of either true science or true religion, for both are founded upon the premises and conclusions of reason, and both must bear its test."[21] In talks made before various audiences during the course of his travels to the West, he explained that a religious belief that was at variance with the power of reason could not be maintained: "Religion must be reasonable. If it does not square with reason, it is superstition and without foundation."[22] However, 'Abdu'l-Bahá also was clear that humanity's power of reason, through which scientific and technological progress occurs, was not enough to ensure the healthy development of society. For this, the moral and spiritual teachings that have always formed the foundations of the world's religious traditions are necessary. In *The Secret of Divine Civilization*, 'Abdu'l-Bahá urged the people of Persia to learn from the industrial, educational, and administrative advances that could be witnessed in Europe, but he also drew attention to how the wealth and new technologies that were being generated through such progress were being used to stockpile armaments and wage war. 'Abdu'l-Bahá found European civilization outwardly superior but deficient with regard to its morality:

> A superficial culture, unsupported by a cultivated morality, is as "a confused medley of dreams," and external lustre without inner perfection is "like a vapour in the desert which the thirsty dreameth to be water." For results which would win the good pleasure of God and secure the peace and well-being of man, could never be fully achieved in a merely external civilization.[23]

The power of reason and understanding is the most valuable of all the gifts with which humanity has been endowed. This uniquely human faculty is the foundation upon which all scientific inquiry is built. Such inquiry aspires to objectivity, to the emergence of a truth that is proven by empirical evidence. Any discussion that occurs in the public arena on a matter of importance would look to the knowledge generated scientifically to shape the contributions being made. However, while there is much to be gained from close adherence to the methods of science, its findings are sometimes cited in defence of claims that, on closer analysis, they do not support. Distinguishing between those claims that are justifiable and those that are not, especially if one is unfamiliar with the scientific field from which the findings emerge, can be challenging. At times, for instance, evidence seems to emerge that is claimed to support what might be called the "fashionable" view—one way of describing a view held by those who occupy positions of power and standing in society. The systematic application of moral and spiritual principles acts as an indispensable corrective to such distortions. An apparent contradiction between such principles and the claims made on behalf of science should at least prompt further investigation and inquiry. The outcome is likely to be a more refined understanding of reality. Being able to weigh knowledge in the balance of spiritual principles constitutes an indispensable faculty demanded of those who participate in public discourse. On the one hand, it discourages them from expressing a dogmatic insistence on a particular line of thinking that seems to accord with a moral principle; if such thinking is not supported by reason and evidence, this might be an indicator of some flaws in their understanding. On the other hand, it protects them from giving uncritical assent to the claims made based on every piece of research put forward as a contribution to a particular discourse. This intellectual safeguard was explored further in a statement prepared by the BIC in 1995:

It is—or by now should be—a truism that, in every sphere of human activity and at every level, the insights and skills that represent scientific accomplishment must look to the force of spiritual commitment and moral principle to ensure their appropriate application. People need, for example, to learn how to separate fact from conjecture—indeed to distinguish between subjective views and objective reality; the extent to which individuals and institutions so equipped can contribute to human progress, however, will be determined by their devotion to truth and their detachment from the promptings of their own interests and passions.[24]

Religion represents a body of knowledge that is complementary to science. It seeks to enable human beings to learn about the moral and spiritual dimensions of reality and to set in motion processes aimed at applying those principles in order to bring coherence to the material and spiritual life of the individual and the collective life of society. In that endeavour, the rational faculty is essential. It implies a systematic approach to learning that is scientific in method. In a range of fields in which Bahá'ís are actively involved, including education and social and economic development, there are clear benefits to be gained from regularly reflecting on action taken and refining plans in light of actual outcomes. The insights arising from such a process often provide the basis upon which contributions to the discourses of society can be developed.

The Spiritual Nature of the Human Being
For the elements of the conceptual framework discussed so far, their implications for Bahá'í participation in public discourse have been considered at the level of objectives, method, and approach. Naturally, however, those same elements help shape the content of any Bahá'í contribution to particular discourses. In this context, another element—the Bahá'í conception of human nature and identity as being fundamentally spiritual—holds special significance.

Understanding human nature in this way opens up a new perspective on reality. It contrasts with materialist concepts maintained on the assumption that human beings are inherently and incorrigibly selfish and aggressive and are governed by animalistic instincts. While acknowledging the potential for human consciousness to become dominated by such tendencies, the Bahá'í perspective maintains that society—as much as its individual members—can, and must, aspire to higher ideals. Whatever the supposed limitations imposed by the circumstances of a particular people, human nature has innate spiritual capacities that allow it to transcend those circumstances.

This central concept opens up consideration of many other areas, such as the role of the individual in society; the balance to be struck between providing for the development of the individual and the progress of society; and a conception of society as being an environment that enables the latent capacities of each individual to flourish. Ultimately, it provides the basis for seeing collaboration, rather than competition, as the dominant means by which social progress occurs.

This perspective on human reality is derived from the teachings of Bahá'u'lláh, who describes the conscious soul as being endowed with the capacity to reflect divine attributes. Naturally, this is an idea that will not be accepted by everyone. Given that so much of Bahá'í thought is founded on this conception, it is understandable that the Faith's contribution to particular discourses is not automatically welcomed everywhere, and consequently, some spaces in the public domain remain closed to Bahá'í participation. This is to be expected and is to a certain extent unavoidable. However, many people are prepared to support a view that there is indeed a unique set of characteristics that distinguishes the human being from all other forms of life, summed up as the "human spirit," with the rational mind being its essential characteristic. This description of human nature, which is entirely coherent with the Bahá'í view of the fundamentally spiritual quality of the human being, forms the basis for common ground on which higher forms of consensus are attainable. Such consensus can, in turn, lead to leaps of imagination as to what human society might accomplish.

Selecting Discourses in Which to Participate

Having surveyed some of the principles that shape the Bahá'í approach to participation in public discourse, it may be worthwhile to consider the nature of those "prevalent discourses of society" in which Bahá'ís choose to become involved.[25] The word *discourse* itself suggests a certain "weightiness": the theme is one of moment and consequence for those who contribute to it, and it sits at the opposite end of a spectrum to those topics that might be thought of as trivial, petty, or frivolous, no matter how much they absorb the collective consciousness. A "prevalent" discourse is not only widespread, but it is well established; it is of lasting importance, and it is meaningful in part because it repeatedly imposes itself upon the public mind. It contrasts with ephemeral subjects that might—for a brief moment in time—appear to hold the attention of the entire world but are soon after quite forgotten. At times, a discourse might be prevalent because it is a controversial or highly divisive issue, and in such instances, Bahá'ís tread cautiously; given that the views of those participating are more likely to be firmly entrenched already, the prospect of bringing about unity and consensus is less bright. Nevertheless, even in such circumstances, Bahá'ís sometimes find that they can help move a discourse in the direction of greater mutual understanding. Finally, for society itself to have ownership of the discourse suggests that it is not solely the concern of a privileged elite, a specialist interest group, or the arbiters of public taste. It commands general interest, even if it might attract very sophisticated contributions from various quarters.

Of course, to distinguish between the numerous topics that vie for the public gaze is not a trivial exercise. Neither is it straightforward. It is a dynamic process subject to the constant flux in social forces at work in the world. The discourse on "governance," for instance, would seem to meet all the criteria outlined above. However, not everything that appears to be associated with that discourse has real value. The political party system of governance often seems inherently obsessed with topics that are insubstantial, fleeting, or chiefly of interest to a limited circle of politicians, journalists, and political enthusiasts. Attempts to justify the level of attention paid to those same topics might be made by exaggerating their relevance to the discourse on governance. Over time, Bahá'ís have found that the ability to participate meaningfully in the discourses of society requires sound judgment in order to discern what is truly important from what is, relatively speaking, inconsequential, even if it does absorb public attention.

One of the criteria by which Bahá'ís judge a particular discourse to hold promise is that the course of its development in society suggests movement in a constructive direction; thus, it might be possible to reinforce a positive trend. The contributions to public discourse made by 'Abdu'l-Bahá offer a potent example in this respect. In his travels to the West, most especially in his public presentations in the United States, he described in unambiguous terms the failings of the society that surrounded him. Racial prejudice, strident nationalism, and discrimination against women were eloquently, but unequivocally, castigated. In the land of plenty that was brimming with confidence in its material advancement and technological leadership, 'Abdu'l-Bahá repeatedly stressed the perils and profound limitations of materialism, and before an audience of one faith, he would unhesitatingly champion the truth of all faiths. Where he found receptivity to a particular Bahá'í teaching, he encouraged his listeners to more fully commit themselves to its promulgation. Naturally, wherever he found receptivity to the Bahá'í Faith itself, he shared the spiritual teachings of Bahá'u'lláh and invited the hearers to identify themselves with the new religion. But more often than not, the addresses he delivered in churches, social societies, universities, and public meetings had the effect of strengthening a strand of public thought that already existed, that was in sympathy with the Bahá'í teachings, and that represented a developing discourse that was already gathering momentum.

On a related point, Bahá'ís do not equate participation in the discourses of society with advocacy or lobbying, at least not in the way that such activities are generally understood, as it is not typically focused on bringing about specific changes in legislation or government policy. Rather, the aim of this endeavour is to make a constructive contribution to a discourse that is prevalent in the public sphere with a view to encouraging consensus. Situations do occur in which, once consensus appears to have emerged, the Bahá'í community is willing to support calls for a change in legislation in a particular area. Nevertheless, this is not the starting point for any attempt to participate in a discourse. Of course, it is well known that Bahá'ís in many countries do, from time to time, make representations to their respective governments requesting that they take action on behalf of Bahá'ís living elsewhere who are harassed, imprisoned, and made to suffer deprivations of all kinds because of their faith. This is an important area of endeavour for various communities, but it is different in nature from the work of contributing to a discourse that is being described here.

Bahá'ís also find value in being able to bring to a discourse a point of view that might not have been expressed before, perhaps because those who are associated with it are yet to organize the concepts, craft the vocabulary, or simply invest the time to articulate it themselves. In this respect, valuable service can be rendered by offering others a voice through which they are enabled to be present in spaces that matter to them, faithfully representing their perspective on a particular discourse and relating it to a spiritual principle. This might even extend to efforts to develop and promote a new discourse that previously did not exist or was not prominent, let alone prevalent. A notable instance of this was the promotion of the discourse, on the international stage and at the United Nations in particular, on the education of the girl child, where the BIC contributed to its emergence as a theme on the global development agenda and offered its experience in the application of this principle as a contribution toward the discourse.

The Individual, the Community, and the Institutions

Bahá'í participation in the discourses of society has, on the whole, been associated more often with actions undertaken by or at the behest of the Faith's institutions, through interactions with government and civil society. This is to be expected, given that at the institutional level there exists the organizational capacity to capture, reflect on, and build upon what is being learned over time. Moreover, it is the institutions that speak on behalf of the community as a whole.

At the national level, Bahá'í participation in discourses is overseen by National Spiritual Assemblies and their external affairs structures, some of whom, owing to the consistent effort they have invested over a number of years, have become trusted and valued contributors to processes that lead to the development of policy. At the international level, such activity is led principally by the offices of the BIC, including the United Nations Office. The contributions made at these levels are, as one might expect, carefully articulated and at times quite elaborate, emerging from an ongoing process of action and reflection that seeks to build capacity for an increasingly effective presentation of Bahá'í thinking on particular discourses that often dates back decades—an iterative process of gradually refining the presentation of a distinctive point of view. They often have a sense of immediacy to them; they are responses to particular events or phenomena, or they are timed to coincide with a formal gathering convened by governmental or non-governmental organizations. They serve to aggregate the worldwide Bahá'í experience, present the insights derived from such efforts in a systematic way, and give a voice to the worldwide Bahá'í community on the national and international stage. So far, it has been less common to see institutional participation in the discourses of society at the regional and local level, but to the extent that it occurs, it arises from a deepening involvement of the Faith in the life of society at those levels and naturally draws inspiration from the pattern provided by the national and international institutions and agencies.

These formal contributions to a discourse are derived from the overarching Bahá'í view of humanity's progress as an ever-advancing process. It is a fundamentally hopeful perspective, but one that recognizes progress occurs through consistent, long-term action and patient adherence to principle. Accordingly, a Bahá'í contribution to a discourse will typically seek to present an expansive vision of the overall aim of work in a particular field, in preference to a discussion of the minutiae of a particular policy or initiative. Its analysis will aim at identifying the root causes of obstacles to progress, which are usually moral and spiritual in nature, and bringing relevant principles to bear upon them. Naturally, the effort involved in addressing the fundamental causes of problems rather than their more visible symptoms is always likely to be considerable, and the Bahá'í contribution to a discourse will acknowledge this reality. But given the view that over time, the very structure of society itself needs to undergo profound organic change, the perspective offered often has far-reaching implications. A contribution to a discourse made by Bahá'ís will typically examine persistent and widespread assumptions about such fundamental matters as human nature and social existence. Notwithstanding the difficulty entailed in challenging deep-seated assumptions, the importance of doing so is stressed because, ultimately, it is their persistence that frequently instills paralysis and impedes progress. Having given a perspective on the issue at hand, a formal contribution to a discourse often goes on to offer pertinent Bahá'í experience. The most notable example of a contribution to a discourse that was structured in this way is "The Promise of World Peace."

Although Bahá'í participation in discourses is typically considered in terms of the actions undertaken by or on behalf of Bahá'í institutions, this is not the only means by which it occurs. Individual Bahá'ís also have a share in this work, and their contribution takes many forms. Yet their endeavours seek to harmonize with the same conceptual framework and share many of the attributes of the efforts of Bahá'í institutions in this arena. On the part of individuals who have achieved a certain standing in their profession or within an academic discipline, such contributions might be as sophisticated and elaborate as any produced under the auspices of the institutions. Indeed, such contributions can at times represent decades of careful study and thought, action and reflection, in an effort to systematically correlate the Bahá'í teachings to contemporary thought in one's own scientific discipline or profession and may represent the fruit of personal effort or of the collaboration of a group of individuals.

Furthermore, individual Bahá'ís from time to time make a contribution to a particular discourse by working together and with others through a Bahá'í-inspired organization. Agencies of this kind are active in such fields as education, the advancement of women, and health and at times are concerned with the advancement of thought in a field that has relevance for the collective life of humanity. Their experience of applying the principles of the Bahá'í Faith to address a particular social or economic question provides them with insights from which a meaningful contribution to the discourse surrounding the issue in question can be made.

Individual Bahá'ís are, of course, also responsible for myriad instances of informal participation in a discourse; in fact, this is arguably an unavoidable and inherent aspect of being a Bahá'í. Simply through interacting with family, friends, neighbours, and colleagues, Bahá'ís are frequently drawn into conversation on the issues of the day in a variety of social spaces, and their response to such situations is naturally informed by insights that emerge from their beliefs. A wide range of social spaces suggest themselves, such as a parent–teacher association, a staff meeting in a workplace, a neighbourhood management committee, a gathering for residents to discuss village affairs, a student union meeting, and so on—any space in which a Bahá'í can make a contribution that is intended to offer a perspective, resolve conflict, or contribute to and advance unity of thought. Here, as much as in seminars, conferences, and other settings for the exploration of a discourse, Bahá'ís contribute by framing the discussion in terms of principle, seeking out points of agreement that lay the foundation for consensus, directing a negative or dispiriting conversation toward a constructive and creative path, and demonstrating all the other attitudes and behaviours that characterize a Bahá'í approach to consultation. Bahá'í youth have been encouraged to be active in this field in an individual capacity; a recent message of the Universal House of Justice encouraged them, once they have taken up an occupation, to "contribute to their field, or even to advance it" in light of the insights they gain from their ongoing study of the Bahá'í writings.[26] Preparing youth to make meaningful contributions to public discourse in this way is a primary concern of the Institute for Studies in Global Prosperity, a non-profit organization established in association with the BIC, which organizes seminars around the world for university graduates and undergraduates for this purpose. These seminars are designed to explore various aspects of the conceptual framework discussed in this paper.

The skills that are required by the individual for engagement in this area of activity relate closely to the capacities that Bahá'ís and others nurture in themselves by participating in the common system of grassroots education that the worldwide Bahá'í community has been developing for about twenty years—the existence of which has now become an established feature of Bahá'í community life in all settings. The curriculum currently used gives considerable attention both to the refinement of spiritual qualities and the enhancement of individual and collective ability for undertaking practical service of various kinds. Of particular relevance here is the capacity for engaging in conversations on meaningful, sometimes complex topics. The habits of study and deep reflection that are cultivated by the materials of this educational system assist participants in developing their ability to express their understanding of profound concepts in such conversations. In the early courses, those taking part are encouraged to apply this capacity to the exploration of fundamental spiritual realities, such as prayer and the existence of the soul. In later courses, the scope of the subjects being considered widens to include analysis of social forces, a Bahá'í perspective on history as process and on world affairs, and insights drawn from the experience of addressing various social ills through the application of Bahá'í teachings. It is expected that the sequence of courses underpinning this educational system will eventually include a course directly concerned with involvement in the discourses of society.

Among other things, this approach to education encourages Bahá'ís to adopt an attitude of learning toward the various areas of activity in which they are engaged—systematically building capacity over time by reflecting on experience as it accumulates and examining it in light of principles that guide their work. To consciously operate in a mode of learning implies a reflective and methodical approach to participation in a discourse. It implies, too, a commitment to refine understanding over time through experience and through interaction with others and with the world. Bahá'ís who are involved in discourses seek opportunities to put their developing skills into practice by identifying the many spaces in which discourses occur and selecting from among them; occasions to reflect upon the outcome, perhaps with others, are created; a profound and ongoing exploration is carried on of Bahá'í teachings that bear on the issues at hand and of the community's experience in the application of those teachings—an exploration that is itself refined through the efflorescence of thought over time; effort is made to understand ever more deeply the way in which discourses are framed by interlocutors and the insights they have gained about them; informed by reflection, choices are made about the next course of action; new opportunities for practice are identified; and so the work is advanced through an ongoing process of learning.

The participation of the Bahá'í community itself, as a community, in the discourses of society is perhaps less obvious at first, but it, too, is indispensable. The followers of the Bahá'í Faith are a community of practice: their efforts to put the teachings of Bahá'u'lláh into effect in their individual and collective lives and to allow the teachings to give shape to a new kind of social reality are of course what informs their participation in the discourses of society at every level. This is an organic process; as the community encounters challenges and difficulties of various kinds, it draws on Bahá'í principles in order to identify solutions. Naturally, Bahá'ís are generally cautious not to overstate the extent to which their experience has given them an increased understanding of particular areas, and they refrain from directing undue attention to initiatives that have not had time to fully mature. Nevertheless, in the gradual emergence of a pattern of Bahá'í community life, one can see a healthy interaction of science and religion, of insights summoned up variously from actual experience, from the exploration of reality, and from the inspiration derived from the spiritual teachings of Bahá'u'lláh. Not only does the experience of community life, where these sources of insight are fused together, enrich the contributions made by Bahá'í institutions and individuals to the discourses in which they participate, but that experience enables Bahá'ís to show their thinking as well as tell it. Where appeals to reason and principle prove unpersuasive, a different outcome can sometimes occur when someone is exposed to the reality of a community that is striving to give effect in deeds to a common set of beliefs. Thus, the pattern of life maintained by the community can itself be a striking contribution to a particular discourse.

Although careful not to overstate the extent of their experience, Bahá'ís nevertheless recognize that in a century and a half of endeavouring to give practical effect to their beliefs, certain insights have been garnered that may be of assistance to others and may therefore constitute a basis for contributing to the discourses of their society. One example that can be cited is the practical implementation of the principle of the equality of women and men, sometimes in societies with entrenched, centuries-old patterns of thought and action. Over the decades and through numerous means, educational as well as structural, the community has learned to draw on its spiritual and moral resources to significantly advance the participation of women in its collective affairs as well as within families and to bring about a profound transformation of individual attitudes—women's as much as men's. The application of the principle of consultation as a means of collective decision-making, creating social consensus, and resolving conflict offers another instance of the application of principle, as does the experience of overcoming deep-seated racial, religious, and class prejudices through the creation of vibrant and diverse communities united in common purpose and committed to acquiring an ever-deeper understanding of the implications of the Faith's pivotal teaching—the oneness of humankind.

As this brief review shows, Bahá'í participation in the prevalent discourses of society takes a variety of forms and occurs at various levels. Although opportunities to engage in this field of endeavour arise naturally as Bahá'ís deepen their engagement in the life of society, it is also true that wherever capacity has been generated and the resources of a community are sufficient, Bahá'ís aim to create such opportunities. They do so by identifying spaces where particular discourses are being explored and assessing the benefits of trying to be present in each space. By making efforts in this direction, it is inevitable that their capacity increases further, and a broader range of opportunities becomes available. Naturally, Bahá'ís wish to invest their limited resources wisely, and they are drawn to those spaces that welcome their perspective; however, they do not shy away from seeking to present the Bahá'í view in the spaces where the most significant exploration of a particular discourse is occurring. For involvement in the public sphere is not an end in itself. The ultimate objective is to improve the lot of humanity through the application of Bahá'í teachings to "the needs of the age ye live in," and this can be realized only if a contribution to a particular discourse comes to the attention of those who are in a position to act on it for the good of all humanity.[27]

At the outset of this chapter, it was explained that the Bahá'í conception of religion accounts for why Bahá'ís attach so much value to involvement in public discourse: religion is understood as the vehicle for spiritual forces capable of transforming both society and the individual. In this regard, correspondence between 'Abdu'l-Bahá and the Executive Committee of the Central Organization for a Durable Peace, an entity based in The Hague in the Netherlands that in 1920 was subsumed into the League of Nations, is particularly illuminating. In the first letter sent to the Committee in 1919—a major exposition of Bahá'í teachings on the subject of peace—'Abdu'l-Bahá praises the aims of the organization and sets out many principles derived from the teachings of Bahá'u'lláh, such as the oneness of humanity, the harmony of science and religion, and the equality of men and women. He states that these principles "must be added to the matter of universal peace and combined with it."[28] "Otherwise," he adds, "the realization of universal peace by itself in the world of mankind is difficult."[29] The committee's reply was courteous, enthusiastic, and complimentary, but it was clear that it could not endorse all the principles explained by 'Abdu'l-Bahá because the organization's work was focused exclusively on the promotion of universal peace, not on spiritual or religious matters. Noting that, at least with respect to the cause of peace itself, they share a common aim, the committee asked 'Abdu'l-Bahá what the followers of the Bahá'í Faith could contribute to its achievement.

The response sent by 'Abdu'l-Bahá was warm and affectionate. In it he acknowledges the existence of a common goal. But he goes on to explain why, from a Bahá'í perspective, the cause of peace is central to the very concept of religion and why the Bahá'í community has been prepared to make the ultimate sacrifice in its pursuit:

> As ye have no doubt heard, in Persia thousands of souls have offered up their lives in this path, and thousands of homes have been laid waste. Despite this, we have in no wise relented, but have continued to endeavour unto this very moment and are increasing our efforts as day followeth day, because our desire for peace is not derived merely from the intellect: It is a matter of religious belief and one of the eternal foundations of the Faith of God. That is why we strive with all our might and, forsaking our own advantage, rest, and comfort, forgo the pursuit of our own affairs; devote ourselves to the mighty cause of peace; and consider it to be the very foundation of the Divine religions, a service to His Kingdom, the source of eternal life, and the greatest means of admittance into the heavenly realm.[30]

For Bahá'ís then, there is a natural alignment between engagement in the public sphere and religious faith. Their conviction gives the strongest motivation for participating in meaningful discourses focused on the betterment of their society.

Notes

1 Bahá'u'lláh, *The Tabernacle of Divine Unity: Bahá'u'lláh's Responses to Mánikchí Ṣáḥib and Other Writings* (Haifa, Israel: Bahá'í World Centre, 2006), 5.
2 Bahá'u'lláh, *The Summons of the Lord of Hosts* (Bundoora: Bahá'í Publications Australia, 2003), 88–96.
3 Shoghi Effendi, *God Passes By* (Wilmette, IL: Bahá'í Publishing Trust, 2004), 342.
4 See Universal House of Justice, "Social and Economic Development: New Field of Bahá'í Service," October 20, 1983, in *Messages from the Universal House of Justice 1963–1986: The Third Epoch of the Formative Age* (Wilmette, IL: Bahá'í Publishing Trust, 1996), 601–04.
5 Universal House of Justice, "The Promise of World Peace," 1985, http://www.bahai.org/library/authoritative-texts/the-universal-house-of-justice/messages/#.
6 Bahá'u'lláh, *Gleanings from the Writings of Bahá'u'lláh* (Wilmette, IL: US Bahá'í Publishing Trust, 2005), 106: 1.
7 Universal House of Justice, "Riḍván 155—To the Bahá'ís of the World," 1998, http://www.bahai.org/library/authoritative-texts/the-universal-house-of-justice/messages/#d=19980421_001&f=f1.
8 Universal House of Justice, "Riḍván 2008—To the Bahá'ís of the World," 2008, http://www.bahai.org/library/authoritative-texts/the-universal-house-of-justice/messages/#d=20080421_001&f=f1.
9 Universal House of Justice, "Riḍván 2010—To the Bahá'ís of the World," 2010, http://www.bahai.org/library/authoritative-texts/the-universal-house-of-justice/messages/#d=20100421_001&f=f1.
10 Universal House of Justice, "Riḍván 2013—To the Bahá'ís of the World," 2012, http://www.bahai.org/library/authoritative-texts/the-universal-house-of-justice/messages/#d=20130421_001&f=f.
11 'Abdu'l-Bahá in a tablet to Dr. Auguste Forel quoted in *The Bahá'í World*, vol. 15 (Haifa, Israel: Bahá'í World Centre, 1976), 43.
12 'Abdu'l-Bahá, *The Secret of Divine Civilization* (Wilmette, IL: Bahá'í Publishing Trust, 2006), 73.
13 'Abdu'l-Bahá, *Selections from the Writings of 'Abdu'l-Bahá* (Wilmette, IL: Bahá'í Publishing Trust, 2004), 298.
14 Ibid., 209.

15 Universal House of Justice to the National Spiritual Assembly of the Bahá'ís of the United States, May 19, 1994, http://www.bahai.org/library/authoritative-texts/the-universal-house-of-justice/messages/#d=19940519_001&f=f1.
16 Bahá'u'lláh, *Gleanings*, 131: 2.
17 Universal House of Justice. "The Promise of World Peace."
18 Bahá'u'lláh, *Tablets of Bahá'u'lláh Revealed after the Kitáb-i-Aqdas* (Wilmette, IL: Bahá'í Publishing Trust, 2005), 143.
19 'Abdu'l-Bahá, *The Promulgation of Universal Peace: Talks Delivered by 'Abdu'l-Bahá during His Visit to the United States and Canada in 1912*, rev. ed. (Wilmette, IL: Bahá'í Publishing Trust, 2007), 72.
20 Ibid., 293.
21 Ibid., 107.
22 Ibid., 63.
23 'Abdu'l-Bahá, *The Secret of Divine Civilization*, 61.
24 Bahá'í International Community, "The Prosperity of Humankind," 1995, http://www.bahai.org/library/other-literature/official-statements-commentaries/prosperity-humankind/.
25 Universal House of Justice, "Riḍván 2010—To the Bahá'ís of the World."
26 Universal House of Justice to the Conference of the Continental Boards of Counsellors, December 29, 2015, http://www.bahai.org/library/authoritative-texts/the-universal-house-of-justice/messages/#.
27 Bahá'u'lláh, *Gleanings*, 106: 1.
28 'Abdu'l-Bahá, *Selections*, 227.
29 Ibid.
30 Previously unpublished.

Bibliography

'Abdu'l-Bahá. *The Promulgation of Universal Peace: Talks Delivered by 'Abdu'l-Bahá during His Visit to the United States and Canada in 1912*. Rev. ed. Wilmette, IL: Bahá'í Publishing Trust, 2007.

———. *The Secret of Divine Civilization*. Wilmette, IL: Bahá'í Publishing Trust, 2006.

———. *Selections from the Writings of 'Abdu'l-Bahá*. Wilmette, IL: Bahá'í Publishing Trust, 2004.

Bahá'í International Community. "The Prosperity of Humankind." 1995. http://www.bahai.org/library/other-literature/official-statements-commentaries/prosperity-humankind/. *The Bahá'í World*. Vol. 15. Haifa, Israel: Bahá'í World Centre, 1976.

Bahá'u'lláh. *Gleanings from the Writings of Bahá'u'lláh*. Wilmette, IL: Bahá'í Publishing Trust, 2005.

———. *The Summons of the Lord of Hosts*. Bundoora: Bahá'í Publications Australia, 2003.

———. *The Tabernacle of Divine Unity: Bahá'u'lláh's Responses to Mánikchí Ṣáḥib and Other Writings*. Haifa, Israel: Bahá'í World Centre, 2006.

———. *Tablets of Bahá'u'lláh Revealed after the Kitáb-i-Aqdas*. Wilmette, IL: Bahá'í Publishing Trust, 2005. Shoghi Effendi. *God Passes By*. Wilmette, IL: Bahá'í Publishing Trust, 2004.

Universal House of Justice. "The Promise of World Peace." 1985. http://www.bahai.org/library/authoritative-texts/the-universal-house-of-justice/messages/#.

———. "Social and Economic Development: New Field of Bahá'í Service." In *Messages from the Universal House of Justice 1963–1986: The Third Epoch of the Formative Age*, 601–04. Wilmette, IL: Bahá'í Publishing Trust, 1996.

———. Universal House of Justice to the Conference of the Continental Boards of Counsellors, 29 December 2015. http://www.bahai.org/library/authoritative-texts/the-universal-house-of-justice/messages/#.

———. Universal House of Justice to the National Spiritual Assembly of the Bahá'ís of the United States," 19 May 1994. http://www.bahai.org/library/authoritative-texts/the -universal-house-of-justice/messages/#d=19940519_001&f=f1.

———. "Riḍván 155—To the Bahá'ís of the World." 1998. http://www.bahai.org/library/authoritative-texts/the -universal-house-of-justice/messages/#d=19980421_001&f=f1.

———. "Riḍván 2008—To the Bahá'ís of the World." 2008.http://www.bahai.org/library/authoritative-texts/the-universal-house-of -justice/messages/#d=20080421_001&f=f1.

———. "Riḍván 2010—To the Bahá'ís of the World." 2010. http://www.bahai.org/library/authoritative-texts/the-universal-house-of-justice/messages/#d=20100421_001&f=f1.

———. "Riḍván 2013—To the Bahá'ís of the World." 2012. http://www.bahai.org/library/authoritative-texts/the-universal-house-of-justice/messages/#d=20130421_001&f=f1.

CHAPTER SEVEN

CONTRIBUTIONS TO INTERNATIONAL DEVELOPMENT DISCOURSE: EXPLORING THE ROLES OF SCIENCE AND RELIGION

MATTHEW WEINBERG

Determining what constitutes meaningful betterment of the human condition and how to constructively transform social reality have been central concerns of both religion and the field of international development. Each in its own way has offered visions that elaborate notions of "the good" and specific pathways for attaining human well-being. Rarely, though, have development objectives and policies explicitly taken into account religious values and perspectives.[1]

This chapter presents a case study of how the Institute for Studies in Global Prosperity (ISGP), a non-profit organization working in collaboration with the Bahá'í International Community (BIC), has sought to reframe and broaden development discourse by considering the interrelationship between community capacity-building processes, the spiritual bases of human action, and social transformation.[2] The complementary roles of scientific and religious resources in defining creative pathways of human empowerment are examined, as well as the means used to undertake this dialogue. Known as the "discourse on science, religion, and development," this decade-long, multi-country initiative represents a measured attempt to raise questions about the salient assumptions and strategies of the development process and to identify avenues of research and action in relation to those questions. The learning emanating from the discourse on science, religion, and development serves to illustrate the deep relevance of religious insight and practice to the exigencies of a rapidly changing world.

The Challenges of International Development

Over the past several decades, theorists, practitioners, and policy-makers have gradually expanded their understanding of many interacting factors underlying social and economic advancement. This evolution in development thought can be seen in the shift in focus from capital-intensive programs aimed at modernizing a society's physical infrastructure; to the prioritization of technological innovation, as exemplified by the "Green" and "White" Revolutions; to programs designed to reduce poverty directly; to initiatives emphasizing local community action.[3] More recently, the development field has emphasized those variables that undergird political and economic stability—the customs, institutions, and procedures that give rise to social cohesion. "Evidenced-based" approaches to development research and policy have also become increasingly prevalent.[4] A range of ideas now underpin development activity, and the amelioration of extreme circumstances of poverty and human health has, in some regions of the globe, been notable.[5]

Although a deepening recognition of the multifarious causes of poverty represents a step forward, it is not at all clear how an integrated and organic approach to development that engages the people most affected can emerge. Incremental or piecemeal measures addressing narrowly defined problems have failed, and likely will continue to fail, to address the widespread physical suffering and social disorder now engulfing significant portions of the planet. Even with a growing emphasis on participatory methods, we are only now beginning to observe the broadest contours of viable patterns of grassroots community advancement. Until truly tangible and sustained improvements occur in the material conditions of the majority of the earth's population, serious questions will remain concerning current development strategies.

Social norms and ideals lie at the heart of individual and collective flourishing. In the main, this aspect of social vitality is not considered in a concrete way by the predominant development paradigm. The role of social relations, social structures, and identity is an integral component of human deprivation. Deficits of well-being are multi-faceted. Economic opportunity can be adversely affected by educational, health, or environmental deficits; social conflict and social exclusion; attitudes about gender; or pervasive corruption in public and private institutions. Indeed, as a United Nations report noted, "the issue of poverty reduction is a great deal more nuanced and complex than the narrow technocratic vision underlying the conventional wisdom."[6]

In many respects, the early development enterprise of "modernization" and subsequent phases of international development programming were concrete expressions of the assumptions and attitudes flowing from aspects of the thesis of "secularization"—that manifestations of religiosity are either a matter for the private sphere only or that religious worldviews are of declining applicability to public affairs.[7] Development theory has generally conceptualized religion as an anachronistic, non-rational system of belief contravening scientific understanding and therefore a primary barrier to development.[8] Consequently, the normative, religious, and culturally contextual dimensions of social development have for the most part been neglected by theorists, practitioners, and institutional actors in the development field.[9] The international development agenda essentially has ignored the fact that the vast majority of the world's peoples do not view themselves simply as material beings responding to material exigencies and circumstances, but rather as beings endowed with spiritual sensibility and purpose. To dismiss the basic self-understanding of the principal stakeholders in the development process is untenable, and for this reason the mainly economic and material criteria now guiding development activity must be extended to include those non-material aspirations and perceptions that inform human action.[10]

In light of the inadequacy of contemporary development approaches, the Institute for Studies in Global Prosperity, over the course of several years, undertook a sustained process of research and dialogue delineating a substantive but radically different development pathway. Drawing on the evolving efforts of the Bahá'í community to learn about the myriad dimensions of social and economic development, the Institute sought to advance a conceptual framework in which the essential spiritual basis of human identity and a constructive articulation of the religious impulse in public life are viewed as central to processes of social betterment.[11] This undertaking to contribute new insights to development work not surprisingly raised a range of questions that could be answered only through a process of collective action and learning involving many different actors. At the core of this learning process was a systematic endeavour to better understand how the powers and capabilities of the human spirit, in conjunction with scientific methodology, can be channelled in original and productive ways.

A New Discourse on Development Emerges

In the 1990s, thoughtful development practitioners were beginning to ask whether the sources and mechanisms of social empowerment could be properly understood without taking religion into account. Especially notable was a project sponsored by the International Development Research Centre (IDRC) in Canada, which sought to analyze the synergistic relationship between scientific, religious, and development worldviews. A penetrating exploration of the topic entitled *The Lab, The Temple, and the Market: Reflections at the Intersection of Science, Religion and Development*, incorporating perspectives from several faith traditions, was one of the main outcomes of this collaboration. A centrepiece of this work drew on the learning and experience of the Bahá'í-inspired organization Foundation for the Application and Teaching of the Sciences (FUNDAEC) in South America. Over a period of many years, FUNDAEC made "a concerted effort to create an alternative development strategy that sought to apply spiritual principles to the transformation of social and economic processes and structures in rural regions."[12] Animating this novel development approach was a conviction that human beings possess a higher nature and that all efforts at technical and social capacity building must be founded on a firm belief in such human nobility. Innovative research and educational initiatives simultaneously sought to cultivate scientific, intellectual, and spiritual capacities of individuals and groups in rural communities. FUNDAEC created the University for Integral Development—an institutional space within which learning processes can be set in motion in a given population. The processes include the search for sustainable systems of small farm production, the establishment of viable systems of formal education, and the strengthening of local economies, all in light of pertinent scientific understanding and cardinal spiritual precepts.

The IDRC project, coupled with the lessons derived from the Bahá'í community's own varied activities in the development field, elaborated a conceptual basis for the first major initiative of the Institute for Studies in Global Prosperity—the promotion of a discourse focused on how the practical application of spiritual concepts can upraise the human condition. That human nature and aspiration cannot be solely understood in limited material terms, that justice and equality are fundamental precursors to social harmony, that enduring social action must be based on universal participation and grassroots learning, that an ethos of service to the common good should permeate all forms of social endeavour, and that unity of purpose in a community is a phenomenon of innovative power capable of overcoming the most intractable of social obstacles were among the insights elaborated in the Institute's conceptual framework.[13] Further, the Institute posited that the primary task of the development enterprise is the raising of capacity among individuals, communities, and institutions across all regions and cultures, with the goal of a creating a civilization in which there exists a "dynamic coherence between the spiritual and practical requirements of life on earth."[14] This recognition of an inseparable connection between the material and spiritual domains of existence gives rise to a foundationally different notion of development.[15]

In its attempt to reassess development thought and praxis, the Institute emphasized that individuals and communities must cease to be regarded as passive "project beneficiaries" and instead be viewed as active protagonists in creating and utilizing knowledge and in tracing out their own path of development, thereby advancing social well-being in a sustainable fashion. In this way, the raising of human capacity is the principal mechanism that serves to bring about salutary personal, community, and institutional change.[16] Human beings are not regarded as a source of endless problems but rather as rich in potential, capable of transforming their individual and collective circumstances. True capacity building involves equipping people with tools and mental models that allow them to effectively address the complex social realities they face. A community, or even a society, progresses by steadily improving its capacity to define, analyze, and meet its own needs.[17] It is a process of action, reflection, and adjustment that aims to bring about consistent patterns of change by drawing on sources of knowledge that not only enhance material welfare but that also deepen human solidarity.

A key underpinning of the Institute's work, then, is that the generation, application, and diffusion of knowledge, rather than economic activity or progress, should be understood as the central axis around which development takes place. If it is accepted that knowledge emanates from both spiritual and material sources, the methodologies of science and the insights of religion can, when working in concert, provide the essential tools for erecting harmonious and equitable social systems.[18] Taken together, science and religion provide the underlying organizing principles by which individuals, communities, and institutions function and evolve. Utilizing the methods of science allows people to become more objective and systematic in their approach to problem solving and in their understanding of social processes, while tapping the spiritual inclinations of individuals deepens social amity and imparts the moral impetus that begets and sustains positive action. Placing the generation and application of knowledge at the centre of development activity makes it possible to study the practical implications of religious imagination and values, particularly the role that these factors play in fostering a unified approach toward effecting social change at the grassroots level.

That many technical development organizations now find themselves focusing on issues of beneficial collective action, social predispositions, and practices reveals the deep connection between the processes of technical and social capacity building. This suggests that meaningful social change results as much from the development of qualities and attitudes that foster collaborative forms of human interaction as from the resolution of specific problems or the acquisition of technical skills. It follows that a complex but vital set of questions concerning human purpose and motivation needs to be incorporated into development thinking.

Capacity-building processes are thus redefined to encompass an array of issues that extend beyond a basic materialistic conception of existence. This, in effect, is a strategy of moral empowerment, of cultivating the moral reconstruction of all human practices—a process that involves the remaking of individual behaviour and the reformulation of institutional structures. From this vantage point, capacity building entails the enabling of the *individual* to manifest innate powers in a creative and methodical way, the shaping of *institutions* to exercise authority so that these powers are channelled toward the upliftment of all members of society, and the development of the *community* so that it acts as a milieu conducive to the release of individual potential, the enrichment of knowledge, and unifying social exchange. The challenge to all three actors is to learn to use material resources and intellectual and spiritual endowments to enhance human well-being. In this respect, the Institute seeks to discern the complementary roles that science and religion—as co-evolving systems of knowledge and practice—must play in this process.[19]

In essence, development activity is concerned ultimately with both the transformation of individuals and the social structures that they create. Hence, to be effective, development work must directly address the inner life and character of human beings as well as the organization of society. Its purpose must be to catalyze a process of social change that engenders mutuality of purpose, compassion, rectitude of conduct, and justice—a transformation that permeates every facet of the relationships that govern human activity.

Development itself is need of new meaning.[20] A systemic betterment of people's lives cannot come about without a unifying vision of life and society. Such a vision must necessarily emanate from the deep-seated metaphysical understanding of the human condition held by a preponderance of the earth's population.[21] While science can offer the methods and tools for supporting social and economic development, it alone cannot set direction; the goal of development cannot come from within the process itself. It is therefore difficult to see how development theory and practice can undergo fundamental change unless the corresponding discourse admits a re-examination of the nature of the human being and the primary aims of social existence. It was this formidable but imperative task that the Institute and its many partners audaciously set out to pursue.

Evolution of the Science, Religion, and Development Discourse: India, Uganda, and Brazil

Beginning in 1999, the Institute launched a wide-ranging inquiry designed to delineate the many dimensions of an integrated pattern of human development. To this end, it has endeavoured to identify new concepts and models of social change, especially by apprehending the essential connections between the moral, spiritual, and material elements of individual and collective well-being. The vehicle for this exploration has been a discourse on science, religion, and development carried out with a spectrum of organizations and practitioners in Asia, Africa, and South America. The overall aim of the discourse has been to generate new perspectives and approaches that can constructively impact development practice and policy.

In India, Uganda, and Brazil, participants used the process to deeply read the complex realities of life in their particular contexts.[22] These participants were involved in virtually every domain of development activity and policy: the advancement of women, environmental preservation, participatory processes, appropriate technology, good governance, education, human rights, health and agricultural training, income generation, and rural development. This collection of development expertise served to nurture several unique and fruitful dialogues and had spillover effects into other national discourses concerning poverty alleviation, primary education, gender equality, public health, and human rights.

India

In early 1999, the Institute for Studies in Global Prosperity and the National Spiritual Assembly of the Bahá'ís of India concluded that it was timely to facilitate a fresh conversation about the development process.[23] With its rich and variegated spiritual traditions, its history as a testing ground for various development theories and programs, and seemingly intractable developmental challenges that continue to confound its intellectual and political leaders, India was a fitting venue for the initiation of a discourse on science, religion, and development. This led to a year-long consultative effort with development organizations and thinkers in many parts of India, eliciting their perspectives on the present state of the development enterprise and their views on the role of spiritual values and resources in bringing about holistic patterns of development. These conversations were facilitated by a concept paper prepared by the Institute, titled "Science, Religion and Development: Some Initial Considerations," which reviews the history of development policies and practice and inviting deeper consideration of how scientific methods and religious perception can work together in enhancing social prosperity.[24]

These preliminary exchanges shaped the emerging dialogue with the many thoughtful observations of the participants, which were incorporated into a document that was released prior to a colloquium held in November 2000 in New Delhi.[25] The document served as a basis for further consultations at the colloquium, particularly those related to the areas of education, economic activity and environmental stewardship, governance and human rights, and appropriate technology. In order to make these views accessible to a larger audience within and outside India, a video featuring a number of interviews and reflections was also prepared.[26] Among the attendees present at the colloquium were representatives of national and international development organizations, academic institutions, government agencies, and research and policy institutes. A message of welcome from Indian President K. R. Narayanan captured the deep-seated concerns of the many development practitioners and decision-makers who had come together to explore a new conceptual framework for promoting an honourable human prosperity: "In order to provide the much needed sanity and strength to our crisis-ridden existence, there is an imperative need to weave the developmental path with the ideals of our heritage and civilization and blend them with science."[27]

The consultative exercises held before the New Delhi gathering confirmed that there was much to be gained by seriously examining how the two knowledge systems of science and religion can work together in raising the capacity of individuals, communities, and institutions. Indeed, a collective verdict emerged: consequential, enduring social change can come only from achieving coherence between the spiritual and material aspects of life. More than five decades of development experience had convinced the diverse spectrum of participating organizations and practitioners that meaningful pathways of social progress cannot depend on political prescriptions or economic recipes alone. The critical process of building human capacity must be all-encompassing, including cultural, social, technical, ethical, and spiritual facets.

In this respect, the colloquium and the conversations leading up to that event were not concerned with religiosity of any particular kind or the relationship between science and religion per se. Rather, their central aim was to discover how the capacities of the human spirit and the tools of science could be harnessed simultaneously so as to allow the masses of humankind to become agents of their own change. Participants concurred that if individuals and communities were to become the principal actors in enhancing their physical and social well-being, they must be able to draw on spiritual tenets and belief systems to give vision and focus to their endeavours. Across cultures, spiritual ideals guide and anchor human behaviour.[28] As one contributor observed: "If the poor were as poor as we think them to be, they would have been dead long ago. The reason they survive is because they have many more resources than we think they have and it's not only material resources... it's the social resources, the cultural resources, their intellectual resources, and more than anything else, their spiritual resources."[29] A clear thesis emerged from the dialogue: if, in fact, a group or community is generating and applying knowledge—knowledge derived from both systematic inquiry and spiritual insights—it will be able to progressively develop the technical, moral, and social capacities that serve its real needs.

The deliberations of the attendees sought to elaborate the practical implications of this vision. The exchanges were wide-ranging, impassioned, and serious. The efforts of those present to understand how the human spirit can be tapped to ensure truly participatory and organic forms of development activity opened many doors. Several key principles and potential lines of inquiry were identified: the imperative of recognizing the web of interconnections among different development issues; the centrality of ethics to development work; the importance of creating systems of economic activity that are value-based, "people-centred," and ecologically sustainable; the need to acknowledge that development failures result as much from the lack of scientific attitudes and methods as from spiritual shortcomings; the necessity of overcoming fragmented approaches at all levels of public education and of developing an integrated set of human capabilities; the need for building partnerships among the many actors involved in the development arena; the benefits of investigating the shape and substance of moral education curricula and their means of implementation; the importance of instituting the equality of women and men in all domains of human activity; the need to raise up institutions of governance that elicit trust and are committed to the ideals of service to and empowerment of those that they represent; the necessity of safeguarding and encouraging acceptance of religious diversity; the indispensability of developing qualitative indicators that assess moral and spiritual variables in the areas of self-reliance, social cohesion, and community participation; the advantages of blending systems of indigenous knowledge and practice in agriculture with modern systems; and the benefits of setting in motion a process of learning about technology so that local communities can raise their capacity for making proper technological choices and can contribute to technological innovation. Lines of action for imparting further momentum to the new discourse also emerged and were summarized in the *Statement of Findings* that was adopted by the participants.[30]

A great majority of those who gathered in New Delhi were pleased to discover how deep the conversation about science, religion, and social development could be. As one attendee observed, "Many seeds were planted here. Now we must nurture them and see them grow."[31] Consistent with this vision, the colloquium itself was characterized by a spirit of openness, sincere reflection, and creative engagement. At the urging of the many organizations present, the National Spiritual Assembly of the Bahá'ís of India established a permanent "Secretariat for the Promotion of the Discourse on Science, Religion, and Development" in 2001. With its partners, the Secretariat co-sponsored several follow-up symposia, disseminating and amplifying concepts of the science, religion, and development discourse to an ever-widening network of development organizations, policy-makers, and academicians across India. This phase culminated in a seminar in 2004. The papers presented there—later compiled in a book—provide a glimpse of both how far the discourse had come and the distance that yet remained to be covered.[32]

The idea of a new model of development that reflected both scientific and religious understanding had been enthusiastically welcomed by many in the Indian development community. But there was also the need to enrich the discourse with a body of knowledge derived from the application of these principles. In 2007, the Institute decided to initiate an action research project to help development organizations articulate some of the primary challenges that arise in their day-to-day work as they strive to apply spiritual precepts and scientific approaches to their plans and programs. The focus was on building their capacity to reflect continuously on their initiatives through an analysis of the suppositions, methods, and values shaping development activity. Some of the issues explored included the balance required in struggling for social change while promoting patterns of cooperation, how to stimulate needed change simultaneously at the individual and social levels, the central role that knowledge plays in raising human capacity and the need for all members of a community to participate in the creation and use of knowledge, understanding the spiritual and material aspects of human motivation, and the appropriate role and uses of wealth and its relationship to honest work. The project was launched with a few organizations, including one that operates extensively at the village level.[33] It is anticipated that significant learning will emerge from the experiences of these organizations as they strive to further their understanding of specific spiritual principles and the implications of how these principles, in alliance with proper methodology, advance development work.

It can be seen from the experience in India that the evolving discourse on science, religion, and development is by its very nature a collective learning endeavour. The complex characteristics of development activity would certainly seem to warrant such an approach of learning through dialogue and reflection. Clearly, an enormous commitment is necessary if we are to move beyond approaches that emphasize narrow material or technical issues to initiatives that embrace truly integrated models of human development.

Uganda

In August 2001, on the occasion of the fiftieth anniversary of the establishment of the Bahá'í Faith in Uganda, the Ugandan president Yoweri Museveni sent a congratulatory message to the Ugandan Bahá'í community praising its valuable work in nurturing social unity and appealing to it to contribute further to the "nation-building" process by championing the equality of women and men, alleviating poverty, and overcoming entrenched patterns of corruption.[34] Partly in response to that call to action, the National Spiritual Assembly of the Bahá'ís of Uganda began collaborating with ISGP in 2002. This collaboration involved sharing with a diverse spectrum of organizations and individuals the Institute's concept paper, previously circulated among development practitioners in India. The elements of an alternative strategy of development drawing on both scientific methodology and spiritual understanding resonated deeply with many who attended related seminars. Among the participants were representatives of non-governmental organizations, religious organizations, academic institutions, the media, scientists, social activists, entrepreneurs, teachers, professors, students, government ministers, lawyers, farmers, village chiefs, and many others who were simply concerned about the future of their society.

For these and numerous other Ugandans, the ongoing failures of development activity reflected the limitations of a materialistic approach to understanding human yearning and collective purpose. In the rich dialogues that ensued, these participants affirmed that true development entailed advancing the intellectual and technological culture of peoples in consonance with their basic spiritual and moral values. A great number expressed the sentiment that this new conceptual framework for development was not idealistic but a real basis for bringing about a just and ethical transformation of Ugandan society.

In a series of events held in different regions of Uganda, discourse participants investigated a range of fundamental questions. Among them: How can participation in development projects be substantive and creative, allowing people the opportunity to gain knowledge and put it into practice? How can such participatory processes be motivated and guided by the application of spiritual principles? How must science and religion both be reconceived in order to support these processes? To achieve development activity that is sustainable, what is the nature of the balance required among technical solutions, social and political interventions, and spiritual factors? In trying to bring about such a balance, what is the interplay between the education and training of individuals, community empowerment, and institutional development? Is social welfare best attained through individual economic initiative and competition or mutual responsibility? Are there strategies of economic development that strengthen family and community structures and reflect moral and spiritual principles? What are the sources of community cohesion? How do patterns of cooperation emerge? How does a community effectively learn from its experiences? What types of institutional mechanisms foster such learning, whether technical or organizational? How can development workers take into account the technological logic and the knowledge base of the people with whom they work? What indicators—social, physical, economic, spiritual—should be adopted to measure effective community learning? What are the particular moral capacities most crucial for development programs to cultivate? How can moral capacity building and technical capacity building be effectively integrated? How does a community go about raising institutions of governance that are devoid of corruption, engender public trust, and strive to uplift all the citizens for which they are responsible? What types of educational curricula can encourage students to become positive social actors and lead lives of service and meaning?

Although the questions and ideas raised were challenging, a sense of optimism pervaded the many discussions, and an ethos of collaboration and collective learning was tangible. The conversations were marked by free exchange, the absence of any ulterior agendas, and a conviction that purposeful social change was an enterprise that can and must engage all members of society. The notion that indigenous knowledge and experience should be referenced in the design, planning, and implementation of development programs was a particular point of emphasis in all the exchanges.

In order to ensure that their deliberations were appropriately structured, participants in the discourse decided early on to focus their reflections on the themes addressed in the ISGP concept paper and to analyze them in the Ugandan context. To these four themes—education, economic activity and organization, appropriate technological use and development, and governance and justice—was added a fifth topic on health, culture, and environmental concerns. In order to benefit from the diverse experience and perspectives of those present, participants were divided into five working groups, with each group addressing a particular theme. The objective was to identify areas of needed research and ultimately to find ways to influence broader policies on these issues.

Over a several-year period, the working groups scrutinized a number of the assumptions underpinning development efforts—particularly in relation to certain initiatives such as the Ugandan government's Poverty Eradication Action Plan and its Universal Primary Education program. As the ideas they gleaned from discussion groups at the various national and regional seminars impacted their thinking, participants observed that earlier tendencies of "dichotomized thought" were being replaced, resulting in changes in their professional and personal lives. Many commented that the influence of the ideas from these discussions was noticeable in national policy discourses on various social themes with which they were associated, such as gender equality, moral education, public health, and the preservation of the environment. The new discourse on development had reshaped understanding concerning human nature and the purpose of social order.

Meanwhile, in 2006, a film entitled *Opening a Space: The Discourse on Science, Religion and Development in Uganda* was prepared that highlights the evolution of the discourse in the country.[35] The video captures the remarkable energy and commitment that motivated participants in the initiative. As they indicate in their comments, this earnestness flowed from the realization that civilization soars on two wings—human reason and rational faith—and that the building of human capacity cannot occur by relying on one wing alone. In short, a pathway out of the morass of current development policy and practice could be seen.

Over time, in addition to the theme-based reflections of the working groups, there came the awareness that the collective deliberations of the participants needed to be taken to a new level. Much more needed to be understood about how development programs that incorporate scientific methods and spiritual principles could be conceived and implemented. The participants in the discourse in Uganda found themselves in a position not unlike the one faced by their counterparts in India just before their endeavours entered a new phase with the launching of an action research effort among partner development organizations. As reflection and deliberation are sustained and learning accumulates, the science, religion, and development discourse will continue to evolve. As one participant observed, "All that we now need to do is persevere—persevere with the confidence that what we are doing is right."[36]

Brazil

In late 2001, when the Institute for Studies in Global Prosperity introduced the discourse on science, religion, and development to Brazil, there was little doubt about the relevance of the theme to the setting. In the vibrant diversity, creative energy, and passions of its people, dazzling future possibilities could be readily imagined, but only if the formidable challenges of gross economic inequality, marginalization of minority groups, and mismanagement of natural resources, among other issues, were directly confronted. The National Spiritual Assembly of the Bahá'ís of Brazil had for many years been directly involved in searching for solutions to these problems in collaboration with various coalitions of like-minded organizations. The introduction of the discourse on science, religion, and development afforded a natural opportunity to place many of Brazil's social dilemmas within a broader context of human capacity building and moral understanding.

This discourse on development was initiated in Brazil with the sharing of the Institute's concept paper and a complementary paper titled "Some Thoughts on the Future of Brazilian Society" prepared by FUNDAEC, one of the Institute's collaborators that has sought, for the past thirty years, to apply understanding from both science and religion to development processes in Colombia. In this paper, FUNDAEC offers some of its own insights for the consideration of Brazilian thinkers who are contributing in different ways to the advancement of their country.

The paper begins by making reference to the way FUNDAEC has conceived of its own efforts in terms of a dual responsibility—to strive to bring prosperity to the people of Colombia and to assist the Colombian people in making their contribution to the well-being of the global community. For Brazilian society to move toward the achievement of these two goals, according to FUNDAEC, its thought leaders and social actors will have to focus on building the capacities of the people of Brazil so that they can become the protagonists of their own emancipation and development. Based on its experience in Colombia, FUNDAEC states that such empowerment can be achieved only through the use of knowledge emanating from both science and religion. The paper then goes on to discuss some of the false conceptions that distort the way science, religion, and development are understood in contemporary social discourse. While providing a new understanding of each of these concepts, the paper makes a few practical proposals for transforming Brazilian society in specific areas such as education, family life, economic activity, and the use of technology.

Over the course of several seminars, the two papers were discussed by individuals representing various segments of the development field in Brazil. In the process, the need for a better understanding of science and religion, as two complementary sources of knowledge for development efforts, became clear to those who participated. A group that included policymakers, social activists, academicians, and development practitioners then undertook a more extensive analysis of the theme. Their discussions focused specifically on the implications of this new understanding for specific matters of concern to the Brazilian people, such as racism, the degradation of the environment, the huge disparities between the rich and the poor, the breakdown of social institutions, the gradual disappearance of traditional knowledge systems due to neglect, and the need to revamp the education system. The results of these deliberations were brought together in a series of papers that were eventually published in a book titled *Ciência, Religião e Desenvolvimento: Perspectivas Para o Brasil* (*Science, Religion and Development: Perspectives for Brazil*).

At the same time, in response to a specific suggestion set forth in FUNDAEC's paper, efforts were made with government leaders to establish institutions at the level of local communities called Centers of Learning, where the development capacity of the population of a given region could be built. These were envisaged as institutions that could become focal points of interaction among scientific and religious as well as modern and traditional sources of knowledge in the promotion of the culture and well-being of a locality. In recognition of the potential impact of such Centers of Learning, the government-supported Casa Brasil project emerged, which in its pilot implementation phase developed a leadership training program that directly drew on the principal concepts of the science, religion, and development discourse.[37]

While the discourse was being enriched by such concrete initiatives, the associated discussions and reflections continued to attract an ever-increasing number of people. Many participants started to use websites and blogs as the means for contributing their thoughts and reflections. Over time, the conversation extended beyond the domain of development as participants began to consider the implications of utilizing scientific and religious insights in areas such as governance, education, gender equality, and human rights. In the area of human rights, for example, civil society leaders and practitioners came together and created a Forum on Human Rights Education, where the subject was approached in the light of experience with the discourse on science, religion, and development. A tangible outcome of this effort was the preparation of pedagogical materials aimed at human rights activists throughout the country.

A dialogue informed by scientific and religious perspectives was of course not new to Brazil. Movements influenced by both the theology of liberation and the Freirean pedagogy of critical consciousness, the participants noted, have been relatively effective in their efforts to interpret the meaning of religious faith in the context of living in a world of oppression, war, poverty, and environmental degradation and seeking to change it with compassion, integrity, and courage. They have been partially successful in discovering the methods that allow individuals and groups to take effective action to transform their surroundings. Some participants, however, felt that even though these efforts have raised consciousness and provided a heartening testimony to the efficacy of insights gained from religious wellsprings in addressing social and economic problems, they have fallen short of providing the masses of Brazil with an appropriate scientific education—one that allows them to resist the forces of social disintegration, to progressively build strong communities, and to pave their own path of development. Many participants expressed their concern regarding the lack of skills in children and youth to analyze critically the enormous quantity of disjointed information to which they are exposed on a daily basis. Some also saw this as a sign of the inability of the larger population to analyze problems methodically; to make proper moral, economic, and technological decisions; and to take effective action to transform their social and physical environments. The route out of the current crisis, according to some of the participants, lies in making use of both scientific and religious resources in developing educational programs that build the ethical and intellectual capabilities of students to become agents of positive social change.

For a great number of the Brazilian participants, understanding what it means to advance a discourse on science, religion, and development was itself a learning process. How is a discourse promoted? How can change be effected in people's thoughts in a non-paternalistic manner? How can individuals and groups be assisted to resist the pervasive pressures of materialistic norms and assumptions and steadily work for the transformation of society? By engaging in the diverse activities involved in sharing concepts associated with the discourse, by pursuing some practical initiatives, and by interacting with an ever-growing cross section of people, participants came to appreciate some of the deeper dynamics underlying social change. Promoting change and going through the learning that it necessitates, as some participants stated, is a complex and difficult process. To set out on a new path requires courage—not an arrogant disposition that demands swift and radical action, but one that is tempered with humility and wisdom. It requires an environment where the dynamics of individual and collective transformation are fully considered; where it is realized that growth and change are organic, that they are gradual and slow, and that they involve constant action, evaluation, and study; and where it is understood that, in pursuing such transformation, one is faced with an ongoing tension between absorbing setbacks and gaining new ground.

Characteristics of the Science, Religion, and Development Discourse

A dedicated social space related to the theme of science, religion, and development has spurred a variety of participants in different parts of the world to engage in an exploration of the many forces that shape the realities and perspectives of individuals, communities, and social institutions. The social space itself served to foster an ethos of humble inquiry, define and reframe fundamental issues, and enrich the conceptual terrain of different development questions. The creation of this space was consequently a critical element in the success of the discourse, as existing development settings for the most part could not begin to locate any role, let alone a primary one, for religious perspectives. Many participants, whether practitioners or policy-makers, indicated that the substantive ideas and vision initially delineated by the ISGP drew them into the process. That this process was seen to be an open conversation facilitated by a religious community committed to reconciliation and mutual understanding among all sectors of society and to real learning about the sources and instruments of social empowerment gave further impetus to the overall initiative. The transparent nature of materials and events, including the active role of participants in shaping discussions, removed any concerns that the effort had hidden objectives. That the Bahá'í community had a demonstrated set of on-the-ground experiences in the development field based on the concepts central to the discourse reinforced the seriousness of the undertaking.

In each country, efforts were made to involve a wide variety of stakeholders in the new discourse—development organizations, citizens groups, practitioners, academics, policy-makers, and religious and community leaders. This approach was taken to ensure that diversity of perspective and richness of experience would illumine the discussions and also to express the very principle of universal participation that must in the end inform successful development endeavours. Indeed, Bahá'í facilitators made systematic efforts, through research and networking, to involve organizations and thinkers that might contribute to the discourse. This networking often continued with the partner organizations themselves. The initial interactions with potential participants often were characterized by surprise at the boldness and depth of the ideas presented and pleasure at the unpretentious and invitational spirit of the effort. It is interesting to note that while the discourse engaged some religious leaders, the great majority of the participants were development or related specialists who recognized the role of religious identity and values in effecting social change.

The distinguishing aspects of the discursive process itself involved raising questions, identifying the need for further knowledge generation, and rigorously appraising prevailing assumptions of development theory and practice. As was seen in India, Uganda, and Brazil, the value of focusing on specific topics such as public health or environmentally sustainable economic activity allowed for more concrete explorations of how religious perspectives, in conjunction with scientific understanding, could lead to new strategies. Another feature of discussions was a deliberate attempt to avoid reductionist thinking and instead to focus on the interconnectedness of social development issues. Whether in identifying connections between community prosperity and the treatment of women, or corruption and the ineffective performance of economic programs, or seeing conceptual links between the human rights and development agendas, the discussions placed emphasis on understanding the web of interrelationships impacting social well-being. Perhaps most important, the extensive use of consultative processes in capturing perceptions and aspirations of participants and in clarifying primary values and attitudes in relation to key problems served to reinforce the spirit of collaboration and solidarity that over time became a distinctive characteristic of the discourse. The participants appreciated that this reliance on generative, consultative methods must as well be a precondition for defining and evaluating actual development policy goals or programs of action. True social transformation can come about only through the creation of new social meanings and attitudes. In this regard, mechanisms of accessible, ongoing community dialogue can lead to innovative social directions and transform arrangements of power affecting community members.[38] The process of probing such social arrangements must also utilize the same discursive methods.

From the inception of the initiative, essential concepts were not presented in an arbitrary or theoretical fashion but were connected directly to practice. The insights that emerged either came from the broad empirical record of development programming or the specific learning of participants, including the Bahá'í community. After some years of the process advancing in India and Uganda, it became apparent there was a need to enhance the substance of the discourse with knowledge gained from the real application of spiritual principles. The action research projects undertaken with a few partners were designed to raise capacity for learning about the role of spiritual principles in development activity and to encourage constructive self-assessment by these organizations concerning the true efficacy of programs and projects. More generally, there exists an integral relationship between public discourse and social action. Participation in public discourse is closely related to real world experience: there is a "complementarity of 'being' and 'doing.'"[39] Discourses are not static because social conditions are not. They evolve and move forward, with different discourses influencing one another. Fundamental spiritual precepts remain the same, but efforts to apply them to social challenges take on new and dynamic forms.

Another facet of learning concerned the value of having a conceptual framework in order to advance the conversation. Such a framework ensures that dialogue, research, and action do not become disconnected and are coherent in overall purpose and approach. The framework that emerged in India, Uganda, and Brazil consisted of certain basic concepts, including the idea of the inherent nobility of human beings, the notion that the generation and application of knowledge is the primary process of social life, and the belief that the purpose of development itself is the raising of capacity among individuals, communities, and institutions. Other elements of the framework were refined over time, such as the methods and strategies used to amplify basic concepts or to generate new insights about development activity. In the end, reference to elements of this framework proved to be an effective way to prevent discussions and lines of inquiry from falling back into dominant modes of development thinking.

Challenges and Future Directions

Over time, efforts to expand and refine the discourse steadily became more systematic and benefited from deepened understanding and elaboration of the concepts central to the initiative. An early stumbling block for some participants was clarifying the role and meaning of religious insight and knowledge, particularly making a distinction between spirituality and religion. Given how vital shared social understandings and values are to human flourishing, it is evident that vague notions of spirituality, or even spiritual change at the individual level, will not be sufficient in bringing about needed changes in social processes and structures. Religion, as a collective expression of spiritual understanding and values and as a phenomenon associated with the emergence of civilizations, was the correct focus of analytic attention if a new discourse on social transformation was to be successful. From a practical perspective, the active expression of the spirituality of individuals and communities, and not their religious affiliation, is likely to be the relevant factor in successful development undertakings. Nevertheless, it is important to appreciate the religious sources of spiritual principles and perceptions. The proposition that religion is a system of knowledge is certainly challenging, but it moves public discussions about religion away from distortions of fundamental spiritual tenets, dogmatic doctrine, or obsession with sectarian identity, and instead brings focus to how the capacities and powers of the human spirit can be channelled to effect beneficial social change.[40] Religion is thus regarded as an evolutionary and civilizing phenomenon addressing knowledge at two principal levels: first, in providing insight concerning human purpose, provenance, and identity; and, second, in informing us as social beings about the essential parameters of social interaction and the very nature of the social order, particularly how it should be constructed to reflect principles of fairness, empathy, and cooperation.[41] It is this framing of religious knowledge that the discourse sought to relate to scientific knowledge and the development of society.

In all three countries where the discourse unfolded, the objective of generating new perspectives and approaches that could meaningfully affect development practice and policy was achieved to different degrees. In India, some of the many organizations that participated in various events were directly impacted by the insights and learning associated with the discourse.[42] Others, including some participants in Brazil and Uganda, were enabled by the discussions on science, religion, and development to make definitive contributions to related public policy debates and in some cases to policy implementation. It was the sense of numerous participants that the first phases of the discourse had opened the way to novel and transformative possibilities of human progress. But real transformation of any kind is the work of generations. New awareness and understanding first leads to new strategies for action, and then additional cycles of reflection, analysis, and action ensue. What is at issue is the raising up of the vital soft infrastructure of communities—an infrastructure created not by outside technical aid or bricks and mortar but by the forces of human motivation, spiritual values, and social unity. It may take years for the seeds of collaborative skill building and organizational capacity building, inspired by spiritual principles, to yield the fruit that could be recognized by current development evaluation criteria. Too often development metrics emphasize near-term technical results over long-term capacity-building and relationship-building processes.[43]

For this reason, the Bahá'í community remains committed to the main premise of the discourse on science, religion, and development—that the set of capacities necessary for building up the social, economic, and moral fabric of collective life is derived from an expanded notion of rationality that references both mind and spirit. By themselves, scientific methodologies will not tell us which ideas or norms best advance a specific social objective or competence. The knowledge, then, that is brought to bear in development work must be multidimensional, encompassing not only techniques, methodologies, theories, and models but also values, ideals, qualities, attributes, intuition, and spiritual discernment. Drawing on both science and religion allows us to satisfy these diverse knowledge requirements and to identify new moral standards and avenues of learning in addressing emerging contexts of social dilemma.

It is recognized that adjustments in implementation will enhance future phases of the discourse. Additional human resources to facilitate learning about the application of core concepts are undoubtedly necessary. This requires individuals who in some way have been associated with development initiatives inspired by spiritual perspectives or who have come to apprehend the potential of these concepts to bring about change across an array of issue areas. The raising up of such resources will also take time and effort and is a focus of current ISGP activity.

Finally, an extension of efforts to affect development policy at the regional, national, and international levels will require new approaches for engaging relevant thinkers and decision-makers. To a certain extent this will involve building a body of examples demonstrating the efficacy of joining scientific methods with religious values, of systematically looking at social problems through the lens of spiritual awareness while also implementing rigorous research strategies. It also will entail applying elements of the conceptual framework enumerated above to other important discourses of social concern.[44] The integration of efforts from all parts of the world will surely give rise to inspired coalitions of individuals and groups convinced that new horizons of peace and prosperity are within humanity's grasp.

That the discourse on science, religion, and development has garnered the enthusiastic participation of a diverse range of key stakeholders and development practitioners in different parts of the globe demonstrates that the civilization-building powers of religion cannot be discounted or minimized in the public sphere. Reframing the assumptions, approaches, and goals of development discourse ultimately reveals a path of social emancipation that expresses the innate, noble potential of the human spirit. Human happiness, security, and economic opportunity are not simple byproducts of material success. Rather, they emerge from a complex and dynamic interplay among the social, cultural, religious, and practical aspects of daily reality. Social development initiatives, therefore, will not lead to tangible and lasting improvements in physical well-being without internalizing those universal spiritual postulates that give direction and meaning to life. For the civilizing virtues of tolerance, compassion, trustworthiness, kindness, and willingness to sacrifice for the common good are not cultivated by the language of civil law or economics but rather by the language of the heart, the voice of conscience and moral responsibility. True prosperity requires both the "light" of spiritual perception and the "lamp" of reflective inquiry.

The persistence of widespread human deprivation and despair speaks to the shortcomings of prevailing social theories and policies. Clearly, new ideas and models are required. For Bahá'ís, a peaceful worldwide polity will emerge only when human relations and social arrangements are infused with spiritual intent, an intent inspired by an all-embracing equity, unconditional love, sound methodology, and a genuine concern for others. It is here where the ISGP, for more than fifteen years, has focused on learning how underlying conceptions and processes relating to social and economic advancement can be reconceived.

In defining such a new path of collective development, the challenge before humanity is to extend its thinking beyond a knowledge framework that is principally materialistic in character to one that examines the nature of human existence in its entirety. What is called for is a fresh exploration of the connections between the scientific and the religious endowments of human experience, between our faculties of reason and those inner predispositions of benevolence and beauty that inspire human beings to action. It is in this sense that a more expansive, holistic approach to human development is being pursued by Bahá'ís and like-minded partners.

Many involved in development work would concur that the source of energy, insight, and confidence that gives rise to individual and collective action, that awakens capacities for constructive change, that promotes community cohesion, and that provides a dynamic, self-sustaining sense of social purpose flows from the stirrings of the human spirit. But what is not clear for most is how the scientific and religious dimensions of human experience can substantively interact so as to transform individual behaviour and social structures. Determining how spiritual precepts and perspectives can be fully integrated into the theory, practice, and assessment of development is no easy task. Much research and learning lies ahead.

Notes

1 Attempts to bring together development and religious institutions to explore mutual objectives and concerns, such as the World Bank-sponsored World Faiths Development Dialogue from 1998–2005, principally served to create awareness of religion's potential role in development work, but it did not lead to meaningful programmatic innovation. Multilateral development agencies and some governments have certainly partnered with faith-based organizations in the delivery of various community services, especially in the public health area, but substantive and sustained collaboration where international development programs explicitly take account of religious perceptions and values in planning, implementation, and evaluation has not occurred.

2 The Institute formally began operating in 1999. To stimulate research and discourse on issues that are global in nature and relevant to the prosperity of humankind, the Institute pursues two interrelated lines of endeavour. First, it has sought to create spaces and cultivate networks in which scholars, policy-makers, and practitioners can reflect together about how the insights of science and religion can be brought to bear upon pressing global challenges, such as development, migration, urbanization, transitional justice, gender equality, and appropriate use of technology. Second, and as a complement to the former line of endeavour, the Institute is working to build capacity among a growing body of undergraduates, graduate students, and young professionals to draw upon scientific and religious knowledge in order to contribute to the advancement of prevalent lines of discourse, research, and practice. For more information, see http://globalprosperity.org.

3 These revolutions greatly raised agricultural and dairy productivity and certainly saved millions from starvation, but they were only partially successful, as overall trends of inequality continued to worsen, in some cases exacerbating patterns of migration from rural to urban areas. See Farzam Arbab, "Promoting a Discourse on Science, Religion and Development," in *The Lab, the Temple, and the Market: Reflections at the Intersection of Science, Religion and Development*, ed. Sharon Harper (Ottawa, ON: Kumarian Press, 2000), 177–205.

4 The efficacy of particular economic, educational, or health interventions in affecting individual and collective behaviour is increasingly assessed by the technique of randomized evaluation. This is a tool that under certain circumstances can inform understanding about human motivation, action, and interaction. See, for example, Abhijit V. Banerjee and Esther Duflo, *Poor Economics: A Radical Rethinking of the Way to Fight Global Poverty* (New York: PublicAffairs, 2011). Critics, though, argue that this technique of analyzing human behaviour suffers from numerous methodological limitations—for example, the effectiveness of specific development interventions will no doubt vary across geographic, cultural, and temporal contexts. Most of all, this analytical technique suffers from a conceptual weakness of promoting a fragmented and static understanding of social behaviour that can discount the role of local knowledge and values in bringing about desired social change.

5 Progress has occurred with respect to reductions in "extreme poverty" and in expanded access to education and basic health care. Still, hundreds of millions of the poorest and most vulnerable on the planet are being "left behind," while those who no longer endure "extreme poverty" continue to face daunting daily challenges. See the United Nations' The Millennium Development Goals Report 2015. It also should be noted that many analysts have criticized the international definition of extreme poverty (of $1.25/day in 2005 international prices) as an inadequate measure of the many dimensions of human deprivation and as too low for even basic human existence.

6 United Nations, "Rethinking Poverty: Report on the World Social Situation 2010," 2010, PDF, 2, http://www.un.org/esa/socdev/rwss/docs/2010/fullreport.pdf.
7 See the discussion in the Introduction by Geoffrey Cameron and Benjamin Schewel regarding the secularization thesis.
8 Gerrie ter Haar, *Religion and Development: Ways of Transforming the World* (New York: Columbia University Press, 2011), 5.
9 See Séverine Denuline and Carole Rakoki, "Revisiting Religion: Development Studies Thirty Years On," *Journal of World Development* 39, no. 1 (2011): 45–54.
10 "It may be argued that, since spiritual and moral issues have historically been bound up with contending theological doctrines which are not susceptible of objective proof, these issues lie outside the framework of the international community's development concerns. To accord them any significant role would be to open the door to precisely those dogmatic influences that have nurtured social conflict and blocked human progress.... To conclude, however, that the answer lies in discouraging the investigation of spiritual reality and ignoring the deepest roots of human motivation is a self-evident delusion." See the Bahá'í International Community, "The Prosperity of Humankind," 1995, www.bic.org/statements/prosperity-humankind.
11 Many elements of this conceptual framework had already been expressed by various Bahá'í-inspired development initiatives with the Office of Social and Economic Development at the Bahá'í World Centre and the Bahá'í International Community, distilling these concepts for the Bahá'í community and sharing them in international development forums. See, for example, the Bahá'í International Community's "For the Betterment of the World: The Worldwide Bahá'í Community's Approach to Social and Economic Development" and "The Prosperity of Humankind."
12 Arbab, introduction to *The Lab, the Temple, and the Market: Reflections at the Intersection of Science, Religion and Development*, ed. Sharon Harper (Ottawa, ON: Kumarian Press, 2000), 6.
13 The genesis of many of these ideas grew out of dialogue with partner organizations and the Bahá'í community's own modest experience in the development area. Over the course of many decades, the application of concepts, principles, and methods set out in the Faith's teachings to a diverse range of social situations has progressively clarified the Bahá'í community's understanding of the complexities of development processes and allowed it to offer its own perspectives to the unfolding international discourse on development. That involvement has provided a valuable opportunity to explore with others the contribution of religious insights to fundamental questions of development. See, for instance, the Bahá'í International Community's "Valuing Spirituality in Development" online at http://www.bic.org/statements/valuing-spirituality-development#fYZWC1vxZPL3ZwiG.97.
14 Universal House of Justice to the Bahá'ís of the World, October 20, 1983, http://

www.bahai.org/library/authoritative-texts/the-universal-house-of-justice/messages/#d=19831020_001&f=f1.

15 Among the world's religious systems, the Bahá'í Faith places a distinctive emphasis on the concept and implications of social "development." In a passage dated in the latter part of the nineteenth century, Bahá'u'lláh avers: "The progress of the world, the development of nations, the tranquillity of peoples, and the peace of all who dwell on earth are among the principles and ordinances of God." See Bahá'u'lláh, *Tablets of Bahá'u'lláh Revealed after the Kitáb-i-Aqdas* (Wilmette, IL: Bahá'í Publishing Trust, 1978), 129–30.

16 This approach shares some of the features of the "human capability" framework set forth by Amartya Sen, but while emphasizing the role of values in human development, Sen does not explicitly consider religious resources or dimensions. See Sen, *Development as Freedom* (New York: Anchor Books, 1999).

17 A process of capacity building in a community is likely more important than any specific project objective because the resulting robust mechanisms of empowerment facilitate new initiatives of greater complexity and impact.

18 Collaboration between religion and science in the development field can take many forms. One obvious example is in the area of moral education. Since moral behaviour is a concrete expression of humanity's spiritual nature, the formulation of educational theories and methods that systematically promote moral development is of particular importance. Learning to apply moral and spiritual concepts to achieve material progress could, in fact, be regarded as the essential prerequisite of all social and economic initiatives. See chapter 4 for an exploration of this point.

19 In its truest form, devoid of dogmatic accretions, religion has imparted spiritual and moral verities that in no way contradict the discovered truths of science. There is no substantive basis to the contention that an intrinsic incompatibility exists between science and religion. The process of scientific discovery itself involves human faculties such as imagination and intuition, in addition to reason, and cannot be regarded simply as a set of well-defined procedures. The historic dichotomy between reason and faith is a false dichotomy. They are complementary faculties of human nature that both engage in the process of discovering and understanding reality; they are both tools that enable society to apprehend truth. See chapter 5 for a detailed overview.

20 Haar, *Religion and Development*, 24.

21 A recent worldwide demographic study carried out by the Pew Research Center's Forum on Religion & Public Life estimated that 84 percent of the world's population identifies with a particular system of religious belief. See Pew Research Center, "The Global Religious Landscape," *Pew Research Center*, article published on December 18, 2012, http://www.pewforum.org/2012/12/18/global-religious-landscape-exec/.

22 Related events exploring the theme of science, religion, and development were also held in Malaysia, Mongolia, and Macau.
23 The National Spiritual Assembly is the democratically elected governing council of the Bahá'ís of India. Among its many responsibilities are the oversight of numerous educational and social development initiatives and the engagement with other social actors and organizations promoting social well-being.
24 The Institute's concept paper, titled "Science, Religion and Development: Some Initial Considerations," simultaneously offered a critique of prevailing development strategy and brought to the fore the potential role of religious insight and norms in effecting positive social change. See globalprosperity.org/library.
25 The document summarized some of the principal issues raised in interviews and submitted papers concerning how development goals and methodology could be constructively reconceived.
26 The video is entitled *Reflections at the Nexus: Science, Religion and Development* and has been shown in several countries around the globe. It can viewed online at http://goo.gl/mmo0VT.
27 K. R. Narayanan quoted in "In New Delhi, a Search for the Missing Ingredient in International Development," *One Country* 12, no. 3 (2000), http://www.onecountry.org/story/new-delhi-search-missing-ingredient-international-development.
28 The challenge for those involved in development is not to prove or disprove the validity of religious beliefs but to harness and integrate their salutary aspects into program planning and evaluation.
29 *Reflections at the Nexus*, op. cit.
30 The document provided a valuable snapshot of the rich array of ideas, concepts, and concrete suggestions put forward during the event and was sent to all members of the Indian Parliament.
31 Personal communication between colloquium participant and author.
32 See Amitabh Kundu and Mariam Tai, eds., *Science, Religion and Development: Advancing the Discourse* (New York: Institute for Studies in Global Prosperity, 2006). Papers in the volume covered topics including education, good governance, ethics and development, traditional agriculture, and the limitations of dominant development models.
33 The learning and insights from one of these valuable exercises was summarized and published in 2010: "May Knowledge Grow in Our Hearts: Applying Spiritual Principles to Development Practice—The Case of Seva Mandir." The document discusses the meaning and implications of working for the "common good," a goal that is present in Seva Mandir programs addressing natural resource management, health, gender equality, education, and participatory decision-making affecting several hundred thousand people. See globalprosperity.org/library.

34 "Bahá'í Community of Uganda Celebrates Its 50th Anniversary," *Bahá'í World News Service*, last modified August 5, 2001, http://news.bahai.org/story/135/.
35 Online at http://goo.gl/h4VOp4.
36 Ibid.
37 Although intended to reach ninety centres around the country, the training program primarily was implemented in the state of Bahia. Due to changes in the federal government's structure in 2005, the program lost its initial momentum and eventually was discontinued in 2007, but it yielded valuable learning in how discourse concepts could be expressed at the program and policy level.
38 Transforming arrangements of power is intimately tied up with social identity and the primary values of a community. These factors directly affect, for example, local governance structures, the station and role of women, attitudes toward education, and the allocation of community resources. Individual and collective behaviour naturally changes, and in a beneficial way, when attitudes and values become clear through community consultation. Some of the more dramatic development successes in recent years—for example, the management of local environmental resources or the elimination of practices adversely affecting young women and girls—have involved the reaffirmation or redefinition of basic social norms through community dialogue. A growing body of research indicates that social capital builds up as a result of discursive or consultative processes in which stakeholders in a given context continually work to elaborate a common understanding of collective objectives.
39 Universal House of Justice to the Conference of the Continental Boards of Counsellors, December 28, 2010, http://www.bahai.org/library/authoritative-texts/the-universal-house-of-justice/messages/#d=20101228_001&f=f1.
40 It is appreciated that if religion is to be the partner of science in the development arena, its specific contributions must be carefully scrutinized. It is unfortunately the case that established religion is often burdened by doctrines and practices that militate against efforts to improve material conditions. Sectarian distortions that encourage passivity, acceptance of poverty, social exclusion, or inequality between the sexes must be weighed against more universal spiritual concepts that emphasize the centrality of justice and the inherent dignity of all human beings. Thus, a new approach to development must also seek to identify traditions of paternalism and other patterns of behaviour that serve to undermine development initiatives.
41 In affirming the profound connection between the material and spiritual dimensions of life, 'Abdu'l-Bahá, the head of the Bahá'í Faith from 1892 to 1921, insisted that religion "must be living, vitalized, moving and progressive." See 'Abdu'l-Bahá, *The Promulgation of Universal Peace*, 2nd ed. (Wilmette, IL: Bahá'í Publishing Trust, 1982). As an essential "expression"

of "reality," religion is not to be dismissed as an atavistic phenomenon irrelevant to the processes of social advancement. Rather, it is a primary force shaping human consciousness, ensuring that humanity's distinctive potentialities, particularly its rational powers, are constructively channelled. It is unsurprising, then, that from the inception of the Bahá'í community, its aims and actions have been informed by an overarching vision of spiritual and social transformation—"to revive the world, to ennoble its life, and regenerate its peoples." See Bahá'u'lláh, *Gleanings from the Writings of Bahá'u'lláh* (Wilmette, IL: Bahá'í Publishing Trust, 1990), 271.

42 Apart from those organizations involved in action research projects relating to the discourse, there were corollary projects. For example, the National Dairy Development Board in India, an organization that has empowered millions of small farmers through village dairy cooperatives, asked the ISGP to provide training to its managers in the areas of consultation and ethical decision-making. It was also significant that a government agency, the National Center for Educational Research and Training (NCERT), was an active participant in the discourse, and as a result of this engagement formally invited the National Assembly of the Bahá'ís of India to become a resource in teacher training programs in the area of values education. Over a several-year period, the National Assembly contributed substantive recommendations to NCERT regarding curricula and training that foster moral development.

43 Identifying appropriate or efficacious policy interventions that can be broadly applied, while important, is not enough; rather, advancing understanding on how local communities everywhere can devise and refine development approaches that continually raise social, technical, and ethical capacity is the more critical issue.

44 Substantive inquiries into the topics of good governance, economic activity, gender equality, appropriate use of technology, and migration have been undertaken by the ISGP in the past few years and are expected to involve a growing number of contributors. Some initial reflections on some of these topics can be found at http://www.globalprosperity.org/library.

Bibliography

'Abdu'l-Bahá. *The Promulgation of Universal Peace*. 2nd ed. Wilmette, IL: Bahá'í Publishing Trust, 1982.

Arbab, Farzam. Introduction to *The Lab, the Temple, and the Market: Reflections at the Intersection of Science, Religion and Development*, edited by Sharon Harper, 1–6. Ottawa, ON: Kumarian Press, 2000.

———. "Promoting a Discourse on Science, Religion and Development." In *The Lab, the Temple, and the Market: Reflections at the Intersection of Science, Religion and Development*, edited by Sharon Harper, 177–205. Ottawa, ON: Kumarian Press, 2000.

"Bahá'í Community of Uganda Celebrates Its 50th Anniversary." *Bahá'í World News Service.* Last modified August 5, 2001. http://news.bahai.org/story/135/.

Bahá'í International Community. "For the Betterment of the World: The Worldwide Bahá'í Community's Approach to Social and Economic Development." 2003/2008. http://bahai-library.com/osed_betterment_world.

———. "The Prosperity of Humankind." 1995. http://www.bic.org/statements/prosperity-humankind#RZ2UzgYfM4xdTMew.97.

———. "Religious Values and the Measurement of Poverty and Prosperity." http://www.bic.org/statements/religious-values-and-measurement-poverty-and-prosperity#Byec0v6AquZcFLPc.97.

———. "Valuing Spirituality in Development." http://www.bic.org/statements/valuing-spirituality-development#fYZWC1vxZPL3ZwiG.97.

Bahá'u'lláh. *Gleanings from the Writings of Bahá'u'lláh.* Wilmette, IL: Bahá'í Publishing Trust, 1990.

———. *Tablets of Bahá'u'lláh Revealed after the Kitáb-i-Aqdas.* Wilmette, IL: Bahá'í Publishing Trust, 1978.

Banerjee, Abhijit V., and Esther Duflo. *Poor Economics: A Radical Rethinking of the Way to Fight Global Poverty.* New York: PublicAffairs, 2011.

Denuline, Séverine, and Carole Rakoki. "Revisiting Religion: Development Studies Thirty Years On." *Journal of World Development* 39, no. 1 (2001): 45–54.

Haar, Gerrie ter. *Religion and Development: Ways of Transforming the World.* New York: Columbia University Press, 2011.

"In New Delhi, a Search for the Missing Ingredient in International Development." *One Country* 12, no. 3 (2000), http://www.onecountry.org/story/new-delhi-search-missing-ingredient-international-development.

Kundu, Amitabh, and Mariam Tai, eds. *Science, Religion and Development: Advancing the Discourse.* New York: Institute for Studies in Global Prosperity, 2006.

Pew Research Center, "The Global Religious Landscape." *Pew Research Center.* Article published on December 18, 2012. http://www.pewforum.org/2012/12/18/global-religious-landscape-exec/.

Sen, Amartya. *Development as Freedom.* New York: Anchor Books, 1999.

United Nations. The Millennium Development Goals Report 2015. PDF, http://www.un.org/millenniumgoals/2015_MDG_Report/pdf/MDG%202015%20rev%20(July%201).pdf.

———. "Rethinking Poverty: Report on the World Social Situation 2010." PDF, http://www.un.org/esa/socdev/rwss/docs/2010/fullreport.pdf.

Universal House of Justice. Universal House of Justice to the Bahá'ís of the World, October 20, 1983. http://www.bahai.org/library/authoritative-texts/the-universal-house-of-justice/messages/#d=19831020_001&f=f1.

———. Universal House of Justice to the Conference of the Continental Boards of Counsellors, December 28, 2010. http://www.bahai.org/library/authoritative-texts/the-universal-house-of-justice/messages/#d=20101228_001&f=f1.

CHAPTER EIGHT

A NEW POLITICS OF ENGAGEMENT: THE BAHÁ'Í INTERNATIONAL COMMUNITY, THE UNITED NATIONS, AND GENDER EQUALITY

JULIA BERGER

The Bahá'í International Community's (BIC's) United Nations Office is the official presence of the worldwide Bahá'í community at the United Nations. Over the course of its seventy-year engagement with this intergovernmental organization, the office has become a respected and valued member of the civil society community, engaging on issues such as gender equality, human rights, sustainable development, peace, and the elimination of racism, to name a few. The formal relationship of this religious community with the United Nations is part of a broader phenomenon of a growing and increasingly visible participation of religious actors in international affairs. This chapter examines the BIC's contributions to the international discourse on gender equality. Specifically, it considers how the principles and vision of the Bahá'í community have found expression in the substance of the community's contributions and the approach it has taken in its engagement with the United Nations.

The Gender Equality Discourse and the United Nations
Over the past seventy years, the United Nations has played a vital role in catalyzing and facilitating an international discourse on the equality between women and men. The conceptual foundations for the United Nation's work in this area are rooted in the UN Charter, which reaffirms "faith in fundamental human rights, in the dignity of the human person, in the equal rights of men and women and of Nations large and small."[1] In June 1946, the United Nations created the Commission on the Status of Women with

a mandate to "prepare recommendations and reports to the Economic and Social Council on promoting women's rights in political, economic, civil, social and educational fields" and to make recommendations "on urgent problems requiring immediate attention in the field of women's rights."[2] One of the commission's first tasks was to contribute to the drafting of the Universal Declaration of Human Rights, which resulted in the inclusion of gender-sensitive language. Over the course of the twenty-year period from 1975–1995, which witnessed four UN world conferences on women, the women's movement gained tremendous momentum and increased its capacity to organize, share knowledge, and sustain growing levels of cooperation. The Declaration of the Elimination of All Forms of Discrimination Against Women and its successor, the convention bearing the same name (CEDAW), were hard-won normative and legal milestones for efforts to advance gender equality.

An Oppositional Dynamic

The advancement of the women's movement has often been characterized by ongoing struggles among opposing parties to secure a greater share of power and resources. The norms of conflict and competition that drive and shape our political, legal, economic, and educational systems have given rise to oppositional modes of pursuing justice, even as they have spawned infinite variations of the "other" against which groups can unite.[3]

Few issues at the United Nations have given rise to more polarizing and contentious debates than the issue of gender equality—in particular, issues related to the family, sexual health, and reproductive rights. Fissures became apparent at the UN conferences of the 1990s. At the 1994 International Conference on Population and Development (ICPD) in Cairo, Egypt, informal alliances between the Holy See and Islamic countries threatened to bring the conference to a halt by objecting to proposed language regarding reproductive rights.[4] "People of [religious] conviction shocked each other and a watching world as they clashed over some of the most volatile topics of the day: family planning and the nature of the family; the rights of women; gender and sexuality; and abortion and birth control."[5] Azza Karam notes that whenever issues such as abortion or homosexuality have been discussed at the United Nations, "conservative alliances have sprung up, cutting bizarrely across denominations and faiths."[6] The divisions are not what one may expect: they are not necessarily dependent on faith (e.g., Muslim vs. Christian, Christian vs. Buddhist), nor do they fall uniformly along national lines. Rather, Karam notes, they are intra-faith and often domestic.[7]

Many criticisms have been leveled against the famously polarized discourses of the 1994 ICPD conference and the disproportionate time and energy that many felt was devoted to reproductive rights at the expense of macro-economic and social issues. At the same time, equally important and constructive realities must be acknowledged: women had gained more professional experience since the 1970s in terms of organizing and advocacy. It was at the 1994 conference that the feminist discourse was prominent for the first time on an international stage.[8] An unprecedented number of civil society organizations had joined in the discussions, shifting the discourse from one focused on population control to one concerned with the empowerment of women.[9]

Over the past several decades, the rising prominence of religious actors and movements has brought new voices to the debate about the rights of women and their role in society. What was once seen as a discourse of "secular" feminists advocating for the emancipation of women from "pre-modern" conceptions of gender has become more complex, with a growing diversity of voices rooted in various ethical frameworks and notions of progress and emancipation. Much of the discourse on gender equality is characterized by frameworks that reinforce a binary view of reality—such as secular vs. religious, modern vs. traditional, conservative vs. liberal, Western vs. non-Western, north vs. south, and the like.[10] The overarching presumption has been that of religion as an anti-modern, anti-secular, or anti-democratic voice in the gender equality discourse and in society in general.[11]

A common presumption among gender equality advocates is that religious practices and related cultural norms are opposed to gender equality and human rights. An example of this challenge is the slate of reservations by member states to the Convention on the Elimination of All Forms of Discrimination Against Women (CEDAW). CEDAW has been described as an international bill of rights for women and is ratified by 186 Member States.[12] However, it has been challenged by over twenty countries seeking exemptions from its legal obligations on the grounds that these violate their religious practices and norms.[13] Similarly, the failure of the 47th Session of the UN Commission on the Status of Women in 2003 to reach agreed conclusions on the issue of violence against women brought to light the tensions in the discourse on gender equality among member states. Iran refused to accept language condemning "violence against women" and refraining "from invoking any custom, tradition or religious consideration to avoid their obligations with respect to its elimination as set on in the Declaration on the Elimination of Violence Against Women."[14] Challenges such as these have contributed to a highly polarized discourse plagued by the perception of "incompatibilities between democracy, human rights and gender equality, on the one hand, and a world in which religious issues and organizations have an active presence in public affairs, on the other."[15]

Fuelling these tensions is some member states' suspicion of and resentment toward the human rights framework as an expression of Western cultural and ideological dominance. Member state representatives put forward arguments about the need to respect the diversity, tradition, and culture of all member states. These are rebutted by others who affirm the universality of the Universal Declaration of Human Rights, both in content and in the cultural diversity of intellectual contributions that lead to its creation.[16] The United Nations has unequivocally stated that "while the significance of national and regional particularities and various historical, cultural and religious backgrounds must be borne in mind, it is the duty of States, regardless of their political, economic and cultural systems, to promote and protect all human rights and fundamental freedoms."[17]

A number of UN agencies and civil society initiatives have begun to bridge the religious-secular divide in creative and practical ways. Among the leading voices is the UN Population Fund (UNFPA), which was the first UN agency to develop formal guidelines for partnering with faith-based organizations, having recognized their strategic importance to UNFPA's mandate in the area of population and development.[18] An Inter-Agency Task Force of Engaging with Faith-Based Organizations for Sustainable Development was created as a mechanism to facilitate the exchange of knowledge and experience in the field of collaboration between the UN and Faith-based organizations.[19] In addition, UNFPA, UNICEF, and the Joint UN Programme on HIV/AIDS (UNAIDS) are also part of the steering group of the Joint Learning Initiative on Faith and Local Communities, which brings together UN agencies, non-governmental organizations (NGOs), and representatives of both academia and the private sector to "build collective understanding of the potential of local faith communities for improving community health and well-being."[20] The creation of mechanisms and spaces for knowledge sharing and deepening understanding, taken together, point to a recognition of the relevance of the contributions of religious communities and a willingness on the part of the United Nations (as well as other actors) to explore approaches to development outside of a secular framework.

Patriarchal Structures and Processes
Despite the major advances in areas of international law, public policy, and public discourse, the United Nations remains a patriarchal institution. Patriarchy manifests itself in relationships and structures that legitimize unequal power relations among men and women. It is reflected in the structures of organizations, in the membership and processes of decision-making

bodies, in the allocation of resources, among other dynamics. A milestone for the United Nation's work in gender equality came in July 2010, when the UN General Assembly created UN Women—the UN Entity for Gender Equality and the Empowerment of Women. Prior to this, the work of gender equality was carried out by four disparate and underfunded entities: the Office of the Special Adviser on Gender Issues and Advancement of Women, the Division for the Advancement of Women, the United Nations Development Fund for Women, and the International Research and Training Institute for the Advancement of Women. Until the creation of UN Women and the appointment of an Under-Secretary General as its head, the issue of gender equality was not represented at the highest levels of UN decision-making.[21] It was only ten years ago that a major outcome document on UN reform made passing references to gender equality and made no mention to improvements to the United Nation's gender "machinery." Of the fifteen members of the Secretary-General's High-Level Panel on System-Wide Coherence, three were women. The disappointment and "outrage" expressed by NGOs in response to this report crystallized into the Gender Equality Architecture Reform (GEAR) Campaign, which successfully lobbied for the creation of UN Women.[22] Today, many High-Level Panels are still organized with few women among their members.[23]

In 1995, member states committed to "tak[ing] all necessary measures to terminate all forms of discrimination against women and girls," but this has yet to come to pass.[24] Patriarchal ideology also manifested itself in the image of the woman that emerged from the gender and development discourse from the UN conferences of the 1990s. Wendy Harcourt describes this image as one of a "colonized, poor and marginalized woman who needed to be managed, educated, trained for work and local decision-making, and controlled reproductively and sexually through multiple series of development processes designed for 'women's empowerment.'"[25] Although references in UN documents to women as actors have increased, women continue to be defined primarily by their capacity as caretakers, caregivers, and providers. "Agency is still mainly masculine," writes Nadine Puechguirbal in her analysis of UN Resolution 1325 on "Women, Peace and Security," noting the "deeply ingrained ... essentialist representation of women as helpless victims" in many UN documents.[26]

One can point to positive developments in the existence and operation (albeit underfunded) of UN Women, in the increased prominence of gender equality in the UN discourse on development, and in the heightened attention to the presence of women on decision-making bodies.[27] Interestingly, Puechguiral notes that:

It is not men-on-top that makes something patriarchal. It's men who are recognized and claim a certain form of masculinity, for the sake of being more valued, more "serious," and the "protector of/and controllers of those people who are less masculine" that makes any organization, any community, any society patriarchal.[28]

In sum, we can see that the United Nations has been a key actor in the international community's efforts to advance and progressively realize the ideal of gender equality. At the same time, however, the gender equality discourse has been plagued by an oppositional, often polarizing, dynamic characterized by rigid binaries. These binaries have obscured the complex identities and points of view that are seeking expression in this discourse. In addition, the enduring patriarchal structures and processes have contributed to an organizational and intellectual environment that has hindered the evolution of the discourse and the implementation of international agreements in this field.

The BIC's Engagement in the Gender Equality Discourse at the United Nations

A distinctive element of the BIC's efforts to advance the equality of women and men is the understanding that social change must be a unifying process, one that engages the partnership of both men and women. The Bahá'í writings state that the "well-being of mankind, its peace and security are unattainable unless and until its unity is firmly established."[29] It is in this light that the contributions of the BIC must be examined and understood.

Building Unity and Solidarity: Non-partisanship and the Practice of Consultation

In its engagement with the United Nations, the BIC has demonstrated an approach characterized by a focus on coherence between the means and ends of social transformation. As the goal of the worldwide Bahá'í community, and by extension the BIC, is to contribute to the process of establishing a unified and equitable world order, the methods employed are intended reflect these characteristics as well. The following dimensions of the Bahá'í engagement are noteworthy: adherence to the principle of non-involvement in politics, the practice of consultation, and the concept of contributing to the discourses of society. The Universal House of Justice underlines the significance and purpose of approaches that enable the Bahá'í community, "in a world where nations and tribes are pitted one against the other and people are divided and separated by social structures, to maintain its cohesion and integrity as a global entity."[30] The Universal House of Justice writes, "It is not possible to build enduring unity through endeavours that require contention or assume that an inherent conflict of interests underlies all human interactions, however subtly."[31]

This poses a challenge to many advocates for gender equality. While the women's movement brought together and empowered increasingly diverse women to advocate for gender equality, it has also struggled against the forces of fragmentation and polarization.[32] This struggle to build and maintain unity, has, according to Devaki Jain, prevented the women's movement from reaching the next stage of development. Jain notes that the emphasis on differences of location, race, class, sexuality, religion—at the expense of commonalities—has suffocated aspirations toward unity, labelling them as untenable or simply unwanted. Yet the challenge exists on another level as well, namely in the overriding paradigm of society as a contest of power between opposing parties. Jain notes that the efforts of the women's movement to become a unified political force has blocked women's capability "to strike back at the empire...the multifaceted empire that includes other dominations within the meta-domination of economic models and forces."[33] The norms of conflict and competition that drive and shape our political, legal, economic, and educational systems have given rise to "us vs. them" modes of pursuing justice, even as they have spawned infinite variations of the "other" against which groups can unite.[34]

The manner in which the BIC has sought to pursue gender equality challenges the utility of the concept of the "other." The relationship between the BIC and the United Nations offers a new perspective on the manner in which gender equality is pursued at the international level. The relationship is rooted in the Bahá'í principle of "non-involvement in politics," a principle that proscribes involvement in partisan political activity. This approach is not intended as a means of objecting to politics writ large. Bahá'ís view government as "a system for maintaining the welfare and orderly progress of a society" and endeavour to be obedient to the laws of the country in which they reside.[35] Rather, the avoidance of engagement in partisan politics protects the Bahá'í community from the structural and ideological divisions and the culture of contest that are coded into the DNA of multi-party political systems.[36]

Despite the limitations associated with adherence to this principle, the BIC has not experienced a shortage of opportunities for full engagement and collaboration in the area of gender equality. Quite the opposite—adherence to this principle has enabled the BIC to make an important contribution in settings challenged by the forces of polarization and fragmentation. An independent research report studying the presence of religion at the United Nations noted that interviewees (members of the

UN community) identified Bahá'ís, along with Quakers, as "key religious actors" at the UN.[37] The report suggests that both organizations are held in "high regard in UN circles" for seeking to build consensus on issues by engaging all concerned parties.[38] "Perhaps most important," it explains, "both operate as facilitators rather than partisan advocates."[39]

In addition to the exhortation to avoid partisan politics in any form, Bahá'ís are guided by their scriptures to adopt the practice of "consultation" in all instances of collective deliberation and decision-making. Michael Karlberg discusses this in detail in chapter 2, as does Shahriar Razavi in chapter 6, in the context of his historical and conceptual overview of Bahá'í participation in the public sphere. Briefly stated, consultation is an approach to collective deliberation that seeks to be unifying rather than divisive. This unity is rooted not in uniformity or conformity but emerges from a commitment to a series of principles that give rise to the effective functioning of the group as a unified entity with its respective interests and goals. Participants engaged in consultation express their ideas freely and constructively; diverse perspectives are solicited to inform and enrich the consultation. Once individual ideas have been expressed, they become the collective resources of the group, who can choose to adopt, modify, or abandon them as needed. The Bahá'í writings further underscore the importance of consultation to the achievement of the social good, stating that, "No man can attain his true station except through his justice. No power can exist except through unity. No welfare and no well-being can be attained except through consultation."[40]

As Karlberg and Razavi note, the consultative approach presents a sharp contrast to the adversarial methods of debate, partisanship, and protest that have become a prevailing feature of contemporary society. Such adversarial methods find expression in the culture of UN deliberations, which are often characterized by entrenched positions, a tendency to dichotomize complex realities, an emphasis on technique over substance, and a predominance of statement-making over meaningful deliberation. The process of consultation tries to shift deliberation away from competing claims and interests to a focus on principle, giving rise to an environment in which collective goals and courses of action are more likely to surface and prevail.

Opportunities for the BIC to apply these principles have been manifold, particularly in its capacity as a facilitator, in executive positions on NGO committees, and as a neutral voice in politically charged environments. For many years, BIC representatives have held executive positions on the NGO Committee on the Status of Women—the largest NGO committee at the United Nations.[41] As chair of the NGO Committee of the Status of Women (1991–1995), BIC Representative Mary Power was a member of the Global Forum Facilitating Committee for Beijing (1992–1995), which organized the (then) largest ever gathering of NGOs. In her report of the conference and the processes leading up to it, Power describes the challenges of seeking to remain neutral and principled when discussions became politicized, when "extreme" and "radicalized" voices dominated, or when tensions rose between NGOs and the organizers of the conference.[42] A further example of this approach can be seen in the BIC's role on the facilitation committee of the Gender Equality Architecture Reform Campaign (2006–2010), which mobilized over three hundred NGOs—both secular and religious—to join together to advocate for the creation of UN Women.[43] Seen as a trusted and non-partisan advocate, the BIC thus has frequently found itself invited to serve, often in partnership with other civil society organizations, as a facilitator and organizer, bringing together organizations and individuals to articulate a common vision and to work constructively toward this end.

The opportunity for the BIC to contribute to building unity and solidarity has also been present in the discourse on sexual and reproductive health. This has been a particularly contentious discourse at the UN, characterized by adversarialism and ideological gridlock.

There is a strong perception among some at the United Nations that this contentiousness is an unavoidable feature of the engagement of faith-based organizations with the topic of gender equality. As the United Nations Research Institute for Social Development (UNRISD) notes, "conservative religious actors see religious moral principles as timeless and non-negotiable, while feminists and other human rights advocates argue for pluralist and rights-based alternatives."[44] A further reflection comes from a BIC youth delegate to the 45th Session of the Commission on Population and Development (2012), which focused on "Adolescents and Youth." Recognizing the challenges of representing a religious organization in a setting where religion is often viewed in opposition to "progress" and human rights, the delegate notes

> the importance of the [BIC] being present within this space as a moderate and informed religious group. Through doing so, we have the opportunity to humbly demonstrate that religion far from being a source of guidance only for the past has a critical role to play in addressing current issues. The most outspoken religious voices at the [commission] currently express extreme perspectives ... and this gives a highly negative view of religion. As Bahá'ís, although we did not enter into the "core discussions" this year (due to apprehension

about being labeled on one side of the debate or the other), we have an important role to play in articulating perspectives that are both ethically based and practically sound.⁴⁵

A further role played by the BIC is that of host, as it not only brings together people to discuss issues of common concern, but it offers its office space to other organizations so that such interactions can take place. Given the shortage of space that resulted from the multi-year renovations of the UN Headquarters and the increasingly restricted access to UN premises for NGOs, the availability of a large meeting space in very close proximity to the UN Headquarters has been of significant assistance to the UN community. From 2000 to 2015, the number of people attending meetings at the BIC has continued to rise; over six thousand people attended meetings at the BIC in 2015. The BIC receives no external funding; the cost of maintaining the large office space is borne exclusively by the worldwide Bahá'í community.

An Orientation toward Discourse
In 2010, in its annual message to the Bahá'ís of the world, the Universal House of Justice introduced Bahá'ís to the concept of "participation in the discourses of society."⁴⁶ It asked the worldwide Bahá'í community to reflect on the nature of its contributions to the material and spiritual progress of society. "In this respect," the House of Justice stated, "it will prove fruitful to think in terms of two interconnected, mutually reinforcing areas of activity: involvement in social action and participation in the prevalent discourses of society."⁴⁷ The Universal House of Justice was not suggesting that the Bahá'í community had not been part of public discourse on various issues and should now begin to engage in them. To the extent that individuals or entire communities are engaged in exchanging experiences, ideas, and perspectives with other individuals and communities, they are part of an ongoing, continually unfolding discourse. The call from the Universal House of Justice was for a reconceptualization of the "nature of contributions" that the Bahá'í community was making to the betterment of the world and an understanding of the protagonists who are helping to establish the new social order. "Indeed," wrote the Universal House of Justice, "the civilization that beckons humanity will not be attained through the efforts of the Bahá'í community alone. Numerous groups and organizations, animated by the spirit of world solidarity . . . will contribute to the civilization destined to emerge out of the welter and chaos of present-day society."⁴⁸

This had a profound effect on the way that the BIC conceived of its role and its methods for engaging with the United Nations. Rather than seeing its role in terms of articulating and sharing a Bahá'í position or perspective on a particular issue, the BIC began to view the United Nations as an arena of discourse, one shaped by many political and economic forces and one that in turn shapes the thinking of those both inside and outside the UN community. We can see an effort to express this new understanding of its role in the international community in the text of the BIC's Quadrennial Report to the United Nations. One of the questions that the United Nations requires accredited NGOs to answer in the quadrennial report is to describe their work in quantitative terms focused on the achievement of the Millennium Development Goals.

> While members of the Bahá'í community, in their respective cities, towns and villages cooperate with others to improve the social and material well-being of their communities, the Bahá'í International Community's work contributions to the UN cannot be easily quantified according to the MDG rubric.
> We believe that our collective advancement towards a more just and peaceful society requires profound alternations of social structures and a broadening of existing foundations of society. Attitudes, thoughts, and conceptions of fundamental issues need to be reshaped as a truly global community emerges and develops in its understanding of the nature of human flourishing as well as the social and material conditions required for such flourishing. We believe, then, that a key part of the transformation that is required must occur at the level of thought ...
> We see ourselves as part of a discourse among the community of nations and seek to contribute to this discourse by offering new ways of approaching issues of global concern, by re-framing the way that certain problems are understood, by identifying assumptions and mental models underlying the understanding of reality and by drawing on insights from the fields of science as well as religion.[49]

The BIC's growing understanding of itself in terms of contributing to prevalent discourses at the United Nations soon found expression in its engagement on the subject of gender equality. At around the time that the Universal House of Justice had introduced this new framing, the Institute for Studies in Global Prosperity (ISGP) was developing a discussion document on the subject of advancing gender equality.[50] The document was divided into five sections, each addressing a particular challenge to the achievement of gender equality: (1) expanding the basis of human identity; (2) overcoming oppression through the acquisition of self-knowledge; (3) moving beyond cultural relativism; (4) transforming economic structures and processes; and (5) redefining power. The ISGP had made it clear that this was not a position paper to be shared in the absence of meaningful conversation. "The purpose of this working document," it stated in the introductory section, "is to invite dialogue and reflection on the challenges that face everyone who is actively contributing to the cause of the equality of women and men, as a means of advancing collective efforts toward the realization of this goal."[51] Noteworthy was the document's use of questions as a discursive tool—thirty-seven questions in all. After studying the document, BIC representatives began to put into practice the methodology of small-group discussions structured around the reading of and reflection on the ideas and questions contained therein.

One can also discern this orientation in the approach taken by the BIC to create a space in which the intersection of religion and gender equality could be explored in a constructive and systematic manner. The BIC's UN Office collaborated with various UN agencies (including UN Women) and a civil society partner to initiate a discussion series titled "The Intersection of Religion and Gender Equality." Each of the discussions in the series, featuring panelists from UN agencies, member states, civil society, and academia, focused on the role and impact of religion at different phases of the life cycle.[52] The BIC's creation of a space in which diverse actors can gather for constructive dialogue, particularly on issues surrounding the often-challenging theme of religion and gender equality, has generated a level of confidence among UN agencies in the approach taken by the BIC. In 2015, as UN Women explored the manner in which to bring together secular and faith-based NGOs, it approached the BIC for input on operational, strategic, and conceptual facets of such an undertaking.

In light of the BIC's evolving orientation toward "participation in discourses" as its overarching framework, the BIC's UN Office also began to reflect on its use of "statements" to the United Nations and whether this form of communication aligned with this framework. Accredited UN NGOs were permitted to submit statements to the United Nations on the themes under its consideration. Yet a "statement" is fundamentally different than "dialogue"—more often than not, the former conveys a particular position, advocates for the implementation of specific measures, etc. While there was still a place for this type of communication, the BIC sought to articulate its ideas in a more invitational tone, seeking to stimulate genuine exploration of a subject and posting questions that it felt were timely and relevant—questions that the BIC itself was seeking to answer. It also began, for the first time, writing "perspective pieces"—less heavy-handed than a formal statement and more open to collective dialogue.

Another element of the Bahá'í approach to participation in discourses is its connection to action. The Universal House of Justice framed "involvement in social action" and "participation in the prevalent discourses of society" as "mutually reinforcing areas of activity."[53] In its 2012 Quadrennial Report to the United Nations, the BIC highlighted this element:

> These contributions and ideas are more than theory or aspiration. While they are guided by the Writings of the Bahá'í Faith, they are equally informed by the efforts of countless individuals and communities around the world working towards this vision of spiritual and material advancement. We believe that every member of the human family has not only the right to benefit from a prosperous civilization but an obligation to contribute towards its construction. In this way, human progress can become increasingly representative of the aspirations and talents of mankind as a whole, and less a process carried out by one group on behalf of another.[54]

Global Structure and Organization
One of the common features of international NGOs at the United Nations, secular and religious alike, is the existence of an international organizational structure. In order to secure UN accreditation, an NGO must be able to demonstrate substantial international reach (along with a mission aligned with the goals of the United Nations); and to maintain its consultative status it must show ongoing international-level engagement, which supports the goals of the United Nations. As such, questions of organizing structure, coordination, and authority assume particular importance.

The administrative structure of the worldwide Bahá'í community provides the overarching institutional context within which the BIC exists. As a federation of over 180 National Spiritual Assemblies, led by the Universal House of Justice, the aim of the Administrative Order is to harmonize and channel the diversity of humanity toward the establishment of a dynamic and unified community.[55] From the local to the global, Bahá'ís over the age of twenty-one vote for the members of their local, national, and international governing bodies, thereby putting in place a system of democratic governance at all levels of society. This structure is the mechanism for a dynamic interplay between the local and the global, balancing the forces of centralization and decentralization along with diversity and uniformity. It defies simple categorization of "top-down" or "bottom-up."

Such an integrating mechanism is apparent in various ways in the work of the BIC. An example of the local-global connection is the correspondence of the Universal House of Justice with National Spiritual Assemblies encouraging Bahá'ís around the world (or in selected communities) to undertake activities to promote the advancement of women. In 1975, designated by the United Nations as the International Women's Year, the Universal House of Justice called upon eighty countries to "stimulate and promote the full and equal participation of women in all aspects of Bahá'í community life, so that their accomplishments the friends [the Baha'i community] will demonstrate the distinction of the Cause of God in this field of human endeavour."[56] That same year, which marked the beginning of the UN Decade for Women, the Universal House of Justice sent letters to National Spiritual Assemblies explaining the goals of the decade and encouraging Bahá'ís to contribute toward these ends. In the decades that followed, National Bahá'í Offices for the Advancement of Women were created and guided by the BIC's Office for the Advancement of Women, which was established in 1992.

Introduction of Concepts to the Discourse on Gender Equality

Many of the oral and written contributions of the BIC have addressed themselves to the philosophical, conceptual, and normative assumptions underpinning the United Nations' understanding of gender equality and the means for its accomplishment. While at times these contributions have been accompanied by concrete policy recommendations, at others they have sought to raise questions, challenge underlying assumptions, and present an alternative reading of the issues at hand. The statements note "a pressing need for a fundamental rethinking and restructuring of society," "a profound adjustment in humanity's collective outlook," and the need for a "fundamental dialogue about the nature of development and 'modernity.'"[57]

Such statements can be understood in the context of efforts to reframe the discourse about the equality of women and men. They endeavour to shift the discourse away from an exclusively rights-based analysis of inequality to one that engages the United Nations in a conversation about gender equality in the context of the development and needs of an interdependent social body that encompasses humanity as a whole.[58] Several concepts introduced by the BIC in its contributions to the United Nations will be explored below: that of gender equality, in the context of the principle of the oneness of humanity; the notion of women as protagonists of development; the idea that the soul has no sex; the nature and purpose of education; and the role of women in the advancement of peace.

Gender Equality as an Element of the Oneness of Humanity
The Bahá'í concept of the equality of women and men must be understood in the context of the pivotal principle of the Bahá'í Faith, the oneness of humankind. It is a principle that addresses itself to relationships at all levels of society: relationships between individuals, within the family, within the community; relationships between individuals and their respective communities and social institutions; relationships between individuals and the natural environment; as well as relationships among nation states. The vision and very goal of the Bahá'í Faith is the creation of conditions—social, spiritual, and material—that enable the oneness of humanity to be expressed in the structure of and relationships at all levels of society.

The BIC has consistently put forward the idea that in light of the interconnectedness of all peoples and nations, the well-being of any one nation, community, or population is rooted the well-being of humanity as the whole. "As long as women are prevented from attaining their highest possibilities," states 'Abdu'l-Bahá, "so long will men be unable to achieve the greatness that might be theirs."[59] Similarly, writing about the Beijing Platform for Action, the BIC stated that, "If the Platform for Action is to win the worldwide support it requires ... the principle on which it is founded ... needs to be understood as an essential aspect of an even broader principle: the oneness of humanity."[60] This principle implies not merely more equitable relationships among the members of society but an "organic change in the very structure of society," a "complete reconceptualization of the relationships that sustain society."[61]

Equality, however, does not imply sameness or identity of function. Herein lies the multi-faceted concept of equality as presented by the Bahá'í community. On the one hand, the equality of women and men is advocated on the basis of their spiritual equality—the equality of their innate humanity. On the other, there are areas in which differences are highlighted; the most prominent among these in the statements of the BIC is that which pertains to education. Mothers are recognized as "the first educators of the next generation" and, as such, their education is granted a higher priority than that of her male counterparts.[62] Distinctiveness, in this case, does not undermine the equality of women and men. When understood in the context of relationships of mutualism and complementarity and the full development of human capacity, this distinctiveness is intended to benefit both women and men alike.

It is interesting, in this context, to note the roles played by male representatives of the BIC in the office's work in the area of gender equality. In the 1980s and 1990s, Giovanni Ballerio was elected chair of the NGO Forum Working Group of the Committee on the Status of Women in Geneva and was secretary of the French NGO Committee on the Status of Women. Ballerio worked with representatives of international NGOs to promote inclusion of the issue of the girl child in the Beijing Platform for Action.[63] It is also noteworthy that of the approximately five hundred Bahá'ís attending the 1995 UN Fourth World Conference on Women in Beijing, nearly one hundred were men. For the past decade, both male and female BIC representatives have been involved in the discourse on gender equality.

Women as Protagonists of Development

Many UN documents cast women as victims, as vulnerable individuals, and as a marginalized population. In a similar way to the United Nations' portrayal of populations living in poverty, this leaves one with the impression that women are primarily a collection of needs waiting to be met and helpless creatures needing to be rescued from their plight. Analyses of various UN documents, such as Resolution 1325—the first UN resolution to recognize the particular situation of women in situations of conflict—has been found to minimize female agency.[64]

The concept of agency is central to the Bahá'í concept of development. In its statement to the 1995 UN World Summit on Social Development, the BIC urged a fundamental rethinking of attitudes and approaches to social and economic development, in particular, "the appropriate roles to the be played by the protagonists" in the process.[65] Acknowledging the crucial role of governments, the BIC noted that in spite of "paying tribute to an egalitarian philosophy and related democratic principles," development planning continues to "view the masses of humanity as essentially recipients of benefits from aid and training."[66]

The BIC refers to development in terms of building the capacity of individuals, communities, and social institutions to contribute to the well-being of society. In a statement on sustainable development, for example, the BIC notes that:

> It is not enough to conceive of sustainable consumption and production in terms of creating opportunities for those living in poverty to meet their basic needs. Rather, with the understanding that each individual has a contribution to make to the construction of a more just and peaceful social order, these processes must be arranged in a way that permits each to play his or her rightful role as productive member of society.[67]

Similarly, in a 2012 statement to the UN Commission on Population and Development, the BIC stated that "the overarching objective" of efforts to foster the healthy development of young people is to enable them to develop their capacities to the fullest so as to "play their rightful role in the transformation of society."[68]

The Soul Has No Sex

Among the concepts that the BIC has introduced in its statements to the United Nations is that the soul has no sex. One element of this assertion is the existence of a spiritual dimension to the human being, a perspective shared by all of the world's religious traditions. Accordingly, the full development of the human being must serve to nurture not only his or her physical and social needs and capacities, but also those that concern the search for meaning, purpose, love, and justice, among others.

The BIC asserts that the very essence of the human being—that which makes us human—is neither male nor female. "The rational soul has no gender," states the BIC's publication prepared for the 1995 UN Fourth World Conference on Women.[69] Echoing this theme twenty years later, in its statement to the 59th Session of the Commission on the Status of Women, the BIC wrote:

> That which makes human beings human—their inherent dignity and nobility—is neither male nor female. The search for meaning, for purpose, for community; the capacity to love, to create, to persevere, has no gender. Such an assertion has profound implications for the organization of every aspect of human society.[70]

Further elaboration is offered in a document titled "Advancing Towards the Equality of Women and Men," used by the BIC in the facilitation of small discussion groups on the theme of gender equality. The document states that "the equality of men and women is a fundamental truth about human reality and not just a desired condition to be achieved for the good of society."[71] This equality is rooted in the equality that exists at the spiritual level. It continues:

> The reality of the human being is his or her soul; and the soul, we firmly believe, has no sex. Men and women exhibit physical differences that undeniably influence some aspects of how they experience the world. Yet, in their essence, in their qualities and potentialities, in those aspects that make human beings human, men and women are without distinction. Neither can claim superiority over the other.[72]

Thus the BIC puts forward the idea that the distinctions between "male" and "female" exist in the physical world at the level of biology but not at the level of our spiritual nature. This perspective challenges materialist approaches that place particular physical or social characteristics at the centre of human identity.

The Nature and Purpose of Education

One of the most consistent themes in the statements of the BIC has been that of education. The Bahá'í writings state: "Regard man as a mine rich in gems of inestimable value. Education can, alone, cause it to reveal its treasures, and enable mankind to benefit therefrom."[73] Furthermore, 'Abdu'l-Bahá states that the "difference in capability between man and woman is due entirely to opportunity and education. Heretofore woman has been denied the right and privilege of equal development. If equal opportunity be granted her, there is no doubt she would be the peer of man."[74]

In these assertions are the philosophical underpinnings of the concept of education as shared by the BIC—that the human being possesses, in a potential state, qualities and capabilities of great value not only to himself or herself but to society as a whole and that it is through the process of education that those qualities and capabilities can be discovered, developed, made manifest, and, ultimately, channelled for the advancement of society as a whole. In 1947, in its first statement to the United Nations on the subject of gender equality, the Bahá'í representation to the United Nations noted that "lack of education has prevented woman from manifesting her value."[75]

The Bahá'í writings place great emphasis on the education of women and girls, instructing that in cases where resources do not allow all children in the family to be educated, priority should be given to girls, as they bear the responsibility of being the first educators of the next generation.[76] In its 1985 statement on peace, addressed to the peoples of the world, the Universal House of Justice asserts: "The decision-making agencies would do well to consider giving first priority to the education of women and girls, since it is through educated mothers that the benefits of knowledge can be most effectively and rapidly diffused throughout society."[77] In terms of the curriculum itself, the BIC states that "daughters and sons must follow the same curriculum of study" and that "there is no natural limit on women's ability."[78] The BIC has also acknowledged some of the challenging family- and community-based dynamics arising from the education of girls. It notes, for example, that "[e]ducating women without educating men in their lives may put women at greater risk of violence."[79] Ultimately, education efforts have to take into account the question of the socialization of men and boys, whose full involvement and support are needed in order for the full benefits of girls' education to be realized in society.

Addressing the UN Commission on the Population and Development on the issue of youth, the BIC states that the "future of today's society will depend to a great extent on the manner in which educational programs and methods are designed to release the latent potential of youth and prepare them for the world they will inherit."[80] In that same statement, the BIC introduces the concept of a "twofold moral purpose" that "provides an important axis of the educational process."[81] This twofold purpose encompasses the development of one's inherent potentialities and one's contribution to the betterment of society.[82]

The importance of knowledge in the advancement of society is a theme that the Universal House of Justice introduced in its 2010 Riḍván letter emphasizing "the centrality of knowledge to social existence":

> The perpetuation of ignorance is a most grievous form of oppression; it reinforces the many walls of prejudice that stand as barriers to the realization of the oneness of humankind, at once the goal and operating principle of Bahá'u'lláh's Revelation. Access to knowledge is the right of every human being, and participation in its generation, application and diffusion a responsibility that all must shoulder in the great enterprise of building a prosperous world civilization—each individual according to his or her talents and abilities.[83]

Since 2010, statements of the BIC have sought to reflect this emphasis on the relationship between access to knowledge, its generation, and the advancement of society.

Gender Equality as a Prerequisite for Peace

From the beginning of its work with the United Nations, the BIC has underscored that progress toward the achievement of the equality of women and men is a prerequisite for peace. In its first statement to the United Nations about gender equality, the BIC suggests that "the present imbalance [between the status of men and women] may be the cause of war."[84] The central role of women in the establishment of peace was addressed as early as 1912 by 'Abdu'l-Bahá, who stated:

> The most momentous question of this day is international peace and arbitration, and universal peace is impossible without universal suffrage.... The mother bears the troubles and anxieties of rearing the child, undergoes the ordeal of its birth and training. Therefore, it is most difficult for mothers to send to the battlefield those upon whom they have lavished such love and care.... Consider a

son reared and trained twenty years by a devoted mother. Having brought him through dangers and difficulties to the age of maturity, how agonizing then to sacrifice him upon the battlefield!... So it will come to pass that when women participate fully and equally in the affairs of the world, when they enter confidently and capably the great arena of laws and politics, war will cease; for woman will be the obstacle and hindrance to it.[85]

On the eve of the UN-designated International Year of Peace, the Universal House of Justice penned a letter addressed to the peoples of the world, titled "The Promise of World Peace," outlining its understanding of the nature of peace, presenting an analysis of the challenges facing the international community, and proposing means for addressing them. By 1989, the letter had been translated into seventy-six languages and distributed to over two hundred heads of state.[86] In unequivocal terms, the statement set forth the connection between the emancipation of women and the achievement of sustainable peace:

> The emancipation of women, the achievement of full equality between the sexes, is one of the most important, though less acknowledged prerequisites of peace. The denial of such equality perpetrates an injustice against one half of the world's population and promotes in men harmful attitudes and habits that are carried from the family to the workplace, to political life, and ultimately to international relations. There are no grounds, moral, practical, or biological, upon which such denial can be justified. Only as women are welcomed into full partnership in all fields of human endeavour will the moral and psychological climate be created in which international peace can emerge.[87]

At the United Nations, it wasn't until 2000 that the Security Council passed Resolution 1325, which stressed, for the first time, the role of women in the prevention and resolution of conflicts, peace building, and peacekeeping. It also recognized the importance of their equal participation in all efforts for the maintenance and promotion of peace and security.[88] Yet, as mentioned earlier in this chapter, a closer analysis of the language of this landmark resolution reveals that women's agency continues to be undermined, as they are most often defined in terms of their vulnerabilities and need for protection. As Cynthia Enloe powerfully warns:

> Perhaps what was not grasped [following the adoption of 1325], and is still not absorbed by the members of the delegation... was the

genuinely radical understanding that informed the feminist analysis undergirding 1325. That feminist understanding is that patriarchy—in all its varied guises, camouflaged, khaki clad, and pin-striped—is a principal cause both of the outbreak of violent societal conflicts and of the international community's frequent failures in providing long-term resolution to those violence conflicts.[89]

This chapter has sought to draw insights from the experience of the BIC's long-standing engagement with the United Nations, particularly as it relates to the international discourse on gender equality. At a time in history when the efficacy of global discourse and decision-making has assumed paramount importance, this research has brought to the fore a largely unexamined constellation of approaches and perspectives of a transnational organization whose goal is to foster conditions for a constructive, progressive, and beneficial discourse. Insights from the BIC's interaction with the United Nations begin to address a number of questions raised by David Palmer in chapter 2 of this volume. Asserting that "civil society is an expression of the spiritual nature of humanity, and releases the powers of a spiritual reality," Palmer asks how civil society organizations can retain their role as spaces for the development of spiritual qualities and capacities, as well as how they can uphold spiritual principles while engaging with government agencies, foundations, and other civil society organizations. This chapter has provided a concrete example of the expression of spiritual principles in the aims, rationale, and approaches of the BIC in its unfolding relationship with the United Nations.

The examination of the dynamics characterizing the gender equality discourse offer a closer look at the challenges facing many religious civil society organizations as they seek to contribute to the discourse at the international level: an oppositional climate, a tendency toward binary readings of reality, the distrust and resentment of religious actors and perspectives, seemingly irreconcilable tensions between human rights-based and faith-based approaches and norms, and patriarchal structures and processes, among others.

This chapter has identified a number of insights that have emerged from the study of the BIC at the United Nations. First, we observe a close relationship between processes and perspectives. For the BIC, the pivotal principle of the oneness of humanity finds expression not only in its conceptual contributions and policy recommendations but also in the manner that it conducts itself in the NGO community—in its relationships with NGOs, with UN agencies, and vis-à-vis member states. Efforts not to become entangled in partisan and/or divisive processes signal a commitment to a particular mode of deliberation, which the BIC considers essential to effective outcomes and, often, their very implementation. This stance is augmented by a commitment to inclusive and open dialogue and to the full participation of civil society in UN processes. To eschew partisanship is not to shy away from diversity or difference of opinion but rather to acknowledge that the quality of deliberation lies not only in the richness of ideas, but also in the culture of dialogue and discourse that it supports.

That the BIC forms part of a larger and continually evolving international administrative and governing structure is also significant. This structure provides an informative example of a manner of operating that allows for flexibility as well as consistency, global-level coordination, and the contributions and expressions of local and national units. As such, it defies simple categorization in terms of "top-down" or "bottom-up" dynamics but strives to operate in a manner that allows for individual-, community-, national-, and global-level flourishing and coherence.

The concepts introduced into the discourse by the BIC have stimulated the consideration of different facets of gender equality: the significance of gender equality within the broader context of the oneness of humanity and the attainment of peace, the identity of women and girls as protagonists of development, the dynamic coherence between the material and the spiritual, the notion that gender distinctions do not obtain at the spiritual level, and the role of education in the advancement of women.[90] The BIC has conceived of its role in the international arena as an active participant in a rich and multi-faceted discourse. As such, these ideas are offered not as "positions" to be adopted by others but as contributions—as insights for public consideration.

The challenge for the international community today is to continue to refine its governing structures and to foster a culture of constructive, inclusive, and effective exchange of ideas and worldviews—even as such exchanges challenge the firmly secular analyses and approaches that once appeared to be the only "game in town." This will require a conscious effort to avoid the conceptual and structural traps that have hindered such efforts in the past. It will require an openness to rethinking the very concept of religion and the operationalization of spiritual values at its core. And finally, it will require a readiness to examine the efficacy of ideas and approaches modelled by diverse organizations seeking to address the most pressing needs of our time.

Notes

1. United Nations, "UN Charter," *UN.org*, http://www.un.org/en/sections/un-charter/index4658.html?page=2 .
2. United Nations, "Short History of the Commission on the Status of Women," PDF, http://www.un.org/womenwatch/daw/CSW60YRS/CSWbriefhistory.pdf.
3. See Janet Khan and Peter Khan, *Advancement of Women: A Bahá'í Perspective* (Wilmette, IL: Bahá'í Publishing Trust, 2003).
4. Jeffrey Haynes, *Faith-based Organizations at the United Nations* (New York: Palgrave Macmillan, 2014)
5. Geoffrey Knox, ed., *Religion and Public Policy at the UN*, 2002, PDF, http://www.catholicsforchoice.org/wp-content/uploads/2014/01/2000religionandpublicpolicyatheun.pdf.
6. Azza Karam, "On Faith, Health and Tensions: An Overview from an Inter-Governmental Perspective," *Heythrop Journal* 55 (2014): 1076.
7. Ibid., 1076–77.
8. Gillian Paterson, "The Catholic Church and Some Discourses on Population," *Heythrop Journal* 55 (2014): 1106.
9. Ibid., 1106. The Vatican partially endorsed the document in 1994, having refused to endorse the 1974 and 1984 documents.
10. See Deniz Kandiyoti, "Disentangling Religion and Politics: Whither Gender Equality?" *IDS Bulletin* 42, no. 1 (2011): 10–14; Sharah Razavi and Anne Jenichen, "The Unhappy Marriage of Religion and Politics: Problems and Pitfalls for Gender Equality (Draft)," in *UN Research Institute for Social Development*, http://www.unrisd.org/80256B3C005BCCF9/(httpPublications)/4ACE883B67ABCDEBC12577690046502C?OpenDocument; and Emma Tomalin (Ed.), *Gender, Faith, and Development* (London: Oxfam & Practical Action Publishing, 2011), http://policy-practice.oxfam.org.uk/publications/ gender-faith-and-development-144042. [Accessed 1 August 2017.]
11. See José Casanova, "Rethinking Public Religions," in *Rethinking Religion and World Affairs*, ed. Timothy Samuel Shah, Alfred Stepan, and Monica Duffy Toft (Oxford, UK: Oxford University Press, 2012), 25–35.
12. "Overview of the Convention." *Convention on the Elimination of All Forms of Discrimination Against Women*, UN Women, http://www.unfpa.org/resources/human-rights-women, accessed August 1, 2017.
13. United Nations Entity for Gender Equality and the Empowerment of Women, "Convention on the Elimination of All Forms of Discrimination Against Women," *UN.org*, http://www.un.org/womenwatch/daw/cedaw/reservations.htm, accessed July 31, 2015.
14. Center for Women's Global Leadership, "No CSW Agreed Conclusions on Women's Human Rights and Elimination of All Forms of Violence Against Women and Girls," *Center for Women's Global Leadership*,

http://www.cwgl.rutgers.edu/download/doc_download/91-no-csw-agreed-conclusions-on-women, accessed July 31, 2015.

15 United Nations Research Institute for Social Development, "Religion, Politics and Gender Equality," *United Nations Research Institute for Social Development*, accessed July 31, 2015, http://www.unrisd.org/80256B3C005BB128/(httpProjects)/3F3D45E0F8567920C12572B9004180C5. The high-profile nature of several of these disputes has given rise to the perception of a clearly delineated binary of religious vs. secular feminist actors permanently on opposite ends of the ideological spectrum, fighting a zero-sum game. Among many at the United Nations, the presumption has been that it is the secular feminist advocates who have secured many of the rights for women, while religious actors have been seeking to undermine the progress that has been achieved.

16 As was noted by many states during the adoption of the Universal Declaration of Human Rights, the values underpinning the Declaration reflected diverse cultures and societies. For example, Ecuador stated that the "multiplicity of origin of human rights could be detected in reading the articles of the Declaration." Pakistan affirmed its full support for article 19, quoting from the Qur'án, stating that Islam "had unequivocally proclaimed the right to freedom of conscience and had declared itself against any kind of compulsion in matters of faith or religious practices." China stressed that Chinese thought had influenced the evolution of ideas of the rights of man in the Western world. Brazil stated that "the Declaration did not reflect the particular point of view of any one people or of any one group of peoples. Neither was it the expression of any particular political doctrine or philosophical system. It was the result of the intellectual and moral cooperation of a large number of nations; that explained its values and interest and also conferred upon it great moral authority." See United Nations Human Rights Council, "Preliminary Study on Promoting Human Rights and Fundamental Freedoms through a Better Understanding of Traditional Values of Humankind," last modified June 1, 2012, PDF, http://www.ohchr.org/Documents/HRBodies/HRCouncil/AdvisoryCom/Session9/A-HRC-AC-9-2_en.pdf.

17 In the Vienna Declaration and Programme of Action, the World Conference on Human Rights stressed the importance of "working towards the elimination of the harmful effects of certain traditional or customary practices, cultural prejudices and religious extremism." See United Nations General Assembly, "Vienna Declaration and Programme of Action," last modified July 12, 1993, http://www.refworld.org/docid/3ae6b39ec.html.

18 The Task Force is a critical space within the United Nations, which convenes over fifteen different offices and agencies, many of which are members of the UN Development Group.

19 There was no one representing gender equality on the UN Secretary-General's Senior Management Group. Under Kofi Annan, the Senior Management

Group consisted of six women and twenty-one men. In 2015, there were twelve women and twenty-seven men.
20 *Joint Learning Initiative on Faith and Local Communities*, http://jliflc.com, accessed July 29, 2015.
21 See note 19.
22 See the Women's Environment and Development Organization's "An Open Letter on Women & UN Reform to the Secretary General and Member States from NGOs present at the 50th Session of the Commission on the Status of Women," *Women's Environment and Development Organization*, 6 March 2006, http://www.choike.org/documentos/open_letter2006.pdf, accessed August 1, 2017.
23 The Ebola Panel, for example, had no women on it. The fifteen-member High-Level Panel on UN Reform originally included only three women, until three more were added following pressure from civil society, raising the ratio of women to men to 1:3.
24 United Nations, "Beijing Declaration and Platform of Action," last modified October 27, 1995, PDF, http://www.refworld.org/docid/3dde04324.html.
25 Wendy Harcourt, "The Global Women's Rights Movement: Power Politics around the United Nations and the World Social Forum," last modified August 2006, http://unrisd.org/80256B3C005BCCF9/(httpAuxPages)/59E3AF8FB95F929FC1257230002F43C1/$file/harcourt-pp.pdf, accessed July 24, 2015.
26 Nadine Puechguirbal, "Discourses on Gender, Patriarchy and Resolution 1325: A Textual Analysis of UN Documents," *International Peacekeeping* 17 (2010): 181.
27 In September 2014, the United Nations reported that women filled over one-third of the fifteen seats on the Security Council—the highest number in the history of the United Nations. See "Record Number of Women Makes History at UN Security Council," *UN News Centre*, last modified September 15, 2014, http://www.un.org/apps/news/story.asp?NewsID=48711#.Vor8wzZTWf4.
28 Puechguirbal, "Discourses on Gender, Patriarchy and Resolution 1325: A Textual Analysis of UN Documents," 179.
29 Bahá'u'lláh. *Gleanings from the Writings of Bahá'u'lláh* (Wilmette, IL: Bahá'í Publishing Trust, 1990), 286.
30 Universal House of Justice to the Bahá'ís of Iran, March 2, 2013, http://www.bahai.org/library/authoritative-texts/the-universal-house-of-justice/messages/#d=20130302_001&f=f1.
31 Ibid.
32 See Devaki Jain, *Women, Development, and the UN: A Sixty-Year Quest for Equality and Justice* (Bloomington, IN: Indiana University Press, 2005).
33 Ibid., 165.
34 See Khan and Khan, *Advancement of Women*.

35 The Universal House of Justice stipulates that this obedience must be carried out in a manner that does not allow Bahá'ís' "inner religious beliefs to be violated. Bahá'ís will not be party to any instigation to overthrow a government. Nor will they interfere in political relations between the governments of different nations." See Universal House of Justice to the Bahá'ís of Iran, March 2, 2013.
36 This principle does not prevent Bahá'ís from voting in local and national elections, as long as they do not have to affiliate with a particular political party in order to do so.
37 Knox, *Religion and Public Policy at the UN*, 37.
38 Ibid.
39 Ibid.
40 Bahá'u'lláh quoted in "Consultation," *Bahá'í.org*, http://www.bahai.org/beliefs/universal-peace/articles-resources/consultation-quotes, accessed August 1, 2017.
41 Between 1990 and 2015, the BIC was elected to serve in various leadership capacities on the UN NGO Committee on the Status of Women, including Chair (six years), Past Chair (one year), Executive Board (three years), Advisor to Executive Board (four years); other elected positions include Vice President of the Conference of NGOs (in 1983), Chair of the NGO Committee on UNICEF (1994–2001), Vice-Chair of the Global Forum of the NGO Committee on UNICEF (1998–2001), Vice-Chair of the UN Decade for Women, and member of the Global NGO Forum Facilitating Committee (of the UN Fourth World Conference on Women, 1992–1995). "The enthusiastic participation of the BIC in UN activities related to women has led to widespread appreciation of the Bahá'í views on the significance of equality in establishing universal peace and social and economic development. The Bahá'í International Community is increasingly identified, as a result, with the worldwide network of people and organizations working in a spirit of friendly cooperation to remove traditional barriers to women's advancement and to encourage and promote positive attitudes vital to the achievement of full equality for men and women." Quoted in *The Bahá'í World*, vol. 18 (Haifa, Israel: Bahá'í World Centre, 1986), 408.
42 Bahá'í International Community, *Report of Bahá'í Participation in the NGO Forum on Women*. Archives of the Bahá'í International Community's United Nations Office, Bahá'í International Community, New York, NY. It is significant to note the BIC's decision at this conference to give up its coveted position as one of fifty NGOs selected to deliver an oral statement in front of member states. At the last moment, conference organizers requested that the slot be relinquished to the Moscow Center for Gender Studies, which was represented for the first time at a world conference. Noting the importance of giving recognition to the challenges facing Eastern European women, the BIC decided to offer its place on the program and distribute its statement in print form only.

43 "An Interview with Members of GEAR's Facilitation Committee," *Bahá'í International Community*, last modified August 2, 2010, http://www.bic.org/news/interview-members-gears-facilitation-committee.
44 United Nations Research Institute for Social Development. "Religion, Politics and Gender Equality."
45 Bahá'í International Community (2012), *Report on the 45th Session of the UN Commission on Population and Development*. Internal memo of the Bahá'í International Community's United Nations Office.
46 Universal House of Justice, "Riḍván 2010," April 21, 2010, http://preview.bahai.org/library/authoritative-texts/the-universal-house-of-justice/messages/#d=20100421_001&f=f1.
47 Ibid.
48 Ibid.
49 Bahá'í International Community (2013), "Quadrennial Report to the UN (2009–2012)." Internal memo of the Bahá'í International Community's United Nations Office.
50 The Institute for Studies in Global Prosperity is a "non-profit organization, dedicated to building capacity in individuals, groups and institutions to contribute to prevalent discourses concerned with the betterment of society.... Founded in 1999—and working in collaboration with the Bahá'í International Community—the Institute also engages in learning about the methods, approaches and instruments which can best be employed to contribute to the discourses of society." See *Institute for Studies in Global Prosperity*, http://www.globalprosperity.org, accessed July 30, 2015.
51 Institute for Studies in Global Prosperity, "Advancing Towards the Equality of Women and Men," *Institute for Studies in Global Prosperity*, accessed May 31, 2015, http://www.globalprosperity.org/documents/ISGP_Advancing_Toward_the_Equality_of_Women_and_Men.pdf.
52 For example, see "Engaging with Religious Leaders Can Help Address Women's Inequality: An Ongoing Conversation."
53 Universal House of Justice, "Riḍván 2010."
54 Bahá'í International Community, "Quadrennial Report to the UN (2009–2012)."
55 The Universal House of Justice is the central governing body of the Bahá'í Faith. It guides national and local elected bodies as they administer the affairs of the Bahá'í community, exercising legislative, executive, and judicial authority. While women can serve at all other levels of Bahá'í administration, the membership of the Universal House of Justice is confined to men. It is a provision that was ordained by Bahá'u'lláh, the founder of the Bahá'í Faith; 'Abdu'l-Bahá, His son and authorized interpreter of His writings, stated that the wisdom of this provision will be clearly understood in the future. The official website of the Universal House of Justice states: "Because the Bahá'í Writings are filled with unequivocal statements about the equality of men and women, however, the question of male membership

of the Universal House of Justice can in no way be regarded as a sign of the superiority of men over women.... The Universal House of Justice is fully committed to advancing this principle—in its guidance to Bahá'í communities worldwide, through the resources allocated to the development and education of women and girl children in particular, through statements presented by the Bahá'í International Community at the United Nations, and by Bahá'í participation in conferences, seminars and other arenas." See "Electoral Process," *Bahá'í.org*, accessed July 26, 2016, http://universal houseofjustice.bahai.org/electoral-process.

56 Universal House of Justice, "To All National Spiritual Assemblies," in *The Bahá'í World*, vol. 15 (Haifa, Israel: Bahá'í World Centre, 1976), 369.

57 See Bahá'í International Community, "The Education of Girls: Constraints and Policy Measures," March 7, 1990, http://www.bic.org/statements/education-girls-constraints-and-policy-measures; "Women's Rights," June 17, 1993, http://www.bic.org/statements/womens-rights; and "Education and Training for the Betterment of Society," February 22, 2011, http://www.bic.org/statements/education-and-training-betterment-society.

58 By 2012, the concept of "reframing" is being used by "Post-2015 Women," a coalition of NGOs co-initiated by the BIC. The coalition describes its goals as "[challenging] and [reframing] the global development agenda." See *Feminist Alliance for Rights*, www.post2015women.com.

59 'Abdu'l-Bahá. *Paris Talks: Addresses Given by 'Abdu'l-Bahá in 1911* (Wilmette, IL: Bahá'í Publishing Trust, 1999), 133.

60 Bahá'í International Community, "The Role of Religion in Promoting the Advancement of Women," September 13, 1995, http://www.bic.org/statements/role-religion-promoting-advancement-women.

61 Universal House of Justice to the Bahá'ís of Iran, March 2, 2013.

62 Bahá'u'lláh, *The Kitáb-i-Aqdas* (Haifa, Israel: Bahá'í World Centre, 1992), 200.

63 He also promoted the importance of the issue at the Economic Commission for Europe Preparatory Conference in Vienna in October 1994 and the final session of the UN Preparatory Committee in New York in March 1995.

64 Puechguirbal, "Discourses on Gender, Patriarchy and Resolution 1325: A Textual Analysis of UN Documents," 173.

65 Bahá'í International Community, "The Prosperity of Humankind," March 3, 1995, http://www.bahai.org/documents/bic-opi/prosperity-humankind.

66 Ibid.

67 Bahá'í International Community, "Rethinking Prosperity: Forging Alternatives to a Culture of Consumerism," May 3, 2010, http://www.bic.org/statements/rethinking-prosperity-forging-alternatives-culture-consumerism.

68 Bahá'í International Community, "Youth and Adolescents Education in Service of Community," February 16, 2002, http://www.bic.org/statements/youth-and-adolescents-education-service-community.

69 Quoted in Janet Kahn, introduction to "The Greatness Which Might Be Theirs: Religions as an Agent for Promoting the Advancement of Women

at All Levels," written by the Bahá'í International Community, August 26, 1995, http://www.bic.org/statements/greatness-which-might-be-theirs-religions-agent-promoting-advancement-women-all-levels.
70 Bahá'í International Community, "Toward a New Discourse on Religion and Gender Equality," February 1, 2015, http://www.bic.org/statements/toward-new-discourse-religion-and-gender-equality-0.
71 Institute for Studies in Global Prosperity. "Advancing Towards the Equality of Women and Men."
72 Ibid.
73 Bahá'u'lláh, "Lawh-i- Maqṣúd" (Tablet of Maqṣúd), *Tablets of Bahá'u'lláh Revealed after the Kitáb-i-Aqdas* (Haifa, Israel: Bahá'í World Centre, 1982). http://www.bahai.org/library/authoritative-texts/bahaullah/tablets-bahaullah/#, accessed August 1, 2017.
74 'Abdu'l-Bahá, "Talk about Women's Suffrage Meeting" (20 May 1912). *The Promulgation of Universal Peace* (Wilmette, IL: Bahá'í Publishing Trust, 1995). http://www.bahai.org/library/authoritative-texts/abdul-baha/promulgation-universal-peace/#f=f9-594, accessed August 1, 2017.
75 National Spiritual Assembly of the United States and Canada (1947). *Bahá'í Statement on Women*. Archives of the Bahá'í International Community's United Nations Office, Bahá'í International Community, New York, NY.
76 Note 76 of *The Kitáb-i-Aqdas* (*The Most Holy Book*) states, " 'Abdu'l-Bahá ... not only calls attention to the responsibility of parents to educate all their children, but He also clearly specifies that the 'training and culture of daughters is more necessary than that of sons,' for girls will one day be mothers, and mothers are the first educators of the new generation. If it is not possible, therefore, for a family to educate all the children, preference is to be accorded to daughters since, through educated mothers, the benefits of knowledge can be most effectively and rapidly diffused throughout society." See Bahá'u'lláh, *The Kitáb-i-Aqdas*, 199–200.
77 Universal House of Justice, "The Promise of World Peace," accessed July 30, 2015, http://www.bahai.org/library/authoritative-texts/the-universal-house-of-justice/messages/#.
78 In 1970, soon after becoming accredited, the BIC submitted a statement to the Commission calling attention to the importance of educating girls. In the 1980s, a strong statement was made to the UNICEF Executive Board supporting the initiative taken by UNICEF's Women's Senior Programme Advisor to advocate for the girl child. The BIC worked closely with UNICEF to promote awareness of the needs of girl children. See Bahá'í International Community, "The Girl Child," April 17, 1991, http://www.bic.org/statements/girl-child. The BIC representative to the UN at the BIC's office in Geneva worked with representatives of the International Federation of University Women (a Geneva-based NGO, now called Graduate Women International) and with other international organizations to promote the

inclusion of the girl child in the Beijing Platform for Action. After the 1995 Fourth World Conference on Women (Beijing), BIC gained representation on UNICEF's NGO Working Group on the Girl Child.
79 Bahá'í International Community, "HIV/AIDS & Gender Equality: Transforming Attitudes and Behaviors," June 25, 2001, http://www.bic.org/statements/hivaids-gender-equality-transforming-attitudes-and-behaviors.
80 Bahá'í International Community, "Education and Training for the Betterment of Society."
81 Ibid.
82 In chapter 4 of this volume, Sona Farid-Arbab addresses in detail the concept of a twofold moral purpose.
83 Universal House of Justice, "Riḍván 2010."
84 National Spiritual Assembly of the United States and Canada (1947). *Bahá'í Statement on Women*. Archives of the Bahá'í International Community's United Nations Office, Bahá'í International Community, New York, NY.
85 'Abdu'l-Bahá, "Talk about Women's Suffrage Meeting," (20 May 1912). *The Promulgation of Universal Peace* (Wilmette, IL: Bahá'í Publishing Trust, 1995). http://www.bahai.org/library/authoritative-texts/abdul-baha/promulgation-universal-peace/#f=f9-594, accessed August 1, 2017.
86 *The Bahá'í World*, vol. 20 (Haifa, Israel: Bahá'í World Centre, 1998), 525.
87 Universal House of Justice, "The Promise of World Peace."
88 United Nations General Assembly, "Women 2000: Gender Equality, Development and Peace for the Twenty-First Century," http://documents-dds-ny.un.org/doc/UNDOC/GEN/N04/486/28/PDF/N0448628.pdf?OpenElement.
89 Cynthia Enloe, "What if Patriarchy *Is* 'the Big Picture'? An Afterword," in *Gender, Conflict, and Peacekeeping*, ed. Dyan Mazurana, Angela Raven-Roberts, and Jane Parpart (Lanham, MD: Rowman & Littlefield, 2005), 281.
90 The BIC is not the only organization to have put these forward. What is unique is the constellation of these concepts taken together, the degree to which these are prioritized by the organization, and how they relate to the broader vision of the Bahá'í Faith.

Bibliography

'Abdu'l-Bahá. *Paris Talks: Addresses Given by 'Abdu'l-Bahá in 1911*. Wilmette, IL: Bahá'í Publishing Trust, 1999.

———. *The Promulgation of Universal Peace*. Wilmette, IL: Bahá'í Publishing Trust, 1995.

Bahá'í International Community. "Education and Training for the Betterment of Society." February 22, 2011. http://www.bic.org/statements/education-and-training-betterment-society.

———. "The Education of Girls: Constraints and Policy Measures." March 7, 1990. http://www.bic.org/statements/education-girls-constraints-and-policy-measures.

———. "The Girl Child." April 17, 1991. http://www.bic.org/statements/girl-child.

———. "HIV/AIDS & Gender Equality: Transforming Attitudes and Behaviors." June 25, 2001. http://www.bic.org/statements/hivaids-gender-equality-transforming-attitudes-and-behaviors.

———. "The Prosperity of Humankind." March 3, 1995. http://www.bahai.org/documents/bic-opi/prosperity-humankind.

———. (2013), "Quadrennial Report to the UN (2009–2012)." Internal memo of the Bahá'í International Community's United Nations Office.

———. "Report on the 45th Session of the UN Commission on Population and Development." Internal memo of the Bahá'í International Community's United Nations Office.

———. "Report of Bahá'í Participation in the NGO Forum on Women." Archives of the Bahá'í International Community's United Nations Office, Bahá'í International Community, New York, NY.

———. "Rethinking Prosperity: Forging Alternatives to a Culture of Consumerism." May 3, 2010. http://www.bic.org/statements/rethinking-prosperity-forging-alternatives-culture-consumerism.

———. "The Role of Religion in Promoting the Advancement of Women." September 13, 1995. http://www.bic.org/statements/role-religion-promoting-advancement-women.

———. "Toward a New Discourse on Religion and Gender Equality." February 1, 2015. http://www.bic.org/statements/toward-new-discourse-religion-and-gender-equality-0.

———. "Women's Rights." June 17, 1993. http://www.bic.org/statements/womens-rights.

———. "Youth and Adolescents Education in Service of Community." February 16, 2002. http://www.bic.org/statements/youth-and-adolescents-education-service-community.

The Bahá'í World. Vol. 18. Haifa, Israel: Bahá'í World Centre, 1986.

The Bahá'í World. Vol. 20. Haifa, Israel: Bahá'í World Centre, 1998.

Bahá'u'lláh. *Gleanings from the Writings of Bahá'u'lláh*. Wilmette, IL: Bahá'í Publishing Trust, 1990.

———. *The Kitáb-i-Aqdas*. Wilmette, IL: Bahá'í Publishing Trust, 1993.

———. *Tablets of Bahá'u'lláh Revealed after the Kitáb-i-Aqdas*. Translated by Habib Taherzadeh et al. Haifa, Israel: Bahá'í World Centre, 1982. Casanova, José. "Rethinking Public Religions." In *Rethinking Religion and World Affairs*, edited by Timothy Samuel Shah, Alfred Stepan, and Monica Duffy Toft, 25–35. Oxford, UK: Oxford University Press, 2012. Center for Women's Global Leadership. "No CSW Agreed Conclusions on Women's Human Rights and Elimination of All Forms of Violence Against Women and Girls." *Center for Women's Global Leadership*. Accessed July 31, 2015. http://www.cwgl.rutgers.edu/download/doc_download/91-no-csw-agreed-conclusions-on-women.

Bahá'u'lláh quoted in "Consultation," *Bahá'í.org*, http://www.bahai.org/beliefs/universal-peace/articles-resources/consultation-quotes, accessed August 1, 2017.

"Electoral Process." *Bahá'í.org*. Accessed July 26, 2016. http://universalhouseofjustice.bahai.org/electoral-process.

Enloe, Cynthia. "What if Patriarchy *Is* 'the Big Picture'? An Afterword." In *Gender, Conflict, and Peacekeeping*, edited by Dyan Mazurana, Angela Raven-Roberts, and Jane Parpart, 391–96. Lanham, MD: Rowman & Littlefield, 2005.

Feminist Alliance for Rights. Accessed May 31, 2015. www.post2015women.com.

Harcourt, Wendy. "The Global Women's Rights Movement: Power Politics around the United Nations and the World Social Forum." Accessed July 25, 2015. http://unrisd.org/80256B3C005BCCF9/(httpAuxPages)/59E3AF8FB95F929FC1257230002F43C1/$file/harcourt-pp.pdf.

Institute for Studies in Global Prosperity. "Advancing Towards the Equality of Women and Men." *Institute for Studies in Global Prosperity*. Accessed May 31, 2015. http://www.globalprosperity.org/documents/ISGP_Advancing_Toward_the_Equality_of_Women_and_Men.pdf.

Institute for Studies in Global Prosperity. Accessed July 30, 2015. http://www.globalprosperity.org.

"An Interview with Members of GEAR's Facilitation Committee." *Bahá'í International Community*. Last modified August 2, 2010. http://www.bic.org/news/interview-members-gears-facilitation-committee.

Jain, Devaki. *Women, Development, and the UN: A Sixty-Year Quest for Equality and Justice*. Bloomington, IN: Indiana University Press, 2005.

Joint Learning Initiative on Faith and Local Communities. http://jliflc.com, accessed July 29, 2015.

Kandiyoti, Deniz. "Disentangling Religion and Politics: Whither Gender Equality?" *IDS Bulletin* 42, no. 1 (2011): 10–14.

Karam, Azza. "On Faith, Health and Tensions: An Overview from an Inter-Governmental Perspective." *Heythrop Journal* 55 (2014): 1069–79.

Khan, Janet. Introduction to "The Greatness Which Might Be Theirs: Religions as an Agent for Promoting the Advancement of Women at All Levels," written by the Bahá'í International Community. August 26, 1995. http://www.bic.org/statements/greatness-which-might-be-theirs-religions-agent-promoting-advancement-women-all-levels.

Khan, Janet, and Peter Khan, *Advancement of Women: A Bahá'í Perspective*. Wilmette, IL: Bahá'í Publishing Trust, 2003.

Knox, Geoffrey, ed. *Religion and Public Policy at the UN*. 2002. http://www.catholicsforchoice.org/wp-content/uploads/2014/01/2000religionandpublicpolicyatheun.pdf.

National Spiritual Assembly of the United States and Canada (1947). *Bahá'í Statement on Women*. Archives of the Bahá'í International Community's United Nations Office, Bahá'í International Community, New York, NY.

Paterson, Gillian. "'On the Other Hand...': The Catholic Church and Some Discourses on Population." *Heythrop Journal* 55, no. 6 (November 2014): 1102–12.

Puechguirbal, Nadine. "Discourses on Gender, Patriarchy and Resolution 1325: A Textual Analysis of UN Documents." *International Peacekeeping* 17 (2010): 172–87.

Razavi, Sharah, and Anne Jenichen. "The Unhappy Marriage of Religion and Politics: Problems and Pitfalls for Gender Equality (Draft)." *UN Research Institute for Social Development*. http://www.unrisd.org/80256B3C005BCCF9/(httpPublications)/4ACE883B67ABCDEBC12577690046502C?OpenDocument.

"Record Number of Women Makes History at UN Security Council." *UN News Centre*. Last modified September 15, 2014. http://www.un.org/apps/news/story.asp?NewsID=48711#.Vor8wzZTWf4.

Tomalin, Emma (Ed.) *Gender, Faith, and Development*. London: Oxfam & Practical Action Publishing, 2011. http://policy-practice.oxfam.org.uk/publications/gender-faith-and-development-144042, accessed August 2, 2015.

United Nations. "Beijing Declaration and Platform of Action." Last modified October 27, 1995. http://www.refworld.org/docid/3dde04324.html.

———. "Short History of the Commission on the Status of Women." http://www.un.org/womenwatch/daw/CSW60YRS/CSWbriefhistory.pdf.

———. "UN Charter." *UN.org*. http://www.un.org/en/sections/un-charter/index4658.html?page=2.

United Nations Entity for Gender Equality and the Empowerment of Women. "Convention on the Elimination of All Forms of Discrimination against Women." *UN.org*. Accessed July 31, 2015. http://www.un.org/womenwatch/daw/cedaw/reservations.htm.

United Nations General Assembly. "Vienna Declaration and Programme of Action." Last modified July 12, 1993. http://www.refworld.org/docid/3ae6b39ec.html.

———. "Women 2000: Gender Equality, Development and Peace for the Twenty-First Century." http://documents-dds-ny.un.org/doc/UNDOC/GEN/N04/486/28/PDF/N0448628.pdf?OpenElement.

United Nations Human Rights Council. "Preliminary Study on Promoting Human Rights and Fundamental Freedoms through a Better Understanding of Traditional Values of Humankind." Last modified June 1, 2012. http://www.ohchr.org/Documents/HRBodies/HRCouncil/AdvisoryCom/Session9/A-HRC-AC-9-2_en.pdf.

United Nations Population Fund. "Guidelines for Engaging FBOs as Agents of Change." PDF, http://www.unfpa.org/culture/docs/fbo_engagement.pdf.

United Nations Research Institute for Social Development. "Religion, Politics and Gender Equality." *United Nations Research Institute for Social Development*. Accessed July 31, 2015. http://www.unrisd.org/80256B3C005BB128/(httpProjects)/3F3D45E0F8567920C12572B9004180C5.

Universal House of Justice. "To All National Spiritual Assemblies." In *The Bahá'í World 1968–1973*. Vol. 15. Haifa, Israel: Bahá'í World Centre, 1976, 614.

———. Universal House of Justice to the Bahá'ís of Iran, March 2, 2013. http://www.bahai.org/library/authoritative-texts/the-universal-house-of-justice/messages/#d=20130302_001&f=f1.

———. "The Promise of World Peace." 1985. http://www.bahai.org/library/authoritative-texts/the-universal-house-of-justice/messages/#.

———. "Riḍván 2010." April 21, 2010. http://preview.bahai.org/library/authoritative-texts/the-universal-house-of-justice/messages/#d=20100421_001&f=f1.

Women's Environment and Development Organization. "An Open Letter on Women & UN Reform to the Secretary General and Member States from NGOs Present at the 50th Session of the Commission on the Status of Women." March 6, 2006. *Women's Environment and Development Organization*. http://www.choike.org/documentos/open_letter2006.pdf, accessed July 30, 2015.

CHAPTER NINE

THE BAHÁ'Í COMMUNITY AND PUBLIC POLICY: THE BAHÁ'Í REFUGEE RESETTLEMENT PROGRAM (1981–1989)

GEOFFREY CAMERON

The chapters in this volume have thus far considered a range of conceptual and practical issues related to the role of religion in public discourse. This final contribution extends this analysis to the realm of government relations and public policy. It examines how the Bahá'í community worked with the Canadian and other governments during the 1980s to facilitate the resettlement of Iranian Bahá'ís rendered stateless by the Islamic Republic of Iran. In the course of narrating and analyzing the development of this program, particular attention is paid to the way that Bahá'í beliefs and principles shaped the approach of Bahá'í institutions and actors to engaging with public policy processes. In addition to proving effective at achieving the specific aims of the Bahá'í community—to provide short-term emergency protection for vulnerable co-religionists—it also exerted a broader positive influence on the early development of Canada's private sponsorship program for refugees.

This chapter focuses on the evolution of the Bahá'í refugee program in the 1980s and the discrete interactions between representatives of the Bahá'í community and government officials over time. It shows how Bahá'í representatives engaged with what public policy scholars call problem formation, issue framing, and agenda setting—which simply refers to the first stage of a policy process, where groups bring issues to the attention of the government.[1] Later on, they also helped advance the final stages of the policy cycle at the level of implementation and administration.

This case study of the Bahá'í community's government relations activity reveals positive practices of policy engagement as well as the absence of a prevalent pattern of public discourse. This latter pattern includes practices such as public protest, criticism, and pressure tactics intended to manipulate public opinion in ways that press governments to yield to the agenda of a civil society organization. These practices are the norm among many civil society organizations—and have been especially prominent in refugee advocacy—but they were absent from Bahá'í efforts to open the doors of various countries to Iranian refugees. What was absent from the discourse and practice of Bahá'í actors, in other words, is just as relevant as what was present.[2]

This analysis of the principles and approaches that inform how Bahá'í actors participate in policy processes, however, should not be confused with describing a strategy for influencing political affairs. Since its early history, the Bahá'í community has carefully modulated its involvement in public policy issues because of core principles about non-interference in politics and non-involvement in partisan politics or debate.[3] The Bahá'í teachings disavow many practices associated with lobbying, particularly the use of manipulative tactics, political interference, and partisanship to advance political goals. These tactics are viewed as means that are inconsistent with the ends that the Bahá'í Faith strives to advance—the broadening of the basis of society and strengthening of the relationships of cooperation and reciprocity that bind people together. Ulrich Gollmer has described the Bahá'í approach to politics as one that "implies a qualitative change in the character of politics.... It must change from strategically oriented action based on shrewd alliances and power politics aimed at asserting particular (individual, group, national, etc.) interests, to action that is directed towards universal understanding."[4] Therefore, the approach of the Bahá'í community to policy processes is informed by underlying principles about the relationship between religion and politics, and it rejects the use of tactics shaped by strategic calculations about achieving political influence.

In one of the most extensive statements on the Bahá'í approach to politics, Shoghi Effendi writes that Bahá'ís should "rise above all particularism and partisanship, above the vain disputes, the petty calculations, the transient passions that agitate the face, and engage the attention, of a changing world."[5] Instead, he writes, they should endeavour "to serve, in an unselfish, unostentatious and patriotic fashion, the highest interests of the country to which he belongs, and in a way that would entail no departure from the high standards of integrity and truthfulness associated with the teachings of his Faith."[6] He continues: "Let them affirm their unyielding determination to stand, firmly and unreservedly, for the way of Bahá'u'lláh, to avoid the entanglements and bickerings inseparable from the pursuits of the politician, and to become worthy agencies of that Divine Polity which incarnates God's immutable Purpose for all men."[7]

This approach to politics is notable by virtue of its distinctiveness from other, prominent models of the relationship between religion and politics. At one extreme is an approach to politics and political theology whereby religious institutions that claim the allegiance of either a majority or a powerful minority assert a privileged role in the governance of the state. At the other extreme is the exclusivist secular state, which governs a supposedly neutral public sphere in which religion is kept entirely private. Religious authorities are discouraged from seeking any role in public policy discourse and are instead expected to attend only to the social and spiritual needs of their members. Between the two extremes is the more common practice in liberal democracies, where religious actors participate in the public sphere alongside other interest groups seeking to advance their policy agendas—their tactics and strategies virtually identical. What distinguishes the approach of the Bahá'í community from these prevalent models is an effort to apply its core beliefs about building unity, fostering cooperation, and promoting deliberation to its methods of government relations on issues of public policy.

The Development of the Bahá'í Resettlement Program

In the aftermath of the 1979 Islamic Revolution in Iran, the newly empowered hardline clerics targeted the country's Bahá'í community with the intention of eliminating it from the new Islamic Republic. Iran's clerical elite had a particular animus toward the Bahá'ís, the country's largest religious minority and followers of a post-Islamic religion—heretics, in their eyes. Bahá'ís were the clearest obstacle to ideological unity in the clerics' project to fuse the state with a radical version of Shi'a Islam.

Following the revolution, the early attacks on the Bahá'ís included more than two hundred executions and "disappearances," which appeared to be coordinated to eliminate those in visible leadership positions in the community. Bahá'í graveyards and holy sites were razed, children and youth were expelled from schools, properties were seized, and virtually all citizenship rights were stripped from Bahá'ís. Writing in the *New York Review of Books* in 1982, Firuz Kazemzadeh raised an alarm: "the threat of genocide hangs over the heads of the Bahá'ís of Iran."[8] Meanwhile, Bahá'ís were banned from leaving the country.[9]

It fell to their co-religionists overseas to communicate accurate information of their plight to their governments and United Nations agencies and to seek their protection by raising international concern and pursuing resettlement for Bahá'í refugees. The first aspect of this initiative, mobilizing global public opinion and activating international legal channels, has been studied elsewhere.[10] The Bahá'ís coordinated an international campaign to focus attention on the executions and disappearances of Bahá'ís, which successfully raised vocal advocates around the world and initiated credible United Nations reporting and resolutions that left no doubt about the actions and intentions of the Iranian government in their treatment of Bahá'ís. The objective of this case study, however, is to focus on the second aspect of this campaign, which was to secure refugee resettlement in dozens of countries around the world for several thousand Bahá'ís rendered stateless by Iranian government actions.

In the wake of the revolution, a significant number of Bahá'ís had been forced to seek refuge in neighbouring countries. Their risky journeys on foot brought them to Turkey, Pakistan, and India, where they lived in a precarious position. Other Iranian Bahá'ís who had been living abroad were unable to renew their travel documents and were stranded without legal status. These stateless Iranian Bahá'ís sought resettlement in countries willing to admit them as refugees.

The Canadian Response
Canada became an early and prominent voice leading an international outcry against the attacks on Bahá'ís. Initially, representatives of the National Spiritual Assembly met with senior officials at the Departments of Immigration and External Affairs with the aim of dispelling misinformation about Bahá'ís spread by Iranian émigrés.[11] These efforts were aided by the unanimous passage of a resolution in the House of Commons in July 1980 that called attention to the persecution of the Bahá'ís in Iran. It was the first such intervention made by a national legislature. With this all-party support from Parliament, Bahá'í representatives helped the Department of External Affairs bring forward a resolution to the United Nations Sub-Commission on the Prevention of Discrimination Against Minorities, initiating a series of interventions by the UN Commission on Human Rights in defence of the Bahá'ís in Iran.[12]

As Canadian government officials became informed about the Bahá'í Faith and the deteriorating situation in Iran, individual refugee appeals brought forward by the National Assembly began to receive more favourable treatment. In 1980, the National Assembly approached the Canadian government more formally with a request for assistance with resettling a larger number of stateless Bahá'ís, offering to verify the status of Bahá'í refugees, assist their resettlement, and guarantee that they would not become public charges.

This approach coincided with the late phases of Canada's massive resettlement program for Indochinese refugees, which welcomed sixty thousand refugees from Vietnam, Laos, and Cambodia between 1979 and 1980. The program was the first to make use of a new provision in the 1976 Immigration Act that allowed private groups to name and sponsor refugees for resettlement in Canada. More than thirty thousand of those who arrived through the Indochinese refugee program came to Canada under the sponsorship of private groups—most of which were affiliated with religious communities.[13] Thus, when the National Assembly approached the Canadian government regarding the admission of Bahá'ís, the new policy framework of private sponsorship had recently been tried and tested. The Canadian government accordingly authorized a program for the resettlement of Bahá'í refugees as the second major refugee program undertaken within the framework of private sponsorship.

Another feature of Canadian refugee policy that had been introduced by the Immigration Act and initially applied in the case of the Indochinese refugees was the concept of a "designated class." When a particular group is identified as a "designated class," members could be treated as refugees without having to show that they met—on an individual basis—the strict criteria of the refugee definition under international law.[14] This kind of recognition allowed the Canadian government and private sponsors to circumvent laborious admissibility guidelines in cases where Cabinet chose to designate specific groups of people as of special concern to the government.

The National Assembly signed a major sponsorship agreement holder with the Government of Canada, which meant that it would assume liability for all Bahá'ís entering under its sponsorship. By identifying Bahá'ís as a designated class, Canadian visa officers were able to bypass the lengthy procedure of determining refugee status through the United Nations High Commissioner for Refugees (UNHCR). Field officers were encouraged to grant refugee status to Iranian Bahá'ís, provided they could verify their status as Bahá'ís. For this, refugees relied on official letters of support from the National Assembly.

As early as 1981, Canada's Department of Employment and Immigration included an appendix to its Immigration Manual that provided visa officers with special directions regarding refugee applications made by Iranian Bahá'ís. The appendix described the relationship between the National Assembly and the Government of Canada and emphasized some characteristics of the program. It explains:

> The situation facing the Bahá'ís in Iran is very serious and unlikely to improve. For this reason, special measures for Iranian Bahá'ís in

Canada are in effect. Following a meeting with the National Spiritual Assembly of the Bahá'ís of Canada, we advanced to the Minister and received his approval for special measures to certain Iranian Bahá'ís outside of Iran and outside of Canada.[15]

The "special measures" described in the appendix applied to two groups of Bahá'í refugees. The first group included those living outside of Iran who faced difficulty renewing their passports as Bahá'ís. The second group was made up of those who had fled to nearby countries (principally Pakistan) and were in particularly vulnerable situations. Many of these qualified as Convention refugees (i.e., those who meet the criteria of the 1951 Refugee Convention), and even those who did not were to "be reviewed as sympathetically as possible with a view to approval by the use of positive discretion whenever reasonable."[16] Cases that could not be approved, the appendix notes, would "require Ministerial concurrence in refusal."[17]

Officers within the immigration service regarded the cooperative relationship between the National Assembly and the Government of Canada positively, but also as an exceptional case. Mike Molloy, a Canadian immigration officer in Geneva, noted in a meeting with Bahá'í representatives that the Assembly's permission to resettle the Bahá'í refugees was virtually unprecedented. Although the participation of a religious community in refugee resettlement was not novel, the degree of trust and cooperation with government representatives was regarded as unique by immigration officers.

Despite the clear policy direction from Ottawa, there were initially lengthy delays and some inconsistency with processing Bahá'í refugee applications. Gerry Van Kessel, a manager in the refugee branch, recalls: "One of our challenges at the beginning was that ... there was very limited recognition [of the Bahá'í Faith] at that time.... The posts abroad were very suspicious of what [Foreign Ministry headquarters was] trying to do."[18] Indeed, according to Dennis Scown, the immigration program manager, the Foreign Ministry headquarters did not have the authority to direct officers to approve specific cases, and some officers resisted the approach of the Bahá'í program.[19] Because field-level officers exercised a high level of discretion when evaluating refugee applications, Bahá'í applications were not always treated with the flexibility that was intended by Ottawa.

In response to this growing problem, the Ministry helped to train two representatives of the National Assembly in its immigration procedures. Mona Mojgani and Carolyn Dowdell began to undertake visits to Canadian embassies and offices in order to acquaint Foreign Service officers with the situation of the Iranian Bahá'ís, to help affirm the policy direction coming from Ottawa. This strategy expedited processing in the early phase of the program, just when the violence in Iran was intensifying and more Bahá'ís were fleeing the country, often on foot and under extremely dangerous circumstances. Pakistan was emerging as a primary destination for these refugees.

When Mojgani arrived at the Canadian High Commission in Islamabad (Pakistan) for the first time, she met with Scown, who initially was unsympathetic to the Bahá'í refugee program and the urgency demanded by headquarters. He first estimated the Bahá'í refugees would be in Pakistan for at least a year because that was how long he anticipated it would take to process their applications. However, following several meetings together, he and Mojgani developed a cooperative approach that helped speed up the processing time. At Scown's suggestion, Mojgani first facilitated the relocation of scattered Bahá'í refugees to Islamabad. She then spent up to twenty hours a day preparing them for their interviews, getting their paperwork in order, and pre-screening candidates who met Canada's resettlement priorities. With Mojgani's help, Scown lowered the waiting time for refugees from one year to two weeks. When Ottawa telexed Scown in February 1985 to ask for a status report on Bahá'í refugee processing out of Islamabad, he replied on the same day:

> Post has gone and will continue to go out of its way to facilitate processing of Bahais. In fact, in past eighteen months have had quota for govt sponsored Bahais raised from fifty to one hundred fifty per year.... Virtually all Bahai cases are interviewed within two wks of applying.... At present we have no/no cases awaiting interview and have informed Bahais wud [sic] welcome more applications from suitable candidates.[20]

Scown recommended increasing the quota of Bahá'í refugees, and he became instrumental in opening up other countries to Bahá'í refugees by advocating informally for their cause with his foreign counterparts.

The positive regard developed for Bahá'í representatives and for the refugees themselves led government officials to prioritize, expedite, and increase Bahá'í resettlement in Canada. Douglas Martin, the Secretary of the National Assembly, communicated with senior officials in the capital, Ottawa. Martin worked with Van Kessel and Kirk Bell, Director-General of Policy at the immigration ministry, to develop the policy framework and to maintain a flow of information about the rapidly evolving situation in Iran. In 1983, Bell approached Martin about increasing the resettlement quota for Bahá'ís, whose quick social and economic integration into Canadian society had impressed officials. While the quota had already been increased several times (which itself was remarkable in the context of an overall drastic reduction in refugee resettlement quotas during the 1980s), Bell suggested something different: the Government of Canada would include Bahá'ís who lacked financial means in a new government-assisted refugee program, while those with more resources would move through the (unfunded) private sponsorship system. However, the Bahá'í community would still manage resettlement coordination in both cases. During the 1980s, the greater part of Canada's Middle East refugee resettlement quota was made available for the resettlement of Bahá'ís from Iran.[21]

As the primary sponsors of Bahá'í refugees, the Canadian Bahá'í community took responsibility for many aspects of the settlement process. One particularly notable feature was the broad distribution of refugees across the country and the avoidance of major urban centres for settlement. While the Bahá'í community in Canada was intensely aware of the humanitarian nature of their support to Iranian co-religionists, they also saw them as contributing members of their growing communities. The response of communities across the country led to the resettlement of refugees in about 220 cities and towns—including the Far North and on islands at both coasts.

The process of settlement and integration adopted by the Bahá'í community was also notable. When a group of refugees arrived in Canada, they would typically stay in an urban centre for less than forty-eight hours before departing for their final destination. This policy was adopted by the Bahá'í community in order to promote local integration. A report prepared after the conclusion of the program made particular note of the reciprocal dynamic of the integration process:

> We have found that when the refugee is not surrounded by an entire community of her own cultural group, she is much more likely to quickly learn the language and customs of her new country. If the Canadians befriending her are sensitive and eager to learn, this does not by any means necessitate her losing her own cultural identity. On the contrary, it provides for a wonderful enrichment of all concerned.[22]

The practice of geographical distribution was also successful in supporting the socio-economic integration of the refugees. A 1985 government memo documented the following: "the employment record of Bahá'í refugees is very impressive. More than 90% find jobs within the first year in Canada—the majority beginning work in the first six months."[23]

The process of settlement was aided by coordination between the National Assembly and local Bahá'í communities identified for resettlement. Government officials were impressed by the scope of national coordination, which they saw as "a nation-wide network of citizens."[24] New arrivals would first be met at the airport by representatives of the National Assembly, after which they would be transferred to a sponsoring local Bahá'í community. Deborah K. Van Den Hoonaard has described an example of this settlement process in the less populated region of Atlantic Canada, where some two hundred refugees initially settled:

> The first Persian Bahá'ís to arrive did not know anyone. Many came in the dead of winter. Three things about their arrival stand out: first, the local Bahá'ís met them at the airport or train station; second, the Bahá'ís treated them like family; third, the host communities let the newcomers know that they were very important to them.[25]

The process by which local Bahá'í communities welcomed refugees contributed significantly to the refugees' settlement and integration into society and the economy. Despite encountering prejudice and racism from certain members of Canadian society, the immediate intimacy of relationships with local Bahá'ís provided both practical and emotional support in the process of settlement.[26]

The program was regarded as a success by the Canadian government, for whom it remains one of the earliest models of cooperative private sponsorship of refugees. It was the first major refugee movement after the Indochinese program to make use of the private sponsorship provisions of the 1976 Immigration Act and to demonstrate their viability as a way to promote cooperation between government and civil society groups in the field of refugee resettlement. Following the conclusion of the Indochinese program, in fact, Canada reduced its refugee admissions and entered into a contentious period of public debate over its moral and legal obligations to refugees overseas. The development and success of the Iranian Bahá'í resettlement program was a significant exception within this period of retrenchment. It generated lessons about the possibilities of trust and cooperation between government and civil society that senior civil servants from that time continue to cite as sources of inspiration in their work.[27] The private sponsorship program flourished under the direction of many of the civil servants who cooperated with the Bahá'í community. It has since become a policy model from which other countries are looking to learn as they grapple with the politics and humanitarian crisis of protracted refugee emergencies around the world.[28]

Expanding the Program Internationally

By 1984, the attention of the Bahá'í community turned to diversifying the destination countries for refugees. Canada had by this time resettled over one thousand Bahá'í refugees, and interventions by both Bahá'í representatives and Canadian officials had helped open up Australia and the United States to refugees coming via Pakistan. According to Martin, Australia established a process for resettling Bahá'í refugees in Pakistan due to persuasion by a senior Canadian official, who testified to the positive outcomes of the refugee program in Canada and urged his Australian colleagues to follow suit. This official also intervened with other Commonwealth governments to seek admission of Bahá'í refugees. With regard to the United States, positive relations between Mojgani and the UNHCR office in Madrid played an instrumental role in leading that country to open an immigration processing post in Islamabad, which helped to increase the number of its Bahá'í admissions.[29]

The successful expansion of the refugee program to Australia and the United States was followed by an international trip by Mojgani to several European countries with a view to opening them up to resettlement. Mojgani visited Belgium, Denmark, Germany, Italy, the Netherlands, and Sweden as a representative of the Bahá'í International Community (BIC) in order to help those National Assemblies find ways to meet with their governments and discuss the possibility of opening refugee admissions for Bahá'ís. Several other European countries were later included in this itinerary (Ireland, Finland, Austria), as well as a number of Latin American countries (Ecuador, Peru, Chile, Bolivia, and Paraguay). As a BIC representative, Mojgani joined meetings held by the representatives of the National Assemblies with government representatives in most countries, serving as an expert to advise on the needs and problems of Bahá'í refugees. In each country, the National Assembly's representatives conducted discussions about refugee admissions and quotas with their own governments.

It quickly became apparent that an international agency would be needed to coordinate the resettlement of Bahá'í refugees on a global scale. In November 1984, the Universal House of Justice wrote to thirteen National Assemblies, informing them of its creation of an International Bahá'í Refugee Office (IBRO) to be based in Toronto:

> It is believed that the resettlement of such refugees could be dealt with more satisfactorily if the effort of all National Assemblies involved were to be coordinated. The House of Justice has therefore decided as follows: The National Spiritual Assembly of Canada, which has con-

siderable experience and success in this field, is charged with coordinating the efforts to settle Iranian Bahá'í refugees. That National Assembly will establish an office for this purpose and appoint a coordinator.... The Universal House of Justice would like to see the Iranian Bahá'í refugees settled in various countries of Africa, Asia and Latin America, as well as of Europe and North America.[30]

The IBRO was established with Mojgani as its coordinator, reporting to the Universal House of Justice. In 1984 and 1985, Mojgani undertook visits to Europe and Latin America, where she accompanied representatives of those countries' National Assemblies to meetings with senior officials in order to acquaint them with the situation in Iran, to share the success of the Canadian program, and to invite them to make an allowance for Bahá'í refugees.

The approach developed by the IBRO to open up additional resettlement quotas in new countries was immediately effective. When the IBRO wrote to National Assemblies in eleven Latin American countries in January 1985, it was already able to report successes from Mojgani's European trip:

> During the course of a trip last month to eleven countries [Mojgani] had the bounty of working with officers of the respective National Spiritual Assemblies in making approaches to their governments. So far, entry for upwards of thirty [Bahá'ís] has been secured to each of six countries (Norway, France, Spain, Ireland, the Netherlands, and Germany). There is also good reason to hope that two others (Belgium and Finland) will also participate.[31]

In her report to the National Assembly of Canada, Mojgani commented on her collaboration with the National Assemblies of European countries, noting that despite their inexperience with government relations and an unfriendly policy environment with regard to refugees, their efforts were rewarded with success.[32]

The achievements of the European trip were shortly replicated in Latin America. Mojgani accompanied National Assembly representatives to meetings with government officials and local UNHCR representatives. Canada's positive response and experience with Bahá'í refugees was presented as a model to other governments, and the advice and assistance of its diplomats was sought in several cases. The IBRO was able to report in April 1985 that at least seven countries agreed provisionally to resettle Bahá'í refugees. Mojgani said she had "good reason to hope" that the following countries would resettle significant numbers of Bahá'ís: Panama,

Venezuela, Bolivia, Argentina, Uruguay, Paraguay, Brazil.[33] Final decisions would rely upon the ability of National Assemblies to follow up with authorities and the willingness of the UNHCR headquarters in Geneva to assist with financing.

At this point, the IBRO was encouraging Bahá'í refugees to take up the openings for resettlement outside of Canada and the United States. While Bahá'ís with personal and family relations continued to move to North America, many others pursued settlement in Europe and Latin America as a means to support the growth and development of the Bahá'í Faith in countries that had smaller Bahá'í populations. (See Table 1.) A review of the correspondence on this process indicates that the Bahá'í institutions recognized the suffering of the refugees but did not treat them as passive victims. Instead, the institutions viewed the refugees as potential resources to support the advancement of Bahá'í communities throughout the world.

By 1989, the primary aims of the program had been accomplished: some eight thousand refugees were resettled in about twenty-four countries. Most stateless Bahá'ís were resettled. And the situation on the ground in Iran was changing. Although Bahá'ís were still denied most basic rights, the violent persecution had tapered off. Therefore, on 22 October 1989, the Universal House of Justice wrote to the National Assembly of Canada to dissolve the IBRO and transfer its remaining responsibilities to the BIC Office in Geneva. The letter noted the historical significance of the efforts of the IBRO, as well as its contributions to the development of the Bahá'í Faith:

> We wish to express our heartfelt thanks to your National Assembly for the ready acceptance of this most difficult, complex, but historic and rewarding assignment to facilitate the resettlement of thousands of Iranian Bahá'ís who have escaped persecution and who, thanks to your assistance, are now able to serve the Cause in many parts of the world.[34]

Many of the countries in which Bahá'ís were resettled were, in fact, not traditional countries of refugee resettlement. The arrival of Iranian Bahá'í refugees were among the first refugees to be resettled in Ireland, for instance, setting the stage for a later openness to receiving refugees from other destinations.[35] Similarly, at the time that Brazil accepted more than one hundred refugees, it too had been resistant to accept refugees nominated by the UNHCR. The extent to which the resettlement of Bahá'ís in these and other countries exerted a positive influence on future refugee admissions is not

Table 1 RESETTLEMENT NUMBERS BY APRIL 1988

Country	Refugees Resettled
Argentina	4
Australia	1369
Austria	17
Belgium	17
Brazil	110
Canada	2257
Chile	*In process*
Denmark	11
Ecuador	7
Finland	*In process*
France	49
Germany	107
Ireland	26
Luxembourg	13
The Netherlands	20
New Zealand	66
Norway	64
Spain	15
Sweden	68
Switzerland	56
Uruguay	2
United Kingdom	274
United States	1268
Venezuela	*In process*

Source: Memorandum of April 1988 from the IBRO to the Universal House of Justice, in Martin, "The Development of Work and the Iranian Bahá'í Refugee Office." Reprinted with permission of the author.

possible to say with certainty. However, at a time when global demand for refugee resettlement is at an historic peak and new modes of international cooperation are being demanded with increasing urgency, these episodes of national hospitality by non-traditional countries of resettlement may be important to recall.

The Bahá'í Faith and the Public Sphere: Insights from the Resettlement Program

This chapter has thus far narrated the response of the Bahá'í community to the Iran refugee crisis, one of its early coordinated, international undertakings with governments. The approach of the Bahá'í community to facilitating this resettlement program reveals characteristics of its participation in the public and political spheres. Two salient features of this public affairs program were non-adversarial engagement and coordinated decentralization. These features are elaborated below.

Non-Adversarial Engagement

One of the most striking aspects of the Bahá'í resettlement program was the non-adversarial approach to government. It is striking because of its contrast with antagonistic or manipulative approaches often used by advocacy groups to influence governments to accept refugees. For Bahá'ís, non-adversarial methods are employed as a matter of principle. Through a closer examination of the refugee program, we can uncover some of these non-adversarial practices in the context of government relations.

The approach of the Bahá'í community to meetings with government officials focused on an appeal to the evidence of the situation facing the refugees and the need for an international response to alleviate suffering. Bahá'í representatives used precise statistics about the numbers of Bahá'í refugees waiting in Pakistan, described the conditions of persecution in Iran and the numbers affected, and stressed that most Bahá'ís have refused to flee their homeland.[36] They emphasized the success of the program in resettling refugees in Canada and identified other countries willing to resettle Bahá'ís. In other words, Bahá'í representatives defined the problem of Bahá'í refugees and framed the issue by appealing to reason and evidence.

Attention was also given to developing trust with government officials over time. Bahá'í representatives built credibility through honest dealings throughout the development and implementation of the resettlement program. Trust was fostered by proactively and individually screening refugee applications, rigorously documenting resettlement processes, and acquiescing to government policy preferences for certain professions or local destinations for relocation. Reflecting on his relationship with a Bahá'í representative, Scown said: "The thing I liked about [her] was that... she gave you the straight goods."[37] He noted the adaptability of the Bahá'í representatives, as well as their willingness to compromise and accommodate government policy even when it obstructed their aims. Another government official in Ottawa commented at a meeting: "the Bahá'ís are the only group whom we have never been burned by. You will find them as concerned about the welfare of this country as they are about their own people."[38] This sentiment is reiterated in other archival materials and interviews with former officials. It reflects not only on the relationships established by Bahá'í representatives, but also on the actions and efforts of Bahá'í refugees to uphold the integrity of the program.[39]

The method and practice of the Bahá'í community is related to core normative commitments that reject adversarialism as a legitimate basis of political action. In this regard, Gollmer states that the Bahá'í approach to political processes is based on the "conviction that human interests are, in principle, non-antagonistic in character."[40] Karlberg describes the Bahá'í community as "an alternative cultural formation" that is distinguished by its unique "non-adversarial principles and practices."[41] He argues that practices of mutuality and cooperation are central to Bahá'í thought and practice: "within this unique cultural universe, its members grow, develop and internalize a coherent set of cultural norms that stand in stark contrast to norms [valorizing] ... contest."[42] Indeed, non-adversarial practices are one way in which the Bahá'í community strives to bring spiritual principle into action.

Recent scholarship on humanitarianism has noted the persistent sense of the sacred within humanitarian action—that is, the desire to act purely for others, without regard to politics or strategy—which is nevertheless eroding in light of practical considerations.[43] For instance, the need to participate in political affairs presents real dilemmas to even secular humanitarian actors who view political engagement as an untenable compromise of principles. Some organizations have responded to these tensions by looking to "sanctify" humanitarianism in a number of ways: by trying to create a space free of politics, by adopting an ethic to act first and ask questions later, by insisting on altruistic motives, and by upholding values above interests.[44] The approach of Bahá'í institutions to working with governments to develop this refugee program is an example of another way in which commitment to spiritual principle is maintained in light of the practical demands of refugee protection.

One might therefore say that, through their commitment to an ethic of non-adversarial engagement, Bahá'ís sought to "sanctify" their practice and "bridge the divide between the sacred and the profane."[45] A core aspect of Bahá'í belief and practice is the call "to build its capacity to contribute to processes that promote peace and unity."[46] The development of non-adversarial approaches in its internal structure and public engagements is part of the mission of the Bahá'í Faith, along with its effort to lend a spiritual impetus to the development of society. Therefore, Bahá'ís do not view the need to relate to governments as somehow sacrificing principles to effect change; instead, government relations themselves are imbued with moral significance through a principled method of engagement.

Coordinated Decentralization
Another notable feature of the Bahá'í resettlement program was its approach to international coordination. Coordination followed the contours of the Bahá'í system of governance, which is organized hierarchically through elected bodies at the local, national, and international levels. The first stage of the resettlement program in Canada took place from 1981 to 1984 under the aegis of the National Assembly, which in turn managed the settlement of refugees through collaborative arrangements with Local Assemblies. As this model of resettlement showed its effectiveness, the Universal House of Justice established in 1984 the IBRO, which acted under its auspices despite being based in Canada. The IBRO collaborated horizontally with other international Bahá'í agencies, such as the BIC office in Geneva, and helped to raise the capacity of other National Assemblies to establish programs of government relations that could facilitate the diversification of the refugee program.

This characteristic of the resettlement program can be called "coordinated decentralization" because the purpose of coordination was not to concentrate authority but to effectively build capacity at lower levels of the system. We can see this characteristic clearly in the direction given by the Universal House of Justice to Mojgani when she undertook her early trip to European countries to share lessons from Canada's experience with resettlement. She was tasked with attending meetings conducted by representatives of the National Assemblies of each country in order to offer advice "on the needs and problems of Bahá'í refugees."[47] The letter also emphasized that policy discussions about refugee admissions and quotas should be conducted by National Assemblies with their own governments. In other words, Mojgani's role was not to control or dictate but to advise and assist other National Assemblies to develop the capacity to engage with their governments on refugee policy.

This approach to coordinating the Bahá'í refugee program provides insight into the Bahá'í community as a transnational religion. Though all world religions are, in one sense or another, transnational communities, this designation can mean a number of different things. On the one hand, we can understand religions as transnational "epistemic communities," sharing common ideas that they attempt to put into practice, including in the area of public policy.[48] Another way that religions can be transnational is through the affective ties they foster, creating "transnational solidarities" that transcend more narrow national identities.[49] A third way is by establishing transnational patterns of religious organization, which is to say by building religious networks and organizations that reach beyond national boundaries.[50] The Bahá'í refugee program demonstrates all three modes of transnationalism.

Rudolph has argued that "transnational religious formations" can be characterized as either hierarchical or self-organized.[51] She also proposes that transnational religion "creates an arena of belief, commitment and practice alternative to the state, draining affect and action from it without replacing it."[52] The Bahá'í community's approach to refugee resettlement resists these characterizations. The process of coordinated decentralization includes features of both hierarchy ("from a centre and from above") and self-organization ("from society and from below"). The Bahá'í community is highly organized within a hierarchical administrative order. However, the process of administration is oriented toward fostering and strengthening a diversity of local practices within a common framework of action. Furthermore, the resettlement program was not aimed at creating an alternative arena of action from the state. Rather, it validated state authority to oversee the process of refugee resettlement. The resettlement program involved working closely with state authorities, not trying to circumvent them.

This chapter's examination of the international Bahá'í resettlement program has illustrated some features of how the Bahá'í community engages with public policy processes. The actions undertaken by the Bahá'í community were informed by principles and beliefs about political order as well as about the appropriate relationship between religion and political authorities. Daniel Philpott argues that when studying the role of religion in global politics, we should begin by looking at the ideas that animate religious actors: "What is important to understand about religious actors is that religious politics, even when it converges with that of the state, emanates from beliefs, practices, and communities that themselves are prior to politics."[53] In a similar vein, Daniel H. Levine encourages scholars not only to look at the political outcome of religious action, but also to consider why religion may have stimulated or sustained action in the first place.[54] In other words, he argues that to understand how religious actors participate in political affairs, we should consider the role of "political theology," broadly defined as ethical justifications for political principles, norms, and practices that are derived from religious thought or scripture.[55]

Underlying the Bahá'í approach to politics is a particular kind of historical consciousness. The Bahá'í writings describe the present moment in history as a time of collective adolescence, when humanity is proceeding through "an unprecedented transition."[56] In this context, it is recognized that institutions, norms, and conventions that were suited to an earlier age are disintegrating at the same time that processes of integration are disclosing new opportunities for humanity to rise to the challenge of collective maturity. Bahá'í institutions thus strive to align their efforts with the forces of integration, which are bringing humanity closer to its promised future of peace and prosperity. This view of history, and the role of the Bahá'í community as an active protagonist in its advancement, informs Bahá'í approaches to politics and government relations.

The Bahá'í approach to involvement in policy processes can be contextualized within this view of historical processes and the role of the Bahá'í community in the collective life of humanity. The Bahá'í teachings offer a number of parameters to guide Bahá'í individuals and institutions in their relations with government. These parameters safeguard the integrity of the Bahá'í community, promote its growth and development, and lend additional impetus to processes of integration. Bahá'ís are bound to behave toward government with "loyalty, honesty and truthfulness."[57] They recognize the basic legitimacy of government authorities and do not associate with political movements that lead to sedition or that adopt methods of conflict and force.[58] This principle is often articulated as "non-involvement in politics," which refers in one sense to "any form of activity that might be interpreted, either directly or indirectly, as an interference in the political affairs of any particular government."[59] Instead, their approach to social change is to "interest themselves in movements which conduce to law and order."[60] Elaborating further, the Universal House of Justice wrote, "[T]heir approach is to avoid conflict and the contest for power while striving to unite people in the search for underlying moral and spiritual principles and for practical measures that can lead to the just resolution of the problems afflicting society."[61]

Non-involvement in politics as an organizing principle for participation in policy processes is striking because it is a boundary principle that limits the scope of possible strategies and tactics to advance political goals. It also disallows the use of inflammatory and emotional language designed to manipulate the reactions of the public. It resonates positively with what James Davidson Hunter has described as a mode of "faithful presence."[62] According to Hunter, religious actors should not try to force their beliefs upon others in public and political settings but rather use their religious perspectives as a source of insight and energy to stimulate constructive processes of social change. Faithful presence involves a "constructive resistance that seeks new patterns of social organization that challenge, undermine, and otherwise diminish oppression, injustice, enmity, and corruption and, in turn, encourage harmony, fruitfulness and abundance, wholeness, beauty, joy, security, and well-being."[63]

The concept of faithful presence is consistent with aspects of the approach the Bahá'í community strives to adopt in relation to policy process. All the endeavours of the Bahá'í community seek in some way to promote the oneness of humankind. This means that, as the Universal House of Justice explains, Bahá'ís cannot strive to "establish patterns of thought and action that give expression to the principle of oneness within their community, yet engage in activities in another context which ... reinforce an entirely different set of assumptions about social existence."[64] Bahá'ís alternatively endeavour to promote change through means that cohere with their commitment to the principle of oneness. In this regard, Bahá'ís are encouraged to "become actively engaged in as many aspects of contemporary life as feasible" in order to "further the cause of unity, promote human welfare and contribute to world solidarity."[65]

This chapter has presented only a brief review of one episode in the development of Bahá'í institutions and their engagement with public policy issues that sheds some light on the question, identified by José Casanova, of investigating "the conditions of possibility for modern public religion."[66] As this case shows, Bahá'í institutions aim to expand those conditions of possibility beyond simply entering into the contest for power or retreating to the private sphere. Future research might significantly extend and deepen these insights by conducting more in-depth comparative studies of non-partisan, non-adversarial action by religious and other groups in their relations with government.

Notes

1 David A. Rochefort and Kevin P. Donnelly, "Agenda-Setting and Political Discourse: Major Analytical Frameworks and Their Application," in *Routledge Handbook of Public Policy*, ed. Eduardo Araral Jr. et al. (Abingdon, UK: Routledge, 2013), 190.
2 Thank you to Michael Karlberg for this helpful framing of a central theme of this chapter.
3 See, for example, Moojan Momen, "The Bahá'ís and the Constitutional Revolution: The Case of Sari, Mazandaran, 1906–1913," *Iranian Studies* 41, no. 3 (2008): 343–63.
4 Ulrich Gollmer, "Bahá'í Political Thought," in *Making the Crooked Straight: A Contribution to Bahá'í Apologetics*, Udo Schaefer, Nicola Towfigh, and Ulrich Gollmer (Oxford: George Ronald, 2001).
5 Shoghi Effendi, *The World Order of Bahá'u'lláh* (Wilmette, IL: Bahá'í Publishing Trust, 1991), 64.

6 Ibid., 65.
7 Ibid.
8 Firuz Kazemzadeh, "The Terror Facing the Bahá'ís," *New York Review of Books*, May 13, 1982, 42–44.
9 See Reza Afshari, *Human Rights in Iran: The Abuse of Cultural Relativism* (Philadelphia, PA: University of Pennsylvania Press, 2001); Dominic Parviz Brookshaw and Seena B. Fazel, eds., *The Bahá'ís of Iran: Socio-historical Studies* (London: Routledge, 2008); and Eliz Sanasarian, *Religious Minorities in Iran* (Cambridge, UK: Cambridge University Press, 2000).
10 See Nazila Ghanea, *Human Rights, the UN and the Bahá'ís in Iran* (The Hague, Netherlands: Martinus Nijhoff, 2002) and Ziya Meral, "International Religious Freedom Advocacy in the Field: Challenges, Effective Strategies, and the Road Ahead," *Review of Faith & International Affairs* 10, no. 3 (2012): 25–32.
11 The National Spiritual Assembly is the elected national governing council of the Bahá'ís of Canada. From here on, I refer to it just as the National Assembly.
12 Ghanea, *Human Rights*, 371.
13 Gerald Dirks, *Controversy and Complexity: Canadian Immigration Policy during the 1980s* (Montreal: McGill-Queen's University Press, 1995), 24.
14 Ibid., 67.
15 Employment and Immigration Canada, *Immigration Manual, IS 26 (Iran)*, Annex II, "Iran: Admission of Iranian Bahá'ís," December 1981, International Bahá'í Refugee Office papers, Bahá'í National Centre, Toronto, ON.
16 Ibid. The 1951 Refugee Convention spells out that a refugee is someone who, "owing to a well-founded fear of being persecuted for reasons of race, religion, nationality, membership of a particular social group or political opinion, is outside the country of his nationality, and is unable to, or owing to such fear, is unwilling to avail himself of the protection of that country."
17 Employment and Immigration Canada, *Immigration Manual*, International Bahá'í Refugee Office papers, Bahá'í National Centre, Toronto, ON.
18 Gerry Van Kessel, personal interview, August 22, 2012.
19 Dennis Scown, personal interview, May 10, 2013.
20 Information obtained from a confidential cable from the Canadian Embassy to Pakistan to the Department of External Affairs on February 5, 1985. Accession No. 177454, Vol. 2, File 85-29-4-BAHAIS, Library and Archives Canada, Ottawa, Canada.
21 R. A. Girard to Hugues Mathieu, February 6, 1985. Accession No. 177454, Vol. 2, File 85-29-4-BAHAIS, Library and Archives Canada, Ottawa, Canada.
22 International Bahá'í Refugee Office, report submitted to Employment and Immigration Canada, June 5, 1988, International Bahá'í Refugee Office papers, Bahá'í National Centre, Toronto, ON.
23 R. A. Girard to Hugues Mathieu, February 6, 1985. Accession No. 177454, Vol. 2, File 85-29-4-BAHAIS, Library and Archives Canada, Ottawa, Canada.

24 International Bahá'í Refugee Office, memorandum to the National Spiritual Assembly of Canada, March 25, 1986, International Bahá'í Refugee Office papers, Bahá'í National Centre, Toronto, ON.
25 Deborah K. Van Den Hoonaard, "The Experience of Iranian Bahá'í Refugees in Atlantic Canada," *Our Diverse Cities* (2008): 105.
26 Ibid., 104–08.
27 See the taped proceedings from the symposium on the "Iranian Bahá'í Refugee Movement to Canada, 1981–1989," held at Carleton University, September 21, 2015, available at http://www.symposium.bahai.ca.
28 United Nations High Commissioner for Refugees, "Canada, UNHCR and Open Society Foundations Seek to Increase Refugee Resettlement through Private Sponsorship," *UNHCR.org*, last modified September 19, 2016, http://www.unhcr.org/news/press/2016/9/57e0e2784/canada-unhcr-open-society-foundations-seek-increase-refugee-resettlement.html.
29 Douglas Martin, "The Development and Work of the Iranian Bahá'í Refugee Office" (unpublished manuscript, 2001), Microsoft Word file.
30 Universal House of Justice to Thirteen National Spiritual Assemblies, November 18, 1984, International Bahá'í Refugee Office papers, Bahá'í National Centre, Toronto, ON.
31 International Bahá'í Refugee Office to the National Spiritual Assemblies of Argentina, Bolivia, Brazil, Chile, Colombia, Peru, Panama, Paraguay, Trinidad, Uruguay, and Venezuela, January 1, 1985, International Bahá'í Refugee Office papers, Bahá'í National Centre, Toronto, ON.
32 Ibid.
33 International Bahá'í Refugee Office, memorandum to the National Spiritual Assembly of Canada, International Bahá'í Refugee Office papers, Bahá'í National Centre, Toronto, ON.
34. Universal House of Justice to the National Spiritual Assembly of Canada, October 22, 1989, International Bahá'í Refugee Office papers, Bahá'í National Centre, Toronto, ON.
35 "Treatment of Bahá'ís in Iran," *Irish Times*, January 23, 2001.
36 International Bahá'í Refugee Office to the Government of Brazil, March 14, 1985, International Bahá'í Refugee Office papers, Bahá'í National Centre, Toronto, ON.
37 Scown, personal interview, August 3, 2012.
38 National Spiritual Assembly of Canada to the Universal House of Justice, June 9, 1983, International Bahá'í Refugee Office papers, Bahá'í National Centre, Toronto, ON.
39 Martin, "The Development and Work of the Iranian Bahá'í Refugee Office."
40 Gollmer, *"Bahá'í Political Thought,"* 468.
41 Karlberg, *Beyond the Culture of Contest: From Adversarialism to Mutualism in an Age of Interdependence* (Oxford, UK: George Ronald, 2004), 129.
42 Ibid., 123.

43 See Michael Barnett and Janice Gross Stein, "The Secularization and Sanctification of Humanitarian Life," in *Sacred Aid: Faith and Humanitarianism*, ed. Barnett and Stein (Oxford, UK: Oxford University Press, 2012), 3–36.
44 Ibid., 8.
45 Andrea Paras and Janice Gross Stein, "Bridging the Sacred and the Profane in Humanitarian Life," in *Sacred Aid: Faith and Humanitarianism*, edited by Michael Barnett and Stein (Oxford, UK: Oxford University Press, 2012), 231.
46 Universal House of Justice to the Bahá'ís of Iran, March 2, 2013.
47 Universal House of Justice to the National Spiritual Assembly of Canada, October 21, 1984, International Bahá'í Refugee Office papers, Bahá'í National Centre, Toronto, ON.
48 Emmanuel Adler and Peter M. Haas, "Conclusion: Epistemic Communities, World Order, and the Creation of a Reflective Research Program," *International Organization* 46, no. 1 (1992): 367–90.
49 Susanne Hoeber Rudolph, introduction to *Transnational Religion and Fading States*, ed. Rudolph and James Piscatori (Oxford, UK: Oxford University Press, 1997), 1–24.
50 Peggy Levitt, "Redefining the Boundaries of Belonging: The Institutional Character of Transnational Religious Life," *Sociology of Religion* 65, no. 1 (2004): 1–18.
51 Rudolph, introduction, 1–24.
52 Rudolph, "Dehomogenizing Religious Formations," in *Transnational Religion and Fading States*, ed. Rudolph and James Piscatori (Oxford, UK: Oxford University Press, 1997), 255–56.
53 Daniel Philpott, "Has the Study of Global Politics Found Religion?" *Annual Review of Political Science* 12 (2009): 193.
54 Daniel H. Levine, "Religion and Politics in Comparative and Historical Perspective," *Comparative Politics* 19, no. 1 (October 1986): 98.
55 See Michael Jon Kessler, ed., *Political Theology for a Plural Age* (Oxford, UK: Oxford University Press, 2013) and Philpott, "Explaining the Political Ambivalence of Religion," *American Political Science Review* 101, no. 3 (2007): 505–25.
56 Universal House of Justice to the Bahá'ís of Iran, March 2, 2013.
57 Bahá'u'lláh, *Tablets of Bahá'u'lláh* (Wilmette, IL: US Bahá'í Publishing Trust, 1988), 23.
58 'Abdu'l-Bahá, *The Promulgation of Universal Peace* (Wilmette, IL: Bahá'í Publishing Trust, 1982), 238–39.
59 Shoghi Effendi, *World Order*, 64.
60 'Abdu'l-Bahá, *Promulgation*, 238–39.
61 Universal House of Justice to an Individual, December 23, 2008.
62 James Davidson Hunter, *To Change the World: The Irony, Tragedy, and Possibility of Christianity in the Late Modern World* (Oxford, UK: Oxford University Press, 2010), 247.

63 Ibid., 247–48.
64 Universal House of Justice to the Bahá'ís of Iran, March 2, 2013.
65 Ibid.
66 José Casanova, *Public Religions in the Modern World* (Chicago: University of Chicago Press, 1994), 39.

Bibliography
'Abdu'l-Bahá. *The Promulgation of Universal Peace*. Wilmette, IL: Bahá'í Publishing Trust, 1982.
Adler, Emmanuel, and Peter M. Haas. "Conclusion: Epistemic Communities, World Order, and the Creation of a Reflective Research Program." *International Organization* 46, no. 1 (1992): 367–90.
Afshari, Reza. *Human Rights in Iran: The Abuse of Cultural Relativism*. Philadelphia, PA: University of Pennsylvania Press, 2001.
Bahá'u'lláh, *Tablets of Bahá'u'lláh*. Wilmette, IL: US Bahá'í Publishing Trust, 1988.
Barnett, Michael, and Janice Gross Stein. "The Secularization and Sanctification of Humanitarian Life." In *Sacred Aid: Faith and Humanitarianism*, edited by Barnett and Stein, 3–36. Oxford, UK: Oxford University Press, 2012.
Brookshaw, Dominic Parviz, and Seena B. Fazel, eds. *The Bahá'ís of Iran: Socio-historical Studies*. London: Routledge, 2008.
Casanova, José. *Public Religions in the Modern World*. Chicago: University of Chicago Press, 1994.
Dirks, Gerald. *Controversy and Complexity: Canadian Immigration Policy during the 1980s*. Montreal: McGill-Queen's University Press, 1995.
Employment and Immigration Canada. *Immigration Manual, IS 26 (Iran)*, Annex II, "Iran: Admission of Iranian Bahá'ís." December 1981, International Bahá'í Refugee Office papers, Bahá'í National Centre, Toronto, ON.
Ghanea, Nazila. *Human Rights, the UN and the Bahá'ís in Iran*. The Hague, Netherlands: Martinus Nijhoff, 2002.
Girard, R. A. Girard to Hugues Mathieu, February 6, 1985. Accession No. 177454, Vol. 2, File 85-29-4-BAHAIS, Library and Archives Canada, Ottawa, Canada.
Gollmer, Ulrich. "Political Theory." In *Making the Crooked Straight: A Contribution to Bahá'í Apologetics*, Udo Schaefer, Nicola Towfigh, and Ulrich Gollmer. Oxford: George Ronald, 2001.
Hunter, James Davidson. *To Change the World: The Irony, Tragedy, and Possibility of Christianity in the Late Modern World*. Oxford, UK: Oxford University Press, 2010.
International Bahá'í Refugee Office. International Bahá'í Refugee Office to the National Spiritual Assemblies of Argentina, Bolivia, Brazil, Chile, Colombia, Peru, Panama, Paraguay, Trinidad, Uruguay, and Venezuela, January 1, 1985, International Bahá'í Refugee Office papers, Bahá'í National Centre, Toronto, ON.

———. International Bahá'í Refugee Office to the Government of Brazil, March 14, 1985, International Bahá'í Refugee Office papers, Bahá'í National Centre, Toronto, ON.

———. Memorandum to the National Spiritual Assembly of Canada, April 9, 1985, International Bahá'í Refugee Office papers, Bahá'í National Centre, Toronto, ON.

———. Memorandum to the National Spiritual Assembly of Canada, March 25, 1986, International Bahá'í Refugee Office papers, Bahá'í National Centre, Toronto, ON.

———. Report submitted to Employment and Immigration Canada, June 5, 1988, International Bahá'í Refugee Office papers, Bahá'í National Centre, Toronto, ON.

Karlberg, Michael. *Beyond the Culture of Contest: From Adversarialism to Mutualism in an Age of Interdependence.* Oxford, UK: George Ronald, 2004.

Kazemzadeh, Firuz. "The Terror Facing the Bahá'ís." *New York Review of Books*, May 13, 1982, 42–44.

Kessler, Michael Jon, ed. *Political Theology for a Plural Age.* Oxford, UK: Oxford University Press, 2013.

Levine, Daniel H. "Religion and Politics in Comparative and Historical Perspective." *Comparative Politics* 19, no. 1 (October 1986): 95–122.

Levitt, Peggy. "Redefining the Boundaries of Belonging: The Institutional Character of Transnational Religious Life." *Sociology of Religion* 65, no. 1 (2004): 1–18.

Martin, Douglas. "The Development and Work of the Iranian Bahá'í Refugee Office." Unpublished manuscript, 2001. Microsoft Word file.

Meral, Ziya. "International Religious Freedom Advocacy in the Field: Challenges, Effective Strategies, and the Road Ahead." *Review of Faith & International Affairs* 10, no. 3 (2012): 25–32.

Momen, Moojan. "The Bahá'ís and the Constitutional Revolution: The Case of Sari, Mazandaran, 1906–1913." *Iranian Studies* 41, no. 3 (2008): 343–63.

National Spiritual Assembly of Canada. National Spiritual Assembly of Canada to the Universal House of Justice, June 9, 1983, International Bahá'í Refugee Office papers, Bahá'í National Centre, Toronto, ON.

Paras, Andrea, and Janice Gross Stein. "Bridging the Sacred and the Profane in Humanitarian Life." In *Sacred Aid: Faith and Humanitarianism*, edited by Michael Barnett and Stein, 211–40. Oxford, UK: Oxford University Press, 2012.

Philpott, Daniel. "Explaining the Political Ambivalence of Religion." *American Political Science Review* 101, no. 3 (2007): 505–25.

———. "Has the Study of Global Politics Found Religion?" *Annual Review of Political Science* 12 (2009): 183–202.

Rochefort, David A., and Kevin P. Donnelly. "Agenda-Setting and Political Discourse: Major Analytical Frameworks and Their Application." In *Routledge Handbook of Public Policy*, edited by Eduardo Araral Jr. et al., 189–203. Abingdon, UK: Routledge, 2013.

Rudolph, Susanne Hoeber. "Dehomogenizing Religious Formations." In *Transnational Religion and Fading States*, edited by Rudolph and James Piscatori, 243–61. Oxford, UK: Oxford University Press, 1997.

———. Introduction to *Transnational Religion and Fading States*, edited by Rudolph and James Piscatori, 1–24. Oxford, UK: Oxford University Press, 1997.

Sanasarian, Eliz. *Religious Minorities in Iran*. Cambridge, UK: Cambridge University Press, 2000.

Scown, Dennis. Personal interview. May 10, 2013.

———. Personal interview. August 3, 2012.

Shoghi Effendi. *The World Order of Bahá'u'lláh*. Wilmette, IL: Bahá'í Publishing Trust, 1991.

"Treatment of Bahá'ís in Iran." *Irish Times*, 23 January 2001.

United Nations High Commissioner for Refugees. "Canada, UNHCR and Open Society Foundations Seek to Increase Refugee Resettlement Through Private Sponsorship." *UNHCR.org*. Last modified September 19, 2016. http://www.unhcr.org/news/press/2016/9/57e0e2784/canada-unhcr-open-society-foundations-seek-increase-refugee-resettlement.html.

Universal House of Justice. Universal House of Justice to the Bahá'ís of Iran, March 2, 2013. http://www.bahai.org/library/authoritative-texts/the-universal-house-of-justice/messages/#d=20130302_001&f=f1.

———. Universal House of Justice to an Individual, December 23, 2008.

———. Universal House of Justice to Thirteen National Spiritual Assemblies, November 18, 1984, International Bahá'í Refugee Office papers, Bahá'í National Centre, Toronto, ON.

———. Universal House of Justice to the National Spiritual Assembly of Canada, October 21, 1984, International Bahá'í Refugee Office papers, Bahá'í National Centre, Toronto, ON.

———. Universal House of Justice to the National Spiritual Assembly of Canada, October 22, 1989, International Bahá'í Refugee Office papers, Bahá'í National Centre, Toronto, ON.

Van Den Hoonaard, Deborah K. "The Experience of Iranian Bahá'í Refugees in Atlantic Canada." *Our Diverse Cities* (2008): 104–08.

Van Kessel, Gerry. Personal interview. August 22, 2012.

ABOUT THE AUTHORS

Farzam Arbab has a PhD in physics from the University of California at Berkeley and has received an honorary doctorate in science from Amherst College. He is a founder of the Fundación para la Aplicación y Enseñanza de las Ciencias (FUNDAEC). From 1993 to 2013, he served on the international governing body of the Bahá'í Faith, the Universal House of Justice. Since his retirement from service on that body, he has dedicated his time to the exploration of questions related to education, science, and belief systems.

Sona Farid-Arbab has a PhD in the philosophy of education from the Institute of Education of the University of London. She has worked in the field of education in China and travelled extensively in that country. From 2002 to 2013, she lived in Haifa, Israel, and served as a Director of the Office of Social and Economic Development at the world centre of the Bahá'í Faith. Since leaving Haifa, she has been engaged in various research and writing projects related to education and development.

Julia Berger served as Principal Researcher at the Baha'i International Community's United Nations Office for eleven years. Prior to this, she was Research Associate at Harvard University's Joint Program on Religion and Public Life. She is pursuing a PhD in Theology and Religious Studies at the University of Kent in Canterbury, UK, with a focus on religious NGOs at the United Nations. She lives in New York City with her husband and twin daughters.

Geoffrey Cameron is a PhD candidate and Pierre Elliott Trudeau Foundation Scholar at the University of Toronto. He has worked with the Office of Public Affairs of the Bahá'í Community of Canada, and served on the Executive Committee of the Association for Bahá'í Studies – North America. He is a co-author of *Exceptional People: How Migration Changed the World and Will Define Our Future* (with Ian Goldin).

ABOUT THE AUTHORS

Michael Karlberg is a professor at Western Washington University in the field of media and public discourse. His research critically examines foundational assumptions underlying Western civilization, including conceptions of human nature, power, social organization, and social change. He is the author of *Beyond the Culture of Contest* and numerous articles that expand on this theme. He is currently working on a book addressing the problem of normative relativism in a world of increasing global interdependence.

David A. Palmer is an Associate Professor in the Department of Sociology at the University of Hong Kong. He has published several books and articles on religion, civil society, and culture in Asia, including *Chinese Religious Life*; *The Religious Question in Modern China*; *Dream Trippers: Global Daoism and the Predicament of Modern Spirituality*; and *The Civil Sphere in East Asia* (co-edited with Jeffrey Alexander).

Shahriar Razavi currently serves as a member of the Universal House of Justice, the international governing body of the Bahá'í Faith, to which he was elected in 2008.

Benjamin Schewel is a Fellow at the Centre for Religion, Conflict and the Public Domain at the University of Groningen and an Affiliate Scholar at the Institute for Advanced Studies in Culture at the University of Virginia. He also serves as a Research and Policy Officer at the Bahá'í International Community, Brussels office. He is the author of *Seven Ways of Looking at Religion: The Major Narratives*.

Matthew Weinberg served as Research Director of the Bahá'í International Community, in Haifa, Israel, and led the initial work of the Institute for Studies in Global Prosperity in contributing to international development discourse. He has worked as a consultant for the Gates Foundation evaluating development programming, and also was a senior analyst with the United States Congress Office of Technology Assessment, in Washington, DC, where he directed studies in the areas of environmental and technology policy.

INDEX

Page references in **bold** indicate a table.

'Abdu'l-Bahá: on attaining higher level of unity, 171–72; on Divine Teachings, 171; on education, 238, 249n76; on engagement in public sphere, 187–88; on equality of men and women, 235; on expression of opinions, 174–75; on faith, 149; on harmony between science and religion, 176; on investigation of reality, 175; on limitations of materialism, 180; on progress of civilization, 176–77; public talks of, 165; on purpose of religion, 14; on realization of universal peace, 187; on science and religion, 23; *The Secret of Divine Civilization*, 164, 176; on sources of knowledge, 176; on supreme need of humanity, 14; tour across United States, 180–81; on women's role in establishment of peace, 239–40
"Advancing Towards the Equality of Women and Men" (BIC's publication), 237
agency, 236
Alexander, Jeffrey, 42, 43
Annan, Kofi, 244n19
Arbab, Farzam, 8
Arendt, Hannah, 103–4

Arguing for a General Framework for Mass Media Scholarship (Potter), 73–74
atheism, 17
axial age, 7, 24–25, 27
"axial" traditions, 10n2

Bahá'í community: approach to politics, 227, 256–57, 271–72; civil society and, 38, 39, 40; collective development, 212; contribution to public discourse, 6, 8–9, 185–86; educational system, 184–85; government relations, 255, 256; growth of, 164, 165; on international arena, 167–68; involvement in social and economic development, 166, 168; Iran refugee crisis and, 257, 262, 268; nongovernmental organizations, 38; promotion of change, 273; public policy engagement, 9–10, 256, 271, 273; social actions, 39–40. *See also* Bahá'í International Community (BIC)
Bahá'í Faith: mission of, 269; nature of, 39; origin and spread of, 5, 6; principles and methods of, 5–6, 159; relation between education and, 97

Bahá'í International Community (BIC): on Beijing Platform for Action, 235; concept of soul, 237–38; concept of "twofold moral purpose," 239; contribution to discourse on sexual and reproductive health, 229; contribution to global development agenda, 181; creation of, 39, 165; engagement in gender equality discourse, 9, 226–33, 234, 241, 242; funding, 230; idea of interconnectedness of all nations, 235; non-government organizations and, 228–29, 241–42, 246n41, 246n42; online library of statements, 168; organizational structure of, 221, 233–34, 242; participation in international forums, 167–68, 228, 230; Quadrennial Report to the United Nations, 233; statement on moral principle, 177–78; statement on sustainable development, 236–37; statements on education, 238–39, 249–50n78; status at United Nations Economic and Social Council, 166; on subject of religion, 23–24; support of Bahá'í refugees, 264; United Nations agencies and, 221, 231–32, 241–42, 246n41

Bahá'í participation in public discourse: aim of, 181, 182–83, 186; calls for change in legislation, 181; conceptual framework, 168–79; epistle to Queen Victoria, 164; forms and levels of, 186; historical perspective, 164–68; at individual level, 183–84; at institutional level, 181; at international level, 167–68, 181, 182; methods and attitudes of, 168–69; moral principles, 177–78; at national level, 182; National Spiritual Assemblies and, 182; preparing youth for, 184; prevalent discourses, 179–81; principle of consultation, 173–75; principle of non-involvement in politics, 172–73; Shoghi Effendi's writings, 165–66

Bahá'í refugee resettlement program: assistance from National Assembly, 260–61; characteristics of, 255, 259–60, 270; development and expansion of, 257–58, 264–67; in Europe and Latin America, 265–66; first stage, 270; immigration procedures, 260–61; international coordination of, 264–65, 270–71; non-adversarial practices, 268–70; success of, 263; transnationalism of, 270–71

Bahá'í refugees: destinations for, 264, **267**; international support for, 257–58; practice of geographical distribution, 262–63; prejudice against, 263; processing of applications, 260, 261; quotas for, 261–62, 265; relocation to Pakistan, 261; resettlement initiative, 258, 263; socio-economic integration, 262–63; sponsors of, 262, 263; statistics on, 266–67, **267**

Bahá'í teachings: on achievement of unity, 171–72, 226–27; axial age thesis and, 27–28; on Cartesian duality, 114; on concept of development, 236–37; on concept of power, 103; on concept of religion, 2, 5, 163–64, 187; on Divine Messengers, 13; on education of women, 238; on evolution of human society, 14, 99, 182, 215n15; on human nature, 52–53, 178–79; on human soul, 114; on limitation of liberal democracy, 78; on mind and spirit, 114; on non-involvement in politics, 39, 246n35, 246n36, 272; on practice of con-

sultation, 79, 80–81, 228; on principle of justice, 58, 79; on purpose of human life, 53; on religious history, 13, 26, 27; on religious truth, 121; on spiritual principles, 54, 55; on supreme need of humanity, 14; on understanding of history, 14, 79, 271–72
Bahá'í World Centre, 38
Bahá'u'lláh: on conscious soul, 179; on divine knowledge, 157; epistle to Queen Victoria, 164; on perfection and maturity, 81; on power to influence, 174; provision on Universal House of Justice, 247–48n55; reflection on religions, 24; on social engagement, 164; Tablet of Wisdom, 174
Ballerio, Giovanni, 235–36
Bayly, C. A., 28
beauty: notion of, 118–19
Bell, Kirk, 261, 262
Bellah, Robert, 20, 28
Ben-Gurion, David, 3
Berger, Julia, 9
Blavatsky, H. P., 20
Bohr, Niels, 159n1
Boy, John D., 27
Brazil: Bahá'í refugees in, 266; discourse on science, religion, and development, 203, 204, 205–6; Forum on Human Rights Education, 205–6; leadership training program, 205, 217n37. *See also* "Some Thoughts on the Future of Brazilian Society" paper
Bruner, Jerome, 106, 107

Cameron, Geoffrey, 9
Camilleri, Joseph, 5
Canada refugee policy, 258, 259–60
capability, conception of, 111, 112–13
Casanova, José, 273
Castro, Fidel, 3

civilization development, 26
civil society: associational dimension of, 41, 56; contemporary discourse on, 46–47; definition of, 7, 37–38, 40, 47; deliberative dimension of, 42, 57–58; emancipatory dimension of, 44–46, 58; expansion of capitalism and, 47; formal organizations of, 56–57; human nature and, 51–52; ideals of solidarity and, 63; impact on political structures, 44–45; informal groups and, 56; institutionalization of, 37, 45; non-government organizations and, 46; in non-Western settings, 47; notion of justice in, 59–60; positive connotation of, 37; power relations in, 52; religion and, 7, 40–41, 48–50; social spaces of, 48–49; spiritual principles of, 51–55, 56, 57, 58, 61, 63; symbolic dimension of, 42–44, 58; voluntary associations and, 41, 48; in Western liberal democracies, 45–47. *See also* global civil society
civil sphere, 42–44
computationalism: conception of, 106
Comte, Auguste, 10n4, 15, 137
constructivism, 107
consultation: practice of, 80–81, 83–85, 173, 175, 228
context of discovery *vs.* context of justification, 138–39
Convention on the Elimination of All Forms of Discrimination Against Women (CEDAW), 223
culturalism: conception of, 107

Dahl, Robert, 101
Darwin, John, 28
Declaration of the Elimination of All Forms of Discrimination Against Women (CEDAW), 222
DeFleur, Melvin, 73

Dennett, Daniel, 15, 28
discourse: definition of, 179
discourse on governance, 180
discourse on science, religion, and development: Brazil case, 203–6, 210; characteristics of, 207–9; India case, 197–201, 208, 210; moral education and, 215n18; Uganda case, 201–3, 208, 210
discourse on spiritual principles, 61–62
Divine Messengers, 163
Dowdell, Carolyn, 260
Duhem, Pierre, 142
Duhem-Quine thesis, 142

education: Bahá'í Faith and, 97; basic elements of, 8; child-centred approach to, 105–6; computational approach to, 106–7; conceptual framework, 97–98; criticism of "banking," 102; language in, 122; in liberal democracies, 101–2; manner and matter of, 105; nature and purpose of, 238–39; notion of capability in, 111, 112; as process, 98; spiritual reality and, 114–15; subject-centred approach to, 105–6; of women, 238; of youth, 239, 249n76
Einstein, Albert, 149
Eisenstadt, S. N., 28
Either/Or (Kierkegaard), 108
emotion, 83
emotivist self, 108–9
Enloe, Cynthia, 240
Ethics and Education (Peters), 105
etiquette of expression, 84
excessive subjectivism, 108–9
Executive Committee of the Central Organization for a Durable Peace, 187
extended reality, 8, 152, 153, 157
extreme relativism, 85

faithful presence: concept of, 272–73
false consciousness: idea of, 101
Farid-Arbab, Sona, 8
Forel, Auguste-Henri, 171
Foundation for the Application and Teaching of the Sciences (FUNDAEC): creation and activities of, 97, 122–23n1; educational initiatives, 112, 118, 194; papers, 112, 204, 205
Freire, Paulo, 102

Galilei, Galileo, 149
gender equality: concept of soul and, 237–38; as element of oneness of humanity, 235–36; as prerequisite for peace, 239–41
Gender Equality Architecture Reform (GEAR) Campaign, 225, 229
gender equality discourse: Bahá'í International Community contribution to, 9, 226–33, 237–38; conceptual framework, 223, 234; controversial issues in, 222; faith-based organizations and, 229, 241; oppositional dynamic, 222–24; United Nations and, 221–22, 225
Glasersfeld, Ernst von, 107
global civil society, 1–2, 45
Gollmer, Ulrich, 256, 269
goods: concept of, 116
Gramsci, Antonio, 44, 101

Habermas, Jürgen, 42, 82, 83, 85
Harcourt, Wendy, 225
Harrison, Peter, 19
Hegel, G. W. F., 20
Heidegger, Martin, 16
Hick, John, 20
Hobbes, Thomas, 102–3
Hodgson, Marshall, 28
homo economicus: concept of, 51–52
human behaviour, 213n4
human capability framework, 215n16

humanitarianism: sense of sacred in, 269
human nature, 51, 52–54, 178
human society: evolution of, 99, 100; globalization and, 1; individuality and, 100; transitional period, 79–80
Hunter, James Davidson, 272
Huxley, Aldous, 20

Ibn Khaldûn, 20
India: discourse on science, religion, and development, 197–201, 208, 210, 218n42
injustice, 59, 60
Institute for Studies in Global Prosperity (ISGP): conceptual framework on development strategy, 191, 193–94, 195, 197, 201–2, 214n11, 216n24; discussion on gender equality, 231–32; foundation of, 213n2; mission of, 184, 213n2, 247n50; research projects, 200, 216n33, 218n44; Spiritual Assembly in Uganda's collaboration with, 201
Inter-Agency Task Force of Engaging with Faith-Based Organizations for Sustainable Development, 224
International Bahá'í Bureau in Geneva, 165
International Bahá'í Refugee Office (IBRO), 264, 265–66, 270
International Conference on Population and Development (ICPD), 222
international development: challenges of, 192–93; "Green" and "White" Revolutions and, 192, 213n3
international development discourse: Bahá'í contribution to, 207, 214n11; capacity-building processes, 196; challenges and future directions, 209–12; collective action and, 195–96; conceptual framework, 209; diverse range of stakeholders of, 207, 211; faith-based organizations and, 212n1; IDRC project, 194–95; key principles, 199; knowledge at the centre of, 195; new perspectives on, 191, 193–96; non-material aspirations, 214n10; notions of spirituality and religion in, 209; scientific and religious resources in, 191; social space for, 207–8
International Development Research Centre (IDRC) in Canada, 193, 194

Jain, Devaki, 227
Jaspers, Karl, 24–25, 26
Joint Learning Initiative on Faith and Local Communities, 224
Josephson, Jason, 19
justice: principles of, 58, 59, 78–79

Karam, Azza, 222
Karlberg, Michael, 7, 42, 52, 228, 269
Kazemzadeh, Firuz, 257
Kepler, Johannes, 149
Kierkegaard, Søren, 20, 108
knowledge: advancement of civilization and, 176; human thirst for, 119; moral empowerment and generation of, 104; religion and, 209–10; sources of, 176–77
Kuhn, Thomas, 139, 143, 144, 145
Kymlicka, Will, 110

Lakatos, Imre, 139, 145–46
language of science and religion, 120–22
Levine, Daniel H., 271
liberal democracy: limitations of, 78
love: as property of human being, 121
Lowery, Shearon, 73
Lukes, Steven, 101, 102

MacIntyre, Alasdair, 4, 16, 108, 116, 117
Martin, Douglas, 260, 261, 264
McNeill, William H., 28
McQuail, Denis, 77
media: art as function of, 80; audiences of, 76; bias of, 76–77; deliberative functions of, 76, 80; in democratic societies, role of, 77; generation of knowledge about, 71–72; normative foundations of, 71, 72, 75, 77–78, 87; political economy of, 75, 76; power of, 84; in public sphere, 7–8, 87; social construction of, 73–74
Media Performance (McQuail), 77
media policies, 75–76, 77
media studies, 7, 72, 73–74, 76–77, 88
Mehra, Achal, 77, 78
Michnik, Adam, 44
Mill, John Stuart, 77
Millennium World Peace Summit of Religious and Spiritual Leaders, 167–68
Milton, John, 77
Mind and Cosmos (Nagel), 152
Mojgani, Mona, 260, 261, 264, 265, 270
moral empowerment, 98–99, 104, 196. *See also* twofold moral purpose
Mumford, Lewis, 28
Murdoch, Iris, 118
Museveni, Yoweri, 201

Nagel, Thomas: challenge to physicalism, 152; criticism of neo-Darwinism, 18; on education and religious orthodoxy, 30n24; explanation of consciousness, 153–54, 156; on extended reality, 8, 151–52, 153; on intentional alternative, 154–55; on natural teleology, 154; on objectivity, 132, 151–52; statement of objectivity, 150–51; on understanding of physical world, 151; view of creationism, 155; works of, 152–53
Narayanan, K. R., 198
Nasser, Gamal Abdel, 3
National Bahá'í Offices for the Advancement of Women, 234
National Center for Educational Research and Training (NCERT), 218n42
National Spiritual Assembly of Canada, 258–59, 260, 261–62
National Spiritual Assembly of the Bahá'ís of India, 197–98, 216n23, 218n42
National Spiritual Assembly of the Bahá'ís of Uganda, 201
natural teleology, 154
neo-Darwinism, 18
Newton, Isaac, 149
NGO Committee on the Status of Women, 228–29
"noncivil" spheres, 43
Nongbri, Brent, 18
normal science: concept of, 144
Normative Theories of the Media (Christians et al.), 77
Nussbaum, Martha, 112

objectivity: conception of, 150–51, 152
Office of Public Discourse (OPD) at Bahá'í World Centre, 169
oneness of humanity: principle of, 55, 59, 78–80, 99, 170–71, 235–36, 273
Opening a Space: The Discourse on Science, Religion and Development in Uganda, 203
oppression: forms of, 59
Osterhammel, Jürgen, 28

Palmer, David A., 7, 241
paradox of protest, 52
Parliaments of the World's Religions, 167
patience: virtue of, 117

perennial philosophy, 20
Peters, Richard S., 105
Phillips, D. C., 107
Philpott, Daniel, 271
Plato's concept of God, 16–17
Popper, Karl, 139–41
positivism, 87–88, 159n2
post-secular, 5
Potter, James, 73, 74
poverty reduction, 192, 203, 213n5
power: examination of concept of, 100–104
Power, Mary, 229
practice: concept of, 116, 117
Press Systems in ASEAN States (Mehra), 77
progress, 176–77, 182, 213n5
progressive revelation, 6, 14, 21–22, 23, 133, 134
public discourse: consultative model of, 82, 83–85; media and, 71; pluralist position on, 4; post-secular approach to, 5; preparation of citizens to participate in, 84; rationalist position on, 3–4, 11n12; realist position on, 3–4; reason, emotion and inclusivity in, 83–84; relational dynamics of, 82–83; role of religion in, 85–87; traditionalist position on, 4. *See also* Bahá'í participation in public discourse
public sphere: concept of, 42, 82, 83; as discursive space, 75; media and, 7–8; place of religion in, 4–5, 86; tensions in theory of, 82
Puechguirbal, Nadine, 225
Putnam, Robert D., 41

qualitative contrasts, 120
Quine, Willard Van Orman, 139, 141–42

racial equality discourse, 38
radical constructivism, 107, 108
rationality, 156

Razavi, Shahriar, 6, 228
reason: as foundation of scientific inquiry, 177; religion and, 176
refugees: definition, 274n16. *See also* Bahá'í refugees
Religion in Human Evolution (Bellah), 20–21
religion(s): approach to development initiatives, 217n40; civilization-building capacity of, 158–59; civil society and, 7, 40–41, 48–50; common themes between different, 133–34; concept of, 18, 24, 60–61; connection to Divine, 133; construction of social realities and, 85; demographic study on, 215n21; development theory on, 192; dispute about progress and, 244n15; divisive aspects of, 49; education and, 97; faith and, 150; historical evolution of, 2, 13, 15–16, 86; knowledge and, 134, 135, 178, 209–10; loss of social influence, 3; main goal of, 218n41; modernity and, 15; narratives of, 15–21; as obstacle to expanding spaces of solidarity, 48, 49; as opposition to progress, 229; origin of concept of, 18–19; as outcome of God's Revelation, 134; perception of order in, 149; politics and, 3, 257, 271; in public discourse, role of, 6, 85–87; in public sphere, role of, 2, 4–5, 86; reason and, 176; in relation to science, 8, 18, 131–32, 134–36, 139, 149–50, 157–58, 215n19; socio-political movements and, 50; as source of values, 40, 48; as system of knowledge and practice, 132–34; as unifying force, 14; as vehicle for spiritual forces, 163–64, 187. *See also* world religions
religious history: construct narrative, 18–19; developmental narrative,

20–21; limitations of narratives of, 28; perennial narrative, 20, 24; postnaturalist narrative, 18; renewal narrative, 16–17; subtraction narrative, 15–16; transsecular narrative, 17
Revelation *vs.* human reasoning, 156
Rudolph, Susanne Hoeber, 271

Sandel, Michael, 110
Schewel, Benjamin, 6
science: changes in paradigm in, 144–45; definition of, 148–49; facts and observations, 136, 137–38; faith and, 149; historical perspective on, 136; ideology of naturalism and, 18; Jasper's idea of modern, 25; limits of, 135; moral and spiritual principles in, 177–78; normative discourse on, 86–87; object of study of, 134–35; pseudoscience and, 139–48; in relation to religion, 8, 18, 131–32, 134–36, 139, 149–50, 157–58, 215n19; as system of knowledge and practice, 132–34; theories of comets, 146–47; wave-particle duality, 135–36
Science, Religion and Development: Perspectives for Brazil, 205
scientific knowledge, 136–37, 138–39
Scown, Dennis, 260, 261, 268
Secretariat for the Promotion of the Discourse on Science, Religion, and Development, 200
Secret of Divine Civilization, The ('Abdu'l-Bahá), 164–65, 176
secularization theory, 2–4, 10n4
self: communitarian *vs.* liberal view of, 109–10
Sen, Amartya, 112, 215n16
Shintoism, 19
Shoghi, Effendi, 22, 159, 165–66, 256
social construction: conceptions of, 72–74, 85

solidarity, 54, 58, 62
soul: concept of, 237–38
spiritual principles: application of, 40, 55–57, 58; as basis for solidarity, 58; concept of, 54–55; discourse on, 61–62, 63
spiritual qualities, 98–99, 116, 119, 120–21
spiritual reality, 114–15, 157
Stroumsa, Guy, 19
Structure of Scientific Revolutions, The (Kuhn), 143, 148

Taylor, Charles, 2, 10n2, 17, 28, 120
teleology, 154
Tocqueville, Alexis de, 41
Torpey, John, 27
Toynbee, Arnold, 20
transnational religious formations, 271
twofold moral purpose, 99–100, 118–19

Uganda: discourse on science, religion, and development, 201–3
underdetermination doctrine, 142–43
understanding: attributes of, 106, 111–12; constructivism and subject of, 107–8; definition of, 104–5; excessive subjectivism and, 108–9; infinite dimension of, 113; permanence of, 115; as process, 105; in relation to spiritual qualities, 115–16, 119–20
United Nations: BIC's engagement with, 221, 231–32, 241–42, 246n41; gender equality discourse and, 9, 221–22, 225–26; gender inequality in, 244–45n19, 245n23, 245n27; mechanisms for knowledge sharing, 224; Millennium Development Goals, 231; non-government organizations at, 228–29, 233; patriarchal ideology of, 224–26; references to women in

documents of, 225; religious actors at, 221, 227–28, 229; Resolution on "Women, Peace and Security," 225, 240–41
United Nations Commission on Population and Development, 236
United Nations Commission on the Status of Women, 221, 222, 223
United Nations Fourth World Conference on Women in Beijing, 236
United Nations High Commissioner for Refugees (UNHCR), 259, 265–66
United Nations Population Fund (UNFPA), 224
United Nations Research Institute for Social Development (UNRISD), 229
United Nations Sub-Commission on the Prevention of Discrimination Against Minorities, 258
unity: as prerequisite to progress, 171; ways to achieve, 172, 173–74
Universal Declaration of Human Rights, 222, 244n16
Universal House of Justice: 2010 Riḍván letter, 239; on building global unity, 226–27; on code of conduct of the press, 81, 91n30; concept of participation in discourses of society, 230; on creation of Bahá'í Refugee Office, 264–65; on education and emancipation of women, 234, 238, 240; encouragement for Bahá'í youth, 184; establishment of, 166; as governing body of Bahá'í Faith, 247–48n55; on involvement in social actions, 233; membership restriction, 247–48n55; on obedience to religious beliefs, 246n35; public statement to world leaders, 22; spiritual messages, 166–68; "The Promise of World Peace" statement, 38, 166–67, 183, 240
Universal Primary Education program, 203
University for Integral Development, 194
UN Women (UN Entity for Gender Equality and the Empowerment of Women), 225, 232

Van Den Hoonaard, Deborah K., 263
Van Kessel, Gerry, 260, 261
Vienna Declaration and Programme of Action, 244n17
View from Nowhere, The (Nagel), 152
virtue: concept of, 116, 117–18
Voegelin, Eric, 27, 28
voluntary associations, 41

Weinberg, Matthew, 9
Western civilization, 16, 17
women: challenges of education of, 238; in establishment of peace, role of, 239–40; patriarchal image of, 225–26, 236; as protagonists of development, 236–37
women's movement, 222, 223, 227
World Faiths Development Dialogue, 212n1
world religions, 19

Books in the Bahá'í Studies series
published by Wilfrid Laurier University Press

Gate of the Heart: Understanding the Writings of the Báb / Nader Saiedi / 2010 / 432 pp. / ISBN 978-1-55458-056-9

Religion and Public Discourse in an Age of Transition: Reflections on Bahá'í Practice and Thought / Geoffrey Cameron and Benjamin Schewel, editors / 2017 / 300 pp. / ISBN 978-1-77112-330-3

www.ingramcontent.com/pod-product-compliance
Lightning Source LLC
Chambersburg PA
CBHW072146100526
44589CB00015B/2110